BACK
FROM
THE
BRINK

THE UNTOLD STORY OF MANCHESTER UNITED
IN THE DEPRESSION YEARS 1919-1932

BY JUSTIN BLUNDELL

EMPIRE
PUBLICATIONS

First published in 2006

EMPIRE PUBLICATIONS
1 Newton Street, Manchester M1 1HW
copyright Justin Blundell 2006

ISBN 1 901 746 47 X

Cover design and layout: Ashley Shaw
Cigarette cards and additional images courtesy of Iain McCartney
Edited by Ashley Shaw and Stuart Fish
Typeset in Friz Quadrata and Berkeley
Printed in Great Britain by Cox and Wyman

TO MY MUM AND DAD

Also, many thanks (for your interest, support, advice and hospitality!) to Dave, Lee, Alec, Richard, Nguk, Len, Sir Matt and the Badgers, particularly Darren, Tanny, Wes, Reg, Kiana, Joanne, Kristian, Matilda, everyone at Empire and Anna.

A NOTE ON THE AUTHOR

This is Justin Blundell's first published book. The idea for a book about this relatively unresearched period in the club's history came after researching the period for a magazine article that was never published.

In Justin's own words he "realised that a) it was interesting, b) it had not really been touched on before and c) it would make a nice change from reading all the usual stuff about the glory years. Not very interesting I know but it's true!"

A lifelong red, Justin's commitment to the cause has produced a book that is different from any other history you will read. Enjoy!

CONTENTS

INTRODUCTION

THE TWENTY-ODD years that separated the First World War from the Second World War have often been referred to as the long weekend. This book follows the fortunes of Manchester United from Friday night to Sunday afternoon. It is the story of how a pre-war giant fell asleep and very nearly did not wake up again. It is the story of record highs and record lows, of protests, punch-ups and revolts, of heroes, villains, wizards and saviours, of great escapes and even greater cock-ups, of joy and pain, tragedy and despair. Amazingly, it is a story that has never properly been told before until now.

By the time the 'Depression Years' era began, in August 1919, United had already been through more than forty years of evolution. Most of what happened in that time belongs in a different book but as a working knowledge of the important names and events from the pre-war era will prove invaluable later on, it seems sensible to kick things off with a quick rundown of the story so far, starting with the Heathen Years.

In 1878 a group of workers from the Lancashire & Yorkshire Railway's carriage and wagon department got together to form a football team, Newton Heath (LYR). Initially, the team, which was based at North Road, Newton Heath, played against other railway teams but it did not take them long to outgrow their competition and start eyeing a move up the football ladder. In 1885, just seven years after their formation, the club turned professional (and dropped the brackets); in 1889 they became founder members of the Football Alliance; in 1892 they were accepted into the first division of the Football League and in 1893 they moved to a bigger and better ground at Bank Street, Clayton (though there were drawbacks to the move, most notably the infamously toxic atmosphere created by the chemical works next door). Then, after spending fifteen years heading in the right direction, the Newton Heath story did an abrupt U-turn. First, the Heathens were relegated, then the crowds started to slide, the cost of moving grounds began to tell and the club were gripped by financial crisis. By 1902, the situation had deteriorated to such an extent that they were on the verge of extinction.

Which brings us to the first critical moment in United's history. A consortium led by local businessman, John Henry Davies, came to the Heathens' rescue, paying off the creditors and pumping in cash. After that, a flurry of other landmarks laid the foundations for the club's first golden era. In spring 1902, Davies was installed as club President, the Newton Heath name was jettisoned in favour of Manchester United and the old green and gold colours in favour of red and white. In 1903 managerial genius Ernest Mangnall arrived from Burnley and began to construct United's first great team. Within a year he had brought in star keeper Harry Moger and assembled the legendary half-back line of Dick Duckworth, 'captain marvel' Charlie Roberts and Alec Bell. Over the next decade or so, a host of other great names, including forwards George Wall, Jimmy Turnbull, Harold Halse and Enoch West, were added to the roster but Mangnall's finest piece of business came in 1906 when he took advantage of the FA's war on Manchester City (as punishment for a bribery and illegal payments scandal, City were forced to sell off seventeen of their players at an auction at the city's Queen's Hotel) to swoop for four members of their 1904 FA Cup winning team; wing legend Billy Meredith, forwards Jimmy Bannister and Sandy Turnbull and England defender Herbert Burgess.

1906 was a great year for Manchester United. In May, they finally climbed out of the second division. The injection of Blue talent then transformed a potentially good team into a great one. Within eighteen months of the Queen's Hotel steal, United had won the league and the inaugural Charity Shield. A year later, they won the FA Cup and in 1911 they claimed their second league and Charity Shield double. Their class and style, as well as their results, made them arguably the finest side the game had ever seen.

At the same time as they were building a club tradition for footballing excellence, Mangnall's champions were also building one for unorthodoxy, rebelliousness and for attracting controversy. The integral role that leading Reds, particularly Roberts and Meredith, played in the formation and subsequent development of the Players' Union inevitably put them on a collision course with the FA, who regarded the fledgling body as a threat to their vice-like grip on the game. Matters came to a head in the summer of 1909 when the entire cup-winning team were suspended for refusing to sign an agreement declaring their loyalty to the FA and its rules. The ensuing 'Outcasts' affair (more of which later) soon blew over but the fallout from it put a strain on the relationship between United and the football authorities which you could claim lasts to this day. It also clouded the judgement of the England selectors to such an extent that most pre-Busby Reds had more chance of producing milk than getting a game for their country.

Six months after the Outcasts controversy, United continued their ascent by moving from Clayton to Old Trafford, the £60,000/80,000-capacity super-stadium which most observers considered the finest in the world. The basic 'bowl' layout of the ground looked pretty much as it did right up to the modern era though there were crucial differences, most notably the fact that only one of the stands (the Main Stand – the present-day South Stand) was seated and covered. The rest of the ground, including the main fans stronghold, the Pop Side (the present-day North Stand), was uncovered and standing only.

The change of address meant that United started the 1911/12 season with the best president, manager, players and ground in the land but instead of cementing the club's position among the game's elite, the expensive move upmarket, rather like the Clayton switch seventeen years earlier, ushered in a period of darkness. Within two years of the second title triumph, financial difficulties had initiated the break-up of the championship team, the talismanic Roberts had been sacrificed and, worst of all, Mangnall had moved to City.

The rest of the pre-war era was spent in a dismal battle against relegation. In 1913/14 the club limped home in fourteenth; in 1914/15 they escaped the drop by just one place and one point. If it hadn't been for the shabbiest affair in their history, they might not have finished that high. On Good Friday 1915, United strolled to a crucial 2-0 win against Liverpool in a curious, non-event of a match at Old Trafford. The lack of passion on show launched a wave of rumours that the result had been fixed. When it later emerged that there had been a rush of bets on a 2-0 score-line, it was blatantly obvious that it had been. An FA inquiry was launched and eight players – four from Liverpool, one (curiously) from Chester City and West and Arthur Whalley and Sandy Turnbull from United – were found guilty of plotting 'to rob bookmakers by criminal fraud' and all of them were banned for life.

There were plenty of influential voices in the game who argued that United should be docked the points they had taken from the squared match and thus be relegated in place of second-from-bottom Chelsea. As there was no evidence of complicity on the part of the United management, the authorities took the view that it would be unjust to relegate either club. Perhaps fortunately, the Reds were still sitting at football's top table when the Depression Years era dawned.

But if United were lucky to be there, they weren't nearly as lucky as Arsenal. In order to reinstate Chelsea, the authorities extended the first division from twenty to twenty-two clubs and handed a free pass to the top flight to one lucky loser. According to precedent, it should have gone to the other relegated club, Tottenham. Instead, it went to the Gunners, the fifth best team in the second division in 1914/15, in recognition of their 'long service' to the game (or, more accurately, their slimy manoeuvring behind the scenes). It is true what they say, then: every silver lining really does have a cloud.

*   *   *

NOW THE HISTORY lesson is out of the way, all that remains for me to do is paint some sort of picture of what the football world was like at the outset of the Depression Years. The basics of the game – twenty-two players, one ball, one ref, two linesmen, ninety minutes, two halves, one rectangular pitch etc. – were the same but the 1919 football vintage clearly had a different flavour to the modern stuff. It was a time when the shoulder-barge was king, when goalkeepers were viewed as fair game and when red cards were often reserved for those incidents which, if they had happened on the street, would have resulted in arrest. It was the era of no substitutes, no play on Sundays, no floodlights, 2.30 kick-offs, no shirt numbers, no goalkeeping gloves, giant shorts, green roll-neck jumpers (for the keepers), thick jerseys (for the rest), lace-up case balls, goal average, two points for a win, two up and two down and (until the numbers were doubled between 1920 and 1921), forty-four clubs and two divisions. It was a time when sports journalists hid behind pseudonyms, when people named John were called Jack, when the FA Cup was seen as the biggest prize of all and when British football was still considered the best in the world.

Enough already. There are really just three things that you need to know before getting stuck into the rest of the book. First, a football manager did not manage the club in the modern sense. The directors/selectors had the final say on playing matters, including which team was picked and which players were bought and sold, and the manager was basically a flunky who carried out their orders and looked after the admin. In Victorian and Edwardian times, managers had been called secretaries and, though their title had changed, in many ways their role had not.

Second, the offside rule at that time required three, rather than two, members of the defending team to be between the attacker and the goal when the ball was played forward to him. And, partly because of Point Two, we have Point Three; the 2-3-5 formation, as outlined below with the numbers that each position was also known by:

1 Goalkeeper
2 Right Full-back 3 Left Full-back
4 Right Wing-half 5 Centre Half-back (pivot) 6 Left Wing-half
7 Right Winger 8 Inside-right 9 Centre-forward 10 Inside-left 11 Left Winger

The 2-3-5 formation looks lopsided now but it was perfectly suited to the rules of the time. As one player could stay behind to mind the back door, as it were, and still catch opposing forwards offside, the backs did not require the constant support of the centre-half (who was expected to look after the opposing centre-forward as well as initiate attacks, a dual role which made him the fulcrum of the team) and the other two half-backs, leaving them free to push up in support of the forwards. And with fewer defensive chores to worry about, teams were able to commit more players full-time to attack.

The formation, in turn, influenced how the game was played. With so many players in advanced positions, there was little point in forwards roaming across the line in search of space because they were almost certain to be left disappointed. Instead, players tended to stick to their own positions and, to a certain extent, only interact with the team-mates closest to them. Thus, each wing went forward in a triangle of wing-half, inside-forward and winger and went backwards in a combination of inside-forward, wing-half and full-back. And when one wing went forward, or back, the rest of the team followed suit, a manoeuvre which conjures up images of old-time football as a battle between two well-drilled troupes of line dancers (though obviously without the yee-haas). Actually, it wasn't quite like that – individual players were allowed the freedom to go out and express themselves wherever they wanted – but there is no doubt that the game was a more rigid and ordered affair in 1919 than it is today. As was the case in society in general, everybody knew their place.

PLAYERS NOT POINTS

ARLY IN THE morning of 11 November 1918, the German peace delegation signed the armistice and the war that the world feared would last forever finally drew to a close. The end of the four-year nightmare sparked scenes of manic celebration across the British Isles, none more feverish than in Manchester where the party people turned the city centre into a giant, red-white-and-blue carnival – and the munitions girls turned teenaged Tommies into men. However, it wasn't long before the drinking, dancing, singing, kissing, copulating and cavorting petered out and the initial rush of euphoria gave way to sober, often gloomy, reflection. So many lives had been lost and ruined that a repeat of the excesses of Armistice Day somehow seemed inappropriate. Perhaps if the troops had landed a glorious knockout blow, or if the conflict had accomplished something really worthwhile, then things would have been different. Instead, Fritz had gone home claiming a losing draw and the continent was riddled with just as many crises and conundrums as before. In the circumstances, it was difficult for even John Bull to shake the nagging feeling that the war to end all wars had been one that no one had really won.

But if the country as a whole were content to mark the end of the fighting with a one-off burst of pissed-up pandemonium, the football community were determined to keep the party going for as long as they could. It isn't hard to see why. In the propaganda battle that had followed the FA's controversial decision to keep on playing in 1914/15[1], the game had played a blinder and scored a thumping victory. Instead of being an unpatriotic and unnecessary distraction, as the self-styled moral gurus from Lord's and Twickenham had alleged, it was now acknowledged that the League matches and the sectional programme that replaced them had provided a welcome release from

1. Other sports, including cricket and rugby union, chose to discontinue competition immediately, a decision they felt would prove their 'moral superiority' over the 'unprincipled mercenaries' of professional football.

the monotony of life on the home front. Even better, the regular kickabouts enjoyed by both troops and workers alike had played a key role in keeping the nation in shape and out of a straitjacket. Suddenly, rather than hindering the war effort, football was taking the credit for helping to win it.

The Manchester-based *Athletic News* added to their unofficial reputation as the chief cheerleaders of the pro-football press by crowing, 'Football was the great sport of our soldiers behind the trenches, at home and at the base, away in foreign theatres of war, and at home through the dreary months of training. It was the great tonic of the boys called on to train and fight, and it was also the great mental tonic and physical "refresher" of those at home who were working night and day and putting every ounce of effort into their work.

'The game answered a great purpose in preserving the pluck, the hope, the faith of the nation. In this great war of nerves football was a great steadying influence.'

In the sporting press's version of world history, the game lagged just behind the sinking of the Lusitania, the glass jaw of the Habsburgs and the peace revolution in Berlin as the reason why German buttocks were not filling the thrones at Buckingham Palace (though, in truth, they already were, regardless of the Royals' sensible, mid-war name change from sausage-smelling Saxe-Coburg-Gotha to Windsor). But if football had made a significant contribution to the war effort, it was nothing compared to what the war effort had done for the game in return. Back in 1914, it had been just another form of recreation, jostling for attention with the old favourites such as cricket, cycling and sleeping with the domestics. Now that a stint in the army had exposed men from every class and every county to the casey, football was the national game, a position it has enjoyed ever since.

Again, the *Athletic News* was on hand to drive the point home: 'Part of the nation knew football before August 1914 and another part knew of it. Now Great Britain realises that it is not just a pastime but an institution typical of the Anglo-Saxon temperament, expressive of the love of fair combat, of a contempt for danger, and of persistent effort in weather fair and foul to achieve a specific object.' Tell that to the next bore who tries fobbing you off with the line, 'well, it's only a game'.

*   *   *

IF FOOTBALL EMERGED FROM the war in fine fettle, there were mixed emotions for United and the working-class lads who formed the bulk of the club's support. The bad news for the Pop Side, of course, was that the war had left them with physical and mental scars that would possibly never heal. The flip side was that it had triggered changes which would make their lives more comfortable than they had been back in 1914. For one, war-related, reason or another, standards of medical care had risen, the welfare system had muscled up, the male workforce had been fully enfranchised and major gains made in pay and working conditions. And even though criminal inroads had been made into the sacred freedom of boozing (was there a worse World War One invention than the afternoon 'gap' in pubs?), most lads were better off socially, too. The transformation of the cinema from fad to nation's favourite had revolutionised their Friday and Saturday nights. Even better, the combination of the growing confidence and independence of single women, the steady rise of the condom and the increasing demand for blokes of all levels of attractiveness (with hundreds of thousands of dead and disfigured men taken off the market, girls could not afford to be as choosy as before) had revolutionised their sex lives. It wasn't exactly the era of free love, but there was now every chance of even the ropiest of Reds picking up some pointers before their wedding night.

Plain-looking Pop Siders weren't the only ones who looked more attractive through post-war glasses than they had done before, either. The wartime break had done wonders for United's image as well. In the wake of the Good Friday match-fixing scandal in 1915 – the latest entry on the longest rap-sheet in professional football – the club's reputation had stood on a par with the Kaiser's. Now that a battle-scarred nation was determined to look forward rather than back United, who might otherwise have been starting the post-war era in the second division, were benefiting from a general wiping of the slate. So, incidentally, were the ringleaders of the match-fixing affair who had their suspensions lifted in recognition of their efforts during the war. Enoch 'Knocker' West was the lone exception, his dogged refusal to admit his guilt leading to his ban remaining in force until the end of the next world war – when he was knocking on for sixty.

Even better, the wartime break had given Jack Robson the chance to rebuild the side that had got the club into strife in the first place. With the backing of the directorate, who recognised that trophies in wartime did not really count (sorry City, that Lancashire sectional title in 1916 lags behind even second division play-offs in terms of prestige), the United manager adopted a new policy with the slogan 'players before points'. Effectively, this involved Robson pillaging junior football for likely lads, throwing them in at the deep end in the first team and seeing how many survived. Several dozen trialists sank rather than swam but the manager's Busbyesque interest in young players did produce some notable results. Four of the wartime finds – defenders Jack Silcock and Charlie Moore, half-back Lal Hilditch and centre-forward Joe Spence – would still be doing the business in a Red shirt in the early thirties.

Robson's philosophy was a bold and imaginative one but the desperate search for fresh-faced talent rather than ready-made stars was a dead give-away that United were struggling for cash. Ever since the costly move to Old Trafford in 1910, the club had struggled to balance the books. The wartime combination of vastly reduced crowds and heavy taxation[2] had turned a financial headache into a

Jack Robson

crisis. As long as John Henry Davies and his fortune hovered in the wings, the club were never in real danger but it was still some effort to keep the business solvent. The wartime posters asked would-be shirkers: 'What did you do in the war?' In Jack Robson's case, the answer would have been two-fold; half the time he was slobbering around the backside of United's bank manager; the rest he spent patrolling the nation's pitches looking for rough diamonds like Silcock and Spence.

It was just as well that he did because precious few of the old guard were still around when the players reported back in the summer of 1919. Though Sandy Turnbull was the only Red to lay down his life for the colours (one death per club was pretty much par for the course), few other sides had been disrupted by the war as much as United. Missing from the regular pre-war team were the

---

2. In May 1916 the government imposed an entertainment tax on all sports and amusements, including football. The tax amounted to 1d of every 6d that came in through the gate. In addition, football clubs agreed to pay a self-imposed charity tax of 10% (on gate receipts). Clubs continued to pay the entertainment tax right up to the late fifties.

goalkeeper, the defence, two thirds of the middle line and most of the forwards. Now that wasn't necessarily a bad thing. Several members of the 1914/15 team were palpably not good enough to be playing first division football. Then again, there were six or seven players whose departures represented a major handicap. They included Big Bob Beale, the best uncapped goalkeeper of his day, the former skipper and centre-half Pat O'Connell, mercurial Irish wing-back Mickey Hamill and two free-scoring centre-forwards, Knocker West and George Anderson. And the biggest handicap of all? The legendary Billy Meredith was refusing to re-sign because of a long-standing argument over his benefit money and was agitating for a free transfer back to City.

Even the A-team would have struggled to do much with the returning pros. Building a tank from a collection of rusty pipes and a roll of chicken wire was once a Saturday night ritual on ITV. Rustling up a top-class outfit out of an outstanding keeper (the regular wartime number one, Jack Mew), a classy but knackered half-back (Arthur Whalley), a clever inside-forward (Wilf Woodcock, the club's top scorer in all but one of the sectional seasons), one bargain-basement summer signing (£100 ex-Birmingham winger Frank Hodges), a collection of journeymen (versatile Jimmy Hodge, doughty half-back James Montgomery and skinny inside-forward Arthur Potts) and a bunch of unproven youngsters would have been dismissed as a gross insult to the viewers' intelligence. No wonder that most pundits felt that Robson's men were headed for a season-long battle against relegation. The most hopeful prediction came from the local *Evening Chronicle* which concluded: 'Youth is well-represented, but there is also a sprinkling of experience in the side, and if the club should strike a winning run early on in the season, the encouragement thus gained will go a long way.' The rest took the Alan Hansen view – you don't win anything with kids.

Watching United stutter their way through the first week back, you could see their point. Derby were robbed of a win on the opening day, the Reds[3] scraping a 1-1 draw in the Midlands courtesy of Woodcock's clever finish, some dogged defending and an exhibition of brilliance from Mew that even his illustrious predecessors, Moger

3. *The team that opened the post-war era at Derby was Mew, Moore, Silcock; Montgomery, Hilditch, Whalley; Hodge, Woodcock, Spence, Potts and Hopkin. In total, the side cost just £100 to assemble.*

and Beale, would have struggled to match. Dreadful Sheffield Wednesday were then allowed to hold on for the dismal nil-nil they had come for at Old Trafford before Derby settled some scores from the Baseball Ground, strolling to a 2-0 victory in the rematch.

But for those who were prepared to scratch under the surface, there were signs even then that Robson's novices were badly miscast as first division whipping boys. In Woodcock and his explosive, if raw, sidekick Spence, the club possessed one proven match-winner and one likely one. And if the rest of the attack looked short of top quality and the midfield lacking in class and legs, the back-line plus the centre-half, Hilditch, was loaded with potential. Everyone knew how good Mew was already. Before the autumn was out, the novices, Moore, Silcock and Hilditch, had all made the critics sit up and take note too. Sadly, Lal, whose classical, polished style earned him an England call-up for October's Victory International against Wales, struggled to sustain his early promise but Mew, Silcock and Moore set standards for defensive resilience that lasted not just for the rest of the season but for the rest of the decade.

Led from the back, the Reds were about to put their difficult start behind them and make the press-box cynics squirm, at least for the next couple of months or so. But what about the Red Army? The return of League football had brought more people out of their homes than the Black Death but for a while it seemed that the post-war boom was passing United by. A quarter of a million people watched the first day of the first division programme but only 13,000 turned up for the Sheffield opener and barely 15,000 for the visit of the Rams.

Even a man as notoriously cocksure as John Henry Davies must have allowed himself a moment or two of self-doubt when United started the season without thousands of their supporters. For a decade, the Reds' sugar-daddy had taken flak over the move from Clayton to Old Trafford, his critics claiming that he had sold the club down the river (the Irwell, presumably); that the old Bank Laners would never come; and that the move had more to do with feeding his own ego than securing the club's future. When the turnstiles stayed silent in the opening week, Old Trafford's transformation from super-stadium to white elephant seemed complete.

Fortunately for president and club, there were good reasons why the Pop Side had more gaps than Dr Crippen's defence. The timing of Wednesday's visit – on a midweek afternoon – made a big crowd unlikely while the gate for the Derby match would have been doubled had it not been for the counter-attraction of race-day at Castle Irwell. When a healthy 20,000 turned up for the Preston match a fortnight later and a record 49,360 squeezed in for the derby in mid-October, it was clear that Davies' justification had arrived. With a new rail link bringing the fans right to the club's doorstep, there were several occasions in the months to come when there was barely enough room on the terraces to swing a rattle, which made a nice change from the early days at Old Trafford when there had regularly been enough room to swing cattle.

John Henry Davies had built his field of dreams and people, like those in the film, would eventually start to come. It did not take long for the club's young forwards to get over their own impotence problems either. The release came with the trip to Wednesday on September 8. In front of 10,000 supporters at Hillsborough, one of whom had made the news by buying two season tickets to ensure that his dog would always sit next to him (imagine how many woolly spectators there must have been at Elland Road…), United cantered to a 3-1 win with maiden goals from Spence and left-half starlet, Tommy Meehan, and another from Woodcock. The ice broken, the Reds were then lucky enough to meet a Preston side whose defence was reputed to be the slowest, most cumbersome and disorganised in the division. Make that doubly fortunate as, under the new fixture arrangements, most teams played each other on a back-to-back basis. Four points were gratefully received. A pair of defensive howlers and Meehan's late drive were the keys to narrow victory at Deepdale. In the Old Trafford return, Robson's fledgling forwards were too quick, eager and elusive for the visitors' plodding backs and indulged themselves to the tune of five goals to one. Spence's sweetly-timed opener was the champagne moment, the first home goal of the season setting the Reds up for their first home win.

When they followed their Preston double with a hard-won draw at classy Middlesbrough (believe it or not, that's not always been a contradiction in terms) on the 27th, the pre-season relegation favourites lay in fourth place in the table and Robson was the obvious candidate for manager of the month. But that was where the story almost ended for the United manager and his young team. In a nightmare journey back from the north-east which could have inspired a Mack Sennett production of Trains, Planes and Automobiles, the team were stranded, almost burnt alive and very nearly catapulted down a ravine. And Steve Martin thought he had problems...

Things started to get interesting when the railwaymen, angered by the prospect of wage cuts, launched a nationwide strike on the eve of the game. That ruled out the train. Then the charabanc that the club had hired to take them home was commandeered by the local authorities to carry food supplies. Without a bus to get them out of Middlesbrough and with no rooms available in town, the party had no choice but to return to their pre-match hotel in nearby Saltburn. That was the cue for a cab journey that packed in more incident than an episode of Wacky Races. In retrospect, it might have been safer to grab a lift off Helen Keller. In a journey of just eighteen miles, all but one of the cabs broke down and one caught fire, the car only being saved from complete destruction by the quick actions of the players who threw clumps of earth onto the flames.

Despite the directors' best efforts to book another coach, United were stranded in Saltburn for most of the week. With the return fixture against Boro looming and desperation setting in, they opted to accept the first lift that came their way. Unfortunately, that meant tackling the Pennines in a rickety charabanc on a foggy night with a driver who forgot the basic rule of moorland travel... to stay on the path. Towards the end of a journey that would have had Harry Houdini reaching for the Valium, the bus left the road and was moments away from ploughing through a low stone wall and down a gully when Mew, who had volunteered to act as a lookout, shouted out the warning that saved the party from a Young Ones-style demise. If only the Titanic had employed a watchman blessed with Jack's coolness and anticipatory talents... On the form he showed in this and other seasons, the cat-like keeper would have steered a path through the icebergs, edged close enough to one of them to replenish the champagne buckets, rustled up a couple of ice sculptures – and still found time to nip down to the hold for a quickie with Kate Winslet.

If anything is calculated to put someone off travelling by bus (except of course the thought of sharing one with Cliff Richard and Una Stubbs) it is the prospect of being pitched into a ravine. It was no surprise, then, that the players refused to clamber back on board after their near-miss and opted to walk back to Manchester where, to top it all, they were mistaken by railway strikers for blackleg engine-drivers in disguise. As on the moors, it was a wonder there were no deaths.

The rematch against Boro was almost as dramatic as the journey to it, Woodcock's last-gasp headed equaliser providing, as Jacques (The *Athletic News'* United correspondent) put it, 'a fitting conclusion to a game which breathed the essence of real football, with all the components of exciting incident to please the appetite of the most insatiable.' But if the Boro draw was a thriller, the Hyde Road derby the following weekend was even better, possibly the best United-City match so far. Ninety seconds in and the Reds were one up, Hodge driving in from Spence's centre. Sustained City pressure climaxed in a predictable equaliser before half-time but United were the better side after it and deserved the lead given them on 66 minutes by a cheeky piece of improvisation from Spence. As City's keeper Smith bounced the ball to avert the basketball-style carrying penalty that applied at the time, the 'Throckley Whippet' nipped in to flick the ball out of his hands and roll it into the empty net. What Bestie pulled off against Gordon Banks in the sixties, Spence pulled off in the derby. And, unlike Bestie's effort, Joe's goal stood.

Perhaps showing their naivety, the Reds then paid the price for ignoring two of football's oldest clichés. One is that it only takes a second to score a goal. Another is that you are never more vulnerable than when you've just scored. United's lead lasted less time than a drunk's erection, City forward Tommy Browell picking up the ball from the kick-off, exchanging passes with a team-mate and smashing a shot past Mew. A third cliché is that lightning never strikes twice. Try telling that to the Kennedys – or to punch-drunk Reds after the events of the final five minutes. Another lung-bursting dash from the irrepressible Spence set up an opening that was greedily snapped up by left-wing speedster Fred Hopkin. But before the local part-timers could turn and head for the exit, Mew was digging the ball out of the net for a third time. The final City equaliser was a doppelganger for the second. Again Browell swung the ball out to the wing from the kick-off and again he was on hand to meet the centre and smash it into the net.

After coming from behind three times, City fans must have enjoyed their Saturday night pints and picture shows and Sunday evening monkey parades[4] more than most Reds. Give it a week, though, and

---

4. *A long-extinct mating ritual whereby groups of lads and groups of lasses would dress up in their best threads and trail each other through the streets and parks in pursuit of one common objective – sharing a bag of chips. At least that's what old-timers like to make out they were after – ever get the feeling that they protest their innocence too much?*

the smiles had switched sides. The Old Trafford derby was a humdrum affair compared with the Hyde Road spectacular but few among that record-breaking 50,000 crowd were interested in aesthetics once United, whose energy and commitment had given them a slight edge throughout, had eked out a 1-0 win. The 64th minute winner was as scrappy as the match itself, City left-back Fletcher making a mess of a routine back-pass and Spence driving the loose ball past the keeper.

When the Reds then took three points from two battles with Sheffield United they were back in fourth place, just three points behind league leaders Newcastle. Kings of Manchester, record crowds, a bank balance that was off the critical list and, now, a place among the finest teams in the land – not even the football comics could have dreamed up a story as good as this. But the season was about to take a sharp turn for the worse. At a freezing cold Turf Moor on November 8, United's two-month unbeaten run ground to a halt with an anaemic performance and a deserved 2-1 defeat. Much, much worse, the club chairman William Deakin caught a chill which developed into pneumonia and put him in hospital. By the following Saturday, when Burnley edged the rematch at Old Trafford, he was in a critical condition; a week later, when goals from Hopkin, Spence and Hodges gave United a bounce-back, 3-0 win at struggling Oldham, he was in his grave. His replacement as chairman was a well-known face around the city, accountant George H. Lawton. As we shall see, it was an appointment that both sides lived to regret.

Three more defeats as November turned into December hardened the opinion that Robson's youngsters had hit the wall. Fortunately, only two of them – back-to-back flops against a rapidly improving Aston Villa – made it into the record books. In the other match, the Oldham return, United were heading for a three-goal thumping of their own when a thick pea-souper came to their rescue, forcing the game to be abandoned with just a quarter of an hour remaining. Though the referee who, by the end, could see less than Arsene Wenger, had no choice but to take the teams off, the visitors were still peeved on two counts. Firstly, that they had lost two certain points (as it turned out they lost one – when the game was replayed in February, the Latics left Old Trafford with a 1-1 draw); secondly, that United had pulled a swift one by refusing the officials' request to cross straight over at half-time. What Oldham folk were muttering under their breath was that the Reds had been given an inkling that the fog was on its way and had delayed the match as long as they could. There had been stories from the club's Clayton days that United had used the foul-smelling fumes from the local chemical works to their own advantage – that a Red-loving stoker would crank up the furnace when the wind was blowing towards the away goal. Despite the change of postcode, and the inherent difficulties in predicting when a pea-souper was going to arrive, the old suspicions lingered on.

It would have done the supporters a favour if United had played all their matches that winter in thick fog. The 0-2 and 1-2 Villa defeats kicked off a ten-week nightmare during which the Reds picked up only a handful of points and rated, at best, three out of ten for entertainment. In that time only the lads at the back, particularly the brilliant Silcock and Mew, continued to impress the football press pack. The team as a whole attracted the sort of condescending write-ups normally reserved for lower division teams still reeling from a thumping in the Cup. The Reds were invariably plucky and enthusiastic; their opponents classy and skilful.

Actually, the writers had changed their stance little all season. Even on their good days United had been criticised for lacking style. If the teams had been chasing women rather than points, other clubs would have been using charm or looks to entice them out of their clothes; the Reds would have needed to use a bundle of bank notes and the back seat of their Model T. For a while the results were the same but it was obvious that United's way lacked class. A great defence, a half-back line that could defend better than it could attack, energetic forwards and a crude long-ball game had underpinned the club's run of success in the autumn. Now that some of the young players had shot their bolt, the energy that was so vital to their no-frills style had dimmed. Falling back on flair and technique was going to be difficult when there were only two or three flair players on the books and it would become nigh on impossible when the most dangerous of them, Woodcock, became embroiled in a losing battle with illness and injury.

The told-you-sos had stuck in hacks' throats in September and October; not so now. They'd said that the team would struggle with the arrival of the heavy grounds and soggy ball: they had. Robson's lightweights falling to what would later become known as the Olsen-Strachan syndrome. They'd said that it would take time for the better sides to find their feet again in proper football: they had. The teams the Reds were meeting now were in far better shape than they had been a couple of months earlier. They'd said that United's no-frills playing style would be found out: it had been. Defences were now mopping up the predictable stream of long balls to the forwards.

Even Pop Side optimists were struggling to come up with reasons for the side's dip in form that differed from the almost universally held belief that the players had been flattered by their early-season results and were now showing their true colours. After the Oldham abandonment, it was difficult to argue that the Reds had been unlucky. There wasn't much to complain about in terms of injuries either; of the likely starters, only Montgomery had spent any length of time on the treatment table. The best theory anyone could come up with was not that the team was cobblers but that the club's cobbler was. The sight of players running onto the pitch a couple of minutes after the start of the second half was nothing out of the ordinary. It had nothing to do with the standard of the pre-match catering either. More likely, it was the result of a lengthy struggle with a pair of pliers and a hammer trying to replace missing studs. According to *The Football Chron*, United were the worst shod team in the league and now the going had turned from good to soft or good to icy it was starting to cost them.

Before the Reds really started to slip and slide, though, there was one last oasis of pleasure for the Pop Side to enjoy. On December 20, Robson's rookies were too fast and furious for classy Newcastle, Mew's latest master-class and close-range finishes from Spence and Hodges clinching what was arguably the result of the season so far. The unexpected good news from Old Trafford was then trumped by unexpected great news from Old Skinny, aka William Meredith. The dispute between the club and its resident legend had dragged on since his 1912 testimonial and most people thought that the 45-year-old would sit tight until the new year, when the final instalment of his benefit money was due, and then retire. Meredith was a contrary sod, however, and it was typical of him that he should agree terms and re-sign just when everyone was expecting him to pack away his toothpick. Not that his adoring public were complaining. As far as they were concerned, Billy's return, after an absence of four and a half years, was bigger than Armistice Day and Mafeking Night rolled into one.

A noisy 45,000 thronged to Old Trafford for the Boxing Day visit of Liverpool in the hope of seeing the start of something special. But if the reception Meredith received was Cantonaesque, the impact he had on the season fell some way short. Those fans who were looking for Billy to inspire a team packed with home-grown talent to levels that the Hansens of the media did not believe they were capable of were forgetting that the Wizard, though still retaining his best tricks (his ball control, dribbling ability and famous defence-splitting backheel), had been well past the veteran stage even before his long lay-off. On a good day, when his inside-forward and wing-back were giving him the right kind of service and when the opposing full-back did not come out of the dressing-room with the attention of ramming his toothpick down his throat, Billy could still conjure up memories of his golden days before the war. However, when he was starved of the ball and roughed up by defenders, he was a luxury that the team could ill-afford. United's pressing game had been blunted even with eleven workers on the field. With ten men and Billy Meredith standing on the touch-line, arms folded, waiting for the ball to arrive on a platter, an already overworked defence became even more stretched.

If anything, the team's form was worse after Meredith's return than it had been before. Boxing Day was a cold turkey sort of an affair, two strong defences grinding out a goalless bore. The following afternoon the Reds were turned over at St James' Park; on New Years Day they scrambled another nil-nil with the Scousers, this time at Anfield. Apart from a narrow cup victory at second division Port Vale, that was as good as January got. United twice fell suckers to Chelsea's John Cock, the burly centre-forward scoring vital goals as the Blues downed the Reds home and away in the space of a fortnight. Sunderland and West Brom, the champions-elect, then extended the club's beaten league run to four and Aston Villa, the eventual winners, knocked them out of the Cup.

From fourth from top in November, United had now slumped to fourth from bottom and positives were as hard to come by as fat people in a Lowry. At best there were two; the hard-core 20,000 had carried on paying their shilling and the defence had somehow maintained one of the best records in the division – just thirty-three goals conceded in twenty-five games. As had been the case almost all season, the real problems lay at the other end. It had been seven weeks since the Reds' previous league win and in that time they had scored just three goals, one of them a penalty. Their effort could not be faulted but every forward was struggling; Spence was temporarily spent, Hopkin inconsistent, Woodcock up and down and Meredith… well he was 45. Depressingly for the supporters, there was little paper talk linking the club with fresh blood. The club had cashed in on the soccer boom but the directors were reluctant to throw money at an inflated transfer market when it was still needed to pay off the contractors and reduce the debt owed to the president, Davies.

When Sunderland turned up at Old Trafford on Valentine's Day, it must have taken some sort of smooth talking for Reds to get their day passes. You can imagine women across Manchester who had donned their best frock for a day out at Belle Vue muttering, 'I wouldn't mind if they were any good' as their husbands slipped out of the back gate. The tens of thousands who risked an earful were at least rewarded for their loyalty. United may have been outclassed for most of the game by a team that played with one eye on their cup-tie against Villa the following week but Silcock and Moore's stand-in, Cyril Barlow, stood firm and two goals in the final quarter from Hodges and debutant centre-half Fred Harris pinched the win.

A week later, United stormed to a Hopkin-inspired 3-0 at Arsenal and although the next two games – the home returns with the Baggies and the Gunners – ended in defeat, a scruffy victory against Everton on March 6 seemed to have secured their top-flight place; with eleven games remaining, the club were eight points clear of the drop zone. Annoyingly, that was the cue for them to embark on a run of form every bit as desperate as their midwinter slump. Five games, three of them at home, yielded two goals and three points. Insult was added to injury when George V took in a football match in the city and ended up at decrepit Hyde Road rather than swanky OT. To save the King from the trauma of gazing on the grim surroundings, City sneakily used their fans to block his view. According to *The Football Chron*, the human mural did the trick: 'With the royal car gliding silently and unseen behind the assembled throng, the king arrived within a couple of yards of the club offices without being aware of the unlovely spot on the other side of the enclosure.'

While 35,000 were singing 'For he's a jolly good fellow' for the benefit of George at Hyde Road, United were losing to a last minute goal at Valley Parade. When they then slumped to a Good Friday 0-1 against the other Bradford club – Park Avenue – they were back in trouble, just two points ahead of second from bottom Blackburn with seven matches left to play. Critically, two of those games would be against their Lancashire cousins; United also had a double bill with another relegation rival, Notts County, to fret about.

For the first time all season, the selectors could smell the bad breath of relegation up close. But just when panic looked like setting in at Old Trafford, two unexpected heroes emerged from the ranks to calm everyone down again. Ageing half-back Jimmy Montgomery had figured just once since September; Billy Toms, a burly centre-forward from the all-elbows-and-knees school, had yet to find the net in his six league appearances. It is not unkind to say that neither player was headed for the United Hall of Fame but in April 1920, when they were brought into the team as part of the post-Bradford reshuffle, they were the right men in the right place. Montgomery's experience and ability to place the ball along the ground brought much needed craft and assurance to the middle line. Toms' weight and willingness to shoot made the attack a more threatening proposition in more ways than one. Mix in the late-season blossoming of the partnership between Meredith and the promising Scot, George Bisset, on the right and the club had stumbled on the recipe for survival. A bad run of results at that time could have taken them out of the division. Instead, the next seven days turned out to be the best of the entire campaign.

Admittedly the jury was still out on the new-look Reds when they were held 1-1 by Bolton on Easter Saturday though Toms wasted little time in making his mark, ending the side's month-long search for an Old Trafford goal with a crisply volleyed equaliser twenty minutes from time. But the home leg of the Wanderers doubleheader was merely the appetiser to the main events; five-star displays both at Bradford PA and in the Burnden return.

In their previous seven matches, United had scored just three goals. At Park Avenue, they had scored as many inside an hour. Meredith was the catalyst for the victory charge and it was from his memory-stoking dribble and cross that Toms banged in the first on 25. The scabby equaliser United conceded shortly after the restart would have derailed them a week earlier. Now it stung them into a devastating three-pronged riposte as young half-back Jack Grimwood drove in via the shoulder of a defender and both Woodcock and Bisset let rip from distance.

And if Bradford was impressive, Burnden was even better, the

Reds climbing off the canvas to rescue a cause that had seemed lost when Wanderers scored with their first two attacks. Bisset levelled things up with a quick-fire double midway through the first half, Meredith found the eye of the needle for his first United goal since December 1913 and Toms side-footed in from Hopkin's pull-back. A team that had recently been drier than Mecca had struck four times in thirteen minutes and though Bolton pulled one back on the hour, Woodcock's late drive made the points safe.

The Reds hadn't quite crossed the finishing line but they were as good as there. That season-ending foursome against Blackburn and Notts County had lost its crunch, at least for United who now had the luxury of influencing which of their opponents would join doomed Sheffield Wednesday in switching divisions. A pair of home draws made the Reds safe; an Ewood roll-over and a Meadow Lane stroll sent Notts down and lifted United to the giddy heights of twelfth. Since survival had been touted by some as a Mission Impossible, it had been some achievement, perhaps Robson's greatest. For next to nothing, his players-before-points policy had produced players who were capable of winning points in the top league. However, it wasn't just the omnipresent critics, their noses out of joint because their relegation predictions had been proved wrong, who were of the opinion that any street parties should be put on hold. Few Reds were pretending that the quality levels had been high; in fact, many of them were still trying to figure out how a team that had regularly played second division football had managed to stay out of it. A two-month spell of good results when other teams were still finding their feet after the war had been United's saving grace. If they were going to keep out of trouble next time, they would need some more tricks of their own.

Roll of Honour

CHAMPIONS: WEST BROMWICH ALBION

FA CUP WINNERS: ASTON VILLA

UNITED: DIVISION 1 (12TH) - FA CUP (2ND ROUND) ASTON VILLA

At the end of each chapter, we have included a profile of every United player who left the club either during or at the end of that particular season. The profiles are arranged in order of which player joined the club first. We have also included extended profiles of the nine 'Depression Years Legends'. These are scattered throughout the book and do not necessarily appear at the end of the chapter which covers their final season at the club

ARTHUR WHALLEY

CENTRE HALF-BACK, JUNE 1909 – SEPT 1920,
25 APPS 0 GLS (IN DEPRESSION PERIOD 1919-32)
(TOTAL UNITED CAREER: 106 APPS 6 GLS)

BY SIGNING FOR the Reds in the midst of the Outcasts furore, Arthur Whalley unwittingly set the tone for his entire United career. Calling it incident-packed barely does it justice. Two years after his £50 move from Blackpool, Arthur picked up a championship medal, a couple of seasons later he was installed as the regular centre-half in place of the departed Charlie Roberts and the following season he starred for the Football League against the Irish and also impressed for the North in the international trial match against the South. A serious knee injury sustained shortly afterwards dashed Arthur's hopes of full international recognition and triggered a short-lived lurch towards the game's dark side. In 1915 he was one of the eight guilty men who were banned for life for their role in the Good Friday match-fixing affair. With his knee and reputation knackered, Whalley went off to war with the Middlesex Regiment as a disgraced former professional.

He returned from it, three years later, with his career and reputation revived. Having risen to the rank of sergeant and taken a bullet in the leg for his country, Arthur had done more than most to earn his FA pardon. But if his return to the United side after two career-threatening injuries, one life ban and near enough a six-year hiatus was the stuff of fairy tales, his final season as a Red was drearily anti-climactic. A virtual ever-present in the first half of the campaign, Whalley barely featured in the second and when the club could not guarantee him a benefit he asked to be put on the transfer list. The Indian summer he went on to enjoy with Southend, Charlton and Millwall suggested that the directors had made a mistake in alienating him. He was some yards short of being the player he had been before his injury but he remained a clever, elegant schemer and an inspiring captain. On top of that, Arthur was the ultimate survivor and United needed someone with his survival skills more than most.

James Hodge

Utility Player (right-winger in 1919/20), May 1910 – Dec 1919, 16 apps 2 gls (total 86 apps 2 gls)

THE SAYING 'too versatile for his own good' could have been coined for Jimmy Hodge who was at his best at full-back but spent most of his United career being shunted around the pitch, appearing at centre-half, every forward position and even in goal. The closest he came to establishing himself as a Red regular was in 1913/14 when he made over thirty appearances at right full-back. A 'J. Hodge' also filled the number two shirt the following year but, in a nightmarish scenario, it was younger brother John rather than Jimmy who got the nod. Christmas at the Hodge's must have been an interesting experience that year... At least Jimmy had the last laugh, playing on for United in 1919/20 while John faded into obscurity but the 28-year-old had grown tired of his utility role and when Billy Meredith reclaimed his wing berth, he opted for regular football with Millwall. The loss of a loyal and enthusiastic servant was regretted but the £1,500 cheque United received for the archetypal 'Jack of all trades, master of none' was large enough to soak up any tears.

Wilf Woodcock

Inside-forward, May 1912 – May 1920, 30 apps 12 gls (total 61 apps 21 gls)

A LOCAL LAD who learned his trade with Stalybridge Celtic, Wilf Woodcock enjoyed a hot spell with United that began in the spring of 1915, when he contributed seven crucial goals to the successful survival scrap, continued through the war years, when he was the club's leading scorer in three of the four sectional campaigns, and ended with a burst of eight goals in twelve matches in the opening weeks of the Depression Years. Before Billy Meredith  strode out of self-imposed exile midway through that first post-war season, wily Wilf was the exception to the unwritten rule that all United forwards had to have more nipples than brain cells.

A combination of illness, injuries and drooping form limited his effectiveness in the second half of the campaign but Wilf had already shown enough pace and artistry to secure himself a place alongside club-mates Hilditch and Mew on the FA's end-of-season jaunt to South Africa. The initial reaction of the club was to wish him well: 'Everyone at Old Trafford was delighted to hear of the honour done to Woodcock, who, apart from being a fast and clever inside-forward, is a gentleman in every meaning of the word,' noted *The Football Chron.* 'His reputation on and off the field is of the highest, and nothing is so certain as that he will do credit to the club he has served so well for years during the tour.' All of which sounded embarrassingly premature a few days later when Wilf, having fallen out with the club over their refusal to guarantee him a benefit, signed for City. For United to lose their ageing skipper, Arthur Whalley, over a benefit disagreement was unfortunate; for the directors to lose their 28-year-old attacking inspiration in the exact same circumstances smacked of carelessness. The lone consolation for disgruntled Reds was that Wilf, despite helping the Blues to the runners-up spot in his first season, never reached comparable heights again although he did provide a couple of reminders of what might have been when he crossed swords with his old club during his two-year (1922-24) Edgeley Park swansong.

Arthur Potts

INSIDE-RIGHT, MAY 1913 TO JUNE 1920,
5 APPS 0 GLS (TOTAL 29 APPS 5 GLS)

ARTHUR POTTS HAD done a good job for the Reds during their successful battle against relegation in the final season before the war but he was only a bit-part player in the first campaign after it. The competition from Woodcock, Hodges and Bisset nudged him out of the running for his favoured inside-right spot and, after playing in United's opening post-war game at Derby, he made just four more appearances all season. Transferred to second division Wolverhampton for £100 the following summer, Arthur's career enjoyed a short-lived Hollywood spell when he was part of the Wolves side that stunned football by reaching the 1921 FA Cup Final, only to lose 1-0 to Tottenham at Stamford Bridge.

JAMES MONTGOMERY

HALF-BACK, MARCH 1914 – OCT 1921
(APPOINTED JUNIOR COACH)
16 APPS 1 GL (TOTAL 27 APPS 1 GL)

JIMMY MONTGOMERY'S INSTANT impact after his midseason transfer from Glossop was one of the key factors – match-fixing and unscrupulous Scousers aside – in United's unlikely escape from relegation in 1914/15. In his second campaign, six years later, the experienced hard man was again instrumental in the club's end-of-season relegation side-step but, just like Billy Toms, he was never given the chance to repeat his heroics. Never a great player, Montgomery's weight and forcefulness were invaluable assets in a dogfight but an ominously full jersey limited his chances of a regular Red berth. The papers were too polite to call Jimmy fat but when they wrote that 'army life had left him burdened with flesh', that was exactly what they meant.

WALTER SPRATT

LEFT FULL-BACK, FEB 1915 – MAY 1920
1 APP 0 GL (TOTAL 13 APPS 0 GLS)

WALTER SPRATT DID some useful donkey-work for the Reds in the months that followed his £175 move from Brentford in 1914/15 but a serious injury sustained whilst playing wartime football (for Clapton Orient, not United*) cost him his chance of a place in Robson's new-look defence and after making just one post-war appearance, in February's home defeat by Arsenal, he was sent back whence he came.

*Clubs still had first claim on their players in wartime football but only if satisfactory arrangements could be made which did not interfere with their war work. Any player – like Wally Spratt – who could not get to play for his normal club could turn out for any club that was 'convenient to his residence or place of work' (or barracks) as long as he got the written consent of either his old club or the League's Management Committee beforehand.

BILLY TOMS
CENTRE-FORWARD, OCT 1919 – SEPT 1920, 14 APPS 4 GLS

THE ARCHETYPAL FOOTBALL journeyman and nomad, Billy Toms swapped clubs a dozen times during his career and set a record when, following his departure from United, he tasted life in all four divisions of the Football League in less than four years. A career spread thinly around the country drew to an end, perhaps appropriately, at a margarine works, C.W.S. in Manchester in the late twenties. It was all a far cry from the spring of 1920 when Billy played a crucial role in United's late-season scramble for safety. After the 24-year-old had claimed three vital goals in as many games, the *Football News* reported that 'Toms is showing very considerable improvement and his weight is an important factor when facing big backs. What, however, is more important still, he is not afraid to shoot, and although he often misses the target, he has so far proved the best goal-getting forward on the side, and his footwork is a real treat to witness.'

Given that sort of write-up, Billy was perhaps unfortunate not to be given another season or two to see if he could cut it in the top division. Instead, he was packed off to Plymouth and the rest of his playing days were spent in the lower leagues. Billy's blend of loud, aggressive but good-natured charisma was certainly missed at Old Trafford even if his abrasive front running was not. Without the former lieutenant's shouts, songs and full-blooded exhortation, the dressing-room would be a far quieter place. As Alec Bell, the former United legend who was Toms' trainer at Coventry, later observed: 'It was one of the hardest tasks to keep Billy from the habitual and violent exercise of his vocal organs. The nearer we drew to the foe the more he let himself go. He usually infected the whole team in the same manner. As a "turn" he was always good, and as willing as he was appreciable. Such a happy disposition as his goes a long way to foster a spirit of good-fellowship among the boys. I have always liked a lad who could sing. He makes my task a light one.'

JOHN WILLIAMSON

RIGHT HALF-BACK, OCT 1919 – MAY 1921, 2 APPS 0 GLS

A MANCHESTER 'PAL' during the war, John Williamson had his cool and thoughtful moments but he was not in the same class as United's regular right-half, Jack Grimwood, and after playing twice against Blackburn at the back end of 1919/20 (the second match, a 5-0 thrashing at Ewood), he faded into reserve-team obscurity. After helping the stiffs claim their first-ever Central League title the following season, John moved on to Bury and then Crewe before finally hitting the big time with British Dyestuffs. Around the same time he and his wife produced a son, John Jnr., who went on to play 59 times for City; honestly, would it have been that hard for him to keep it in his pants?

JOHN PRENTICE

LEFT-WINGER, NOV 1919 – JUNE 1920, 1 APP 0 GLS

IT IS FAIR to say that John Prentice did not risk a mobbing whenever he walked through Albert Square. Only the most ardent Red would have known who he was. Recruited from Manchester Amateur League football in the autumn of 1919, John made one senior appearance the following Easter, did not fancy another stint as Fred Hopkin's surrogate and took himself off to Swansea Town at the season's end. A year later he dropped out of league football for good.

BOOMTIME

I N THE RUN-UP to the election in 1918, the government had promised to build a land 'fit for heroes'. Once the short-lived post-war boom had come and gone, it was being said that they had kept their word – only heroes would put up with living there. The railway strike that had almost brought the United squad to a sticky end on Marsden Moor was merely the precursor to a couple of years in which an average day at work meant standing at the gates and hurling abuse at blacklegs. That was if you were lucky enough to have a job. By the summer of 1921, over two million people were signing on, food was short, so was money and the tough times before the war were beginning to look like one long round of parties and piss-ups. Still, it could have been worse. In Germany and other European countries, inflation was so bad that bank notes were proving handy as toilet paper, the Russians were still reeling under the effects of their Civil War while in America the poor bastards could not even get a drink.

The football world, however, continued to turn at a different pace. If the first season of post-war football had been a major success, the second was a record-smashing triumph with huge crowds and huge profits at virtually every club. For United, in particular, things had never been so good. Forty thousand crowds were now the norm, 50,000-plus no longer a rarity while the Villa match on Boxing Day pulled in the long-standing record United record of 70,504[1]. When the Reds were at home, the centre of Manchester had the pulling power of a foul-mouthed leper – or St James' Park before the Keegan era. Even the reserves became accustomed to playing in front of big crowds with the visit of Bolton in January attracting a Central League record of 17,000.

1. *The record stood for 85 years until April 2006 when 70,908 watched United's 2-0 win over Arsenal. At the time this book went to press the record stood at 73,006 against Charlton on 7th May 2006 but this was likely to be bettered in 2006/7 now that Old Trafford's capacity has reached 75,000.*

Even before the records started tumbling, the money-men at the club found themselves in a win-win situation similar to the plc's position in the mid-nineties when Sir Alex was filling the stadium, the trophy room and the megastore without the board having to cough up for superstar wages. Minimal investment in the team in 1919/20 and a season of mediocre football had still brought in a five-figure profit. If the fans would turn up in their thousands anyway – and many Reds would have sacrificed their Saturday afternoons just to watch Billy Meredith's wife hang his pants on the line – what was the point of splashing out on new players in the hope of improving the team? As long as they stayed in the top division where the big crowds were, it made better financial sense to use the profits to help clear the club's still-hefty debts.

It was with this bold and ambitious strategy in mind that United prepared for 1920/21. Instead of shopping at Deansgate's finest, Jack Robson had to make do with rooting through the Piccadilly pound shops. While the rumour mill linked him with moves for highly-rated forwards in Stevens of Hull and Preston's Roberts, the five new arrivals were all in the promising novice class. In fact, ageing novice would be a more appropriate description of Billy Goodwin and Teddy Partridge, the two players being touted as the solution to United's attacking problems. When they landed their dream moves from Exeter City and Ebbw Vale respectively, the duo had a combined age of 57.

As a result of the club's transfer policy, Robson's squad was bottom heavy with players who had yet to make a name for themselves and inadequately endowed with players who had. For a crack at the Central League, the United manager was perfectly placed. For a crack at first division glory he was as ill-prepared as the woman who goes out with Mike Tyson without her can of mace. The *Athletic News* reported that there was a 'quiet confidence at Old Trafford', a statement that was met with incredulity by all who read it... What, exactly, were the club quietly confident about? Not needing the key to the trophy room? Struggling more than last year? Making City look like footballing gods?

In fairness, it did not take the directors long to realise that their penny-pinching approach would at best mean another nine months of ball-crushing mediocrity – and, at worst, a year or two sharing the same division as dross like Rotherham County, South Shields and

Leeds United. After a predictably poor start to the season – a draw and defeat against both Bolton and Arsenal – they gave Robson the green light to do some serious shopping. After six years of frugality, he needed no second bidding. In early September, he snapped up Harry Leonard, an experienced (i.e. old), free-scoring centre-forward, from Derby for £800; days later, he splashed out another £2,000 on Liverpool's Scottish international forward Tommy Miller and in mid-October he made it a hat-trick by signing William Harrison, a midget right-winger whom he had been chasing for the best part of twelve months, from Wolves.

For John Henry Davies, the near-£5,000 transfer treble was a means of repaying the public for their recent tremendous support. In particular, it was a tribute to the 50,000 fans who had turned up for the 3-2 opening-day defeat by Bolton and in the process generated League record receipts in excess of £3,300. 'When I saw that crowd,' Davies said, 'I made up my mind that if new players were needed, we would get them no matter what the cost. The directors feel that with such magnificent support as we are getting, and indeed as we got last season, when we made £12,000 profit, it is their duty to the public to do their share towards making the season a success.

'The club is still handicapped financially for reasons pretty well known, but the great following the team has makes it clear that there ought to be a wonderful period of prosperity before Old Trafford. We hope that Leonard and Miller will make our forward line one of the best in the country. Indeed we owe it to that splendid young defence of ours to see that other departments are all right.' The intentions were honourable, the results anything but...

*   *   *

WHEN THE HAT-TRICK of new signings made their first appearances together in the goalless draw at Preston on October 30, the forward line was virtually unrecognisable from the one that had misfired its way through the previous campaign – or even the one that had started the season. Of the regular forwards from 1919/20, only Hopkin survived. Woodcock, who had fallen out with the directors over his benefit, had taken his wily ways to City; Toms and his elbows had left for Plymouth while Meredith and Bisset, who had apparently taken a Sheringham-Cole-style dislike for each other, had been dropped. Goodwin, the biggest close-season buy at a meagre

£640, had been given just one opportunity to impress while Spence and emerging inside-left George Sapsford, both of whom had been virtual ever-presents in the opening couple of months, had also been demoted to the reserves. United's front five on the opening day had consisted of Meredith, Bisset, Goodwin, Sapsford and Hopkin. Once the selectors had sunk their teeth into it, it lined up thus – Harrison, Miller, Leonard, Partridge and Hopkin.

The team's results in their autumn fixtures raised hopes that the new-look attacking unit would indeed live up to their president's billing. Leonard flew out of the blocks, scoring three goals in a week as the Reds belatedly got their season going with back-to-back wins against Chelsea but it was Tommy Meehan who really took the eye on both occasions, the significance of which would become clear later in the season. Miller flopped badly as his United career kicked off with home and away defeats by Spurs but an outstanding performance, and goal, in the 4-1 thumping of Oldham eased the fears that the Scousers had passed on dodgy goods. A thrilling 2-2 draw in the Boundary Park return was then trumped by Harrison's winning debut against Preston before a tight 2-1 against Sheffield United and draws in the Deepdale and Bramall Lane returns extended the side's unbeaten run to six matches.

But the good sequence of results concealed the fact that many of the old problems still remained. United owed most of their points to good fortune, the occasional moment of inspired play in attack, stacks of effort and the continued excellence of Jack Mew and the rest of the defence. Of the £5,000 trio of forwards, only Miller hinted at living up to his price tag. In his few appearances, Harrison had earned comparisons with a cat's tongue such was his penchant for disappearing up his own backside. Already there was talk that Meredith could do a better job. As for Leonard, it had not taken long for him to become the player the Pop Side loved to loathe. Five goals in his opening six games was, on the face of it, an impressive return but he was clumsy, a poor leader of the line, perpetually offside and the slowest thing Old Trafford had seen for years. When Harry ran for the ball he looked like someone who is attempting that pants-round-your-ankles shuffle from the toilet to answer the phone.

At least there had been signs of promise on the left flank with Hopkin starting to add some consistency to his undoubted pace and panache and Sapsford, and then Partridge, showing glimpses of genuine quality at number ten. Behind them, Meehan was showing something like his best form while Silcock had recovered from a slow start to the season to reaffirm his status as the best left-back around. But the strong left half of the team could not cover for the deficiencies of the right forever and it was inevitable that a listing ship would take on water eventually. With the derby doubleheader against City to come, there could not have been a worse moment for United's season to show signs of starting to sink.

*   *   *

IT IS ALWAYS DANGEROUS to take on-going derby-day superiority for granted. If recent blunders show anything, it is that United fans are never more than a Neville or Silvestre disaster away from a weekend they would rather forget. Still, you wouldn't have blamed younger Reds for believing that derby games come with a victory guarantee. Those who were just too young to be tainted by the '89 catastrophe enjoyed the rare privilege of passing through their entire school careers without experiencing a genuinely gut-wrenching derby moment. The 1-1 draw in '92 when City played the part of Zola Budd to United's championship-chasing Mary Decker might just have made them think about bunking off. Otherwise, there was no need. Generally speaking, the nineties chapter of the series between Manchester's Little and Large was as closely fought as contemporary Ashes series, with United discovering a whole host of ways of rubbing Blue noses in it (winning from two goals down in '93, strutting to 5-0 the following year, being gifted that FA Cup penalty in '96...) and City finding as many ways of making us laugh (time-wasting their way to relegation in '96, the Forward with Franny nonsense, Peter Swales' hair...).

Earlier generations of Reds, especially those who were around in the late sixties and early seventies, were not so fortunate. Denis's backheel was by no means the only painful moment of an era when United were in their post-Busby decline and City were enjoying one of their occasional spells when their name and the word that best described them did not rhyme; there was also a 4-0 League Cup thrashing in '75, a seven-year period when the Blues won six times at Old Trafford and the Mancunian one-two of 1968 when City pipped United for the title – though that was a mere wet dream compared with the multiple orgasm that was Benfica at Wembley.

Reds in the early twenties had yet to experience anything as bad as March '68 or April '74 but their first serious derby beating in fourteen years would at least have enabled them to understand why their hairy descendants invaded the pitch. It wasn't just the defeat and woeful performance that hurt, it was the fact that the team had under-performed on such a big stage; in almost thirty years of Manchester derbies, there had never been a game that had roused as much interest as this one.

In wider football terms, the derby doubleheader wasn't even that important. Only a point separated the two clubs in the table but City were eighth and United were eleventh – it wasn't as if the league title was at stake. The reason why the games were as big a talking point around town as Lady Godiva's taste in topiary once was in Coventry had more to do with burning issues off the pitch than the footballing contest on it. In early November, the Hyde Road grandstand had provided the setting for the city's most spectacular bonfire and, in the fallout from the incident, relations between Manchester's big two had been strained to breaking point. Traditionally, they had been the sort of neighbours who enjoy a cup of tea and a chat over the garden fence. Since the blaze, they had become the kind who only raise their heads above the parapet to pour creosote on the roses.

To get to the bottom of the bust-up, we have to rewind a month, to the moment when John Henry Davies, who had been 'impressed by the dangers of overcrowding at Hyde Road, the numbers that had to be turned away and the risks to the football-loving public'[2], had made the unique and generous gesture of offering the Blues the use of Old Trafford for free. At the time, the City board, whining about the disadvantages of playing their 'home' games away and worried about the possibility of a fan backlash, had poo-pooed the idea. Once Hyde Road came to resemble something from Pudding Lane, they suddenly decided that it wasn't such a bad offer after all but when they informed

2.   With only one means of getting to and from the ground, a fire hazard for a main stand, and barriers that would have struggled to contain an excited pack of brownies, Hyde Road was reputed to be one of the most dangerous grounds in the country. The club were fortunate that they had never had a really serious incident to deal with but a catalogue of near-misses had been reported – for example, there had been a small blaze in the grandstand during the King's visit the previous spring – and, as a result, many people were apprehensive about going to watch City play (though not as apprehensive as later generations of Blues would be…).

Davies of their change of heart, they found that he was no longer in the mood to play ball. City had missed their chance of relocating for nothing. If they wanted to use Old Trafford now, they would have to accept the President's new terms and that meant trousering the same gate money as they had from the corresponding matches the previous season. Any surplus would go to United.

As gates had gone up by 30% across the board, neither that offer nor the alternative proposal of the usual 10% terms (for using another club's ground) made the City directors damp with excitement. Instead, they vowed to stay on at Hyde Road and patch up the ground as best they could. With a sympathetic press behind them, they revelled in the role of Angie Watts to United's Dirty Den. The *Athletic News*, a regular Red-beater in previous years, led the attack: 'Manchester United did not in our opinion manifest the much vaunted league spirit [by withdrawing their offer]. They missed a great opportunity to make the club popular by a fine sporting act... the followers of Manchester City have greater affection for the old club than ever. And they have formed a just appreciation of their neighbours.'

The Official United programme, which, I suppose, could fairly be accused of some bias, was the lone voice in support of United's standpoint. They felt that Davies had already shown the 'real fraternal feeling which ought to exist among all clubs, and especially neighbours' (another line from the anti-Red rant in the *Athletic News*) when he made his original offer and that his subsequent decision to do an Oliver Twist and ask for more was entirely understandable in the circumstances. After all, if you turn down a girl once because there are better options open to you, you cannot then bank on the same girl dropping her knickers at a later date, not unless she drops them for a living. The attitude of the United directors was summed up thus: 'I offer you a free loan of a thousand pounds and you say you do not want it. Then you meet with disaster and come and say you want a renewal of the offer. To which I reply that you turned it down when you thought you could do without it and now you ought to pay reasonable terms.'

And though the terms were not over-friendly, they were not that unreasonable either, especially as the City management had assured Davies that they had no intention of benefiting financially from the move to Old Trafford. Pull the other one; Captain Hardy told less of a porky when he promised Nelson it was only a scratch. Held back by

Hyde Road's limited capacity, the Blues had no hope of maximising their earnings if they stayed where they were. By moving to Old Trafford and playing rent-free, they were bound to cash in.

HYDE ROAD, NOVEMBER 27, 1920
MANCHESTER CITY 3 UNITED 0

JUDGING FROM THEIR PERFORMANCE in the Old Trafford appetiser, City's players would have relished a permanent switch across town. The Reds were completely outplayed but Mew's typical brilliance ('The Wonder of Mew' was the pre-Elvis headline in the *Athletic News*), added to a set-piece header from Miller, salvaged an unlikely 1-1. More noteworthy than the game itself, though, were the scenes surrounding it, the likes of which would not have looked out of place at the other end of the century. Old Trafford had hosted huge crowds before but the levels of congestion both inside and outside the stadium were unprecedented.

'Attendance records were broken at Old Trafford when the two Manchester teams met,' reported The *Guardian*. 'Every inch of accommodation appeared to be occupied, and it is estimated that some 66,000 people passed through the turnstiles. The approach to the ground resembled a vehicle park at a great racecourse. Tramway traffic was heavily impeded and on either side of Warwick Road transport of every description was lined up – charabancs (extemporised and deluxe), taxis, private motors, motor-cycles, and even a number of horse-drawn coaches. Hyde Road had sent a young army of supporters, and wherever one sat, opinions and criticisms were instantly challenged or vetoed by an opposing partisan. But it was all in the best spirit.' There is something about those final sentiments, though, which does not quite ring true. If, as the report suggests, the *entente cordiale* between Reds and Blues remained intact for part one of the derby double, it had certainly disappeared by the time the Reds were getting their butts whipped in part two.

In fairness to the United players, the trip to Hyde Road must have been a confusing experience. Few people believed that City would have the ground ready in time and a vastly reduced attendance seemed inevitable. But Mangnall, who had pulled a few rabbits out of his hat in his time with United, had other ideas. In the time it would have taken Fred West to redo his patio, an army of builders had erected new dressing-rooms and offices, built a twenty-five tier uncovered stand and adapted the old Stoneyard Stand into a temporary sitting area. When the work was finished, the ground capacity stood at thirty-five thousand and that was five thousand or so more than it had been before the fire. Instead of the vastly reduced crowd and subdued atmosphere they had been expecting, the Reds walked out into a Blue bear-pit. Psychologically, City were one-up before the game had even kicked off.

When the United players took to the pitch, the band struck up 'I wouldn't leave my little wooden hut for you' and 'Home, Sweet Home'. That may have been innocent enough but the general atmosphere was as unfriendly as anyone could remember and the Reds shrivelled in it. Although Mew was again on form and the defence played stoutly, at least in the first half, United were outclassed, outpaced and eventually overwhelmed. Compared with the fast-moving combination play of the home half-back line and attack, the Reds were hopelessly slow and inept. A goal behind in no time, United were two down at half-time and then conceded again just five minutes into the second half. The third goal proved too much for Mew who became embroiled in an 'unpleasant incident' with City forward Browell, a player with whom he had waged a running battle. Unfortunately, since the press used the phrase 'unpleasant incident' to cover anything from an accidental trip to full-scale war, we cannot be sure what exactly it was that they got up to.

Even though it had been two months since United's previous stumble, the scale and manner of their first Hyde Road defeat since 1906 made casualties inevitable. Few Reds, though, would have dreamt that Tommy Meehan would have been one of them. After a mediocre start to the season, the flame-haired Mancunian had emerged as the one constructive talent in a half-back line desperately lacking in creativity. In both games against City he had stood out like a diamond in a sea of turd yet the directors were still eager to cash in. When Chelsea, who had been vastly impressed with Meehan's contribution to United's two victories over them in September, came in with a £2,000 bid, the 24-year-old was effectively bundled out of the door. He did not fancy a move to London – or anywhere else for that matter – and resisted staunchly for ten days but eventually was pressured into the deal and moved to the Bridge.

The papers and supporters were astonished that a player of

Meehan's youth, skill and versatility had been allowed to leave for what amounted to a bargain price. Unfortunately, it was merely the first sign that the directors had not familiarised themselves with the first rule of football management – keep the class and dump the clowns. After Meehan, the Reds would be involved in plenty more transfer deals which would have only made sense had the players concerned been caught in the missionary position with the club priest.

Less controversially, the City debacle also marked the beginning of the end for tortoise-paced centre-forward, Harry Leonard. The *Evening Chronicle* summed up his performance at Hyde Road thus: 'Leonard was little more than useless: his passing was poor, weak and ill-directed, and he was unconscionably slow on the ball.' Not good then. The same line would have made a fitting epitaph for Harry's short-lived United career. He would only play once more for the first team and indeed spent most of the second half of the season back home in Derby, picking up his £9 a week without even turning out for the reserves. As falls from grace go, his was particularly spectacular; a year after performing in front of record crowds at Old Trafford, he was eking out the last drops of his career in front of one man and his dog at non-league Heanor Town. Not even Neil 'the postie' Webb fell so far, so fast which was just as well given the extra baggage the Neil-y man was carrying at the end of his United career – the impact of his landing could have triggered a second Ice Age.

Having dumped Leonard, the selectors pushed Miller across to his favoured centre-forward position and gave recent recruit Joe Myerscough a shot at cementing a place at inside-right. If both men ultimately deceived in their new roles, they did at least deliver a few weeks' flattery beforehand – in their first three outings together, the duo shared an impressive eight goals. The half-back line got a post-derby makeover, too, Tommy Forster taking Meehan's old position on the left and Grimwood ousting Hilditch from the centre-half berth. Both newcomers went on to enjoy excellent seasons – Forster won the hearts of the fans with his weekly impression of a Jack Russell on steroids while Grimwood's all-round style and dynamism made him the latest prospect to be hailed as the new Charlie Roberts – but it was asking too much for them to come into the side and straightaway fill the creative void left by Meehan. The inevitable result was that the half-back line – and the team as a whole – continued to do most of their best work in their own half rather than in attack.

Admittedly, there did not seem much wrong with the new-look Reds as they racked up eight points out of eight in early December. Bradford Park Avenue were swept away on successive weekends by the Myerscough-Miller goal deluge, Newcastle were turned over 2-0 at Old Trafford and Aston Villa were edged out at Villa Park in a seven-goal Christmas Day thriller. But the Newcastle game was the only one in which the side demonstrated anything resembling top-flight quality. Beating the cup-holders, Villa, on their own turf was no mean achievement but the 4-3 win was a triumph for commitment and stickability rather than class. If the two keepers had swapped sides, the hosts would have strolled to the points – Stephen Hawking would have made a more formidable barrier between the sticks than Villa's inexperienced third choice, Spires. As for the Bradford wins, well everyone stuffed Bradford – at the halfway stage of the season they had already conceded almost fifty goals. Both Park Avenue and fellow stragglers Derby seemed hell-bent on taking the wooden spoon which was great news for the other teams who had been tipped as relegation possibles. With twenty-four points on the board already, United were well clear of a bottom two who had claimed just eighteen between them. Whatever happened in the second half of the season – and little of it was pretty – survival was more or less guaranteed.

The Advent wins made the return game with Villa on Boxing Day a must-see event. The 70,000-odd fans who turned up for the match set a new record for the provinces and also gave the club a better idea of how many people Old Trafford could safely hold. The answer was rather less than that amount; large numbers could not see the action and a number of barriers gave way under the pressure. There was also the invisible menace that was the inevitable result of thousands of people filling their necks with turkey, sweets and booze one day and then being crammed into a confined space early the next. Anyone who held a lit match for too long ran the risk of going the same way as the Hyde Road grandstand. (Incidentally, the belly-churning prospect of sitting near someone with ripe guts is never a consideration when the television companies switch kick-off times to midday. It would be appreciated if lads who were probably still wrestling with a greasy donner in the early hours were allowed the chance to do some serious damage to the porcelain before they set off for a game. The atmosphere at early kick-offs is invariably poor in more ways than one.)

As for the match itself, United continued a trend stretching back to the opening day of the ground – when Liverpool pooped the party by winning 4-3 – of under-performing in big games at Old Trafford. This time Villa brought along a goalkeeper who had a decent grasp of what to do and, with United's attack suffering an overdue off-day, that virtually guaranteed an away win. Wright, the fit-again Villa keeper, denied both Harris and Myerscough with top-drawer saves in the first half when the Reds were in the ascendancy. United then fell to a sucker blow just before the break and fell apart thereafter. Walker, the visitors' centre-forward, grabbed a couple and Stephenson secured the points with a third minutes after Harrison had brought United back into the game with his second goal in as many days (I should stress that it was the only purple patch in Billy's season – otherwise, most reports conveyed the impression that he could not have been more tightly shackled if he had been locked in a box at his local madam's).

What many people had predicted would happen after the humiliation by City instead materialised following the disappointment against Villa. United lurched into a sequence of results even more desperate than their run of form at the same stage of the season the year before. In 1919/20, the Boxing Day draw with Liverpool had been the prelude to a run of seven wins and eleven defeats from twenty-six games which included defeat at the hands of Villa in the fourth round of the Cup. In 1920/21, the Boxing Day defeat by Villa was followed by a sequence of six wins and fourteen defeats from twenty-four games which included defeat at the hands of – you've guessed it – Liverpool in the Cup. The difference this year was that United bade farewell to the competition at the first, rather than second, hurdle though they were unlucky to lose (2-1 in the replay) after outplaying the Scousers in the original tie. That game was memorable for a goal from Miller that was described in the *Athletic News* as 'a veritable masterpiece of individual brilliance'. Receiving the ball in midfield, he beat two defenders 'with delightful ease and drove the ball past Scott without ever losing control or making a false move'. It was the work of an artist; unfortunately, it was the last time that Tommy would step to the canvas in United colours. After a desperate dip in form in the second half of the season – and no goals in his final twelve league appearances – he joined Harry Leonard in passing through the exit door in the summer.

A 6-3 hammering at Newcastle on New Year's Day provided the first hint of the horrors to come. Despite being lame for most of the game and conceding plenty, Mew was rated among the two best Reds so you can imagine how good the other nine were. The other innocent party was Partridge who earned the penalty from which Silcock clattered in his first-ever senior goal, set up his flying wing-partner, Hopkin, for the strike that tied the scores momentarily at two apiece and then netted a late consolation. United would be grateful for the continued good form of Partridge – and Hopkin – in the weeks to come as the rest of the forwards regularly gave the impression that they were being paid by the opposition. Most of all, though, they would be thankful for the uncompromising work of the defence. The St James' indignity was matched a fortnight later when the Reds were rolled over 4-1 by reigning champions West Brom but that was it as far as humiliating beatings went, at least for the next couple of months or so. Thanks to a rearguard that would soon feature two England internationals (Silcock and Mew[3]), United's half-dozen defeats in dismal February and March were invariably by the slenderest of margins.

And on those odd occasions when the forwards clicked, the side's defensive solidity usually guaranteed at least a point. A week after the West Brom lesson at home, the Reds turned the tables with a shock victory in the Black Country. Hopkin was the architect of the decisive goals from Myerscough and Partridge but Mew and his full-backs, Silcock and Cyril Barlow, were the architects of the win – Jack was so good that the West Brom directors made a point of visiting the dressing-room after the game to congratulate him. The Sunderland game, a winless month later, was another personal triumph for the brilliant 31-year-old. Mew kept a 'clever and dashing goal', picked up more than £1,000 from his share of the 40,000 gate and also ended up with a rare win bonus as the Reds romped home 3-0. The introduction of a trio of forwards – Goodwin, Sapsford and Irish winger James Robinson – from the successful reserves made all the difference. Of the new boys, Robinson enjoyed his day in the sun the most, scoring one goal and setting up another.

3.   *Mew made his England debut in the 2-0 win over Ireland in October 1920. Silcock won his first cap in the goalless draw with Wales the following March.*

The youth formula also worked in the Roker Park return as United survived a late Sunderland onslaught to claim their third 'double' of the season but the rookie-inspired revival was derailed by the Reds' midweek defeat at Goodison Park and all but forgotten by the end of their dreary doubleheader with Bradford City a fortnight later. Both games ended in undeserved draws and the United reporter from the *Athletic News* must have been tempted to re-hash the line he had penned after watching the home failure against Everton the previous month: 'I would like to pay all kinds of compliments to Manchester United, but they have deprived me of the most pleasant part of a critic's function – the opportunity to bestow praise.' In the 1-1 draw in Bradford, the forwards were weak and ineffective; in the 1-1 draw at Old Trafford, they produced their poorest exhibition of the season. Given the competition involved, it must have been a display of ineptitude to compare with the White House interpreter who allowed JFK to (supposedly) announce to the world that he was a jelly doughnut[4]. At least United did their battered image a favour by becoming the first – and only – club to donate the gate money to the fund dedicated to ex-servicemen. Unfortunately for the veterans, that did not guarantee as large a cheque as it would have done earlier in the season. By the time of the Bradford match, gates were down to a hard-core of between twenty and thirty thousand.

Considering what was being served up on the pitch, twenty thousand was still a good crowd. The Easter fixtures presented United at their worst. On Good Friday they were edged out by a single goal at Burnley, the following day they were trounced 5-2 at Huddersfield and on Easter Monday the Clarets completed a swift double by romping to a 3-0 in Manchester. It was relegation form but the Reds were never so bad that they allowed themselves to be sucked into the battle for survival. Both Derby and Bradford picked up their game in the second half of the season but neither could make up for their abysmal starts. In the end, the Tykes won the race for the wooden spoon and United finished in fourteenth place, a comfortable fourteen points ahead of the second-from-bottom Rams.

Perhaps the lack of pressure played its part in the side's insipid form. Perhaps, as the eccentric (i.e. batty) Ted Dexter once said to explain why the England cricket team had been steamrollered by the

---

4.   ('*ich bin ein Berliner*')

Aussies, it was caused by Venus being in the wrong juxtaposition with somewhere else. More clued-up Reds would admit that the lack of quality in the team was at last being reflected in the results. That the club were enjoying the rare pleasures of a dead season was down to the fallibility of others as well as that fortunate run of results over weaker teams earlier in the season. A glimpse at the final league table showed that United had kept their place at the top table by feasting on the small fry. Of their fifteen wins, only three had come against teams who finished above them. Like Mussolini in the thirties, the Reds had maintained their status by beating the King Zogs and Abyssinias of the division rather than any of the big boys.

United only got the better of one team that ended the season in the top ten; Middlesbrough on April 9. By then, the directors had decided to phase out the new players they had introduced during the season and revert back to the previous year's model. Time was running out for the high-price flops. Leonard, who had been brought back for the second Burnley defeat, would never darken United's door again, Miller would play just twice more and Harrison once, although he, at least, had another season at Old Trafford left in him. Spence, who had been banging them in for the reserves, was given another chance at centre-forward while Bisset was called up after an eight-month absence and pitched in alongside Meredith.

The shake-up inspired a revival of sorts as United ended the season by taking seven points from their final seven games. Moreover, it gave Meredith, who featured in all but one of those matches, the opportunity to embark on a well-deserved valedictory tour. Despite making enough of an impact to endorse the frequently aired opinion that he remained one of the club's best forwards, Billy was granted his free transfer in the summer. After sixteen years, 332 games, 35 goals, countless headlines, five trophies and as many suspensions, the great man was gone. But not finished. Even though he would never see 45 again, there was never any doubt what Billy would do next. When the 21/22 season kicked off he was back wearing the blue of City.

It was undeniably the end of an era. The Wizard's departure cut all links with the great days under Mangnall before the war. Then, United had been all about style, stars and silverware. What was left was an outstanding stadium, a huge and loyal support and a team that did not match up to either. At least there was hope in the form of the talented reserve side that had romped to the club's first-ever

Central League title but the Reds had been down the youth route before and had almost finished the season in a different division from the one they had started in. The alternative was to throw more money at the transfer market in the hope that the next big-name signings did not turn into big mistakes like Leonard and co. But with £5,000 effectively pissed down the drain, the directors were understandably reluctant to put their hands in their pockets – their participation in that summer's market would be minimal. Yet by keeping their money where it was they were effectively playing Russian roulette with the club's future. And after hearing clicks in the previous two seasons it was surely only a matter of time before their number came up.

ROLL OF HONOUR

CHAMPIONS: BURNLEY

FA CUP WINNERS: TOTTENHAM HOTSPUR

UNITED: DIVISION 1 (13TH) - FA CUP (1ST ROUND) LIVERPOOL

Thomas Meehan

Wing-half back, June 1917 – Dec 1920
53 apps 6 gls

In terms of bad ideas, selling Tommy Meehan to Chelsea was right up there with Michael Hutchence's decision to spice up his last thrill. Everyone who had seen the little craftsman (he was just 5ft 6in) play – bar, it seems, the United directors – knew that he was going to be something really special. How frustrating it must have been for Reds to read and watch as he fulfilled all that early promise – and more – at Stamford Bridge. Within three years of his move down south, the reluctant Blue had won some of the game's highest honours (one England cap, two call-ups for the Football League side and a Charity Shield appearance for The Professionals against The Amateurs*) and earned the admiration of press, fans and peers alike. In 1924, the *Football News* did a piece describing him as 'a marvel for his inches and a real ornament to the game'. That same year Everton's Sam Chedgzov nominated him as one of his most dangerous opponents, telling the readers of the *Topical Times*: 'Tommy Meehan, of Chelsea, is only a little fellow, but one of my biggest worries; I never know where I am with him. He is a most deceptive half-back. His tactics always baffle me, and there is no limit to his capacity as a worker. Meehan worries the life out of me all the time. He is like a jack-in-the-box and sometimes when I think he should be nowhere near me, up he pops in front of me, kicks the ball between my legs, and is off before I rightly know what is happening. Yes, I should say that the ex-Manchester United player is one of my greatest worries, because I never know what he is up to.'

The tragedy for Meehan's many admirers was that the great times did not last long. In the latter stages of the 23/24 season he contracted sleepy sickness and in August that year he died in London's St George's Hospital, aged just 28. The whole of football mourned. A crowd in excess of 2,000 attended his funeral at Wandsworth Cemetery and a benefit fund was immediately set up to support his wife, four children and invalid parents. A match between Chelsea and Tottenham was arranged and, in total, a sum of £1,580 was raised.

* *The Charity Shield adopted a number of formats in its early years. When it began, in 1908,*

it was contested by the champions of the Football League and the champions of the Southern League (United won the first and fourth Shields, beating QPR 4-0 in 1908 and Swindon 8-2 in 1911). Over the next thirty years it was contested by the cup winners and the Corinthians, by the league champions and the cup winners and, on five occasions (1913 and 1923-26), by the Professionals and the Amateurs.

FRED HOPKIN

LEFT-WINGER, MAY 1919* – MAY 1921, 74 APPS 8 GLS

*Hopkin, then a Darlington player, guested for United
in sectional matches from March 1916

IN HIS EARLY DAYS, the papers could never decide whether to call United's left-winger Fred Hopkin or Fred Hopkins which was understandable because for most of the time there seemed to be two of him. In some games, the number eleven shirt was filled by a pacy raider – the 'Darlington dasher' – who would burn off the fastest defenders and send over a never-ending stream of enticing crosses; in others it was worn by the Darlington ditherer, a player blessed with an abundance of pace but with seemingly little idea of how to use it.

Two seasons into his United career, it was clear that Hopkin had stopped taking the Jekyll-and-Hyde pills and had developed into one of the most consistent and dangerous outside-forwards in the top division. He would never have been mistaken for a really classy ball player and his goal return did not do justice to a thumping shot but he was brave, direct and a fine assists merchant. His pace remained his main asset, however, and it was a sad indictment on the passing ability of the rest of the side that in some games he saw less ball than Eva Braun; with Fred around, there was every chance of a clueless lump up the pitch being turned into a defence-splitting through-ball.

As Hopkin had the potential to develop into one of the best outside-forwards in the country, it was a major surprise when he was sold to Liverpool for £2,500 in the 1921 close season. The official explanation for the transfer was that 'the player was unsatisfied' at Old Trafford. That may have been so but the directors were in no position to let him go, particularly for such a low fee. Less than six months after cutting their own throats with the Meehan deal, they had done it all over again.

George Albinson
Wing-half, May 1919 – May 1921, 1 app 0 gls

A LOCAL BOY who did not quite make good, languid left-half George Albinson was never able to make the leap from Central League stalwart to first-team contender and left United after making just one senior appearance – in the unfortunate 2-1 cup defeat by Liverpool in January '21. Subsequent moves to City and Crewe did not work out for him either and in 1925 he gave up on his League career and joined Cheshire side Witton Albion.

Frank Hodges
Inside-right, Aug 1919 – June 1921, 20 apps 4 gls

Frank Hodges arrived from Birmingham via St Mirren (for whom he had starred in wartime football) with a reputation as a clever schemer with a deft touch. He just about lived up to it in his first season as a Red but a disagreement over terms led to him falling out of favour in 20/21 and, after making just two appearances all season, he was shown the door. Frank's next move took him to Wigan Borough who had just been accepted into the newly-formed third division north. His double against Nelson on the opening day of 1921/22 were the first goals that the Pie-Eaters ever scored in League football.

Harry Leonard
Centre-forward, Sept 1920 – June 1921, 10 apps 5 gls

'LEONARD IS A real centre-forward,' swooned *The Football Chron* when Harry was snapped up from Derby. 'He keeps his position. One does not find him all over the place, running about needlessly. When the ball arrives in the centre he is there. Long experience has given him a cool head. It will be surprising if he does not prove a success at Old Trafford.' Oops...

...What United actually got for their four figure investment was an over-the-hill 34-year-old who still knew the way to goal – five goals in ten appearances was no mean return – but usually looked in need of a bus pass to get him there. A summer of inactivity following a bust-up with his former employers had done nothing for his efforts to roll back the years and neither did the road accident he was involved in shortly after moving to Manchester. Knowing the speed of Harry's reflexes, he was probably hit by a runaway milkfloat.

TOMMY MILLER

FORWARD, SEPT 1920 – JULY 1921, 27 APPS 8 GLS

TOMMY MILLER WAS the most successful of the hat-trick of disastrous signings that Jack Robson made in early 20/21 but, paradoxically, also the most disappointing. Harry Leonard and Billy Harrison were known to be on the slide even before they proved it in such spectacular style. By contrast, Tommy arrived, apparently in his prime, with a reputation as one of the best inside-forwards in the game and left, three decent months and seven bad ones later, as a homesick misfit. The homesickness excuse smacks of a red herring; after all, the Scottish international had been plying his trade south of the border for nigh on a decade. But it was the best explanation that anyone ever came up with for his failure to make his class tell at Old
Trafford. A bright start – four goals in three games – after succeeding hapless Harry at centre-forward was followed by a long drought and by the time he was helping Scotland to their famous 3-0 Hampden victory over England in the spring of '21, Tommy was a Red irregular. Perhaps uniquely, he did more for the United cause before he joined the club than he did when he was on the books. As one of the guilty Scousers in the infamous 1915 match-fixing affair, Tommy had played a material role in saving the Reds from relegation.

Depression Years Legend

Billy Meredith

Right-winger Oct 1906 – July 1921
35 apps 3 gls (total 332 apps 35 gls)
b. Black Park, near Chirk, Wales
30th July 1874
d. Withington, Manchester
19th April 1958
Height: 5' 9" Weight: 11st.4lbs.
Debut: United 1-0 Aston Villa 01/01/07

Career: *Black Park (Chirk) 1890, Northwich Victoria (am.) 1892, (pro.) Sept 1893, Manchester City Oct 1894, United Oct 1906, Manchester City player-coach July 1921-1924, United coach Sept 1931*

International career *(for Wales): 48 apps (including 3 official post-war apps): (Wales 2-2 Ireland at Belfast 14/02/20, Wales 1-1 Scotland at Ninian Park 26/02/20, Wales 2-1 England at Highbury 15/03/20) 11 gls*

The greatest winger of all time? The greatest British footballer of all time? Simple. If you are a Red and are still breathing it is George Best. If you were a Red and are long gone it is Billy Meredith. In a career spanning four decades, the Welshman bestrode his profession like no other. Even twenty years after his retirement it was blindingly obvious that the game had seen no better. Don't just take my word for it either. His contemporaries were queuing up to say the same sort of thing. When the *Topical Times* ran a series in the early twenties in which the stars of the day nominated the game's greatest ever player, Billy's name dominated like no other.

Pre-war Newcastle great Colin Veitch led the plaudits, enthusing: 'Meredith was without equal as a right winger amongst all the wing men I have ever seen. I shall long remember his speciality in legs [steady, Colin!] and his bosom pal, the toothpick! Associated with these were superb command of the ball, individual brilliance, and excellence in combination with his partner and the moving half behind him. As for his centres – well, if anything more perfect has been known in that particular branch of the game, I should like to know of it. If, perchance, the ball was not well and truly delivered in front of the goal when he finished with it somehow one felt that the ball must be to blame, so rarely was anything but the correct flight forthcoming.'

Steve Bloomer, England's then record goalscorer, added: 'As long as I can remember him, he has been a wonderfully brilliant winger. His close dribbling and elusive feinting, his centring while on the run, his desire always to do the best thing in the quickest and shortest way, and his beautiful ball control were things of joy.'

England goalkeeper Sam Hardy nominated Billy as the best player he'd ever seen, explaining: 'There never was a player who could manipulate the ball like Billy, and there never was a winger who could centre like him'. The Wizard's own keeper, Jack Mew, concurred: 'As a player I place Billy on a pedestal of his own and far above anybody else, because it is my firm conviction that he is easily the best player who has ever kicked a ball… I unhesitatingly state that there never has been a player who had the ball control Meredith has, and I have seen a few tricky forwards in my time. Has any exponent of the game ever brought that wonderful backheel touch to the state of perfection Billy did? Has there ever been a winger who could place a centre with the deadly accuracy of Meredith? I very much doubt it.'

A man never known for his modesty, Billy would no doubt have endorsed all of the above. But he was honest and farsighted enough to recognise that his brilliance as a player would ultimately be overshadowed by his most famous habit. In his memoirs, he wrote: 'It is wonderful what trifles help to make a man famous. Long after my fame as a football Internationalist has become dim, my name will be remembered as the man who required a toothpick to help him play football.'

Billy's toothpick had long been the subject of popular speculation and debate. In the next breath he gave the definitive answer to why he played with one permanently attached to his lower lip. It was, he said, an offshoot of his Welsh roots, specifically the decade he spent working down the mines in his native Chirk: 'Welsh miners chew tobacco. I chewed tobacco. When it got worked up I made more steam than I could consume. The groundsman swore that if Billy Meredith did not stop chewing twist there would not be a single blade of grass on the ground next season. One opponent observed, "I don't mind a fellow taking the game seriously. Still there is no reason for him to froth at the mouth."

'It wasn't nice I quite admit, but habit had made it necessary to chew something while getting coal, and habit is more than second nature. My pals tried to help me. Some suggested thistles [they weren't pals, Billy...], and I tried straw. But I ate straw too quickly. By accident I took a wooden toothpick from the table where I had lunch one Saturday. Putting it between my teeth I discovered that I had discovered it. I could nibble away, and by the time I had got through with it the ref had whistled us off the field. Since then, the partnership of Meredith and his toothpick has become famous.'

What Billy could not possibly have envisaged, however, was how fresh his name would remain today, almost half a century after his death. Whereas his contemporaries have mostly been forgotten, the deeds of William Henry Meredith have become established in football folklore. Maybe if Bloomer, Veitch and the rest had had a famous prop, their names would have lived on, too. Then again, the toothpick was only a small part of the makeup of the Meredith legend. Billy's incredible star quality and individuality, his politics, reforming zeal and taste for controversy, as well as his immense talent, were equally important ingredients.

So was his astonishing longevity. Few players have given old Father Time the run-around that the Wizard did. When he kicked his last ball for United, in the 3-0 rout of Derby on the final day of 20/21, he had been playing professionally for twenty-seven years and was just weeks away from his forty-fifth birthday; when he enjoyed his fairy-tale hurrah with City in their run to the FA Cup semi-finals in 1924 he was closing in on fifty. This at a time when players did well to stretch their careers into their thirties.

Billy himself would claim that his incredible durability, and apparent immunity from injury, was the result of the eight years he spent down the pit in his native Chirk, starting at the age of twelve when he was given the job of unhooking the tubs at the bottom. But if nature and the mines had made him tough, speedy, well-balanced and wiry, years of meticulous self-devotion ensured he stayed that way. Whereas other players lived as hard as they played, Billy shunned the booze and the fags, his only luxuries being an occasional glass of claret and his pipe. Treating his body as a temple became a Meredithian obsession. Massages, herbal remedies, heat treatments down the Hydro, his favourite 'dog fat' rub and regular hot baths placed Billy years ahead of his time in terms of professionalism and preparation.

His team-mates, particularly his wing partners, may have given another explanation for Meredith's staying power; that he looked as fresh as he did because he was a wizard at delegating the donkey work. The way Billy played, the relationship between the outside-right and his inside man was conducted on a master and servant basis; he mastered, his partner served. The role did not suit everyone. Harold Halse, an outstanding player and goalscorer who played 124 games for United between 1908 and 1912, was too much of a free spirit to tie himself down to the job of Billy's Man Friday. Pre-war, Meredith developed a far more intuitive understanding with John Picken, a relatively unsung plodder. But if partnering the Wizard was a potentially odious task, playing on the other flank offered a taste of footballing nirvana; a procession of beautifully crafted centres that were practically begging to be banged into the net. Billy and inside-left Sandy Turnbull dovetailed as effectively on the pitch as they did for their Beadlesque pranks[1] off it, a Meredith dribble and cross and a decisive header from Sandy being as regular a cause of communal orgasm among United fans as a Bobby dazzler or a Denis scissors-kick decades later.

In his defence, Billy would have argued – with some justification – that his job as a winger was not to scrap for possession but instead to hold his position on the flank and cause havoc whenever the ball arrived at his feet. But it was an undeniable fact that the older he got, the more time he spent doing next to nothing on the touch-line. In some of the matches Billy played for United after the war, a shooting-stick would have been as appropriate an accessory as his toothpick. After one game, at Chelsea in January 1920, the *Football News* reported that 'it was almost pathetic to see him standing in idleness on the halfway-line with his arms folded and chewing his indispensable quill.' And the less work Billy did, the easier it was for defences to snuff him out. Throughout his career there had been the odd detractor willing to buy the line that he did not enjoy being closely marked – as if any player does. Once he entered his forties, it was an undeniable fact that he could be negated by any back who was strong, quick and mean enough to rough up a national treasure.

1. *Before Turnbull's death in the war, Billy and Sandy formed a two-man Crazy Gang, cutting up socks, tying sleeping team-mates to their chairs and generally running schemes to embarrass and annoy. In their most famous wind-up, Sandy would dress up as a woman and stand at the hotel bar with his back to the room, Billy would tell a team-mate that the 'lady' at the bar was asking for him and, if the player showed any interest, Sandy would spring out from beneath his disguise and land a smacker on his lips.*

Gratifyingly, things never got to the stage where the Meredith circus degenerated into a freak show. He wasn't the player he once was, that much was as inevitable as it was obvious, but he did not get picked on reputation alone. On his day he could still turn it on. In City's cup quarter-final with Cardiff in March '24 it was silver-haired Billy who held the attention of the crowd and laid on the game's only goal. When he left Old Trafford he was still considered the best right-winger on the books. All the same, there were signs that even the Wizard had outstayed his welcome. It was not unknown for ironic cheers to break out on away grounds when he belatedly got himself involved in a game or for a blasphemous minority on the Pop Side to heckle him if he was having an off-day at Old Trafford. It was perhaps a mistake that Billy did not call it a day when United refused him his free transfer in 1919. Thereafter there was always a suspicion that his heart, which he famously said was always full of it (meaning football), was no longer in it (meaning United). And it was an avoidable shame that the Wizard, by taking his career into its 'Old Skinny' (unsurprisingly, a nickname that Billy hated) phase, crossed the line from being a wonder of his age to being a wonder for it.

Where he did get his timing right, however, was in leaving the club when he did. Like Bobby and Denis in the seventies, Billy sidestepped career-tainting relegation by just one season. Like Denis, he moved to City on a free transfer and went on to play a leading role in a derby nightmare. The key difference was that Billy was spared the trauma of having to kick – or backheel (a classically Meredithian method of torture) – the Reds when they were already down. No, as we shall see, the only Mancunian blood Meredith ever felt on his fingers was Blue.

*   *   *

LOOKING BACK, IT IS astonishing that City ever wanted Billy back. During his first spell at Hyde Road he had done more than any other player to transform the club from bankrupt nobodies into cup winners. Then again, he had also done more than anyone else to bring them crashing right back down again. In the battle between City and the FA that obliterated their 1904 cup-winning side and led to the balance of power in Manchester swinging decisively from Blue to Red, Billy was by far the most prominent figure.

In fairness, the war was by no means all of his own making. Professional football had been around since 1885 but the game remained a sea of unresolved issues; a battle between professional and Corinthian values, the FA and the Football League, gentlemen and the working classes and the concept of football as a game and of football as a business. Not even the stalest old fart at the FA could deny that the sport had taken massive strides forward since turning pro but the authorities' thirst to clamp down on professionalism, to preserve the 'sporting' nature of the game and, most of all, to counter the 'destructive greed' of the players remained undiluted. So, in an age when entrepreneuralism was all the rage, when ordinary workers could bank on freedom of contract and movement and the right to sell their labour to the highest bidder, footballers remained stuck in a modernised form of serfdom. They could not move unless their club were prepared to release them, they carried a price tag on their heads and their earning potential was restricted by the FA-enforced maximum wage which, in Edwardian times, stood at £4 a week, including bonuses.

The inherent contradiction of football – that of a professional game being run by a body that really wanted it to be amateur – made it inevitable that the FA and the professionals would collide at some stage. Two factors made Hyde Road the standout choice for the battleground. The first was the widespread suspicion (which was later proven) that City's success owed as much to bribery and corruption as it did to the quality of their football. The maximum wage had created a thriving black market at virtually every big club, including United, but it seems that City's directors were the worst offenders. An elaborate system of rule-dodging devices – under-the-counter payments, unexplained expense accounts, bulging slush funds et al. – allowed them to stuff as much cash in the players' back pockets as they did in their official wage packets. In 1904, none of the cup-winners were on less than £6 a week (50% more than the regulations allowed) while at least one player was taking home £8. In addition, the club paid out £650 in bonuses at roughly £50 a man.

The second factor was Billy Meredith's emergence as a political as well as a playing colossus. The enslavement of footballers had caused massive resentment throughout the game but most players, worried about the consequences of making a stand, opted to keep their grievances to themselves. Meredith was different. Having earlier won a battle with his conscience over the rights and wrongs of playing a game for money, he was determined that every professional footballer should have the right to get out of his career all he could. Using his fame as his platform, Billy soon turned himself into the campaigner for player rights *nonpareil*. No Meredith interview or article was complete without him launching a scathing attack on the FA and putting over the moral and financial case for a shake-up of the system. Put simply, professional footballers were full-time skilled workers, not part-time players. They were not playing for enjoyment, they were playing for their clubs and to support their families. And the bottom line? They were citizens of this country and deserved the same rights as everyone else.

Meredith's campaign for player rights raised the spectre of the players rising up en masse against the FA. City's flagrant flouting of football law raised the possibility of the clubs joining suit. With the whiff of revolution burning their nostrils, the authorities decided to launch a pre-emptive strike. Two weeks after the Blues beat Bolton to win the cup (with Meredith – who else? – scoring the [offside] winner) they stormed into Hyde Road and demanded to see the club's books. The subsequent investigation, which lasted for two months, nailed one player and a quartet of directors for making illicit signing-on payments but – to the evident disappointment of the FA – failed to uncover any evidence of illegal wages or bonuses. City and their most famous player had slipped the noose this time. Given the sums involved, however, they could not hope to evade detection forever.

A year later, a bad-tempered match between championship-chasing City and Aston Villa gave the authorities another excuse to go on a fishing expedition around the club's affairs. This time they landed the catch they wanted. What began as an inquiry into a fracas involving Villa's Alec Leake and City's Sandy Turnbull swiftly lurched into a gloves-off, open-ended interrogation as unsuspecting witnesses were brought before 'secret courts', plied with questions and pressurised and manipulated into singing from the Commission's song-sheet. When the FA's findings were published on August 5, 1905, they provided the biggest sensation the game had ever known; Meredith, the itch the Establishment had longed to scratch, had been found guilty of offering Leake £10 to throw the match and had been suspended for eight months.

The immediate reaction of most was a mixture of shock, dismay, sympathy and confusion. Many people were stumped as to why an inquiry into a fracas in which Billy had not even been involved had ended with him being hit by a bribery charge. The typical northern viewpoint was that he had been stitched up. The bribery allegation had been made by an 'unnamed Birmingham gentleman' who said that he had overheard the conversation in which Meredith had made his offer to Leake. Billy admitted that such a conversation had taken place but maintained that he had only been joking. Leake also thought it had been a wind-up and had consequently not seen fit to mention it at first. It was only when he was called back before the commission that he admitted that something sinister had indeed taken place. When Turnbull was banned for a month for his role in the fracas and Leake was let off with a slapped wrist, the obvious conclusion was that the FA had done a deal with the Villa captain to get him to talk.

It was by no means the only part of the investigation that stunk like tramps' plums either. Once Meredith was within their reach, the FA had no qualms about riding roughshod over the legal necessity of *habeas corpus*. Thus Billy was informed of his punishment without ever getting the opportunity to defend himself. Clearly the word of a gentleman carried far more weight than that of a mere player, particularly a Welsh one. The press demanded to know why they were not at least allowed to see the evidence. The answer was twofold. If the FA had made their evidence public they would have left themselves open to the laws of libel and slander. Also they did not have to. The FA's power over the game was as arbitrary as it was absolute; they did not have to answer to anyone and the players did not have the right to bypass them and fling themselves at the mercy of the law of the land. Billy hadn't had a trial and now had no right of appeal. The Wizard could not have been treated less justly if he had been tried like a medieval witch – found guilty if he floated, innocent if he sunk.

Meredith's reputation and clean record – and also the suggestion that he was too tight to offer £10 for anything – stood in his favour; the arrogance and secrecy of the Commission told against the FA. Even though he had been found guilty, Billy's stock, post-verdict, was probably stronger than that of his accusers. As for City, the only damage they had sustained was being deprived of their star forward for a season. And that was the way things would have stood had the Blues not made one of their trademark disastrous decisions, reneging on an agreement to support Billy financially throughout his suspension and then reporting him to the FA when he continued to pester them. Yet another FA commission was set up to investigate the Meredith feud and within days every City player and official was neck-deep in scandal.

Previously, Billy had been prepared to stay silent and do his time; now he had been betrayed by his club, he developed a nasty case of verbal diarrhoea. In a dramatic U-turn, the Wizard abandoned his protestations of innocence over the bribery charge but insisted that he had only approached Leake at the prompting of the City management and with the full knowledge of the rest of the team. Other incriminating information was volunteered, most of it concerning the massive irregularities in the payments City had made to their players. With that, the whole house of cards collapsed, the players as a body issuing a confession and flinging themselves at the mercy of the FA, who must have felt like the hungry grizzly who returns home from an unsuccessful day's hunting to find a salmon pie baking in the oven and Goldilocks and her open-minded sisters getting warmed up in his bed.

The opportunity to quash their greatest enemy was too tempting for the authorities to be swayed by thoughts of mercy. Their judgement was unique in its brutality. At a stroke, City were all but destroyed. The entire board of directors were suspended, the secretary and chairman were banned for life, several players were banned for a season and all of them were forbidden to play for the club again. It was the pivotal moment in Manchester's football history thus far. City had already won the Cup and had just finished a failed bribery attempt away from claiming their first title. There was no reason to suggest that they would not have gone on to further cement their position as the city's finest. Instead, they had to watch from close quarters as newly-promoted United first matched and then surpassed their achievements. Within three years, the Reds had won both the league and Cup and built a reputation for style and class that underpins the club's claim to greatness to this day. Within those same three years, City had gone down.

Given the events of 1906-9, it is little wonder that a tendency to bitterness has taken such a firm hold (along with hairy palms) in the Blue gene pool. City's demise, and United's simultaneous rise, were reason enough for chips to start sprouting on Blue shoulders. How much more galling it must have been to know that the Red revival was achieved on the back of City-reared talent. Ernest Mangnall was far too cunning a fox to allow the subsequent auction of players at the town's Queen's Hotel to be conducted along the lines of the Queensberry Rules. A pre-auction whisper in the ear secured the services of three of City's biggest talents – Herbert Burgess, Jimmy Bannister and Sandy Turnbull – before any other club had even had the chance to make a bid.

Meredith, whose ban had been extended by another nine months, became the fourth Blue to join the cross-town traffic when he was snapped up on a free in the 1906 close season. It was the final indignity for the City management who had originally demanded £600 for the man whose vengefulness had destroyed them. Yet again, a previous undertaking returned to haunt them, Billy producing a letter, signed by the board, which guaranteed him a benefit match and a minimum sum of £600. When the FA, whose thirst for Blue blood remained unquenched, informed the City management that they would force them to honour the agreement, Billy got his wish of a free transfer. He did not lose out on his benefit money either as a 'gentleman' acting on United's behalf slipped £500 into his pocket and also paid his £100 fine. Thus the hypocrisy of the situation was exposed. By punishing City for illegal payments, the FA had benefited other clubs (in this case, United) who were just as crooked, if less stupid, than they were. If it had been anyone else but the Blues, you'd almost be tempted to reach for the violins...

United were the big winners in the bribery affair; City, obviously, the main losers. Meredith ended up somewhere in the middle. He lost eighteen months of football at a time when he should have been at his prime. Despite his fastidious attention to his body, he must have feared that he was now drinking from the last dregs of his career. Inevitably his reputation had lost some of its sheen and a place on the moral high ground was no longer his for the taking when he spewed forth on player politics. But his misdemeanours had done nothing to undermine his status as the hero of the working classes, the only telling difference being that his most ardent supporters now wore differently coloured scarves. His debut for United alongside the other ex-City recruits, against Aston Villa on New Years Day 1907, caught the imagination like nothing else in the club's history. *The Guardian* reported: 'When Roberts led the United team with its famous recruits on to the field there was a scene of wonderful enthusiasm. A greater roar of cheering has probably never sounded over a football ground, nor probably has a football crowd ever been seen in more remarkable animation. The vast motionless expanse of faces which stretched upward from the snow-heaped sides – over 40,000 there were in all – became suddenly moved and transformed, almost as a sea under a hurricane, and one saw nothing but an amazing tumult of waving arms and handkerchiefs.' Typically, Billy rose to the occasion, setting up his old buddy Turnbull for the only goal of the game. The opponents and score-line may have been different but it was just like Eric's return ninety years early.

That the Welshman and the Frenchman shared an ability to bring Manchester to a wet-panted standstill says it all really. Bestie had a lot of Billy in him but, of all the latter-day heroes, it was Eric who probably came closest to replicating the impact that the Wizard had on the Red psyche. The parallels between the two are striking. Both were football geniuses who came with an instant glory guarantee; both were pinched for a song from fierce rivals; both were absolutely committed trainers and professionals; both were bêtes noires of the football authorities – the famous line about the smell of sulphur following Eric wherever he went could

just as easily have been applied to Billy. Unprecedentedly in the latter's case, both were able to elevate themselves above their station as mere footballers and transform themselves into national celebrities in their own right. Billy's star quality as a player provided the base; the endorsement deals, personal appearances, newspaper columns, music-hall sketches, cartoons, film roles (in 1926 Billy starred, as himself, in the 'sporting picture', *The Ball of Fortune*; previously, he had appeared in his own training film) and, of course, his famous toothpick gave him a celebrity on a par with the music-hall greats of the day. If anything, his very public fight with authority and his long suspension enhanced his image. After all, he was never going to be a popcorn superstar in the mould of Best or Beckham; like Eric's, Billy's charm lay in his eccentricity and dark, brooding rebelliousness. Fifty years before Rock Around the Clock and Jimmy Dean, Billy provided the very definition of a rebel with a cause. Nike would have loved him.

*   *   *

CLEARLY THE FA, REVELLING in a bubble of self-congratulation following the rape of Hyde Road, underestimated the depth both of Billy's rebelliousness and his belief in his cause. Otherwise they would have taken the opportunity the bribery affair had handed them to suspend their long-time nemesis *sine die* or, at the very least, refrained from lending him a helping hand in securing the transfer he wanted. For Billy had not just swapped one team that had been unable to fulfil their full potential for another that would fulfil theirs in glorious style. He had also swapped the one club that had given the establishment more aggravation than any other for another that, in time, would make City seem like the class swots.

If anything, the bribery affair had sharpened Billy's political instincts and his antipathy for the game's authorities, the 'little shopkeepers who control our destiny' as he pointedly called them. When he moved to United, he found his spiritual home. Led by skipper Charlie Roberts and reserve goalkeeper Herbert Broomfield, the Clayton dressing-room was already amongst the most militant in the country. Meredith's arrival was the springboard which turned talk into action. Just months into his new career, Billy, Roberts and Broomfield led player politics on its next logical step, the formation of a Players' Union. The FA had only just succeeded in their drawn-out pursuit of City; now they were faced with more Mancunian mayhem, this time a band of Red rebels whose motive was not to side-step the rules that tied them, but to destroy them.

Meredith set the ball rolling by sending a circular to all professional players canvassing potential support. Finally, on December 2 1907, the Players' Union was established at a meeting at the city's Imperial Hotel. That it was a Mancunian, and specifically a United, dominated body was blatantly obvious. Players from a dozen clubs were represented at the Imperial but Clayton provided the fledgling PU with its secretary (Broomfield), its president (the incurably rebellious John Henry Davies) and its popular face (Meredith and Roberts).

The PU's first manifesto contained some familiar demands: an end to wage restrictions, the introduction of freedom of contract and access to the law of the land rather than the arbitrary justice of the FA. They were fundamental rights of the sort that were being granted to workers across the country but the player's wish to get tooled up with the full power of trade unionism was met with ridicule by a conservative press. Dismissing their demands as pie-in-the-sky, the papers blasted the players for their self-interest and greed. What they failed to acknowledge was that the professional game was pulling in thousands of pounds at the gate but only a fraction of that money was finding its way into the players' pockets. Someone was doing very nicely out of football, and it wasn't the men on the field.

The threat that a strong Union posed to the cosy world of 'masters and servants', as one bare-faced FA official summed up the relationship between club and player, was obvious. When the PU began urging its members to join up with workers from other fields under the umbrella of the General Federation of Trade Unions and even advocated strike action, the league clubs, many of whom had been sympathetic to the players' requests for better pay, rushed to align themselves with the FA. To cement the alliance, the authorities declared a devilish amnesty that blew holes in their claims to be the moral guardians of the game. In return for the clubs' unconditional support in the fight against the PU, the FA promised to overlook any past misdemeanours. No longer would directors live in fear of players following Meredith's lead and exposing their indiscretions.

With the clubs in their pockets, the FA pushed ahead with their plans to quash the Union. While the Reds were celebrating their 1909 cup triumph, the authorities were inserting a clause in all players' contracts which forced them to disown the PU and declare their undying loyalty to their 'masters' at the FA. A crushing victory/defeat beckoned. Faced with the alternative of being prevented from earning a living, the players had no option but to accept the clause. Or did they? In a show of heroic self-sacrifice of the sort that prompted Captain Oates to nip out for a stroll with the penguins, one set of players put their careers on the line to fight for their principles.

Some PU die-hards, recognising that they could not hope to

launch a counter-strike until the season started, decided to resign from the Union, collect their wages all summer and then rejoin in September. The cup-winners, led by Meredith and Roberts, opted against fighting underhand tactics with more of the same. En masse they refused to sign the contract clause. The FA responded by suspending the entire side *sine die*. The Reds were now, famously and uniquely, the Outcasts, the name concocted in a moment of inspiration by their captain.

Despite their PU-sympathies, the United management, their arms tied by the majority decision of the League to support the clause, could not support their banned stars. It made no difference to the players who rented out a pitch at Fallowfield and carried out their pre-season training as normal. Their plan was to sit tight until the new season and hope that the spectre of a disrupted fixture list and the anticipated ground swell of support from other pro-union players would force the FA into a humiliating climb-down.

As the season loomed into view, it was clear that the Outcasts' brinkmanship had paid off. A sizeable number of players, many of them from the militant north-east and Merseyside, returned from the summer break and immediately pinned their colours to the Red rebels' cause. Backed into a corner, the FA cooked up a typical piece of fudge, promising to lift all suspensions, recognise the Union and give some provision for players to take their grievances to court but only if they put an end to 'this nonsense' about staying affiliated to the GFTU (and, by doing so, renounce the right to strike). When the compromise deal was put to a vote, the PU's 640 members voted by three to one to accept it. The Outcasts' leaders were mortified. The union they had fathered had been saved but it was not the mighty body it would have been had the membership as a whole shown the guts that the United lads had. The authorities had lost the battle but they remained streets ahead in the war; it would be another fifty years before player power – and Jimmy the Chin – forced them to make any major concessions on pay and conditions.

*   *   *

MEREDITH LAMENTED THAT 'the bulk of the players have not shown much pluck in the matter'. Pluck was something he himself could never have been accused of lacking, nor could dedication to his cause.

Billy's appetite for the battle and his distaste for the power enjoyed by the 'little shopkeepers' lasted longer even than his career. He was still niggling away, bemoaning the game's injustices and attempting to put the world to right (and chewing on his toothpick), when he was in his seventies.

Billy's knack of attracting controversy did not fade either. In 1914, five years after the Outcasts furore, he was suspended by the United board for 'insubordination' for leading a threatened mutiny against their decision to fine and ban Sandy Turnbull for a verbal assault on the caretaker manager, J.J. Bentley. A year later he was dragged into another match-fixing scandal, the Good Friday affair, even though this time there was no evidence that he had been anything more than a peripheral figure in the plot to rig the crucial Liverpool match (his past record and close association with the guilty Turnbull were enough for many people to convict him regardless).

Less spectacular was Billy's long-standing dispute with United over his benefit money and also the stalemate arising out of the club's decision to deny him his free transfer back to City in 1919. The Wizard's observations that 'the selling of players is a degrading business' and that he 'would rather have ended my career as a footballer than allow any club to sell me, even for a pack of woodbines' were still as worthy as ever but by the time the war had come and gone, his moans and groans must have sounded gratingly familiar.

There was more to Billy, though, than the perpetual malcontent. Admittedly he could be moody, quick to take offence, vain and aloof, particularly amongst people he did not know. Throw him in amongst team-mates, friends and family, however, and a far more appealing and groovy side to his personality is exposed. Talent aside, the secret of United's success in the Mangnall era lay in how well the players got on with each other off the pitch. Billy was at the centre of this close-knit band of brothers, and the hot-pot suppers that his wife Ellen served up made a get-together at the Merediths one of the highlights of their social itinerary.

Had they known the consequences, the FA would have confiscated Ellen's crock-pot. The football and political discussions that took place over her dinners were the breeding ground for the Players' Union as well as the tactical ploys that made United's football style so cutting edge. When the nights took a turn for the merrier,

Billy, of course, would opt out of the boozing and possibly because of his sobriety would content himself with a watching brief when Sandy Turnbull led the rest of the lads in their usual raucous sing-song. But if he was private and taciturn, at least in comparison with the abrasive, outspoken and humorous Turnbull, he was also one of the lads, an intriguing mix of boyish fun, silly pranks, practical jokes and head-turning opinions.

Inevitably, dressing-room relationships changed as the generation gap between Billy and his team-mates widened into a chasm. Doubtless many of the younger generation of Reds were intimidated by the old master, or at least confused by the sight of a living legend who was old enough to be their father getting up to the sort of tricks[2] that even their kids had grown out of. A scandal-hungry press gleefully reported rumours of dressing-room rifts and of team-mates purposely starving Meredith of possession. In all probability the reality was somewhat different. The service to United's forwards was regularly so poor that you could make a case that each of them was being intentionally ignored while Jack Mew, for one, was clearly fond of Old Skinny, saying that he always found him 'a jovial fellow and a real sport'.

One thing is certain, though. For Billy, as well as United, things were never the same again once the Outcasts began to break up. The death of Sandy Turnbull in the war was perhaps the final straw. Compared to ten years earlier, the Old Trafford that Meredith returned to when the fighting was over must have seemed a lonely and depressing place. Viewed in those terms, his desire to leave does not carry the same whiff of betrayal. Billy would always be Red at heart but it was clear that there was nothing to gain from him playing on with United but soured memories. It must have been frustrating for him that it took the club another couple of seasons to arrive at the same conclusion. Against his will, the Wizard's United career was extended by another

2.   *He might have lost his Crazy Gang partner, Turnbull, but Billy remained the king of practical jokes at Old Trafford right up to his departure. Joe Spence's prized whippet was his most famous target, the poor mutt being kidnapped and mummified in bandages while Joe went spare looking for him. But if travelling and training with Billy could be tiresome, his team-mates could count themselves lucky that they did not have to live with him. The Wizard, who had a pub in Longsight, got up to all sorts of tricks in his spare time, including letting ponies loose in the barmaids' quarters, but he saved his best work for his strait-laced sisters. Recognising that any bad language would have them reaching for the hair shirts, Billy first taught his parrot to spout filth and then, when his wife let the foul-mouthed bird loose, paid his nephew to run around the kitchen shouting 'bugger!' at them.*

thirty-five, largely cameo, appearances and three goals. In the context of a prodigious career his contribution to the Depression Years was a minor one but there is no anomaly in him taking such a prominent part in this book. The Billy Meredith story is not just the story of a great player and Red icon, it is also a means of understanding the path that the Manchester giants, and the professional game in general, trod in their formative years. Without Billy, United's transformation into football's answer to Camelot might never have taken place. Sadly, now he was gone, Camelot was a Wizard short of greatness. Come to think of it, there weren't too many shining knights left either.

ANNUS HORRIBILIS

JACK ROBSON HAD made his name by being the man whom clubs called in before the receivers. Throughout his career he had taken on struggling organisations and turned them into viable concerns without spending any real money. When he took on the United job in December 1914 he already had an impressive record of turning sows' ears into silk purses. At Middlesbrough he had overseen the leap from amateur to professional status while at both Brighton and Crystal Palace he had managed football's equivalent of a boob job, taking clubs that were not blessed with much and leaving them in better shape than they had ever been before.

Despite mediocre league finishes of eighteenth, twelfth and thirteenth, Robson's reputation had been enhanced during his spell at Old Trafford. For many Red-watchers, he was nothing short of a miracle-worker. He had led the club out of its financial crisis, built a new team and a vibrant reserve set-up out of – and for – virtually nothing, kept the side in the top division and at the same time attracted record crowds to the ground. But the situation at the club was changing and Robson's face did not necessarily fit in the new era. The Reds were not completely clear of their financial worries but they no longer needed a manager whose forté was keeping clubs afloat. What United needed was someone who could take them to the next level, someone who could attract the big names and make them the talk of the football world as had been the case before the war. In short, they needed a Mangnall. And the one thing that Robson lacked was Mangnall's mastery of publicity and promotion. As the late United chairman W. Deakin said: 'Robson knows a player in the rough. He can find them. His only fault is that he is not a showman.'

Perhaps Robson sensed that he wasn't the right man to take the Reds to this next level. Certainly he felt that the demands of the job had become too great for him, particularly since his health remained a major concern (Jack had a long history of chest problems and had indeed spent most of the summer fighting a serious illness). Whatever his reasons, by early October Robson had decided to relinquish his role as manager-secretary and accept the newly-created position of assistant manager. For United, the logic was sound; they could bring in the showman they needed without losing Jack's know-how, his administrative skills and his player-spotting genius. Sadly, there was no time for the new arrangement to bear fruit. In January, United's great servant died from pneumonia. Tragically, his friends, who had always told him that a man with his chest should not be living in smoggy Manchester, had been proved right.

*   *   *

THE IMPACT OF ROBSON'S health problems on United's season were felt even before a ball had been kicked. Old-school managers did not always have the final say on the hiring and firing of players but if Jack had been around he would surely not have stood for the transfer chaos that enveloped the club during the summer. Those people who thought that the weakest forward line in United history could not get any worse had just found out that, where this board were concerned, it was better never to say never. Out had gone Miller, Meredith, Hopkin, Hodges and Leonard. In had come Arthur Lochhead, a promising but unproven centre-forward from Hearts, John Scott, a veteran left-half from relegated Bradford Park Avenue, and another collection of unknowns and reserves from clubs of the magnitude of Darwen, Eccles and Walkley. For a net return of just £1,500, United had lost five experienced forwards and replaced them with none.

Admittedly, a certain amount of dead-heading was necessary. Neither Hodges, who had been on the transfer list ever since a contractual dispute the previous summer, nor Leonard were likely to feature again so it made sense to knock them off the wage bill. It might just have been good business to cash in on the homesick, out-of-sorts Miller as well. But there was no defending the rest of the pruning. Meredith was undoubtedly a fading force but, as the papers pointed out, if he was good enough for the Blues (the League runners-up in 20/21), he was more than good enough for the Reds. Hopkin's £2,500 move to Liverpool, meanwhile, was a mystery in the Tommy Meehan class. Quality outside-lefts were difficult to find, it would have taken far more than £2,500 to buy any of them and there was no proven replacement on the books. The selectors' plan to switch Partridge to the far left and bring in the talented Sapsford alongside him was fatally flawed. Partridge was too plain in style to be a wing-man and his inability to adapt to his new role initiated a sharp decline in status from danger-man to joke – or from Teddy to Alan. The outlook on the right was equally cheerless. Harrison's was the basket that most of the selectorial eggs had been placed in post-Meredith but another year's exposure to the midget former Wolf would only confirm the suspicion formed the previous season that, even at 5ft 4in, he was as big a waste of space as Harry Leonard.

You do not need to be a tactical genius to recognise the dangers of flying without wings. And if the worst pair of outside-forwards in the top flight wasn't a handicap enough, the midfield was screaming out for a refit too. Robson had uncovered a crop of promising half-backs, with Welsh grafter Ray Bennion the latest to elevate himself into contention, but none of them had developed into the inspirational leader and pivot that the team desperately needed. Both Lal Hilditch, who seemed to have lost a yard of pace, and Jack Grimwood, whose upcoming quiet spell would silence the 'new Roberts' talk, had work to do to live up to the great expectations that had been heaped upon them. The *Football News* estimated that the squad was two wingers and two half-backs short of being competitive in the top flight. The *Chron*'s verdict was that this team made the 20/21 version look like world-beaters. When United lost defensive pillar Charlie Moore to a serious ankle injury sustained in a pre-season charity match at Northwich, everybody's verdict was that they were going down.

The redoubtable rearguard of Mew, Silcock and Moore were the main reason why the Reds had survived the previous two seasons. Now that the famous trio had become a duo, the consensus was that a new era of defensive slackness was about to dawn over Old Trafford. By the end of August, it looked like it had already arrived. In their opening two matches United shipped eight goals, five to Everton and three to West Brom. Goodison, in particular, was a disaster. Two down at half-time, the Reds leaked three more goals after it and were thankful for the referee for dubiously chalking off another three. Not even Michael Knighton managed as embarrassing an opening-day performance as that.

Fortunately, the theory about the defence cracking up sounded far more convincing in the wake of the Bank Holiday defeats than it did just a month later. By then, the answer to the right-back problem had risen, unexpectedly, from the ranks. It wasn't Frank Brett, the highly-rated novice who had come, seen and been conquered on his debut at Goodison and had never really recovered. More improbably, the player to ride to United's rescue was Charlie Radford, a former Walsall centre-forward who hadn't even been getting a game in the reserves before a chance switch from centre-forward to full-back. Charlie II made the most of his big break, forming a partnership with Jack Silcock that would not be embarrassed by subsequent comparisons with Silcock and Moore. Radford left the silkier side of the defender's art to his partner but he was tough, energetic, kicked like a mule and at the very least gave forwards something to think about – such as how it would feel to spend the rest of the season with a limp. The end of season statistics may hint at a different conclusion but, on their day, the new-look rearguard of Mew, Silcock and Radford was as good as any in the league. As ever, the real villains of United's campaign played up front, not at the back.

In fairness, the forwards did not always perform like they had won their places in a raffle. The Everton return was one of those exceptions, Harrison and Spence firing the Reds to a swift piece of revenge. However, Tityrus, the Up-Pompeii-sounding correspondent from the *Athletic News*, got it right when he cautioned, after the side's 2-1 win: 'The United exceeded expectations, but even so it would be folly to think that they can remain in their class with such football as they showed. It would be ridiculous to assure the directors of the United that they have found a team; it would be a great illusion.'

The Reds proved as much by failing to win any of their next half-dozen fixtures. Falling back on their concrete rearguard, they lost only one of those – 3-2 at Preston after giving, ironically, their best exhibition so far – but drab draws were clearly not what stretched Mancunian underpants. In perhaps the most tedious ten days in their history, United scrapped their way to a hat-trick of anaesthetising nil-nils, the first at the Hawthorns and the next two against Chelsea. The home leg of the Chelsea bore-double attracted Old Trafford's fourth successive sub-30,000 gate. The identical fixture almost twelve months earlier had pulled in over forty thousand. The post-war football bandwagon had only been rolling a couple of years but here were signs that the new, fickle supporters were already starting to jump off. In order to win them back, plans were drawn up to remedy Old Trafford's glaring fault – the lack of cover on the Popular Side – but the directors balked at the anticipated bill of twenty-odd thousand. It was an oversight that would haunt them for years. Hordes of Reds were prepared to hand over their shilling to watch the least stimulating football in the division but few were keen on being made mugs of and getting drenched at the same time. And wet weekends in the city aren't exactly unusual...

United's poor start and the volley of criticism it triggered must have made Robson's decision to stand aside that much easier. As his successor would not be installed until early November, the players now had a month to come up with a decent leaving gift. A shock selectorial brain-wave involving Lochhead and Spence at least helped them cobble together something vaguely suitable.

In the opening weeks, the former had been used exclusively at centre-forward and the latter at inside-right. Swapping them around, as the directors did for the trip to Spurs on October 8, was good news all round. Spence had yet to smooth all his rough edges – or fully recover from the second season syndrome that had blighted him in 20/21 – but he was strong, quick and willing and had a keen eye for the half-chance. Lochhead was perhaps Spence in negative. He was a classy bag of tricks but lacked the physical tools for a scrap. Pushing him to inside-right not only gave him more opportunity to utilise his undoubted talent and vision, it also spared him the donkey work that formed the bulk of the centre-forward's job, particularly south of the border.

Lochhead settled into his new role with a series of attractive cameos, Spence by seizing centre stage. Apparently desperate to show his gratitude to the man who had saved him from the pit, Joe embarked on an October goal frenzy, scoring seven times in that month alone. Annoyingly, the first sustained attacking threat of the season coincided with the first lengthy run of games without a clean sheet. Still, Joe's goals helped the Reds double their end-of-September points tally and ensure that whatever problems Robson left behind, a position in the bottom two was not among them. With eleven points from their opening dozen fixtures, United would start life under their fourth (permanent) manager in fifteenth place, three points clear of second-from-bottom Cardiff and six ahead of Arsenal.

Of the five matches that wrapped up the Robson era, two were drawn, one was lost and two were won. The Lochhead-inspired comeback against Spurs which gave the Reds their second victory of the season, six long weeks after their first, was thrilling enough to have been almost worth the wait but the real moment to treasure was the derby turnaround on the 29th. The previous weekend, the Red Army had staggered away from Hyde Road in the manner of a prisoner who can't catch soap. Inspired, inevitably, by the skinny old bloke on the right, the Blues had nailed the Reds 4-1, Horace Barnes netting a rare derby hat-trick. In front of 56,000 at Old Trafford, the balance of power flipped 180 degrees. City led early but the game was United's from the moment, midway through the opening half, that Spence equalised from Hilditch's flick-on. A scruffy second settled the match but it took a brilliant third, again from Spence, to really get the Pop Side jumping. Merging skill and swerve with lightning pace, Joe slalomed past three men before completing his masterpiece with an extravagant lob over the keeper. For now, the film of the Robson years had its happy ending. How much better viewing it would have made had the final twist been left on the cutting-room floor...

FOR THE FIRST TIME in their history, United opted for a Scot as their next manager (now that would be a policy worth persevering with...). John Chapman was the Jock in question, lured from Airdrieonians after fifteen years spent transforming them from perennial strugglers into a major force in the Scottish game. As he had been more than the club's manager – according to the *Athletic News*, he had also been 'a guide, philosopher and friend' – it

John Chapman

had clearly been a major wrench for Chapman to sever ties and it is probably fair to say, as it was with Alex Ferguson decades later, that only the lure of a club of United's reputation and potential could have enticed him away.

What set Chapman and Fergie apart however was the size of the task awaiting them. Eighteen months earlier, the team that Fergie inherited from Big Ron had won the Cup; a year earlier, they had been tearing up the record books with their league form. The biggest weakness (Davenport, the Gibsons and Higgins apart) of the class of '86 was that a few hours earlier the spine of the team had probably been in the pub. By contrast, the class of '21 had so many weaknesses that the man most likely to be found drinking away his problems in the city's bars was their new boss.

United's latest manager was well thought of in boardrooms either side of the border and when the Reds got their man he was viewed as quite a catch. He brought with him a reputation as an astute, experienced manager with a knack of finding and bringing through new talent. He also had experience of operating within a strict budget having taken over at Airdrie when the bailiffs were hovering. But was Chapman the showman that United needed? A quick glance at his CV suggested not; many of his strengths were similar to those of his new assistant. And instead of being known for Mangnallian qualities such as flamboyance, pushiness and style, his most obvious character traits were stereotypically Scottish. No, not ginger, tight-fisted and drunk but shrewd, dour and confident. Instead of acquiring the next Ernest Mangnall, United appeared to have got themselves a younger version of Jack Robson.

Chapman got off to a bad start in more ways than one. His comments that 'there is only one person who thinks more about the game than I do and that's the wife' were far too close to the unintelligible witterings of Kenny Dalglish for the comfort of any modern Red though Mrs C was obviously a useful asset at times. 'When I could not come to terms with a player I used to send for the wife,' John revealed. 'It's wonderful the persuasive powers of a woman. She once signed in a few minutes a chap I had argued with for a week.' Meanwhile, Middlesbrough welcomed him to England by handing his new team a double football lesson. Three goals down inside 38 minutes at Old Trafford, United narrowed the gap to a single goal before the hour but eventually subsided 5-3. One hack called it the 'best exhibition of vigorous, clever football he had seen for ten years'. He was talking about the visitors. At Ayresome, United reverted more to type, defended stoutly, hardly threatened and lost again, this time by a more prosaic 2-0. They were now just two points clear of danger.

Generally, new managers like to at least give the impression of giving the players they inherited a chance to impress. Chapman, anxious to avoid the ignominy of being the first man to take United down, did not have the time or the inkling to be fair. When Aston Villa rolled over his new side with chastening ease at Villa Park on November 19, he obviously decided he had seen enough. In the days that followed he threw himself into a transfer binge and, given the tartan flavour to his roots, it was no surprise where he went shopping. Had he been handed a blank cheque, Chapman would have re-crossed the border with a list that ran to a couple of new half-backs, a smattering of reserve backs and four or five new attackers. Instead, he had to focus on hunting down the bare essentials; a right-winger, a strong centre half-back and a quality centre-forward. Hilditch, Grimwood and Spence had enjoyed some vividly bright spells in the central roles but none of them had played well enough for long enough to convince the hierarchy that they were yet the permanent solution.

Initially, Chapman struggled to persuade clubs to part with their best men. He was desperate to land his old Airdrie outside-right David Ellis but United were told to stick their £3,000 bid where certain film stars stick their hamsters. Motherwell's Hughie Ferguson, who had cracked a century of goals in just three seasons, was another prime target who turned out to be untransferable. Eventually, though, money – or was it Mrs Chapman? – talked. In the space of a week, Chapman set up deals worth an estimated £6,250 for his old centre-forward Willie Henderson and Ayr United centre-half Neil McBain. Both were heralded as excellent buys. Henderson was a brave and direct runner who had just scored thirty-six goals in his first season in senior football. McBain was an all-round class act whose powerful tackling, running and heading had put him on the wish-list of just about every club in the country.

The 26-year-old's price tag matched his billing as Scottish football's next big thing. Most reports put the transfer fee at a club record £4,500; the *Evening News* ran a story that the twin deals for McBain and Henderson had 'made a hole in £8,000' which would have made him the most expensive player ever. That did not make losing their star man any less bitter a pill for the Ayrshire public to swallow. As far as bombshells go it was in the Hiroshima class and Chapman would have been well-advised to pack a false nose and beard on his next trip Ayr-way; he was as welcome in town as an erection in a convent.

Back in Manchester, Jack Robson would have been forgiven a tinge of envy when, in his first three weeks in the job, his successor was given as much money to spend as he had in seven years. But there was no bottomless pit at Old Trafford and by paying top dollar for McBain, Chapman had exceeded his transfer budget. Instead of bringing in the right-winger the team desperately needed, the new manager was forced to cash in on one of the men who could have done a job there. The decision to sell George Bisset to Wolves for £1,200 registered on the press's stupidity-monitor somewhere between the Meredith and Meehan deals. In his two years of in-and-out action at United, George had developed into a favourite cause of the local hacks, most of whom could not understand why a man with his potential had not been given more chances to fulfil it. Their frustration was exacerbated by the fact he had been flogged to Wolves, the club that, twelve months earlier, had lumbered the Reds with Harrison. It had been some swap.

In time, Bisset would join the oft-repeated list of players whom United had been mad to let go but, for the time being, Red eyes were focused on the new boys' debuts in the Villa return on the 26th. Chapman could not have stage-managed them better if he had bought the referee. The longer McBain played, the more impressive he looked and by the second half he had his man in a stranglehold and was looking a class act with the ball at his feet. Henderson did not look so comfortable but a few missed passes and untidy pieces of control were struck from the memory in the instant it took him to crack in his late winner. 'The light on this Gargantuan ground was growing grey,' wrote Tityrus, 'when Harris flashed the ball to William Henderson, the well-built centre whom the Airdrieonians secured from Edinburgh St. Bernard. As quick as thought, Henderson, fully twenty-five yards from goal, drove with his left foot. This swift, skimming, straight shot was only arrested by the back of the net, a mighty cheer rending the air as Jackson tried to catch the ball. This was a bolt from the grey, and if Jackson could not see the ball, Henderson could see the goal, and pierced it.'

With the spine of the team strengthened, Chapman's breakthrough win as United boss would be the first of many – or at least that's what the beer was saying in Red pubs that night. As it happened, the good times lasted barely longer than the hangovers. Aroused, by the record-breaking transfer flurry, to levels of excitement that had not been seen for a decade, the Reds exploded in their pants and their hitherto poor form drooped even further. It had taken the new regime a month to claim their first victim. It would take another two for them to claim a second.

The Villa win proved a false dawn for the two Scottish lads as well. A slice of perspective had gone amiss amidst the hype that surrounded their arrival in town. Adding new players to the team in mid-season and expecting them to turn things around is normally a recipe for disappointment even though there is a certain French exception to the rule. Also, there was a huge difference between Scottish and English football. Effectively, they were two different games. The tartan version was all about short, sharp passing and tanner ball players; the Sassenach version had its skilful elements but often boiled down to blood and guts. Scottish players who tried their luck south of the border had to learn that they had to earn the right to play and McBain, despite his muscular reputation back home, struggled with the physical side of the game. Only when he was pushed out to left-half, where the physical demands were not quite so high, did he make a sustained impact in United red. Forget the fanfares and wild predictions that had accompanied his record-breaking transfer, the search for the new Charlie Roberts was back on.

Henderson's struggles were even more pronounced. Admittedly it was not all his own fault. He had been in top-class football for all of two minutes (all right, eighteen months) and here he was in the middle of a relegation scrap alongside forwards who would have made Pelé look like Terry Gibson. But he was raw, cumbersome, wasteful in possession and increasingly ineffective in front of goal. Willie hit another pile-driver in the home draw with fellow strugglers Bradford on December 10 but did not find the net again until the following September. The move to Old Trafford had well and truly cured him of the goalscoring diarrhoea he had experienced with Airdrie the previous year. Donning a United shirt was rapidly becoming football's answer to overdosing on prunes.

So United had a pricey centre-back who could not quite handle it in the centre, and a centre-forward who could not score. Just like the previous autumn, a transfer binge had been wasted. By the turn of the year, many a Red was arguing that the directors should have stuck with the players who had creamed City and invested the money in that Pop Side roof instead. December's results – and cats-'n'-dogs weather – made it hard for anyone to disagree. Defeat in the away leg of the Bradford doubleheader dropped United into the bottom two for the first time. A home nil-nil and Anfield 1-2 against title-chasing Liverpool sentenced them to spend Christmas there and ever-deteriorating results in the remainder of the festive programme – four defeats, three of them resounding – left them bottom of the pile. The relegation candidates that John Chapman had inherited two months earlier were now viewed as relegation certainties.

*   *   *

AS HE CELEBRATED HIS FIRST Mancunian hogmanay, Chapman would have been forgiven for asking himself, as Fergie must have done in '89 (and Robbo the season before), why he had exposed himself. He had sacrificed a long and happy marriage for a fling with a racy number down south only to discover that the honeymoon period lasted barely long enough for the consummation. Still, he was fortunate that he lived in gentler times when there were no tabloids to bay for struggling managers' blood or turn their faces into vegetables. In today's football it would have been tin-hat time already. And at some clubs, and with some chairmen, a similar start would have cost the gaffer his job. Let's not get too worked up about the lot of the modern manager, though. Admittedly the job is a stressful one (try being a supporter) but what other profession, apart from the oldest one, gives so many opportunities to people who would struggle to pass the two star stage at McDonalds? Any system that keeps a liability like Alan Ball in work for so long has to be seriously flawed. Then again, given Ol' squeakie's outstanding contribution to the Moss Side comedy club in 95/96, who's complaining?

To a certain extent, the United manager got away with putting his miserable start down to bad luck. Most regulars agreed with him when he said that the performances had often been better than the results. Failure to beat either Burnley or Liverpool at home, when the Reds were the better side on both occasions, remained a source of festering frustration; McBain's penalty miss against the Scousers was particularly galling. Given the restricted squad he inherited, Chapman could ill afford the injuries he picked up either. As well as the one, long-term casualty (Moore), Hilditch, Silcock, Radford and Grimwood were all regulars on Jack Pullar's treatment table.

McBain moaned: 'What have we done wrong? We could not have had more ill-luck had we killed a policeman.' But the statistics did not lie. In the nine weeks between Chapman's first win and his second, United played eleven games and scored just seven goals; between

Christmas Eve and January 14, they fired blanks in five of their six league outings. The change in manager had not solved any of the old problems in attack; the wingers still could not get the ball across, the unlucky Partridge remained in purgatory on the far left while the lack of combination between the forwards seemed to confirm the whispers – hotly denied, of course – that certain members of the team did not see eye-to-eye. Apparently, Chapman's efforts to 'create a social atmosphere among the players' by organising whist drives and smoking concerts, and making them have tea together after each game, had only made matters worse.

An embarrassing third round defeat at home to Cardiff begged the question whether the club had hit rock bottom. Having watched the Welsh side romp to a 4-1 win, few Reds were prepared to buy the line the management were peddling about an early cup exit being a blessing in disguise. If it was a disguise it was a f***ing good one. No one wanted to concentrate on the league when the table made such a depressing read. But Cardiff was no nadir. Five days later, United lost Jack Robson.

*   *   *

THE NEWCASTLE MATCH THE following Saturday was played out amidst the eeriest atmosphere Old Trafford had yet known. Unlike the Everton game in '94, the first gathering after the passing of Sir Matt, there was no sense of celebration and thanksgiving to take the edge off the overriding emotions of sadness and grief. It did not help that Robson's old boys played dismally and lost again, to an early breakaway. It was a victory that surely ranks among the emptiest in Newcastle's history. The scorer, in particular, must have felt like the sort of lowlife who goes to a funeral and steals from the collection plate. As for the crowd, they were faced with the most poignant afternoon of their Red-watching lives. On their way down Warwick Road they would have passed the house in which their former manager's body lay. Thus the walk to and from the ground was transformed into an impromptu wake featuring an army of mourners twenty thousand strong.

The following Monday, several hundred people braved the wintry conditions to attend Jack's funeral at Southern Cemetery. As the snow swirled around them, his casket was carried to the graveside by the two trainers, Pullar and Jones, and, fittingly, by five of the young players

(Hilditch, Mew, Silcock, Sapsford and Grimwood) who owed the great talent-spotter their United careers. Days later, the FA paid their own respects to one of football's most admired figures by announcing that March's international trial match at Old Trafford would double as a testimonial game in his honour. Ironically, it was Mangnall, the man whose achievements at United Robson could never quite match, who acted as secretary of the testimonial fund which raised £2,000 for Jack's wife and family.

No one could have predicted how the players were going to react following the death of their old mentor. The club had never been in a similar situation before, or since – the only other managerial casualty thus far has been Wilf McGuinness's hair. The early signs were that at best it was not going to help. Defeat at Roker Park pushed the Reds even further round the relegation U-bend; they were now three points shy of second-from-bottom Bradford and a further point behind the Gunners in twentieth. Depressingly, United had played a game more than both. But just when there seemed nothing to stop the Reds' slide towards the second division, their favourite opponents showed up at Old Trafford to offer them a lifeline.

Sunderland had played United in Manchester on ten occasions and had been beaten every time, often convincingly. In both seasons since the war, a visit from the Mackems had helped pull the club out of a mid-season tailspin. On January 25, history repeated itself once more. Within five minutes the Reds had doubled their goal tally for the whole of the month, Spence leaping highest at the back post to head in Robinson's centre and Lochhead driving in just as emphatically from the edge of the box. A swift Sunderland reply hinted at more Red disappointment but Sapsford, increasingly spoken of as the side's most vibrant attacking force, made the points safe with a second-half third. For many supporters, the feeling that night was akin to getting it on with Gloria Swanson and listening to their 1,000-1 yankee come in all at the same time. One 'enthusiast' made the papers by arriving home after the game with a couple of canaries, a coconut won at the local shy and tickets for the second house at the theatre. Apparently, his standard post-match routine that winter had involved storming in, shunning his tea and refusing to take the family to the pictures – and presumably giving the dog a good kicking as well.

The feel-good factor easily survived the fortnight's break before United's next fixture, at home to Huddersfield. A crowd of thirty thousand, ten thousand up on the wintry norm, thronged to Old Trafford to watch Spence earn the Reds a point with a late equaliser. The timing of the goal – just moments after Joe had swapped places with Henderson in the centre – and the identity of its scorer was not lost on either the crowd or the selectors. For some time there had been a theory doing the rounds that the only thing keeping the big Scot in the side was his price tag. His Huddersfield flop marked the moment when Willie was turfed out of the last chance saloon. When United travelled to St Andrews the following weekend, Spence was back in the number nine shirt in which he had been so prolific pre-Chapman and Henderson was in the reserves.

Joe would not be so productive again but he, and Sapsford, were key figures as United's revival passed through February and stretched into March. In the next four matches, Chapman's SAS combination claimed four goals, all of them vital. Joe was the match-winner at Birmingham, making up for an earlier open-net howler by side-footing the goal that ended the Reds' ten-month wait for an away win. A week after the miss of the season, Sapsford netted the goal of the decade in the drawn Old Trafford return. Standing well out wide when a wayward centre came to him hip-high, he collected the ball with one foot and drilled it into the opposite corner with the other. At Huddersfield two days later, another, less spectacular, finish from the slippery inside-left earned the Reds the point they needed to clamber out of the bottom two for the first time in three months. Against Arsenal on the 11th it was Spence's turn once more to keep the wheels of revival revolving, his neat finish settling the first of the great relegation battles.

But if Joe and George were the headline acts, the foundations of United's scramble for freedom were laid by the dynamic defence. Somehow, the three alchemists, Mew, Silcock and Radford had turned eight goals into nine points. As an exercise in making the most of what you've got it was in the Posh Spice class (and I'm talking tits as well as talent – has anyone with hair ever got so much use out of toupée tape?). The Arsenal game was emblematic of the side's defensive resilience and capacity to guts it out. Behind early when Bennion dribbled and Spence gobbled his goal, the Gunners then pounded themselves into impotence on the Reds' granite chin.

By mid-March, United's position had been transformed from hopeless to hopeful. With ten matches to play, they were two points and one game ahead of Bradford and three points and two games ahead of Arsenal. Another month of their recent form and their season would be saved. But just when the Reds looked to have mapped a way out of trouble, they managed to get themselves lost again. Not even their heroic defence could save them when the forwards dried up all together. Old Trafford defeat by Blackburn on the 18th dropped the club back into the bottom two; a 3-0 mauling at Ewood coupled with unexpected victories for both the Bantams and the Gunners returned them to bottom place. From then on they never looked like surviving. Bolton emulated Blackburn's single-goal victory at Old Trafford and should have won by more. The point of no return was reached at Highbury on April 5 when the Reds shrivelled in another do-or-die affair. Lochhead did at least end their six-hour wait for a goal but it was the merest of consolations. Displaying the survival instincts of a suicide bomber, United, who conceded a bad goal just before the break and two more just after, had already rolled over.

Four weeks earlier, all Reds had hoped that the home leg against Arsenal would define and decide United's season. Instead, it was the 3-1 Highbury leg. Technically there was still hope but the manner of the Arsenal, and previous, defeats suggested that the side had already become reconciled to their fate. The rest of April became a question of 'when' rather than 'if'. Another poverty-stricken display at Burnden received its just desserts; a week later, Oldham swatted their hosts aside at Old Trafford. With five damaging defeats at the hands of their county cousins, it was clear that the Reds had been cast in the role of Julius Caesar to Lancashire's Brutus. A knife in the back was the thanks they got for helping save Blackburn's neck in 1919/20.

A valedictory win against Sheffield United in front of an impressive Easter crowd of 30,000 only delayed the inevitable. Five days later, confirmation of the club's ticket to the second division arrived, perhaps fittingly, at Boundary Park (Ice Station Zebra being as suitable a venue as any to receive such chilling news). Only a United victory and an Arsenal defeat in the north London derby would have kept the Reds breathing. Instead, United drew and the third-from-bottom Gunners won to move out of range. And if the club's relegation wasn't gut-wrenchingly painful enough, Liverpool, inspired, as they had been all season, by Freddie Hopkin, chose that same afternoon to clinch the title. You can stick your royal family divorces and Windsor fires. Scouse champions, Red relegation, Robson's death... 1922 truly had been an *annus horribilis*.

Suddenly it seemed like a long time since the club had been

celebrating their second league title in four years. In fact it had only been seven first-class seasons. In terms of a riches-to-rags story, the road to United's first-ever relegation was almost as dramatic as the 1968-74 version. As in '74 there were plenty of people who traced their demise back to the glory days. The Reds had spent beyond their means to build their famous side while the move to Old Trafford and then the war had almost crippled them. Mangnall's team had been allowed to grow old, Mangnall himself had moved on and his successors had not had the cash to rebuild.

Add in the more immediate causes of death – the disruption caused by losing Robson both as a manager and a man and the injury problems that had plagued the club throughout the winter – and you have the gist of the argument, oft-repeated at the time, that relegation had been a juggernaut that United had no chance of side-stepping. It would have been a persuasive one, too, had Robson not pulled off his miracle and kept the 'players-before-points' team up in 1919/20. Since then, the foundations of the club had been reinforced and the financial muscle provided by their record-breaking supporters had given them a golden opportunity to book themselves a permanent place on football's top table.

Frankly, they had blown it. Despite the £10,000 transfer spree of the previous eighteen months, the forward line, the side's Achilles heel, still suffered from a chronic lack of imagination, combination and quality. Since the war, the Reds had yet to spend big on a player who had been a genuine success while several players who would have done a good job for the club had been allowed to leave. If the Reds had retained even a couple of Meehan, Hopkin, Woodcock, Miller, Bisset or even Meredith, they would not have been facing life in Division Two. Worryingly, there were no signs that the board were any nearer to getting the message. In the closing days of the season they took the bizarre decision to sell Sapsford, the club's brightest attacker, to Preston. The move seemed to confirm the widely held view that the directors would not recognise a class player if he hurdled the hoardings and kung fu kicked them in the chest. Like the supporters, the *Athletic News* were spitting feathers when they heard the news: 'At such an hour the United part with an inside-forward of the proved capacity of George Sapsford who scored two for Preston at Birmingham on the final day of the season. Still a club that could dispense with Hopkin could do anything.'

Returning would not be easy...

ROLL OF HONOUR

CHAMPIONS: LIVERPOOL

FA CUP WINNERS: HUDDERSFIELD TOWN

UNITED: DIVISION 1 (22ND) - FA CUP (1ST ROUND) CARDIFF CITY

LESLIE HOFTON

FULL-BACK: JULY 1910 TO MAY 1913
& SEP 1919 TO FEB 1922
1 APP 0 GLS (TOTAL 18 APPS 0 GLS)

LESLIE HOFTON WAS widely tipped to be England's next great defender when he moved to United from Glossop for a hefty £1,000 in the summer of 1910 but a succession of bad knee injuries – the worst of which he sustained whilst playing for the Football League in 1911 – denied him the opportunity to fulfil his vast potential and forced him into retirement at the age of just 25. By the  time League football resumed after the war, Hofton's knees had recovered sufficiently for him to successfully negotiate a trial and earn a new contract at Old Trafford but – understandably enough – he was never quite the same player the second time around and, as a result, never really threatened to make himself a first-team regular. Instead, he spent the second half of his United career as captain of the club's championship-winning reserve team.

TOMMY FORSTER

WING-HALF, JAN 1916 – SUMMER 1922, 36 APPS 0 GLS

A 5FT 6IN terrier who had impressed alongside the equally diminutive Tommy Meehan in wartime football, Tommy Forster was a disappointingly marginal figure in his first season as a pro, mainly because of his inability to recover his extraordinary stamina following his delayed demobilisation from the army. A summer's training knocked him back into shape and in 1920/21 he bridged the gap between sectional and league football, emerging as a rare plus point in a season full of minuses (none bigger than the sale of his old midfield buddy, Meehan). In February, the *Football News* wrote approvingly: 'After his return from the army, Forster appeared to have slowed down very considerably. In recent games, however, the Northwich man has made great strides, and at present he is the most improved man in the side. For a small player he is a rare tackler, and a big point in his favour is the fact that his work is always clean. His work is not showy, but he is a player who ignores the word beaten, and he is the best feeder of the line...After losing Meehan, United are fortunate to have a reserve of Forster's class.'

Towards the end of the season, the same rag added: 'Forster does a lot of fine work which is rarely noticed. With three or four inches in height he would make a great player.' In truth, Tommy did not quite possess the constructive ability to reach Meehan class but he was plainly good enough to hold down a place in United's midfield. Surprisingly, he was only given limited opportunities to build on his strong start. The arrival of John Scott and, later, Jack Grimwood's switch from pivot to left-half, restricted Tommy to just four appearances in 21/22 and at the end of the season he returned to Northwich Victoria, the club that Jack Robson had plucked him from six years earlier.

GEORGE SAPSFORD

INSIDE-LEFT, APRIL 1919 – MAY 1922, 53 APPS 17 GLS

BEARING IN MIND the Meehan and Hopkin deals from the previous year, George Sapsford's ill-timed move to Preston was the completion of an ignominious treble. As Teddy Partridge was the only other recognised inside-left on the books (and he was needed on the wing), George's £2,500 switch would have smacked of stupidity had he staggered from the same footballing gene pool  as William Prunier. He had not. In fact, the tricky Mancunian was highly rated and, considering his inexperience, seemingly set for bigger and better things. Already, after just a season and a half as a first-team regular, he had forged a reputation as a schemer with a soft touch and a salmon's leap while a strike rate of one in three had gone some way to silencing the accusations that he was not much of a goal-scorer.

Fortunately for the directors, their foolhardy decision to cash in on Sapsford did not backfire on them to the same extent as the other two sales. George scored on his Preston debut but fractured an ankle shortly afterwards and was restricted to just thirty-five league appearances in his three seasons at Deepdale. Moreover, Arthur Lochhead emerged as an impressive replacement for him at Old Trafford. However, the supporters and papers never allowed the club to forget how they had discarded three of their brightest talents. Sapsford's was one of the names that the directors would be beaten with for years to come.

JAMES ROBINSON
LEFT-WINGER, JUNE 1919 – JUNE 1922, 21 APPS 3 GLS

THE REGULAR UNDERSTUDY to Fred Hopkin during his first two seasons at the club, James Robinson was given an unexpected opportunity to cement a permanent place in the side when Hopkin was controversially sold to Liverpool in the summer of '21. In a run of six successive starts that autumn, he did not embarrass himself but nor did he do enough to win over the selectors. For the rest of the relegation season Jimmy returned to the role of understudy, this time to Teddy Partridge, and the following summer he moved to Tranmere on a free. He did not get much of a look-in there, either, and after two more frustrating seasons on the sidelines, the former Irish junior international dropped out of the professional game for good.

GEORGE BISSET
RIGHT-SIDED FORWARD, NOV 1919 – NOV 1921, 42 APPS 10 GLS

GEORGE BISSET CHOSE a bad time to try his luck in English football, his move from Third Lanark coinciding with the Reds' transformation from hopefuls to hopeless, the arrival of the kind of playing conditions that would have tested the balance of a mountain goat and the return from self-imposed exile of the King, Billy Meredith. The extra weight that the recently demobbed winger was carrying did not help his cause either and a combination of all of the above persuaded the selectors to ditch him after just a handful of appearances.

A strict training regime which removed an X or two from his short size and cut chunks out of his sprint times brought Bisset back into contention and a chance switch to inside-right won him a ticket back to the first team for the closing stages of 1919/20. George's subsequent vibrant performances won him a small army of admirers. In April, *The Football Chron* wrote: 'Bisset has now established himself as a forward of proved ability. His footwork contains real craft, and is as quick as it is clever. He has also found increased speed since he came to Old Trafford and no doubt his friends over the border would be both surprised and pleased if they saw him.' The *Athletic News* went a step further, predicting in their 20/21 preview that 'if Bisset is kept at inside-right he will probably be one of the forwards of the season'.

Actually, his season never came close to living up to its billing. A month after the *Athletic News* made their grand prediction, George was out of the team and by the turn of the year he was officially on the missing list. Eleven months later he was transferred to Wolves. According to the gossipmongers, Bisset's strained relationship with resident legend Meredith was his undoing. More likely, he was the victim of the muddled thinking and transfer market incompetence of the directors who, after wasting thousands on Harrison, Miller and Leonard, first had to play them and then had to balance the books. One easy solution was to cash in on an under-employed but bankable asset like George. For his admirers it was a bitter blow that the finely built Scot's potential would never be realised at Old Trafford. Their criticism of the club only abated when Bisset, despite a bright start at Molineux, failed to realise it anywhere else.

CYRIL BARLOW

FULL-BACK, DEC 1919 – OCT 1922 (AMATEUR FROM JULY 1914),
30 APPS 0 GLS

RECRUITED AS AN amateur from the Northern Nomads in the summer of 1914, Newton-Heath-born Cyril Barlow was forced to wait five years to sign his first professional contract and another three months to make his United debut. By then he was 31 years-old and lacked the pace, if not the tackle and temperament, to hack it in the first division. Compared with Jack Silcock, a souped-up sports car of a defender, and Charlie Moore, who was a tough and reliable Volvo, Cyril was one of those light-blue three-wheelers that pensioners used to totter around in in the seventies – useful in an emergency but something you would rather keep in the garage. After making just three appearances in 21/22, a move to New Cross in October ensured that Cyril stayed garaged for good.

FRANK HARRIS

HALF-BACK, MAY 1920 – SUMMER 1923
(SIGNED AS AMATEUR FEBRUARY 1920),
49 APPS 2 GLS

AN URMSTON OLD Boys old boy, Frank Harris was still an amateur when he marked his United debut with a bullet header against Sunderland on Valentine's Day, 1920. It wasn't all downhill from then on but nor was it a sign of things to come. A broad-shouldered worker, Frank was a regular on the right of midfield for most of 20/21 but lost his way during the relegation campaign and did not feature at all the season after. Too defensive and too crude, he left professional football just three years after joining it.

BILLY GOODWIN

CENTRE-FORWARD, JUNE 1920 – AUG 1922, 7 APPS 1 GL

A DELICATE FIRST touch, powerful shot and a well-honed sniffer's instinct earned Billy Goodwin a stack of goals both in the Central League and also in the lower divisions with Exeter and Southend but his lack of speed told against him in the top flight and he left Old Trafford with just one goal to his name, his headed winner at Roker Park in March 1921. Billy did have some lasting impact at the club, though, as it was his excellent form for the stiffs that triggered Charlie Radford's transformation from non-playing centre-forward into first team full-back.

GEORGE SCHOFIELD

WINGER, AUG 1920 – MAY 1922, 1 APP 0 GLS

A BLOND AND slim wide-man who was comfortable on either flank, George Schofield owed his one shot at stardom (in the 1-1 draw at Bolton in September '20) to the club's frenetic attempts to find a successor to Billy Meredith. He wasn't the answer and within three years of his Burnden run-out he was playing for Altofts W. R. Colliery which must be a dream for any player.

WILLIAM HARRISON
RIGHT-WINGER, OCT 1920 – SEPT 1922, 46 APPS 5 GLS

TECHNICALLY, UNITED'S SCOUTS delivered on instructions when they were told to find the club a younger alternative to the soon-to-depart Billy Meredith. However, as William Ewart Harrison was almost 34 when he was enticed from Wolves, he did not exactly represent one for the future. The first in a long line of right-wingers who were unable to cope with the ghost of Meredith, Harrison wasn't a complete disaster in the Harry Leonard mould but nor was he any sort of success. As the *Football News* observed, in November 1920: 'He [Harrison] is nothing like so clever as he was a couple of seasons ago. He certainly possesses greater speed than Billy Meredith but this is about the only advantage he has over the famous Welshman, whom many of the club's supporters would like to see in the team again.' The general feeling was that Harrison was the right man, years too late. For a veteran he was explosively quick but he was nothing like the player he had been in his pre-war heyday when he had been a shining light in the Wolves team that lifted the 1908 FA Cup.

FRANK BRETT
RIGHT FULL-BACK, FEB 1921 – AUG 1922, 10 APPS 0 GLS

WHEN HE WAS given first shot at replacing long-term injury victim Charlie Moore in August '21, Frank Brett had the key to a regular first-team place in his hands. Within three weeks he had lost it down the back of his sofa and a promising career was never the same again. A year of bit-part action later, the then 23-year-old left the Reds to join Aston Villa and within a year he had moved on again, this time to Northampton Town, where he became a minor legend, clocking up over 250 appearances.

Nothing that Frank did at Old Trafford or beyond quite justified the fuss that surrounded his £300 move from Birmingham district side Redditch in early 1921. Before joining Redditch as a professional, Frank had signed amateur forms at Villa Park. It says much for the iniquitous system that governed players' rights at the time that he remained tied to Villa regardless of the fact that they had never pursued their initial interest in him. When United moved in for Brett, Villa dug out his old registration documents and demanded their slice of the pie.

What happened next was a tiresome and drawn out argument between the two clubs that threatened to run longer than The Mousetrap. To cut a long story short, United ignored Villa's claim for compensation, the FA fined them ten guineas for registering a player before they had obtained his transfer from his former club, the Reds tried to come to terms with the Villains, the negotiations were unsuccessful and the authorities eventually stepped in and forced a compromise. All of which must have spiced up the negotiating process no end when Brett rejoined Villa and their midfield iron man, Frank Barson, moved in the opposite direction just eighteen months later...

PERCY SCHOFIELD

INSIDE-FORWARD, MAY 1921 – SEP 1922, 1 APP 0 GLS

A DEPUTY FOR the injured George Sapsford in United's 3-2 defeat at Deepdale (in October '21), Bolton-born Percy Schofield did not play another senior game for the club and subsequently faded into non-league anonymity, first with Eccles United and then with Hurst F.C..

RICHARD GIBSON

RIGHT-WINGER, JUNE 1921 – APRIL 1922, 12 APPS 0 GLS

RICHARD GIBSON WAS signed for £250 from Birmingham to act as cover for Billy Harrison. I wonder, has there ever been a clearer sign that a footballer's career is going nowhere? Twelve mid-season appearances later, the midget wing-man had his boots hung up for him when he was one of the dozen players binned in the Reds' post-relegation clear-out.

JOHN SCOTT

LEFT-HALF, JUNE 1921 – JUNE 1922, 24 APPS 0 GLS

A LEFT-HALF with a long-standing reputation as a cool customer and wily playmaker, John Scott was brought in from Bradford Park Avenue to add experience and sang-froid to a fresh-faced half-back line and also to aid in the development of the promising left-wing partnership of Sapsford and Partridge. In hindsight, his £750 fee would have been better spent elsewhere. Scott had experience all right but he no longer had the legs and when he was faced with a pacy right-winger he was powerless to do anything bar wave him past. Given the captaincy at the start of the campaign, John was an ever-present in the first half of the season but was dropped for good following the 3-0 thrashing at Newcastle on New Year's Eve. United's eventual relegation in 21/22 completed an unwelcome double for the plodding Scot as he had gone down with Park Avenue the season before.

WALTER TAYLOR

RIGHT-WINGER, DEC 1921 – APRIL 1922, 1 APP 0 GLS

FROM NEW MILLS to the first division in two short weeks, Wally Taylor's rise from junior football was meteoric but his fall was equally swift. Tossed into a relegation-bound side and left to sink or swim, Wally sank, the *Football News* describing his debut/farewell performance (in January's 2-1 defeat at Bramall Lane) thus: 'Taylor may be a useful forward, but he is a mere boy, lacking considerably in weight...To put him against opponents like Uttley and Sturgess is certainly courting disaster. It was unfair to Taylor and the rest of the team.' At the end of the season Wally was released on a free transfer and he then disappeared from the professional game altogether. One of many one game wonders (the wonder being how they ever ended up at Old Trafford in the first place) during the Depression Years, he could at least have comforted himself with the thought that it is better to have played and failed than never to have played at all.

THE RED DEVIL

BEFORE THE PREMIER League and Sky joined forces to trample on the last vestiges of community spirit that remained in the game – and in the process extend the gap between the divisions from an arm's length into a gaping chasm – there was a school of thought which argued that relegation wasn't necessarily a bad thing. Handled the right way, a short spell in the footballing shadows would allow clubs the opportunity to cut out the cancer that had helped put them there and also to reorganise, rebuild and rid themselves of their losing culture. In short, a stint at a lower level could provide perennial strugglers with a five-star ego-massaging service similar to that enjoyed by the Glazers when they undergo a 'grilling' on MUTV.

There is no better example of this Obi-Wan Kenobi effect – 'if you strike me down [Darth] I shall become more powerful than you can possibly imagine' – than United's dramatic revival under Tommy Doc. The vibrant young side he led out of the second division in 1975 bore little or no resemblance to the backwards-looking strugglers he had taken into it. There are those who would argue that the transformation would have taken place anyway and that the Doc's new signings just needed time to settle in. What is undeniable is that the manure of the second division made the perfect seed-bed for the next wave of Red heroes. Young, gifted and cocky, they got used to winning right from the off and, at least until Tommy went and Dave Sexton came in, they hardly ever stopped.

But the 'blessing in disguise' line only worked for clubs that bounced straight back. With no televisions, never mind television money, relegation in the twenties was not the financial disaster that it is today but a club with the overheads of United could not cope with reduced crowds and reduced income for ever. Add on the difficulties in keeping their quality players (what few there were) happy and attracting others to the club and it was vital that the Reds did not allow the second division to become their Hotel California. They already knew how hard it was to leave; the last time the club, in its Newton Heath guise, had fallen from the top table they had not got their seat back for another twelve years.

With only two promotion spots available, it was a difficult division to get out of at the best of times. Depressingly, United's stature made it doubly so. Imagine – but don't bother if you've just eaten (...in the past month) – being stuck in an all-nude hot tub with Ann Widdecombe, Cherie Blair and that old girl with the bell from Maine Road. Then imagine the same hot tub with a Cindy or a Kylie added to it. If you could not get out of the tub yourself, clearly the next best thing would be to make sure that she could not get out either. United, believe it or not, were the Kylie of Division Two though admittedly they were from her fresh-out-of-Neighbours phase rather than the classic falling-out-of-hotpants one. Second division chairmen, most of whom were used to surviving on a meagre diet of visits to, and from, footballing Widdecombes such as Rotherham, Clapton and Leeds could not believe they had been so lucky. Having the Reds around meant there would be two bumper pay-days for the clubs and a pair of cup finals for their journeymen pros. Motivation, it has to be said, was never going to be a problem.

Given United's record in knock-out football – one victory in three seasons – the prospect of nine months of cup-style battles made most Reds understandably nervous. And that was not the only reason why promotion was by no means taken as red either. According to the promotion handbook, teams had to be strong enough to cope with the physical demands of the division if they were going to dig their way out of it. Apart from the lads at the back, this United side did not possess the tools. If it came to the survival of the fittest what hope was there for lightweights like Partridge and Hilditch? And what were the Scottish lads going to make of it? The transition from the Scottish to the English leagues had been tough enough; what awaited them in the second division would make life in the first seem like a gentle stroll. It was just as well they could go commando under their kilts. Had they worn pants, they would have spent the summer months filling them.

As Prince Charles found out at boarding-school, a big name does not necessarily save you from having your dinner money nicked and your head flushed down the bog (and with those ears it must have been a hell of a job for him to get it out). But those fans who approached the new season with similar concerns about the Reds were about to have their brows unruffled. Frank Barson, the Aston Villa colossus, was on his way and when Frank arrived, the club had the sheriff they needed to deal with the varmints and vagabonds of Division Two. The million dollar question was whether his new posse had the firepower they needed to back him up...

*   *   *

ONE LOOK AT FRANK BARSON would tell you that he was not a man to be trifled with. Jack Mew was 5ft 8in tall and weighed a fraction over twelve stone but at a time when nutrition-deficient diets were still churning out generations of midgets he was spoken of as a heavyweight. Barson packed thirteen stone of muscle into his six foot frame and would have cut a fearsome figure even today when six foot-plus defenders are the norm. A nose that was spread across his right cheek said all that was needed about a career spent going in where it hurts. Or, more to the point, where his opponents got hurt. Frank took the knocks unflinchingly (his ability to play through pain was legendary) but he was principally famous for handing them out – many an opponent had cause to regret finding themselves on the wrong end of a Barson shoulder charge. Meet him on the wrong day and a forward was likely to find out how Tony Underwood felt when he was run over by Jonah Lomu. Except there was no lucrative pizza commercial to look forward to, just a month or two of eating meals through a straw.

Barson's arrival at OT was the climax to a saga that had intrigued the sports press for the best part of two years. Initially, he and Villa had been the golden couple, the Bogey and Bacall of post-war football. Within months of moving from Barnsley in the autumn of 1919, Frank had led the era's first crisis club on a magical mystery tour which began with a meteoric rise up the table and climaxed in Cup Final glory. It is no exaggeration to say that the Cup was as much Barson's that year as it was Matthews's in '53 and Gazza's in '91. But it hadn't taken long for the relationship to turn sour. The *casus belli* were the board's demands that every player live in the Birmingham area. Frank, who had business interests near his Sheffield home, had refused to comply, the club had kept pushing him and, after first going through the separate beds phase, he had sought a divorce.

Getting one had not been easy. The maxim that you do not keep an unhappy player did not apply to the same extent in those days. The clubs' hold on their staff was so tight that they could squeeze the fight out of most malcontents. Even if a player refused to sign a new contract, the club still retained his registration and without his registration the player could not play for, or, more pertinently, be paid by, anybody else. That was the corner that Frank had been backed into the previous summer when Villa had refused to countenance his transfer request. Faced with a season without either pay or football he had been left with little choice but to backtrack and re-sign.

A year on, however, he had made it clear that nothing save a kidnap attempt would get him back to Birmingham. In the knowledge that their iron man was not for turning, Villa had reluctantly decided to cash in. Cue the biggest transfer scramble in years – and United's biggest coup. The big guns were all interested but Barson was apparently desperate to become a Red even though that meant dropping down a division. How reassuring that United's pheromones remained strong enough to reach the nostrils of the very best though Frank's head may have been turned anyway by the interesting package that was placed before him. Neatly side-stepping the regulations on bonuses and the maximum wage, the directors promised him his own pub if he led them to promotion. Funnily enough, they also forgot their recently-announced pledge to make every squad member live in town.

Barson was one of those players whom rules are made to be broken for. At 31 he was supposedly in the twilight of his career but by common consent he remained the finest all-round centre-half in the game. In effect, Frank was three players – strong, aerially superb defender, midfield playmaker and general enforcer – rolled into one. He was also a captain in the 'marvel' class and United had lacked one of those since Charlie Roberts's day. Recently, the directors had gone in for choosing Mike Brearleys – good leaders who wouldn't otherwise have been guaranteed a place in the side – which is why the captain's armband had been passed on quicker than syphilis at an orgy. In the past season alone, the management had tried out three different skippers; Hilditch, McBain and Scott. They had also picked five players at centre-half. At the very least, Barson's arrival would mean that selection meetings no longer dragged on so long.

But it wasn't his talent that underpinned Frank's standing as just about the most talked-about figure in the game. It was his notoriety. When he signed for the Reds he was already well on his way to a career total of at least twelve sendings-off. In an era when red cards were thought to bring shame on the player, his club and even struck a blow against the English sense of fair play, that made him more or less unique. His backers argued that, with Barson, things were never as bad as they seemed. The theory was that the difference in power and essential hardness between Frank – the former blacksmith with arms like Popeye and a face that looked like it had doubled as the anvil – and other mortals turned the slightest physical contact into a potential case for the CPS. The alternative view was that he was an out-of-control psycho who derived some perverse pleasure in handing out pain. Ever the conservatives, the England selectors subscribed to the Satan-in-shinpads standpoint which is why Frank's potentially lengthy international career had stalled after just one game. Classy, controversial and under-used by his country – he was never going to have any difficulty fitting in at Old Trafford was he?

*   *   *

THE LOOSE ENDS OF his £4,000 transfer were tied up on the season's eve but, having missed out on pre-season training, Frank would not be ready to make his debut for another couple of weeks. Not even his absence, though, could stifle the first outbreak of Barson fever at Old Trafford for the Crystal Palace game the following day. If the season had kicked off without a major transfer coup, the takings that afternoon would possibly have fallen short of Frank's monthly bar bill (like another, latter-day Captain Marvel, he was known to be fond of the odd pint or eight). Now that the post-relegation gloom of the summer had been usurped by big-signing euphoria, the gate was an impressive 36,000. That Barson-swelled crowd was the clearest vindication yet of the 'speculate to accumulate' policy that the supporters had advocated since the war. If they spent big to bring in the best, the directors wouldn't just improve the team, they would claw back the money they invested through the gate. Frustratingly, the lesson went unlearned. By the time the Depression Years entered their Prozac stage, the Barson effect had long been forgotten.

With Frank absent on the opening day, the limelight settled

instead on John Wood, a £1,750 summer recruit from Dumbarton, and only about the twentieth player to be touted as the solution to the right-wing conundrum. A brilliant debut goal, as United made short work of the Eagles, suggested that the square-jawed Jock might actually live up to his billing but it was a cruel illusion. Wood had arrived with a reputation as a goal-hungry flier – the twenty-five goals he scored in 21/22 had earned him third place in the Scottish First Division scoring list – but his first goal as a Red would be his last. By Christmas he had been branded the club's least successful right-winger yet.

Hillsborough, two days later, was as frustrating as the Palace, Wood and Barson news had been uplifting, United being denied a deserved last-gasp equaliser by a Clive Thomas[1] moment from the referee. But that, and a 2-0 ambush at Coventry on September 23, were the only blemishes on an otherwise exhilarating reintroduction to life in the second. Six wins in five weeks lifted the club into second place and sealed their best start to a season in a decade. And scanning the top half of the table for United's name wasn't the only stimulating new experience for match-going Reds. The prospect of turning up at that gate and expecting to be worked up into a rich lather of excitement was a new experience. For those who were bothered, there was still plenty to grumble about in terms of the team's style and combination. For anyone who loved their matches packed with thrills, spills and, most of all, last-gasp goals, September 1922 was just about as good as it gets.

Four of those September matches were settled when they were close to burning out. Joe Spence started the trend at Selhurst Park, bundling and smashing in two goals in the final half-hour as United came from behind to win 3-2. But the real story of the afternoon was provided by Charlie Moore who completed another stage of his remarkable recovery from career-threatening injury with a steadfast display in place of the unfit Radford. A new contract followed soon after but the final phase of Charlie's resurrection, a regular first team place, would not be completed for another year. For most of the season, the selectors kept faith with the Silcock-Radford partnership from the year before.

1.   In the 1978 World Cup, the controversial Thomas hit the headlines for blowing for time just as Zico was heading Brazil's 'winner' in a vital group game against Sweden.

It was also the afternoon when United discovered at first hand the realities of lower league life. After the relative splendour of Hillsborough, Selhurst offered the first, grim reminder of the cultural gap between the divisions. Players and pressmen alike were shocked to discover 'a little wooden stand, a remarkably uneven pitch and a stable-like dressing-room with a sort of box as a bath' – clearly Palace's ground was as splendid then as it is today. Second-class surroundings are not the only local tradition to have survived either. John Chapman, still coming to terms with United's pulling power, was astounded by the large numbers of London-based Reds that he saw in the crowd. Fifty years before the terrace (and train) wars made them famous, the Cockney Reds were already a force to be reckoned with.

Another Spence winner rescued a turgid midweek encounter with Wednesday and earned United swift revenge for their Hillsborough setback. The selectors' decision to give Joe a sustained run at centre-forward was proving a good one. He had notched four goals in four games already and would end the month with six in eight. But nothing he nor the other players could do could deflect attention away from Barson. A fortnight of communal salivation finally ended when Frank kicked off his United career away to Wolves on the 9th. Molineux gave him a predictably unfriendly welcome, his links with Villa amplifying the jeers and catcalls that he usually received on away grounds. As ever, it was so much wasted breath. Hostile fans were no problem; when you are the least popular player around, they tend to come with the territory. Ring-rustiness was the real concern, Frank's lack of football explaining why his performance was steady rather than five-star. Still, he did enough to be rated the pick of the half-backs. There cannot have been much wrong with his stamina either as it was his run and shot that paved the way for United's late winner, thumped in on the rebound by another summer signing, inside-left Harry Williams.

Wolves were the second victims of the Reds' last-gasp goal rush. They were also the third, losing to an even later effort at Old Trafford the following week. 'Almost on the point of time Manchester United snatched a lucky victory at Old Trafford on Saturday in the return match with Wolverhampton Wanderers and the players were so overjoyed that they raced from all parts of the field to shake hands with the scorer,' wrote Jacques. A disappointing spectacle was granted an extraordinary denouement when Spence met a luscious centre from McBain with a full-length diving header. Which explains why the players were so 'overjoyed' that they ran over to... shake Joe by the hand (those boys in the twenties sure knew how to let themselves go). The rattle-wavers on the Pop Side reacted with less restraint. The performance may have been a C-plus but the excitement factor at the finale was definitely Class A and Old Trafford had not been treated to as big a high for months. You can stick your 5-0s, every fan knows that the best way to win a football match is by scoring a goal in the last minute – and, as every Scouser and Bavarian knows, the worst way to lose one is by conceding two.

Defeat at Highfield Road was a shock but Old Trafford was back jumping again when Spence netted late to claim another slice of instant pay-back in the rematch. It was another cracking strike, too, a Sparky-style volley from the edge of the box. Given that 28,000 Reds had again been left in a state normally brought on using a belt and a syringe, it was perhaps the wrong time for the club to invite them to gather in front of the main stand to hear the plans for the re-formation of the Supporters' Club. The results were predictably anarchic. Thousands of Reds swarmed onto the pitch and the handful of policemen on duty were powerless to stop the raggy-arsed fans treating themselves to an unofficial tour of the plush main stand.

The Red rascals were clearly intent on enjoying the moment but the more philosophical match-goer was still troubled with old doubts. Goals remained hard to come by, with Spence just about the only player who was getting any. Despite the step down in class, the side were still struggling to express themselves – the thrilling climaxes could not hide the fact that much of the foreplay had been typically tedious. There was also a nagging feeling that United were enjoying the calm before the storm. The fixture list had handed them an easy start in more ways than one. None of the teams they had played so far were likely to feature in the promotion equation. Worse than that, only Coventry, at Highfield Road, had given the players a proper taste of lower league hurly-burly. And the 0-2 score-line suggested that they had been unable to stomach it.

*   *   *

THE SEPTEMBER SUCCESSES HAD been built on the sand of late goals. The next couple of months provided the answer to the question the worriers had been posing of what would happen if it started to rain; a shot-shy attack scored just five times and the team set off on a dismal eight game run without a win. But if it was a mini-crisis in football terms, in other walks of life it wouldn't have even registered as a blip. The fireworks had fizzled out at Old Trafford but the political landscape both at home and abroad remained a minefield. Like a spotty teenager's face, no one knew where it was next going to blow.

Ireland, in particular, was a disaster zone. The government's excessively brutal reaction to 1916's failed Easter Rising had driven three-quarters of the country into the arms of Sinn Fein and also triggered a chain of events that linked the formation and rise of the IRA, unsuccessful attempts to bring in Home Rule, a vicious war between the British and the republicans, Bloody Sunday, countless other atrocities and a torrent of deaths, with close on 1,000 assassinations between 1919 and 1921 alone.

The most recent attempt at an Irish solution – the creation of the Irish Free State as a self-governing dominion within the Commonwealth – had merely replaced one war with another. The refusal of the six north-eastern states to countenance the split from the mother country led to an eruption of IRA violence in the North. Meanwhile, in the South, the Anglo-Irish conflict was superseded by a brief but horrendous civil war as those Republicans who were unwilling to settle for anything less than a completely independent and united Ireland battled it out with those who were. The murders continued apace; in 1922 alone, another 230 people were killed. As he himself had predicted when he put his name to the Anglo-Irish treaty, Michael Collins headed the list of victims. Four days before the season started, the father of the IRA was assassinated by members of the very movement he had made infamous. To paraphrase one of the T-shirts printed in the wake of Roy Keane's expulsion from the Irish squad in the build-up to the 2002 World Cup, another Cork hero had been shot in the back.

Elsewhere, the French, increasingly frustrated by the inability of the Germans to meet the reparation payments imposed on them at Versailles, were on the verge of invading the Ruhr while the British almost came to blows with Turkey over their efforts to claw back the land they had lost in the post-war Treaty of Sevres. Eventually, though, a war-weary government opted to turn a blind eye, prompting the famous line that the country 'cannot act as policeman of the world'.

Domestically, the Carlton Club meeting of the Conservatives brought down the wartime coalition government, banished its leader – the other Welsh wizard, David Lloyd George – into the political wilderness and initiated a process that would lead to the first Labour government. Other countries, by contrast, were heading towards the far right. On October 30, Mussolini and his fascist army marched on Rome and seized power to the accompaniment of enthusiastic crowds. An increasingly nationalistic Germany would eventually embrace Hitler in similar style though his first putsch, in Munich the following January, ended in embarrassing failure and a taste of porridge for the future Fuhrer. Russia, meanwhile, was set to lose Lenin to his second stroke, paving the way for the pogroms, purges and concentration camps of the Stalinist era. With evil Joe on his way in Russia, evil Adolf making waves in Germany and Il Duce already installed in Italy, the pieces of a nightmarish jigsaw were already falling into place. Not that many people in this country were too bothered about it at the time. Given the seriousness of the post-war economic crisis, they were more worried about putting food on the table than the emergence of swastikas in Berlin.

*   *   *

BY THE TIME THE Brown Shirts marched on Rome, the Red shirts were already in retreat. Billy Harrison, the player the fans had loved to hate before his summer move to Port Vale, returned to Manchester to gain his revenge, scoring a screamer as his new club shocked his old. A horror show in the Potteries led to Red-faced defeat in the return and the first major reshuffle of the season. Partridge was moved back to outside-left in place of the inexperienced Harry Thomas; McBain, who had just started to show his Ayr form in midfield, was controversially pushed forward to partner him and Grimwood was brought in at wing-half. The new-look left flank added some spark to the forward line but did nothing to correct the old failing of wasting chances. United made plenty but converted just one en route to a pair of draws against Fulham and were again victims of their impotence as they drew home and away against Clapton Orient and were held 2-2 at Gigg Lane.

When Bury pulled them out of their drawing sequence by winning at Old Trafford on November 25, United were down in ninth and, in terms of points, closer to the bottom of the league than the top. It was a ludicrous position for the club to find themselves in, particularly as two of the three sections of the team were genuinely first division class. The defence had occasionally been guilty of taking their eye off the ball but could cope with the best the second league had to offer in their sleep. Barson was now well into his stride and when he and McBain lined up alongside each other, the half-back line looked as strong as any in the country. But Frank had already found out that you could take United's forwards to the toilet but you could not make them piss. Lochhead, as expected, had struggled to impose his class on the rollerball football of the second division, Wood had yet to reveal any class and gave the impression that he would struggle in any division, Partridge was being wasted at outside-left and Spence, without a goal in seven weeks, had rolled out of his purple patch and into a dry one. Henderson, meanwhile, needed surgery on his ankle and would be the latest player to be ruled out for a year through injury.

Fortunately, the cupboard wasn't completely bare. Centre-forward Ernest Goldthorpe had been an unheralded free transfer when he had arrived from Bradford a month or so earlier but he wasn't unheralded any more. A debut goal at Clapton, a brace at Bury and two performances that resonated with star quality endorsed what those in the know had always maintained, that the club had a potential steal on their hands if only they could keep him fit. In his early days, before he sustained the serious knee injury that cost him three years of football, Goldthorpe had been rated a certain International and the intoxicating combination of pace, skill, tenacity and ruthlessness he brought to the rest of United's season made it easy to see why. It would be an exaggeration to claim that he was a one-man cure to all of the side's attacking ills but when Ernie played well, the forward line looked stronger than at any time since the war.

But if the Clapton trip marked the moment that the club found a striker, the home leg of the Bury double marked the moment when they almost lost one. Before the game, Billy Sarvis, the back-up inside-right, was knocked down and critically injured as he ran along Chester Road to catch the reserve-team bus. The head injuries he sustained were so severe that the feeling at the scene was that he would not even make it to Salford Infirmary. Thus the game kicked off with his club-mates, several of whom had witnessed the accident, fearing the worst.

Given the circumstances, the Reds' insipid contribution to Bury's big day was easily explained. Happily, they need not have worried; Sarvis proved harder to finish off than War and Peace. After several days on the critical list, weeks more in hospital and a year's recuperation back home in Wales, the Taffy Lazarus stunned both his doctors and the United directors by writing in and requesting a return to training. Billy was eventually re-signed but the miracles did not extend to him adding to his lone first team appearance. A couple of seasons of Central League graft later, the great survivor moved on to Bradford.

*   *   *

DESPITE THE COMPETITION FROM the Manchester races and Salford's big cup game at the Willows, the Bury match still attracted a crowd of 32,000 to Old Trafford. By then, the pre-season jibes that the Red Army would not fancy it in the small time sounded frankly ludicrous. An average gate of around 25,000 was well down on the rib-crushing figures of a couple of years earlier but at a time when the trade depression was sending crowds crashing down across the board, it still made United one of the top six or seven best supported clubs in the country.

The figures speak for themselves which is just as well because the enduring loyalty of United's support did not get much of a mention in the press. T'was ever thus. So-called sleeping giants stir from their slumber, thousands of their hitherto unseen supporters remember the way to the ground and in the time it takes them to say 'howay the lads' football writers are in full brown-nose mode. United, by contrast, have been pulling in the biggest crowds for decades – in good times and bad – yet have rarely experienced the 'greatest fans' treatment.

Admittedly, they have not always deserved it. Those who survived them will tell you that the seventies were a golden age for the fans but it is highly unlikely that anyone who had dealings with tanked-up (or worse, tank-topped) Reds in brick-throwing mode would welcome them back. The football specials bringing the Doc's Army into town were as welcome a sight for the nation's shopkeepers, policemen and car-owners as Viking long-boats were for Anglo-Saxon virgins. And if seventies Reds were guilty of taking their devotion to the cause to criminal lengths (with the worst of their crimes being against fashion), the latest generation stand accused of not caring enough. Since Fergie started delivering titles on a conveyor-belt basis – a glory spell that coincided with football as a whole becoming fashionable again – Old Trafford has been at the centre of the fickle fan debate. Will the glory-hunters and corporate brigade hang around once the bubble bursts or Glazer milks us dry? Probably not, although there is something to be said for giving them the benefit of the doubt. The latest additions to the Old Trafford stands will not get the chance to prove they are genuine fans until they experience the bad times as well as the good.

To be honest, most Reds would prefer not to be showered with praise anyway. Who needs the backing of a two-faced press that luxuriates in the knowledge that anything to do with United sells regardless of whether it is good, bad, true or false? Given the siege mentality that the club and fans are comfortable with, constant praise would be difficult to handle. At least when people stick to the 'nobody likes us, we don't care' approach, everyone knows where they stand. More tellingly, there is the insinuation in the media's reluctance to dish out the compliments that somehow the supporters do not deserve it. You would not, after all, lavish praise on Jennifer Lopez's nipple-tweaker (supposedly she has one for photo shoots) for never taking a day off or on Simon Le Bon for staying faithful to his missus. It follows that you do not trumpet the loyalty of fans who have the privilege of supporting a club with a name and team as glamorous as any in the game. Take it a step further and, by withholding their praise, the media are inadvertently admitting to Red supremacy. Give me that over any tin-pot loyalty accolade any day.

*   *   *

THE HARD-CORE 20,000 WERE back inside Old Trafford as United finally pulled themselves out of their two-month slump with a 3-0 stroll against Rotherham County but any hopes of a December leap up the table were dashed as the Reds served up a mixed bag of results. A draw at Rotherham followed by a 1-0 win in the fog-bound derby with Stockport made it five points in three games but apart from a fortuitous Boxing Day win at Upton Park there was little to rouse the supporters out of their festive stupor. The home defeat by West

Ham made it a bah-humbug sort of Christmas Day, the final fixture of an unhappy year produced a depressingly inept loss at Hull but the worst moments of all came at Edgeley Park on the 23rd. For Stockport, Christmas really did come early. The lure of the Reds plus the presence of thousands of travelling fans swelled the attendance to an Edgeley record of 25,000. Meanwhile, an indifferent display from the United half-backs and a Lucanesque vanishing act from the forwards handed Stockport as big a result on the pitch as they enjoyed off it. And to add acid to the burning pain of the 1-0 defeat, the Reds had Spence, the latest right-wing experiment, sent off in the final moments for what the *Empire News* described as 'an alleged attempt to bring down an opponent.' Typical that; United could not even get their fouls on target.

The year ended with the Reds in mid-table, a hefty four wins adrift of joint leaders Notts County and Bury. By then, other clues – apart from the lack of goals – were starting to emerge to explain why a season that had looked set to return the club to the top flight had wandered so far off track. Rumours of dressing-room discontent had been sweeping town for weeks with even a notoriously conservative press picking up on the 'Manchester United sensation'. Now the fingers were being pointed at just one man, the former skipper Neil McBain.

In typical United style, the directors initially did their best to put the press and supporters off the scent. So when McBain was left out of the Rotherham trip on December 9, the uninspiring 1-0 against Barnsley on New Year's Day and then the Hull return five days later, the Official Programme wrote that, 'McBain, who has been a versatile man of the team, and has done well in every position he has been played in, was given a well-earned rest.' That did not tally with the story doing the rounds in Red pubs which claimed that a number of influential players had gone in to see the directors and informed them that they would refuse to play if the Scot was picked. The directors had sided with the disgruntled majority, dropped McBain from the side and in the process drawn a line under his United career.

Responding to the rumours, the management strenuously denied that they had ever been approached, let alone influenced, by a cabal of 'dressing-room dictators' and accused the Scot of being over-sensitive. Whatever the truth, the facts are that McBain issued a public statement saying that he did not think he was receiving fair treatment, the directors announced that they would not let a player dictate to them and then quickly ended the affair by packing him off to Everton for £4,200. Given the corner they had been backed into, it was a useful piece of business. Initially, the directors thought they would have to swallow a big loss. In the end, they recouped most of the money they had originally paid out.

Even so, the McBain saga was an embarrassment for the club and particularly for John Chapman who had always been keen to foster a strong sense of unity among his players. It was clear that his team-bonding exercises – the whist drives, dinner dances and smoking concerts – had not paid off. Actually, the inference from the press reports was that the dressing-room atmosphere could not have sunk much lower if Chapman had arranged a series of wife-swapping parties . . . with the gaffer baggsying the physio's wife, of course. It was also a major blow to the supporters who were desperate not to lose a player who had been arguably the biggest influence on the side after Barson. The fledgling Supporters' Club even went as far as sending a delegation to the board to plead for a reconciliation only to be told, in the politest possible terms, to keep their noses out of club affairs. But the players, one bad cup moment apart, seemed to flourish now that Neil was out of the way; in the next five weeks they got their league campaign back on track and, in the process, produced three contenders for afternoon of the season – a thriller against Hull, a vital win at Leeds and a goal-fest at Meadow Lane.

The Hull game, of course, came in the midst of the McBain affair and the ninety minute orgy of excitement that both teams served up provided the perfect antidote for those fans who had been rocked by the news of the club's latest Scottish disaster. Two goals down inside the opening quarter of an hour, the Reds roared back to level with short and long-range strikes from Goldthorpe and Lochhead before Radford netted the winner with a deflected screamer. As impressive as the fighting spirit and character in the team was the performance which, by general consent, was the best of the season so far. United were strong, quick and clever, the half-backs were dominant in both construction and destruction and even the forwards earned good reviews, particularly Partridge and Lochhead on the left flank. Teddy got the rattles swinging with his thrilling runs and centres, Arthur with his clever footwork and repertoire of flicks and back-heels. Everyone knew that United's inside-left was too good a player not to make some sort of impact on the second division. Since his recall to the side on Christmas Day he had been doing just that – his goal against Hull was his sixth in his last five games.

Eleven days later, memories of an indifferent display in the original tie at Valley Parade were erased as Goldthorpe's exquisite dribble and drilled finish knocked his old club Bradford out of the Cup. As the Empire Stadium was preparing to host its first Final[2], Wembley fever was in the air for the first time but before the Red Army could catch a dose of it, a fourth round trip to White Hart Lane acted as a vaccine. The papers argued that it was no disgrace to lose, even by 4-0, to a side containing six internationals but for a team with promotion aspirations, such as United, the gap between the divisions had seemed frighteningly broad. Another humiliating afternoon, this time at Hyde Road where the Reds were slaughtered 5-0 in the 'friendly' derby, raised more, uncomfortable questions about their ability to hack it in the top flight. For now, though, the debate was an academic one; first, the players had to prove they had the pedigree to make it there.

Three points from the doubleheader with the table-topping Tykes was a persuasive start. The old United disease of weak finishing cost them in the Old Trafford leg, the ultra-negative visitors holding on for an undeserved nil-nil. Elland Road the following week was far more satisfying, a single Lochhead strike sending the 25,400 locals home bleating. Incidentally, that was yet another record crowd for an away ground – more fuel for the 'only come to see United' point of view. The goal itself was nothing special, the simple facts being that Goldthorpe was taken out in the area, Lochhead smashed his spot-kick straight at the goalkeeper and netted from the rebound. More noteworthy were the shenanigans of the Leeds players beforehand. When Arthur stepped up to take the kick, they crowded behind him so he could not get a decent run-up. This jostling tactic had

---

2.   *Surprising as it may be for anyone who has been brainwashed into believing that Wembley really is the home of football, the FA Cup was already fifty-one years old when it moved to the stadium in 1923. Previously, the Cup Final had been staged at seven different grounds: Kennington Oval (in 1872 and between 1874 and 1892), Lillie Bridge (1873), Fallowfield (1893), Anfield (1894), Crystal Palace (1895-1914), Old Trafford (in 1915 Sheffield United beat Chelsea 3-0 in a match dubbed the 'Khaki' Final because the majority of the 49,557 crowd were in uniform) and Stamford Bridge (1920-22). There had also been replays at the Baseball Ground (1886), Burnden Park (1901), Goodison Park (1910), Old Trafford (in 1911 when Bradford City beat Newcastle 1-0) and Bramall Lane (1912).*

only recently been introduced to the game by Sheffield United and would not last long as the FA quickly took steps to eradicate it. Still, it remains as possibly Yorkshire's most lasting contribution to the sport. To prevent opponents blocking the penalty-taker's run-up, the design of the pitch was altered to give him an area where only he could stand – had it not been for the furtive Tyke, that otherwise useless arc at the edge of the box might never have existed.

The Elland Road 1-0 narrowed the gap between the Reds and the promotion zone to three points, cost Leeds their place in the top two and cleared the way for Notts County to reclaim top spot. They did not hold on to it for long. On their next outing, the Reds raised eyebrows to Roger Moore levels by pulverising the Magpies by six goals to one. In hindsight, it was obvious that someone was going to catch it from United eventually – the team had been making chances all season and even the goal-shy forwards were due a good day some time. But you would have needed an inspired run of form with the tea leaves to have predicted that the division's top dogs would be the ones to bear the brunt of the Red backlash. Especially when they dominated the opening stages and took the lead through Cock, a forward who did not piss away good chances. But this time neither did United. Goldthorpe hooked in a right-footed equaliser on fifteen, his teeth-loosening barge on the home keeper set up a tap-in for Myerscough midway through the half and when Joe scored again on the stroke of half-time, United were cruising at 3-1. Cruising but not finished. Driven forward by Barson in one of his untouchable moods, the Reds doubled their tally in the second half, Goldthorpe bagging all three in an amazing 4½ minute goal flurry. Not since John Picken achieved the feat against Middlesbrough in 1909/10 had a United player scored four goals in a match. As for the team, they had not been so goal happy since Blackburn were swatted aside by the identical score in a fifth-round cup tie back in 1909, the year that Charlie Roberts had got his hands on the trophy.

In the space of six weeks, United had turned their season on its head but having worked so hard to get themselves back into the promotion race, the side immediately fell victim to a springtime stitch. Three questions were asked of them in the wake of Meadow Lane. Were the forwards capable of repeating the ruthlessness they had shown against County? Could the team as a whole perform as well against the weaker sides as they had against their promotion rivals? And were they capable of reproducing their impressive away form at Old Trafford? In all three cases, the answer was an emphatic no; in the rest of February and the first three weeks of March, United played six matches – including four at home – and picked up just five points. Having been a mere point behind the leaders on February 10, the Reds approached the Easter fixtures a distant sixth.

The side's disastrous form at Old Trafford was the biggest puzzle. How could a team that had just won away at Leeds and Notts County then proceed, in the space of a fortnight, to draw at home against mid-table Derby, draw again in the return with the shell-shocked Magpies and then surrender their two month unbeaten record by losing to an ordinary Southampton? In the forlorn search for an answer, H.P.R, writing in the *Football News*, reached for an old Mancunian favourite; he blamed the Scousers: 'I often think that Liverpool, who opened the ground at Old Trafford, and who carried off the spoils, must have created some ill-fated atmosphere which still hangs over the club.'

Others repeated the point made earlier that playing at a sporting Mecca like Old Trafford inspired United's opponents while the pressure of playing in front of a large and demanding home crowd perhaps inhibited some Reds. The side's lack of success at the ground brought the papers out in a rash of reminiscences about the supposed good old days at Clayton. United had always had a formidable record there partly because visiting sides were unaccustomed to playing on a surface that could have doubled for no-man's land at Ypres. Throw in that vomit-inducing stench from the adjoining chemical works and United had basked in as big an advantage as Oldham and Luton did when they played on plastic.

No one seriously wanted a return to the Bank Lane days but the question of what would have happened to the club had they stayed put still made an interesting 'what if?'. In the short term, they would clearly have been better off financially. Without a plush new stadium to pay for, the belt-tightening of recent years would not have been as extreme, leaving enough money in the coffers to build the next great team. No guarantees of course but, without the cost of moving, the Reds would possibly have got more use out of the trophy room and almost certainly would not have gone down. Then again, had it not been for the move to Old Trafford, United would have lacked the base they needed to launch their bid to join the football elite – and football superstardom was where the club were headed even if Reds in the twenties had to take that on trust.

FEBRUARY'S DISAPPOINTMENTS CONVINCED THE directors to break into the seven grand they had raised from the cup ties and the sale of McBain and splash out on a couple of new forwards, Ken MacDonald from Cardiff and Huddersfield stalwart Frank Mann. This time there was no repeat of the summer's Barsonmania; initially Frank and Ken left the fans colder than a summer in San Francisco. It isn't difficult to see why. Instead of the right-winger or Cantona figure the supporters craved, the club had invested in a bustling, cumbersome centre-forward (as if they had not been down that route enough times already) and an inside-right who looked like Joe Spence's dad rather than his prospective partner on the wing. It makes you wonder whether United's scouts could not read Chapman's handwriting; there had to be some reason why, like Chris Eubank when he visits a steak-house, the management constantly ordered one thing and got another.

In fact, despite his aged appearance and bald head, Mann, the inside-right, was only in his early thirties and would serve the club well although it would take time and a positional switch for Reds to begin to appreciate him. As for MacDonald, he always looked like a stop-gap signing and in the end he did not stop for long, moving on to Bradford in October after just nine games and two goals. He worked hard and did not mind throwing his weight about but he lacked speed and style (and if we're honest, talent) and United had far better options on the books in Goldthorpe and the promising Glaswegian, David Bain.

Neither new boy made much of an impact on 22/23. MacDonald deputised for Goldthorpe in the Southampton disaster and scored United's goal in the frustrating draw at the Baseball Ground but then made way for the fit-again Ernie at Valley Parade. The rest of his season was spent in the reserves. Mann was brought into the side just as MacDonald was dropping out of it and was an ever-present in the final ten games of the season without ever making a cast-iron case for his continued inclusion ahead of Myerscough. In general play, Frank's vision hovered between the good and the exceptional but he had a blind spot where the goals were concerned; it would be another seven months before he worked out where they were. Yet another non-scoring attacker was the last thing that United's promotion challenge needed. Goals continued to arrive in drips, home and away 1-1s with Bradford extending the Reds' latest drawing rut. The reviews after the Old

Trafford stalemate were uncomplimentary to both sides, *The Guardian* commenting that 'two poor teams in Manchester United and Bradford gave further evidence of the weakness which caused them to leave the first division.'

Most people were booking United in for another season outside the top flight. With just eight games remaining they lay four points adrift of the top two and to stand any chance of gatecrashing the promotion party they would need to match, or even better, their January form. A pair of 3-0 strolls in their Easter doubleheader against South Shields at least got them going again but the events at Blackpool on Easter Saturday appeared to confirm the suspicion that this wasn't going to be their year. Conceding the only goal of the game in the closing minutes was bad enough, losing Barson to injury made the pain of defeat even worse. What could have been a celebratory weekend away for the trainloads of travelling Reds instead turned into a communal wake – with candyfloss and rock in place of the customary sandwiches and sausage rolls.

More injury misery followed in the Old Trafford return as Goldthorpe sustained a fractured collarbone. It could have been worse – it could have been his suspect knee – but the break still ruled him out for the rest of the season. Flicking two fingers at adversity, the ten men roared back from 1-0 down to take the points with two goals in four second half minutes. Then, after a stultifying nil-nil at the Dell, they continued their revival by smashing and grabbing a shock win at promotion rivals Leicester. Bain, preferred to MacDonald as Goldthorpe's replacement, stole in to nudge the Reds ahead midway through the first half. After that, they sat back in defence and allowed the Foxes to bang their heads on the brick wall thrown in front of goal by the defence and half-backs. Silcock and Radford made a heroic last line but Hilditch was the afternoon's undisputed hero. After another in-and-out season, Lal was belatedly prospering as Barson's deputy, so much so that the skipper, despite being fit again, had insisted that the selectors keep him in the side.

The Filbert Street surprise lifted the Reds into third place, level on points with fourth-placed Leicester and second-placed West Ham and two points adrift of Notts County. With only two games left compared with the Hammers' five and the others' three, United's promotion chances remained slim but, for Pop Side optimists at any rate, there was still reason enough to dream. West Ham were due to meet Bolton in the 'White Horse' Cup Final at the end of the month and, that distraction apart, were faced with a daunting schedule featuring six league matches in just eighteen days. There was always a chance that they would blow up, particularly if they lost (as indeed they did, 2-0) at Wembley. Meanwhile, if the Reds beat Leicester in their return game at Old Trafford they would travel to Barnsley on the final day of the season in the knowledge that a victory – and their superior goal average – would make it impossible for the Foxes to catch them.

Instead, United ended a season of Old Trafford mediocrity by giving perhaps their worst home performance yet. After a chanceless first half, Leicester strolled to victory in the second, scoring twice through Duncan and Grimwood's brother-in-law, Smith. As far as the papers were concerned, the team had not been equal to either the opposition or the occasion. Listening to Barson's pleas to keep faith in Hilditch had been a fatal mistake; they were the selfless actions of a good egg but the team sorely missed his presence and leadership. The absence of Goldthorpe had been the other major handicap. In what was only his fourth senior start, Bain's lack of experience had been horribly exposed.

On the same afternoon that Leicester snuffed out United's final hopes of sneaking a promotion place, Hopkin's Liverpool nailed their second championship in succession. Having gone down on the day that the Scousers clinched the title the previous year, Reds were getting used to recurrences of the Mickey Thomas syndrome – where one bad moment (being caught in a lovers' lane with a married woman) is swiftly followed by another (being stabbed a dozen times in the backside by her husband). At least the atmosphere was lighter this year than it had been the last. Admittedly, frustration and disappointment still reigned. How could it be any different considering that United could, and should, have gone up – if they had played just a half-decent season at home they would have romped to promotion. But there had been enough rewarding moments this time to send the supporters away for the summer contemplating something other than self-harm. And while they did not yet have a team to be proud of, at least they now had a warrior to idolise. In United history there have only been a handful of players – Meredith, Roberts, Best, Robson, Cantona... – who have momentarily seemed bigger than the club. He had only been around for a matter of minutes but big Frank Barson – a true Red Devil in every sense – was already well on his way to joining that list.

Roll of Honour

Champions: Liverpool

FA Cup Winners: Bolton Wanderers

United: Division 2 (4th) FA Cup (2nd Round) Tottenham H

Depression Years enigma

Neil McBain

Centre Half-back
Nov 1921 – Jan 1923 43 apps 2 gls
b. Campbeltown, Argyllshire
15th November 1895,
d. 13th May 1974
Height: 5' 8" Weight: 12st.3lbs.
United Debut:
United 1-0 Aston Villa 26/11/21

Career: *Campbeltown Academicals, Hamilton Academicals, Ayr United 1914 (Portsmouth and Southampton during WW1), United Nov 1921, Everton Jan 1923, St. Johnstone July 1926, Liverpool Mar 1928, Watford Nov 1928, appointed player-manager May 1929-1931, manager to Aug 1937, Ayr United manager 1937-38, Luton Town manager June 1938 – June 1939, New Brighton secretary-manager June 1946, Leyton Orient ass't. manager Feb 1948, manager Apr 1948, Estudiantes de la Plata (Argentina) coach Aug 1949, Ayr United manager 1955-56, Watford manager Aug 1956 – Feb 1959, Ayr United manager Jan 1963*

International career *(for Scotland): 3 apps (Scotland 1-0 England at Villa Park 08/04/22, Scotland 1-0 Ireland at Windsor Park 03/03/23, Scotland 0-2 Wales at Ninian Park 16/02/24) 0 gls*

Rumours of dressing-room unrest were legion in the Depression Years but the stiff upper lip mentality of most players made it easy for the club to play them with a straight bat. Only when Neil McBain was unceremoniously bundled out of the Old Trafford exit midway through 22/23 did a story escape their defensive prod. McBain himself was in no mood to go quietly and the *Topical Times*, the only paper either interested or daring enough to delve deeper into the latest United controversy, gave the disgruntled Scot ample opportunity to embark on a can-of-worms-opening exercise. In a statement published in the paper on January 12 1923, McBain waxed lyrical on his belief that he had been made the victim of a player-led, anti-Jock putsch:

'I have asked to be placed on the transfer list, and I hope that the directors and officials of the club will accede to my request. I realise that I cannot find happiness at Old Trafford. For some time past I have suffered criticism at Old Trafford. I hesitate to name the critics, but I think I am entitled to say that I have not been fairly treated by several of my clubmates and directors. There had not been open hostility till the Monday on which we were due to play Rotherham. On that day I was chosen, as usual, for the first team. I say "as usual", because I am under no apprehensions as to the merit of my play. I have done well by the United; I have invariably put club interests first.

'When Barson came to the side I was asked to leave my own position. This I did, though I recognised that my playing in a 'foreign' position would imperil my chances of receiving a cap. Reverting to the matter of the game with Rotherham. Till just before the match I understood that I was to play. Then I was informed that I was to be 'rested'. I was certainly not satisfied with the explanation. However, I waited until the conclusion of the match, when I interviewed Mr Chapman, our manager.

'Here I wish to say that Mr Chapman has always treated me with the most absolute fairness. I asked Mr Chapman why I had been 'dropped' – for dropped I had been. Mr Chapman was only able to inform me that I was being 'rested'. I told him that I considered myself above the Old Trafford Reserve team class. To this he agreed. Thereupon I told him of my desire to change quarters. Then I learned that immediately prior to the match certain players waited upon our directors and told them that they would not take the field if I were permitted to play. I cannot blame the management for refusing to play me; they were placed in a very unenviable position. But either the players who demanded my resignation from the premier team or I myself must go.

'The reasons which prompted their amazing action? Frankly I do not know, unless – well, I have refused to consort with them outside football hours. I am also a 'foreigner', and there has been jealousy over my playing in the side – I cannot say more. The directors will decide this week whether I am to be retained or not; I can only say that I do not wish to be retained. I hope that another club is found for me soon. Were I able to discover a Scottish club able to afford such a 'luxury' as myself I should return home. But an English club will do. I do not think that one signing me would regret the action.'

In reply, the club spluttered indignantly about not surrendering to player power and reiterated that McBain had been rested rather than dropped. The week after their McBain exclusive, the *Topical Times* interviewed United director George Bedford to ascertain the club's side of the story:

'I cannot understand Neil's statement at all. In fact, I did not know that there was any serious disagreement between the players. I cannot think of any incident bearing any resemblance to that which Neil alleges took place. I will be frank. I recall that after the match with Hull City – which we lost – there was some chaffing in the dressing-room.

'Certain of the players thought fit to tell Neil that Barson would have filled his place to better advantage. They were not criticising McBain seriously – it was only dressing-room talk. And you know what that is. Neil must be over-sensitive. Some of his mates simply said that Barson was more suited to the heavy ground – on which the match was played – than he.

'Of course we have done the only thing possible in placing McBain on the transfer list. We cannot permit a player to bring allegations against us.

'Revolt at Old Trafford? And dictation to the directors by the players? No! You've got hold of the wrong end of the stick. Why, when several of the men objected to training shortly before the holiday games – they alleged that they required a rest in preparation for the strenuous time – they were treated summarily. They were told that unless they obeyed the orders of their trainer they would be required to appear before the board. Not perhaps a very serious threat – but one sufficient to cause them to abandon all idea of resistance.

'I'm telling you all this in order that you may understand that the directors at Old Trafford are – directors. And not likely to tolerate demands similar to those which McBain says were made to them.'

The supporters' club deputation was informed that 'leg-pulling' had lost McBain to Old Trafford. At the time, they had enough faith in the board to believe them. Fortunately for Neil, the *Topical Times* had additional information to contradict the general perception that he was more paranoid than a schizophrenic on acid. First, there was evidence that, even before McBain asked for a transfer, United had been in touch with other clubs in an attempt to move him on. Unofficially, the word was that the directors were 'greatly relieved' when Everton came in for him. Intriguingly, the paper's 'Special

Commissioner' also learned from a source inside the club that one player had tendered an apology to the directors 'for the part he played in the proceedings which led up to McBain's determination to get out quick'. Suddenly Neil's theories did not seem so far-fetched; certainly the 'Special Commissioner' was of the opinion that he was more hot than cold. And when another Scot, John Wood, was dumped on the transfer list and apparently 'sent to Coventry' by his team-mates, the leg-pulling excuse began to stink of a cover-up.

But if there was an Anglo-Scottish split in the camp, the evidence is at best circumstantial. There is a story that Arthur Lochhead once refused to play alongside Frank Barson but Arthur's aversion to his skipper was apparently based on Frank's tendency to juice up his sentences with liberal doses of swearing rather than any suspicion that he was keen to re-enact Bannockburn in the showers. Perhaps there was a racist element to the treatment that McBain and Wood received at Old Trafford. If there was, it would help explain why so many highly-rated Scots flopped in a United jersey. More likely, the primary issue was not that they were foreigners but that they were dressing-room outsiders. McBain himself admitted that he had made no effort to socialise with his team-mates away from football. Actually he went further, saying that he 'refused to consort with them' as if he would rather eat his own excrement than join the boys for a bonding session down the pub. As an exercise in social suicide it takes some beating.

Neil's aloofness inevitably set him on a collision course with the dressing-room in-crowd and particularly its most influential figure, Barson. Unless it was catching him sniffing his jockstrap, it is difficult to think of anything that could have wound Frank up more than the Scot's no-shows at the bar. The fact that both men were competing for the same jersey inevitably accelerated the process. Although Neil excelled both at left-half and inside-left, it was obvious from his outburst in the press that he wasn't best pleased about his move from the centre. In all probability, he had already shared his frustrations with his team-mates and it is a relatively straightforward task to link the chain of events from there – McBain shouts his mouth off about why he, and not Barson, should be playing in the centre, he gets his chance in his specialist position in the holiday fixture at Hull, he plays poorly in United's defeat and the pro-Barson faction jump at the opportunity to put him in his place.

If all that amounts to an educated guess, any attempt to put the last chain into place inevitably involves, like Clapham Common in the early hours, some stabbing in the dark. If, as seems likely, some of McBain's team-mates were prepared to risk their own necks by issuing their 'he-goes-or-we-do' ultimatum to the directors, the obvious question is why. The obvious answer is that no one (still living) knows. McBain hinted at racism and jealousy; a study of his later career suggests that he himself may have been the problem. To become embroiled in one dressing-room controversy can be written off as bad luck; to become embroiled in another, as Neil was at Everton less than eighteen months later, hints at something more sinister. Then again, the rumours that he did not get on with his Goodison team-mates could have been a consequence of giving a dog a bad name. Certainly, Neil was at pains to stress that there was no friction in the camp and that the Toffees were a 'very happy family'. He did ask to leave the club but was adamant that homesickness, not controversy, was the motivating factor.

If McBain was as homesick as he said he was, mind, he had a strange way of dealing with it. Everton refused him his transfer and, apart from two seasons as a player with St Johnstone and another two as manager of his former club, Ayr, he did not make it back home for another forty incident-packed years. During that time he saved the Scotland team from perishing in a plane crash (to cut a long story short... the Scotland players were about to embark on an aerial sightseeing trip during a tour of the States when Neil, a racing enthusiast and an expert mechanic, spotted something he did not fancy about the plane's engine. Following his lead, the rest of the squad refused to go on the trip and then watched from the ground as the plane took off and then crashed in a nearby field), became the oldest player to appear in a Football League match when he played for New Brighton as an emergency goalkeeper aged fifty-one years and four months and, during a nomadic managerial/coaching career, enjoyed a six-year stint as coach of Estudiantes, the Argentine club that infamously kicked their way to victory over

United in the World Club Championship in '68.

In his post-United playing career, McBain also established himself as one of the finest centre half-backs in the British game. An artist in attack and sound in defence, he scored well enough for skill, pace, tackling, dribbling and heading for the Analyst to dub him 'the model centre-half'. To a certain extent, then, he must go down in Depression Years history as yet another one who got away. Good as he was, though, McBain was never as good as Barson and when it became clear that he wasn't prepared to sacrifice himself in a foreign position in the long-term, a parting of the ways became inevitable; Old Trafford simply wasn't big enough for the both of them.

*   *   *

JOHN HOWARTH

RIGHT FULL-BACK, MAY 1921 – SUMMER 1923 (AND BEYOND),
4 APPS 0 GLS

SADDLED BY THOUGHTLESS parents with the middle name Thomas, John Howarth came but never quite conquered Old Trafford. An injury crisis gave him a taste of first team action towards the end of the relegation season but he was never called upon again. Signed, along with George Haslam, from his hometown club Darwen for a combined £750 fee, John never came close to enjoying the United career that even his old team-mate did*. He did, though, manage to drag out his United days almost as long, albeit by default. Slapped on the transfer list in May '23, John was still on it four years later. 'Not with a barge pole' was clearly the attitude of prospective employers.

*'Tiny' Haslam spent most of his six years as a Red skippering the reserves

JAMES PUGH

LEFT FULL-BACK, APRIL 1922 – JULY 1923
2 APPS 0 GLS

TWO PLAYERS JOINED United from Welsh League sides in 1922. One of them, Harry Thomas, played for United for nine years and was capped by Wales. The other, James Pugh, made two appearances in the senior side as a stand-in for Jack Silcock, spent the rest of his only season as a Red in the Central League and then signed for Wrexham. The *Athletic News*' description of his performance in his final match against Fulham made a suitable epitaph for Jimmy's short-lived United career. As they pointed out, he was 'only a moderate left-back'.

HARRY WILLIAMS

INSIDE-LEFT, MAY 1922 – SEPT 1923, 5 APPS 2 GLS

THE OWNER OF possibly the squarest head and biggest ears of any United player ever (had his lugholes been lit from behind, he could have guided planes in with them), Harry Williams failed to make a similarly large impression with his feet, making just a handful of appearances in his one season as a Red and then dropping out of the game altogether in his mid-twenties. After scoring important goals against Palace and Wolves in September '22, Harry was perhaps unfortunate not to be given a longer run in the side but he was nudged out of contention by the selector's decision first to give Neil McBain a try-out up front and then to move Arthur Lochhead from the right flank to the left. A year later, Harry took himself and his ears to Brentford where, for two seasons, he formed an effective wing partnership with 'Patsy' Hendren, the celebrated Middlesex and England cricketer.

JOHN WOOD

RIGHT-WINGER, MAY 1922 – SUMMER 1923, 16 APPS 1 GL

1922's ATTEMPT AT solving United's problem right-wing position was no more successful than 1920's (Billy Harrison), 1921's (Richard Gibson) or 1923's (David Ellis). The 'other Scotsman' in the McBain affair, John Wood was sent, metaphorically, to Coventry in January 1923 before returning, permanently, to Scottish football that summer. After half a season's rehabilitation with Lochgelly United he moved on to St Mirren where he rediscovered the scoring touch he had mislaid so badly at Old Trafford.

BERT CARTMAN

RIGHT-WINGER, MAY 1922 – JUNE 1923, 3 APPS 0 GLS

IN A SEASON when the Reds went through more right-wingers than Stalin, Bert Cartman was one of a quartet of players who were tried out for a handful of games and then discarded. At £350 from Bolton he was perhaps a gamble worth taking but it did not pay off for either club or player and Bert was shipped off to Tranmere only a year after arriving. In nine seasons on the Wirral he made a name for himself as one of the best wingmen in the bottom division. Considering where he had come from, the accolade was on the empty side, rather like being nominated the best actress in a porn film.

DAVID LYNER

RIGHT-WINGER, AUG – DEC 1922, 3 APPS 0 GLS

IRISH INTERNATIONAL DAVID Lyner was the most disappointing of the clutch of signings that John Chapman made in 22/23 which was no mean feat given the competition from the likes of Henderson, Wood and Williams. After a run of three games in late September he entered the bowels of the Central League and six months after joining United from Glentoran he was dumped on Kilmarnock; few people noticed he had gone.

WILFRED LIEVESLEY

RIGHT-WINGER, OCT 1922 – AUG 1923, 3 APPS 0 GLS

A MEMBER OF a famous footballing family, Wilf Lievesley was one of three brothers who played the game professionally and the uncle of Leslie Lievesley who had a one-year stint as a Red in the early thirties. Neither Lievesley had much of a United career – between them they managed just five appearances – but Wilf did at least get to sample the big-match atmosphere (in January '23), playing in the promotion doubleheader with Leeds and also the big cup-tie at White Hart Lane. The *Athletic News* initially liked what they saw, writing after the Leeds 0-0: 'The forward picture is not all black. In the absence of Spence, Manchester United introduced Lievesley, a local product and he proved his ability. Well-built with plenty of pluck, he beats a man well without too much embroidery and unless it was that his centres would have been more useful had they been placed further away from the goalkeeper, his display was full of promise.' Wilf also shaped up reasonably well in the Elland Road return but the Tottenham humiliation brought his progress to a crashing halt and, following a close season move to Exeter, he spent the rest of his career, along with the host of other Red rejects, in the lower divisions.

ALBERT BROOME

FORWARD, JAN 1923 – JULY 1924, 1 APP 0 GLS

THROWN INTO THE first team for the final game of 22/23 at Barnsley, Albert Broome earned rave reviews for his 'excellent ball control and quickness of foot action' but never got another sniff of first-team action. Another one-game wonder, Albert left United for Oldham the following summer but only lasted three months as a full-time professional at Boundary Park before he took up a job as a commercial traveller.

CURSED

I N NOVEMBER 1922 the Lord Carnarvon-Howard Carter digging team pulled off the archaeological result of all time when they unearthed the final resting place of the Egyptian boy-king, Tutankhamun. Four months later, Carnarvon died after a short and sudden illness and a legend was born; the 'curse' of Tutankhamun had claimed its first victim. From that day on, the demise of anyone even remotely linked to the find was seized upon as proof that the curse existed. Some of the goings-on were strange enough to intrigue even the stoutest sceptic. As every schoolkid knows, at the precise moment of Carnarvon's death, the lights went out across Cairo while back home in England, his terrier, Susie, let out her last howl and dropped dead. Others were less persuasive. When an Egyptian, Ali Kemel Fahmy Bey, was killed in the Savoy shortly after visiting the site, the wrath of a long-dead pharaoh did not stand out as the principal cause of death, not when his wife was caught holding the gun she had just used to nail him with. The family of Richard Bethell, Carter's secretary, became well-versed in tragedy when Richard and his dad died in quick succession and then the hearse carrying Bethell senior's body knocked down and killed a small child. But Richard did not die until five years after the find while his dad, whose only connection to Egypt was a small collection of antiquities, killed himself. And if the curse really was responsible for killing the monkey, why did it take so long to deal with the organ-grinder? Like the nine other people who were present at the unwrapping of the mummy, Carter survived well into the thirties.

If Scooby-Doo taught us anything it is: a) that if you take as many drugs as Shaggy clearly did (come on, he had a laughing dog...) then you will always be susceptible to attacks of the munchies (remember the size of those butties?). b] that when you are walking through a haunted house never, ever go last in line and c] that no matter how strange things may seem, there is almost always a rational explanation (usually involving the caretaker). In time, the curse of Tutankhamun seemed less and less convincing. It wasn't just that so many of the dig team survived, there were sound reasons for writing off the main events as one massive coincidence. Carnarvon had been a funeral waiting to happen ever since a motoring accident in 1901. What did for him in the end was an infected mosquito bite followed by a bout of pneumonia. Susie had spent months pining for her master back home (and even longer hobbling around on just three legs) so her final howl wasn't entirely unexpected either. As for the lights going out, my guess is that that was as much a part of everyday life in Egypt as treading in camel shit.

Things were different back in 1923. Curses were the in-thing and there were plenty of influential people – with the novelists Marie Corelli and Arthur Conan Doyle among the most vocal – prepared to swear by them. Even United got in on the act, floating, in a desperate attempt to explain why they were making such a dog's behind out of getting out of the second division, the theory that Old Trafford was cursed. Joe Spence made the suggestion that the ground should be dug up to see if they could find 'the remains of a policeman or a Jew or something of the sort that was perhaps casting an evil spell over the club's doings'. Which must have gone down a storm in Prestwich and other kosher areas of town though it has to be said, in Joe's defence, that he was only using what would have been considered a regular expression at the time. It sounds bad now but it did not exactly make him Manchester's answer to the Führer.

Unquestionably, Old Trafford had been a magnet for bad luck. Since the move, United had been hit by war, an explosion of taxes, financial crises, season after season of dross, eventual relegation and the death of two former managers, Bentley and Robson. 1923-24 turned out to be little better. Chapman was dogged by a remarkable series of family bereavements, including the deaths of both his father and brother. Sarvis returned but the grim Reaper was determined to make up for the one that got away; tragically, the season would be the final fling for one of the club's most popular characters. As for injuries and suspensions, the problem was not how many players were affected as which ones. Had he been asked to nominate his four most influential players at the start of the season, Chapman would have looked no further than the spine of Mew, Silcock, Barson and Goldthorpe. Between them, the awesome foursome totalled just forty-three appearances.

You do not have to be superman to understand the impact of a broken spine. Mew was perhaps missed least; his detractors had always said that his rashness would lead to self-destruction and so it proved, Alf Steward seizing the opportunity to realise some of his much-trumpeted potential. The absence of Silcock and Barson would have left a gaping hole in the best of teams but Moore and Grimwood, both of whom enjoyed their most effective seasons to date, did at least show that the Reds could breathe without them. Given the club's record at uncovering effective centre-forwards, Goldthorpe was probably the biggest loss. Shorn of his leadership, presence and goals, the side spent large chunks of the season gifting opposing goalkeepers their clean sheet. In their Persil-sponsored campaign, the misfiring forwards failed to score in no fewer than seventeen matches.

Overall, it would be a season short on goals and overburdened with 'if onlys'. If Goldthorpe and the three Internationals had not missed so many games, if the directors had had a real go at strengthening the squad in the summer, if Chapman had been able to call on an experienced, reserve centre-forward, the supporters may have had their Hollywood ending. It would not, after all, have taken a massive improvement on the previous year's showing for United to regain their top flight place – the same again plus four less points dropped at home would have done. Instead, Reds were stuck in the blackest of black comedies – and all the best jokes were on them.

Joke 1: United stumble to their worst league finish yet. Joke 2: the story of the season makes as attractive viewing as a mucky movie starring your dog and your granny. The relegation campaign was a tortuous experience but at least the supporters had been gripped by its plot. 1923-24 suffered a stroke early in the New Year and drifted aimlessly from then on. Not even the apathy-soaked atmosphere of spring '89 had anything on spring '23. Admittedly, 1989 was the year of Leighton, Milne and 23,000, going on 18,000, against Wimbledon. But it was also the year of the Fledglings' cup run, the comeback victory against the Scousers and Michael Thomas' championship winner at Anfield. In 1923, similarly redeeming features were thin on the ground. Possibly the one saving grace for Red egos was that City did not pile on the agony by winning the Cup but, driven on by the ageless Meredith, they had a damned good try, reaching the semi-finals before bowing out to Newcastle. Add on the image-(and coffers)-boosting impact of their move to Maine Road and the identity of the true Kings of Manchester was becoming depressingly clear.

Yet all that misery seemed a long way off when United started the season with a decent set of results, a home win and away draw against Southampton and a winning double against Bristol City. Never mind the points, just playing Bristol promised to be a happy omen – for both clubs. The last time they had shared the same division (in 1911), United had claimed their second title, the last time they had been in the second division together (in 1906), both clubs had secured promotion while the last time they had met in the Cup (in 1909), Bristol had been the bridesmaids to Roberts's cup-winners.

Clearly, though, the omens had passed their sell-by date. The Robins, who ended up taking the wooden spoon by a distance, were one of the few clubs who would remember the season less fondly than the Reds. A far more accurate sign of things to come was the absence of Silcock. The ruptured thigh he sustained in a pre-season friendly made him the first of the Fab Four to be hit by the injury jinx and all but ended his season before it had started. He would not be fully fit for four months and even when he was ready to return, the selectors decided, wisely or not, that it would be unfair to split up Radford and Moore.

Even the good results were misleading. The Reds' bright start to the campaign had been a limp rather than a procession with all but one of the wins belonging in the 'how the fuck?' category. Bristol could easily have reversed their 2-1 defeat at home while Southampton, who wasted enough chances to have won by a landslide at the Dell, should have taken the points they lost to a typical piece of Goldthorpe opportunism at Old Trafford. Other sides, starting with Bury at a fiery Gigg Lane on September 8, would not be so lenient although the result of the 'junior' derby almost got lost amid the barrage of shock-horror headlines it generated.

Another rum United-Bury affair was a throwback to Newton Heath times when derby games – actually, most games – were mere excuses for brawling on the pitch and vein-throbbing aggro off it. For the record, the Shakers won the points with two goals in the final half-hour. But it was the Reds who won the war. Old Heathen monsters such as Bob Donaldson, Harry Stafford and Caesar Llewellyn Augustus Jenkyns (whose parents were clearly bastards) would have nodded approvingly at the pugilistic spirit shown by the side, Mew in particular. Barson had the wilder reputation but the sight of Jack in full bull mode – head down, steam coming out of his ears – was as fearsome as anything the sport has provided, Peter Beardsley's smile included.

Bury's Robbie and Bullock were roughed up early in the game before Mew's clash with the latter turned into a running battle – the Bull versus the Bullock. Bullock had the satisfaction of stealing his side's second, Jack the consolation of saving his earlier penalty – and also landing a couple of crunching haymakers. That the two men only had eyes for each other was evident from the build-up to the penalty award, given for hands by Moore. While the United defence were desperately trying to prevent a goal, their goalkeeper was twenty yards away knocking seven shades of shit out of his favourite Bury forward.

Mew pulled off a stunning one-handed save to keep out Bullock's spot-kick but then added another blot to his copybook by making what Jacques described as 'a rude and childish gesture towards the unsuccessful marksman'. A sizeable section of the 19,000 crowd had been in a barely controlled frenzy all afternoon; Jack's gesture almost started a riot. At the end of the game, he was pelted by objects, including a glass bottle, and when the players were due to leave the ground, the police were sufficiently concerned about the prospect of a disturbance that they provided them with an escort. In the end there was no trouble, the home crowd satisfying themselves with a lengthy chorus of boos.

But there were serious repercussions for Mew. Dragged in front of the directors to explain his actions, Jack admitted that he had let his feelings run away with him and also expressed his regret. As a result, he was dropped for the return match the following weekend, a decision which created the odd situation of the veteran keeper having both his wrists and his back slapped in the same week (on the Wednesday between the Bury games, Mew was rewarded for his decade's service at Old Trafford with a second benefit match, against Hearts). Jack was back between the sticks for the next game, at South Shields, but time was running out for the club's long-standing number one. Alf Steward had been the best keeper in the Central League for the past three years and deserved his chance in the first team. Mew was still very good, almost great, but at 34 he was fighting a losing battle against time as well as his talented apprentice and his cantankerousness gave the selectors the excuse they needed to ease him out of the picture. The axe fell for good in early October and 'Jack the Cat' spent most of the remaining three years of his United career in the reserves.

*   *   *

THE POST-WAR SCHEME whereby games were played, like the Bury matches, on a back-to-back basis had been introduced in order to simplify the task of the League fixtures department. What the authorities had not appreciated, in their eagerness to look after their own, was the ill-feeling the arrangement would cause. The smaller clubs, many of whom relied on their 20% cut from away gates to keep their doors wolf-free, had the biggest gripe. Those of them who were drawn against a glamour outfit, like the Reds, at a time when crowds were traditionally at their peak were now guaranteed a pair of bumper pay days; those who played them at other times of the year (towards the end of the season or just before Christmas) lost out. But it wasn't just the minnows who felt penalised. All clubs suffered if their roast-beef fixtures were bunched together towards the start of the season, meaning their fans only had the dregs to look forward to later on. Fag-end finales and profits went together like slugs and salt, as United were about to find out.

The clubs' dissatisfaction with the 'pairs' scheme helps explain why it was dumped at the end of 23/24. But the real reason for the change had more to do with fisticuffs than finance. When the games were spread out, there was every chance that players who left Part One with a grievance would have forgiven and forgotten about it by the time of Part Two – unless, of course, they possessed a Keanesque lust for revenge (remember, it was almost four years before Alfie 'he deserved it' Haaland received Roy's stamp of disapproval). With the rematch following right on the heels of the original, turning the other cheek did not carry the same appeal.

The revenge factor did have one beneficial spin-off, though, in that nothing pulls in the punters quite like the prospect of a slugging match (while all fans enjoy a good, clean game, most of us prefer a good, dirty one). Which explains why 43,000 supporters descended on Old Trafford for the second round of United's spat with Bury on September 15. The pre-match hype was dominated by predictions of blood being spilled but possibly because Mew was confined to the stands, there was no need to clear space in the local infirmary. Instead of a war, the two sides served up an afternoon of thrills and United served up their best performance of the season. Still, it was not enough to see off opponents that the Reds had not beaten since 1911, a solitary defensive cock-up allowing the Shakers to steal the points with the only goal of the game.

The South Shields trip the following Saturday was another hard luck story although United only had themselves to blame for losing a match they should have won by a landslide, the forwards repeatedly turning gilt-edged chances into goal-kicks and Radford smashing a penalty almost into North Shields. It wasn't until the Old Trafford return on the 29th that the September goal drought finally drew to a close but on a bittersweet afternoon the bitter memories far outweighed the sweet. Lochhead's sumptuous free-kick earned United their first point in four weeks and Mew reached a unique milestone when he became the first man to play five hundred games for the club (a tally that included appearances in all competitions and at all levels) but Goldthorpe and Barson both picked up bad injuries. The moment in the first half when Ernie went down clutching his suspect knee was, by a distance, the worst of the campaign. The cartilage damage he sustained not only finished his season, it effectively ended his top-class career.

After going under the knife for a make-or-break operation, Ernie was considered fit enough to make a comeback the following August but the first game that season would be his last in United colours; one year and a series of breakdowns later, he moved to Rotherham. For nigh on a year the strapping Tyke had looked like the transfer steal of the century. What a tragedy – for Ernie, United and possibly England – that his career was curtailed at the age of 25 when there were still so many goals left in his boots.

Barson's back strain was far less serious but it would still be a couple of months before he was fit enough to return. It was symptomatic of the way the cookies were crumbling for the Reds' skipper. If anyone was affected by a United curse it was Frank. When he left Villa, it had been on the basis that they would pay him a percentage of the transfer fee. A Football League inquiry had subsequently released his old employers from their promise because, 'by his conduct and demands', Barson had forced them to transfer him (there's justice for you...). On top of losing his slice of his transfer, his wife was seriously ill, he was getting abuse wherever he played for supposedly overdoing the physical stuff, referees were forever on his back (Mancunian apologists were incensed by the treatment Frank was receiving; because of his bad-lad reputation he had as much chance of winning a decision as a black defendant in Klan country) and when he turned up for one game sporting a shiner he found himself at the centre of a fresh outbreak of claims that all was not well in the camp. Predictably, the club denied that any other player was involved though it should have been a relatively simple task to find out if that was indeed the case. A quick rundown of the latest arrivals at the local hospitals should have sufficed...

A week after losing their skipper, the rudderless Reds lost a freak game at Boundary Park, Oldham defender Jack Wynne scoring twice for both sides and, just as bizarrely, featherweight Teddy Partridge getting sent off for fighting. Their fourth defeat in a month left the club languishing in fifteenth, an embarrassment that begged the question whether Reds should stop talking about promotion and start fretting about relegation. But the season had slid to its autumnal nadir. Aided by a large-scale cull and a hitherto unseen cunning plan from the selectors, John Chapman was about to put a smile back on the Pop Side.

Of the eleven players who lost at Boundary Park, only six survived for the return game the following week. Mew was the biggest name casualty. Like a captain waiting for a batsman to reach his century before declaring, the directors had waited until Jack reached his appearance milestone before issuing their own declaration – that he was dropped. His replacement, Steward, headed a list of four players who were promoted from the reserves but he, and Scottish centre-forward David Bain, were the only ones who hung around for long. Billy Dennis, a left-back, and 'Tiny' Haslam, a strapping centre-half, lasted just four games before Radford and Grimwood were brought back in their place.

Unsurprisingly, given a scoring record that would have embarrassed a fifty-year-old virgin, the biggest shake-up was in attack. The axe fell permanently on McDonald and Myerscough both of whom were packed off to Bradford City. McDonald's passing went as unnoticed as a silent and odourless fart (as befitted the impact he had made), Myerscough's aroused more comment. Joe might not have featured since March but the squad wasn't exactly brimming with inside-forward talent and he could have been a useful asset later in the season. At the very least he was worth more than the price – £1,500 for the pair – he was sold for. The consensus was that, like Partridge before him, Myerscough had been badly messed around by the selectors and that he was a better player than he had recently looked.

Another player to get the Anne Boleyn treatment (as in the axe rather than a seeing-to by a fat bloke with gout) was David Ellis, a long-term Chapman target who had finally arrived at Old Trafford in June via a short spell at Maidstone. An ever-present at right-wing in the opening couple of months when Spence was used in place of Mann at inside-right, Ellis hardly featured again and was flogged to St Johnstone in the summer. A lack of robustness did for him in the end which made him the umpteenth tartan signing to flop at Old Trafford because of difficulties adapting to the vigorous English style. When were United going to learn that buying Scottish brought as many pitfalls as buying centre-forwards from Brian Clough?

When the blood-letting was over, the attack lined up with Bain in the middle and Spence and Mann on the right. Lochhead and the season's big discovery, Frank McPherson, continued on the left. Mann's lack of goals eventually cost him his place but for a time that winter, the Frank & Joe double act was the nearest the club had come to an effective right-wing pairing since Halse and Meredith were tearing it up under Mangnall. As a couple they were perhaps not in the Come Dancing class but at least they did not spend the whole time treading on each other's toes. Meanwhile, McPherson, the 'Bullet' from Barrow, and Lochhead, the wily Salford schoolmaster, had already formed a Rogers-Astaire understanding on the opposite flank. In the heady days of mid-season, there were those who claimed that the blend of Arthur's skill and Frank's speed made them the best left-wing pairing around. That was probably taking things too far but there was little argument that the play on – and supply from – both flanks reached a level that had not been seen at Old Trafford for years. If only Goldthorpe had still been around to take advantage...

The upshot of all this chopping and changing was that the selectors had finally stumbled on a forward line capable of firing the imagination of the support. Their cunning plan was to pack away the scalpel. Instead of reshaping the side on a result-by-result basis, the management at last showed the good sense to give the new-look team an opportunity to gel. What was more, out went the old tactic of trying out round pegs in square holes; every one of the new players was playing in a position he was comfortable in. As a result, the side was as well-balanced as it had been for years. United may have lost their stars but, for a couple of months at least, they had a real team.

It helped that the changes had an immediate impact. Oldham were swept aside by a tremendous second-half showing in front of 26,000 at Old Trafford. Bain in particular grabbed his chance to impress, a thumping header and a close-range stab immediately moving him into second place in the scoring charts alongside his beaten marker Wynne. The forwards as a whole showed up better than at any time all season and the passion and quality that vibrated through the team prompted one fan to predict, in a letter to *The Football Chron*, that 'if only they could play like that always, the gates would never be less than 50,000'. A slight exaggeration, perhaps, but a still impressive 32,000 returned the following week as the Reds roared to a 3-0 win against Stockport. Bain scored again but the afternoon really belonged to Mann whose two-goal performance shone as brightly as his polished pate. A tap-in on the half-hour finally got rid of the no-goals monkey that had been clinging, rodeo-style, to his back while the swerving run and clipped finish for his second conjured up memories of his Huddersfield prime.

After their sour September, Reds were enjoying themselves again. According to the *Chron*, there had never been so much public interest in the club: 'One hears their doings and affairs discussed by all classes during the week'. That included women – Old Trafford was renowned for the number of ladies who sat in its stands. But the side's autumnal recovery was not entirely gremlin free. Away from home, results remained indifferent. Matches at Stockport, Leicester, Coventry and Leeds yielded just three points and the Midlands police should have been making enquiries about the robbery of two of them. At least the 0-0 at league leaders (and champions-elect) Leeds was a solid afternoon's work, the return of Barson and the continued excellence of Moore, already a shoe-in for Red of the year, providing the key to a useful point. But the one step forward was swiftly followed by two in the other direction as Frank picked up an illness that ruled him out until the New Year.

Back in Manchester, though, the Reds were nigh on irresistible.

Leicester gave the most stylish exhibition by a visiting side all season but, like Oldham and Stockport before them, they were simply brushed aside, Mann's late volley sealing another three-goal romp. Then, on December 8, Leeds were relieved of their three-month unbeaten record in the course of a beating as savage and one-sided as anything seen outside the roughest of night-clubs – and that includes the Majestyk. The *Chron* put it nicely, writing: 'Leeds United were outplayed, outmatched, outrun and almost thrown out of Old Trafford.'

In the opening half-hour, in particular, the Reds played almost perfect second-division football, a mixture of free-flowing passing and snarling, ankle-snapping aggression. Lochhead was the conductor-in-chief, now dropping off the play to parade his repertoire of flicks and shimmies in midfield, now firing raking passes out to the wing fliers, now launching devastating runs into the area. Midway through the first half, a run timed with Robsonian precision culminated in him thundering in Spence's low centre. Ten minutes later, Bain and McPherson cooked up a similar opportunity and the outcome was the same, Arthur driving in his second from six yards. Leeds pulled one back when a corner wasn't properly cleared but McPherson's second-half run and finish settled it. Describing Frank's goal as a run and finish barely does it any sort of justice; it was like a scene from one of those poorly-conceived football movies, the sort where the opposition dive out of the way as the 'hero' takes the ball half the length of the field, beats twenty-five defenders and bicycle kicks it into the net. Except this was for real. McPherson's potential was there for everyone to see. He was just about the quickest thing in long shorts, he had strength, heart and a left foot like a hammer. Admittedly there were questions about his first touch and the number of tricks he had in his armoury but there remained more than one pundit who was prepared to back his claims to an England place.

But if the Bullet made the weightier contribution to United's revival, history shows that Joe Spence's emergence as the side's other winger of substance was much the bigger story. Despite topping the club's League scoring list in each of his four seasons, the pacy centre-forward had so far struggled to cash in on the talent that had made him the most hyped of all the Robson discoveries. Instead of being one of the first names on the team-sheet, he had spent long stretches of his apprenticeship being shunted along the front line or dumped.

But those who had championed the Whippet's cause ever since he burst onto the scene with four goals on his wartime debut were about to receive their full pay-off. Once he was recast permanently as a right-winger, Joe abandoned the path leading to squad-player obscurity and discovered that he had the knack of turning full-backs into panting wrecks. It was still early days, but time would show that the October reshuffle was a seminal moment in the development of Joe Spence from an honest foot soldier into a Red legend.

*   *   *

THE LEEDS PERFORMANCE WOULD not be surpassed all season but you would have had to search hard to detect a drop in standards as Port Vale were handed home and away football lessons in the run-up to Christmas. The only thing missing from a swaggering display of superiority in the Potteries was a bagful of goals, the Reds contenting themselves with a long-range howitzer from Grimwood. It did not matter; the locals still considered Chapman's side the most impressive outfit they had seen at Hanley all season. Seven days later, the players took the same form into the return match in Manchester and this time the goals flowed like tears from a Geordie. Bain banged in a hat-trick and Spence and Lochhead also netted as United strolled to their biggest win since the Meadow Lane 6-1.

From their position among the division's pond-life, the Reds had now risen to an encouraging fourth, just two points behind joint leaders Derby and Leeds with a game in hand on both. The side's revival lent December's Annual Shareholders Meeting an almost bullish feel, John Henry Davies taking the opportunity to pay tribute to 'the keenness and promising play of the team' whilst also stamping on the on-going rumours that they were 'disUnited'. Chapman, Davies stressed, was surrounded by 'a loyal group of players'.

The club were absolutely determined to paint a picture of camaraderie. On Christmas Eve, Mew was presented with a gold watch to mark his 500 appearance milestone. Conveniently enough, the ensuing pleasantries made it into the papers. Accepting the gift, Jack said that 'no one could wish to belong to a better club or wish to be under better management' and that 'no club could have a more conscientious or better manager than Jack Chapman'. Ramming home the point, he then asked his manager to accept the international medal he had been awarded when he was selected for the FA tour of South Africa in 1920.

In reply, Chapman thanked Mew for 'a gift that he would always treasure' and added that he had 'never had charge of a more loyal body of men', that 'they gave little or no trouble' and that 'on the field every man was out to play the game and give of their best for the club'. It was a smart piece of propaganda but putting a Richie Cunningham spin on events did not really wash. It was fairly obvious that they had not all been happy days. Mew himself had only just picked up the toys he had lobbed out of the pram after being dropped (his immediate reaction had been to slap in a transfer request; surprisingly, there had been no takers), Barson's black eye remained unexplained and as the rumours of unrest had lasted long after his departure, it seemed more and more likely that Neil McBain had been made the fall-guy.

*   *   *

IN A SENSE IT IS STRANGE that clubs should go to great lengths, as United did that Christmas, to promote the idea that the management and team are one big happy family. After all, football clubs, just like any other workplace, are always going to have their fair share of good eggs and total wankers, friendships and feuds. In the twenties in particular, the scope for tension and hostility was immense. Unregulated by the manager, who ran the club from his office not the training-ground, the first-team dressing-room often provided a haven for back-stabbing, bitterness and bullying. The senior pros, not the trainer, ran the show for most of the week and if they were bastards then life could be made miserable for the other players, particularly up-and-coming youngsters (in other words, potential threats), who were frequently relegated to the role of untouchables.

The bottom line, of course, is that it does not matter if players are bosom buddies (Gary Neville and Becks), home video co-stars (Bosnich and Yorke), lovers (nothing has ever been proven but the strongest rumours point to Upton Park via Maine Road), silent partners (Cole and Sheringham) or sworn enemies (take your pick: Keane and ....) as long as they are doing the job out on the pitch. Happy dressing-room or not, for two and a half months the Reds had been doing exactly that. But the season was about to turn ugly. Just hours after making his Christmas Eve speech, Chapman would be rendered helpless as United's scheduled flight back to the first division experienced engine difficulties. By mid-February, it had crashed and burned.

What a dismal Christmas 1923's turned out to be. In the space of eight festive days the Reds won one point and frittered away seven. Barnsley were outplayed home and away but won both games, United falling to breakaway goals on each occasion. An ordinary Coventry side ('87 apart, has there ever been any other kind?) stole the points in similar style in the first match of the new year. Perhaps the players were not taking the threat posed by lesser teams seriously enough. 'No doubt the secret of United's success against more formidable opponents such as Leeds and Leicester is that less risk is taken in thinning the defence,' observed *The Manchester Guardian*. The other holiday fixture featured the long-thirsted return of Barson but not even he could inspire the side to anything more than a point at Valley Parade. It did not help that, because of an incident on the line, the players had to change into their kit on the train and virtually run from their taxis straight onto the pitch. United started well but faded after half-time though Bain wasted two late opportunities to win it.

He made amends a week later as the Bantams were thumped 3-0 in the return but the good times didn't last, the Reds dropping three points in a week to Fulham. The witless defeat at Craven Cottage proved too much for Barson, two of the home side's forwards needing smelling salts after 'accidental' (the press's word; the Fulham fans begged to differ) collisions with the United skipper. There was controversy of a different kind in the Old Trafford return, the referee, a Mr Bryan, blowing for time before the ninety minutes were up. Ordinarily that would not have mattered but as a drive from Lochhead was heading for the onion bag at that very moment, the Red Army had every reason to feel aggrieved.

Aggrieved but not anarchic. Not yet, anyway. For now, they had a mouth-watering home cup-tie to look forward to. McPherson's early drive and Steward's late penalty save had stolen the Reds a 1-0 win against Southern League Plymouth in the third round. Awaiting them in the fourth were Herbert Chapman's Huddersfield Town, a side that in the next three seasons would make football history by becoming the first ever to clinch a hat-trick of titles. Chapman's sleeping giants versus Chapman's history-makers; clearly it wouldn't take much of a patter to shift tickets for this one. In the end, 66,678 crammed into

Old Trafford, setting a record for a home FA Cup tie that stood until the Barthez-Di Canio match in 2001, but the bean counters were just about the only ones left smiling as the game went depressingly to form. One up after barely ten minutes, Huddersfield extended their lead on the half-hour and deepened the sense of anti-climax by running in a third after half-time. It was as emphatic a defeat as the previous season's at White Hart Lane, the difference in class as brutally obvious as ever.

In the aftermath, time to question a couple of extravagant gambles by the selectors. After standing by him for three months, they had finally run out of patience with Bain. Which was fair enough; as he had bombed as often as he had scored, the young Scot's hold on the centre-forward slot had long been a limp-wristed one. But bringing in Willie Henderson as his replacement? Which gin bottle had that one come from? Henderson, you will remember, had flopped badly following his move from Airdrie in 21/22. Since then he had been dogged by injuries and had made as many appearances on the surgeon's table as he had in the first team. He had not featured since the Port Vale ignominy sixteen months earlier but here he was being asked to lead the line against the champions-elect. As expected, the gamble did not pay off, Jacques being particularly scathing about his performance: 'Henderson at centre-forward was never an effective figure. He did not feed the wingers, he made but one shot of note and generally seemed an industrious worker never getting anywhere.' Swapping Silcock for Radford, meanwhile, would have made more sense if it hadn't been Jack's first senior outing for seven months. Understandably rusty after his long lay-off, he was badly caught out for the third Huddersfield goal and, like Henderson, was dropped for the next game.

It is amazing the deflationary effect – on both players and fans – of a bad cup defeat. At the start of February, United still had an outside chance in the league – they had sunk to tenth in the table but lay just four points off a promotion place. By its end all hope had gone. Four league games in the month yielded two points, no goals and another bad injury to Barson. This latest one, a knee ligament tear sustained in the 3-0 spanking at Derby, finally put Frank's nightmarish season to sleep. Typically, he refused to listen to the doctors who wanted him to stay in hospital overnight, insisting instead on joining his team-mates for their evening meal before hobbling home in the charge of fellow Sheffield resident, Mann.

There was still a third of the season to go but many United fans took the cup setback as their cue to abandon ship. You could hardly blame them. In the midst of a trade depression a shilling was a lot of money to fork out on a team that was busy going nowhere. On top of that, nine out of ten Reds had to travel a distance to get to the ground (even then, the club were wide open to taunts about the number of local fans) meaning they had to find another half-shilling for the tram. Fifty thousand supporters disappeared in the week between the Huddersfield tie and the Blackpool nil-nil alone. In the desperate last weeks of the season, 15,000 was the standard crowd. By its end, attendances had sunk even lower. Those pre-Christmas predictions of another record financial season suddenly looked ridiculously premature – for the first time in years, United were heading into the red.

Frustratingly, the team was still playing as much good football as any in the division. Some experts actually felt they were playing too well and advocated a switch from their favoured close passing game to the kick and hope stuff that had taken Derby, Leeds and Bury into the top places. But the principal failing was an old one; 'the man without a shot', as Tim Bobbin, Jacques's stand-in, put it. After the Huddersfield defeat, the selectors reverted to type, persistently shuffling and reshuffling the attack, but no combination of Henderson, Ellis, Partridge, Kennedy, Evans and new boys Tommy Smith and Jock Miller (a £1,100 pair of inside-forwards from Leicester and Grimsby) could provide the solution to the team's lack of goals.

The only discernible impact of the selectorial version of blind man's buff was the way it unsettled the established members of the front line. Spence was perhaps the only one who maintained his form until the season's end. Lochhead was the worst hit, his confidence destroyed by an ill-considered switch back to centre-forward, a position he had floundered in ever since his move down south. Most reports gave the impression that Arthur could not have retreated further into his shell if his missus had taken out a full-page spread in the *Evening News* detailing his shortcomings in the bedroom (and if the Scot made love like he played there would have been plenty – for all his fancy flicks he was not always renowned for his end product). Abruptly deprived of his partner's pandering, McPherson also endured a dramatic slump in form, his breakthrough season ending with him resembling a headless chicken rather than a future international, though with some England managers that would have made him an automatic choice.

Kennedy scored United's first goal in ten long hours as the team ended their seven match winless run with a cruise against no-hopers Nelson on March 1. But with neither promotion nor re-election realistic propositions, the season had already lost its point. Over the final two months the club would have nothing to play for except pride. And the results suggested that the players weren't overly fussed about salvaging any. The Reds won just two of their last eleven games: a 5-1 thumping of Palace in which Spence matched Goldthorpe's feat of the previous season by bagging four and a stroll in the sun against Wednesday in the final home game. The same match provided the season with its Wimbledon '89 moment as only 7,500 fans bothered to turn up.

Otherwise, pick a most embarrassing moment out of these; Old Trafford defeat in the Nelson return, a pair of draws against hopeless Hull or the 3-0 hammering at the Victoria Ground where Stoke hadn't won since Christmas. The Nelson debacle should have just about nicked it as defeat by relegation-bound nobodies, United's clueless performance, Radford's sending-off and a gate under 9,000 (an embarrassing 68,000 fewer than City pulled in the same afternoon for their cup quarter-final against Cardiff) painted the perfect picture of Red disaster. But most humiliating of all was United's final league position of fourteenth which left them looking up the skirts of clubs of the size and anorexic resources of Stockport, Clapton Orient and South Shields.

Wins in dead rubbers would not have changed what had been a desperate season, but a good finish to the campaign would at least have raised Red spirits. Instead, United sent the supporters into the summer break with their chins scraping along Warwick Road. How much better it would have been if they had followed the lead of the Labour government that had recently squeezed into power (for the first time ever) courtesy of a decent election performance and a hung parliament. Like the Tories before them, the new regime could have been brought down at any time but Ramsay MacDonald and his party used what little time they had to prove, first, that they were not a bunch of closet commies intent on ripping apart the fabric of British society and, second, that they were up to the job.

Chapman's Reds had not made it back up this time but they should have been sending out signals that they were worth backing in the future. Already, the supporters were growing tired of the hard luck stories; in a late-season letter to the *Chron*, 'Popular Sider' spoke for the man on the terraces when he wrote that 'the bad luck explanation is becoming monotonous and has lasted too long and it is high time the club occupied its right place in the football world.' Maybe, though, there was some truth in those curse theories after all. In the close season, United were hit by their most savage blow yet as Charlie Radford was killed in a motorbike accident, aged just 24. The loveable giant with the heart and strength of a lion would leave a huge void behind him, off the pitch as well as on it. As the Wanderer said: 'We shall sadly miss poor Charlie with his dark hair, eager face and magnificent physique, his merry disposition, quaint sayings and many songs on the journeys of the campaign.' Less than three years after burying Robson, Old Trafford was in mourning again.

ROLL OF HONOUR

CHAMPIONS: HUDDERSFIELD TOWN

FA CUP WINNERS: NEWCASTLE UTD

UNITED: DIVISION 2 (4TH) - FA CUP 2ND ROUND (HUDDERSFIELD)

DEPRESSION YEARS LEGEND

JACK MEW

GOALKEEPER SEPT 1912 – SEPT 1926
195 APPS 0 GLS
(TOTAL 199 APPS 0 GLS)
B. SUNDERLAND 30TH MARCH 1889
D. BARTON IRWELL AREA OCTOBER QTR. 1963
HEIGHT: 5' 8" WEIGHT: 12ST.2LBS.
DEBUT: UNITED 2-3 MIDDLESBROUGH
01/03/13

Career: *Blaydon United, Marley Hill United, United (am.) July 1912, (pro.) Sept 1912, Barrow Sept 1926, Lyra F.C. (Belgium) trainer-coach Oct 1927, Lima F.C. (Peru) coach June 1928*

International career *(for England): 1 app (England 2-0 Ireland at Roker Park 23/10/20) 0 gls*

TWO GREAT UNITED keepers had more reason than most to rue the timing of the war. When it began, big Bob Beale stood on the cusp of the England team. When it ended, he stood mainly behind the counter of his dad's furniture shop in Maidstone, his only connection with his former existence being an occasional and long-distance run-out with the reserves. Beale's wartime transfer to the Western Front did at least enable his understudy, Jack Mew (whose work as a driver and engineer for a local car manufacturers kept him in Manchester and out of the trenches), to establish himself as United's first-choice keeper but by the time League football restarted he was just about the oldest 'next-big-thing' in the business. Before the war, Beale's excellence had limited Mew to just four senior appearances. When the league programme was resurrected he was already the wrong side of thirty and time was running out for him to make an impact commensurate with his abundant talent.

Fittingly for a player who could have caught bullets (or at least turned them around the post), Mew grabbed his shot at the big-time and held on to it, at least for the next four years or so. During that time, when he and Jack Silcock formed the backbone of the United side, there was no more admired keeper in the country. Nor was there one who made a greater impression on the psyche of opposing forwards. Like Peter Schmeichel decades later, Jack was a sleep-disturbing mix of goal-shrinking presence and senses-jangling aggression. If his natural brilliance as a shot-stopper wasn't enough to make forwards weep, his bull-like charges out of the area invariably did the trick. Not since God borrowed one from Adam to make Eve had male ribs faced a comparable threat.

It was because of this obvious relish for the physical side of the game that some critics, in his early days at Old Trafford, didn't rate Mew as a man who would make a real name for himself. Mistakenly, they had interpreted his inexperience, enthusiasm and essential hardness as crudeness, indiscipline and a lack of cool. Once the 'Blaydon Bull' had had his rough edges knocked off him in the Central League, it was clear that United had pulled off a major coup in stealing him from under the noses of Sunderland, his home-town club.

At 5ft 8in, Jack might have been on the short side for a keeper but his superb technique easily compensated for his lack of inches. His handling and positional play were top-class, his powers of anticipation simply uncanny. Often it appeared that the ball was being hit at him when in fact it was an illusion created by his intuition and power of divining his opponents' intentions. Later, old team-mates would nominate this ability to make keeping look easy as Jack's greatest strength. They also raved about his physical gifts, notably his muscle-packed frame, his wrists of iron (at a time when a wet ball at the wrong feet could be a dangerous weapon, he would warm up for games by fisting away shots belted at him from close range) and his speed and agility. Jack's running-style was described as 'quaint' so it can be assumed that his sorties out of goal were not a thing of beauty, as befits his image as a rampaging bull, but for a hefty man he was remarkably nimble-footed, an asset that Jacques captured in memorable style in the wake of another match-saving display, this time at Oldham in 1919: 'Jack Mew, like a cat on his feet, and splendidly sure, strong and quick with his hands.'

An apparently pathological disregard for his own physical well-being completed the set of goalkeeping essentials. If the old saying about keepers being nuttier than squirrel shit still holds true today when they are in danger of being smothered by over-protective referees, we can only imagine how deranged they must have been in Jack's day when they were expected to cope, uncomplainingly, with everything from a mild barge to a Glasgow kiss. Whereas outfield players were playing a game that was purely association football, Jack and his roll-neck contemporaries remained stuck in the days when football was a mix of the association and rugby codes. Picking the ball up was an open invitation to be shoulder-charged to the ground by a square-jawed centre-forward while diving for the ball in a goalmouth scrimmage (even the name resonates with memories of the game's rugby past) was an open invitation for a kicking.

In the circumstances it was understandable that some keepers, Jack in particular, opted to get their retaliation in first. The Mew bull-charge wasn't just a means of preventing an opponent from scoring, it was also a means of paying him back for past or even future injustices. Inevitably his abrasive approach did not endear him to all. It was quite common for Jack's brilliance to inspire demonstrations of adulation, even among opposing supporters. Then again, it was not unknown for one of his juicier challenges to leave an away crowd on the verge of a riot. In that respect, Gigg Lane in September 1923 was perhaps the defining moment of his career. That, you may remember, was the game in which Jack left his goal for a punch-up, returned to it in time to save the penalty that had been conceded in his absence and then rubbed in his superiority by inferring, with a hand gesture, that the unsuccessful taker was (and I'm speculating here) a tosser.

One lunatic taking on the whole of Bury surely represents one of the goalkeeping images of the decade. On the basis that the capacity to inspire adulation and provoke enmity simultaneously is the preserve of the great, that afternoon may have also backed Jack's claim to legendary status. The directors did not quite see it that way. After dragging Mew before them to issue a grovelling apology, they suspended him for a week and shortly afterwards dropped him for good. Apart from a mini-encore in the midst of the 25/26 cup run, Jack spent the rest of his United career out of the limelight. Aged 37 when he had the last in a series of transfer requests granted, he then embarked on a short-lived burst of nomadism, accepting playing and coaching positions at clubs in Belgium, Barrow and Peru, before settling down somewhere genuinely exotic; Cheetham Hill, where he made his living as a boiler mechanic.

Perhaps Jack's 'eccentric' side held him back in terms of gaining England recognition. Perhaps, in a theme we will return to time and again, the main stumbling block to his international aspirations was the club he represented. He did play once for his country, against Ireland in 1920, and also represented the Football League in 1921 but that, and the consolation prize of a place on the 1920 FA tour of South Africa, was scant reward for his talent and a source of great frustration to him personally.

Certainly Jack did not lack for backers amongst his fellow players or in the press. In December 1919 the so-called 'Prince of Goalkeepers', Villa's Sam Hardy, embraced him after a match and told him that he should have been named in that season's inter-league side. In the *Topical Times* a couple of years later, 'Fuse' wrote: 'All round the country I hear professionals and others passing the word round – "Isn't Jack a fine fellow?" And what a goalkeeper! Jack Mew has done something like carry the Manchester United defence on his back for some time.' Jack Sharp went even further, raving, in the same rag: 'Jack Mew is possibly the best goalkeeper in the world today. Many good judges tell me he is, and what I have seen of him makes me believe that he is just now at his finest point of play.'

As with so many great Reds at that time, Jack had to settle for the adulation of the Manchester public rather than the recognition of his country. When, in 1923, he became the first United player to be awarded a second benefit, he was hailed not only as one of the club's greatest servants but also as its finest ever keeper, which was no empty accolade considering the trio of 'Bank of England' custodians – Scottish international Frank Barrett, the long-limbed Harry Moger from the championship sides and also Big Bob – who had gone before him. Perhaps he remains the greatest even today. After all, every great United keeper has saved their team on the pitch; only Jack – and Harry Gregg – can claim to have saved their team-mates off it.

*　　　　　*　　　　　*

CHARLES RADFORD

RIGHT FULL-BACK, MAY 1920 – SUMMER 1924, 96 APPS 1 GL

HIS TWELVE STONE of muscle squeezed into a magnificently toned 5ft 9in frame, Charlie Radford played exactly as he looked – hard. It was this apparent indestructibility as well as his infectious personality that made the news of his death so difficult to digest. In more recent times, the story of his motorbike accident would have dominated the front pages. In the less sensationalist and sports-hungry times in which Charlie lived and died, it hardly got a mention. He deserved better. He was never going to play for England, admittedly, but for two seasons he was an inspirational, tough-as-Barson (the two titans roomed together – has there ever been a room-mate pairing less likely to be made the target of late-night japes?) figure at the heart of United's defence. His main strength was exactly that, his strength – Charlie's shoulder-charges were just as frightening as Frank's – but he could also play a bit, his kicking being strong and sure with either foot. His chief flaw was his tendency to rise to the bait and overdo the physical stuff. After one particularly brutal foul against Nelson (in March '24) had earned Charlie first use of the soap and a six week suspension, the *Football News* wrote that he was 'wholehearted but prone to losing control of himself'. In the context of his fatal crash, the words were eerily prophetic.

JOE MYERSCOUGH

INSIDE-RIGHT, MAY 1920 – OCT 1923, 34 APPS 8 GLS

IN NOVEMBER 1922, the *Football News* wrote of lanky Lancastrian Joe Myerscough: 'Myerscough has the height, speed, and that very essential, the pluck, for an inside-forward. Not a Buchan* by any means, but he possesses a powerful shot.' Unfortunately for Joe, his accuracy did not match his power and it was his poor goal return (just four goals in his final thirty matches) that cost him his chance of nailing down a regular place in the side and finally convinced the board to cash in when Bradford came knocking in early 23/24. For all that, many Reds regretted the loss of a player who had played 'many fine games for both the first and second elevens' and had apparently impressed everyone with his 'enthusiasm, unselfishness and modest demeanour'.

* the quote refers to Charles Buchan, the famous England and Sunderland inside-forward

SIDNEY TYLER

RIGHT FULL-BACK, MAY 1922 – MAY 1924, 1 APP 0 GLS

SYDNEY TYLER WAS only eighteen when he made a 'thoroughly satisfactory' debut for United (in the 3-0 rout of Leicester in November '23) but those teenage kicks were the only ones he got at Old Trafford. A move to his hometown club, Wolves, did not work out either and it was only when Sid dropped down to the third division south with Gillingham and Millwall that he found his feet as a pro.

JOHN BARBER

INSIDE-RIGHT, MAY 1922 – MAY 1924, 4 APPS 2 GLS

SALFORD LAD JACK Barber could have been a contender but instead goes down in history as another Red bum. A cup goal against Bradford City in only his third senior appearance (in January '23) was a potential breakthrough moment for the then 22-year-old but an ill-timed run of injuries, including a dislocated elbow, slammed shut his window of opportunity. By the time Jack had got himself fit, Frank Mann had arrived from Huddersfield. If the shiny-headed Mann had no need for a Barber, the feeling was mutual. After making just one first-team appearance in 23/24, Jack began a decade-long trawl around the lower leagues with Southport, Halifax, Rochdale and, finally, Stockport County.

DAVID BAIN

CENTRE-FORWARD, MAY 1922 – JULY 1924, 23 APPS 9 GOALS

FOR HALF A season it appeared that the selectors had struck gold by throwing rookie Scot, David Bain, at the problem centre-forward position. In a run of sixteen games in the middle of the 23/24 campaign he scored eight goals, including a classy hat-trick at home to Port Vale. The *Football Chron* were impressed enough to write of the 23-year-old that 'more and more he convinces that he has solved the centre-forward difficulty. He shows intelligence and judgement in his play'. To the *Chron* went the award for speaking too soon. By the end of March they had changed their tune, reflecting: 'At one time David

Bain seemed likely to solve the centre-forward question with much success, but his form gradually went back and he lost his place in the line.' That Bain had hit the wall following his first taste of regular football should have come as no surprise. The obvious prescription for him then was to give him a spell in the reserves, a long rest over the summer and another opportunity at the start of 24/25. Instead, United sold him to Everton. At Goodison, Bain was converted into a half-back, a role he played successfully for the rest of his career.

KEN MACDONALD

CENTRE-FORWARD, FEBRUARY – OCTOBER 1923, 9 APPS 2 GLS

WHEN UNITED WENT shopping, in the spring of '23, for a forward to get their stalled promotion push moving again, Ken MacDonald, a strong and bustling type from Cardiff City, wasn't exactly what class-starved Pop Siders had in mind. A dreadful debut, in a dreadful defeat (by Southampton) pushed him even further down in their estimation and nothing he could do from then on could stem the taunts of the terrace grumblers. In hindsight, though, the fans might have been more supportive. After he was rescued from his Old Trafford nightmare by Bradford Park Avenue, Ken went on to embarrass them by embarking on an astonishing scoring spree that bagged him 135 goals in just 145 league games. It took his old United team-mates the best part of three years to score as many.

BILLY DENNIS

LEFT FULL-BACK, MAY 1923 – FEB 1924, 3 APPS 0 GLS

PLUCKED FROM STALYBRIDGE Celtic when they dropped out of the league in 1923, Billy Dennis was destined for a blink-and-you'll-miss-it United career. Three appearances in the midst of a defensive emergency (in October '23) brought him mixed reviews and it was not long before he was loaned out to answer a similar crisis at Chesterfield. By February, the switch had been made permanent. A lower-league journeyman for the rest of the decade, Billy was also a good enough quickie to play cricket professionally in the local leagues. His other claim to fame was that he was one of the select (most would say, jinxed) band of footballers who saw action in both world wars.

David Ellis

Right-winger, June 1923 – Sept 1924, 11 apps 0 gls

An old Chapman favourite from Airdrie, David Ellis came with a reputation for lightning pace and left, for St Johnstone, with the same reputation as John Wood. Bought for £1,250, sold for just £500; throw in his wages and each of the Scotsman's appearances cost the Reds in excess of £100. Who could blame the directors, then, for standing their ground when Ellis claimed a 50% cut of his transfer fee? He had taken them for a long enough ride already.

James Miller

Forward, March – summer 1924, 4 apps 1 gls

It is difficult to understand the thinking behind United's £500 plunge for Grimsby's Jock Miller in the spring of '24. After appearing in four consecutive games at the end of the dead 23/24 season he was back in third division football, where he always excelled, when the Reds kicked off their next campaign. The cynical argued, convincingly, that he had only been brought in to keep the Pop Side interested during a meaningless spring.

THE RETURN TO THE QUEEN'S HOTEL

'IT WAS THE best of times, it was the worst of times, it was the age of wisdom, it was the age of foolishness, it was the epoch of belief, it was the epoch of incredulity, it was the season of light, it was the season of darkness, it was the spring of hope, it was the winter of despair, we had everything before us, we had nothing before us, we were all going direct to Heaven, we were all going direct the other way.' So ran Charles Dickens's paradox-sodden slogan for the years leading up to the French revolution when England was rotten and France was even worse. At a stretch it could also have been used to sum up Red experiences in 1924. For United, it truly was the year of all the emotions. The first seven months had been the worst of times for the club, Radford's tragic death setting the seal on a season of darkness. Quite unexpectedly, the next five would provide some of the best and if the Reds were not headed directly for sporting heaven, at least they managed to position themselves on the stairway towards it. In a reversal of the Dickensian catch-phrase, it had been a spring of despair. After a summer when it had seemed that they had nothing before them, United were set for a winter of hope.

It is not difficult to see why only dreamers – and the drunk – were confident that Barson would get his pub this time around. United had just trailed home in fourteenth place, no new names had come in to replace either Bain, who had been surprisingly transferred to Everton, or Radford, leaving the squad even weaker than it had been the previous year, the old weakness at centre-forward was glaring brighter than ever and because of the number of strong outfits in the division, promotion had never looked more difficult. Chelsea, Middlesbrough, Southampton, Portsmouth, Leicester, Sheffield Wednesday, Derby and Bradford City were all fancied to do well. Against that, the most persuasive argument for optimism was – yawn – that the club had been unlucky last season and that they could not be as unlucky again.

They could not afford to be. Just three months of meagre crowds had been enough to turn an anticipated hefty profit into a £1,500 loss. If the missing thousands were to stay away for good, the financial implications did not bear thinking about. Already, the club were starting to feel the pinch; the directors had made it quite clear that the transfer embargo they had imposed in the summer would remain in force for the foreseeable future. A pity that; in the autumn, their fiscal timidity would rule them out of the race to sign the most sought-after young player in the country, Tranmere's Dixie Dean. Fortunately, it did not cost them any of their established stars. To the relief of all, nothing ever came of the persistent stories linking Barson with a move to West Brom. Like Eric's decision to stay put in the traumatic close-season of '95 (when three favourites – Hughes, Ince and Kanchelskis – were moved on and even the most devoted Fergie-ites were left wondering whether the great man had lost the plot), the news on Frank drew some of the sting from a painful summer.

Even so, the season started with the Pop Side split into two camps – those who were happy with the direction the club were heading in and those who got out of the bath to shit. The latest [strained] analogy would have been given added appeal had Louis 'the Meat King' been perched on the Old Trafford throne (the Edwards era would not start for another forty years) but seditious chatter was seeping into the conversation in Red pubs much as it had in the cafés and taverns of eighteenth century France. The Supporters' Club and the newly-constituted Shareholders Association had been formed with the avowed aim of supporting the club rather than interfering in its business but the rank underachievement and fiscal limpness of the last two years had already caused a shift in the goalposts. It would be misleading to suggest that the supporters were planning to roll out the guillotine (not at this stage, anyway) but they were certainly keen on having some say in how the club was being run.

The directors, for their part, were keen for the fans to pay their money at the turnstiles and then, frankly, to piss off. The shareholder-supporters' early-season request for a boardroom voice received a terse put-down, leaving them with the same dilemma that has always faced dissident fans. If the directors weren't prepared to play ball, they would have to be made to. But how do you put pressure on the board without simultaneously damaging the prospects of the team?

The AGM provided just about the only forum in which to

achieve the former and avoid the latter but making the suits squirm for an evening provided a momentary kick rather than meaningful progress. The directors only had to expose their heads above the parapets for one evening a year and, when they did, they were able to extricate themselves from verbal snookers by ruling difficult questions out of order. So it did not really matter that the supporter-shareholders and their leader, George Greenhough (the Leon Trotsky of the Mancunian Red Army), transformed this year's meeting from a gentle picnic, replete with cucumber sandwiches and nice words, into an interrogation as fierce as Kenneth Starr's grilling of Bill Clinton. When they were faced with tough questions such as how they planned to use the club's money, players – or even their cigars – the directors simply hid behind the Fifth.

But if their major goals proved beyond them, the supporters' groups at least managed to demonstrate their potential as a nuisance the club could do without. In previous years, the re-election of directors Harold Hardman and Joseph Yates to the board would have been a mere formality. This time, heavy opposition from the floor left the pair reliant on John Henry Davies's casting vote to get back in. As it turned out, Matt Busby, then an up-and-coming youngster at Maine Road, would have appreciated it had Hardman, for one, not enjoyed his president's support. When the hard-nosed solicitor took over the reins himself, in the early fifties, he became the antithesis of everything that Busby felt his chairman should be - unyielding, opinionated, careful with money and ultra-conservative. As Busby was on a mission to turn United into the biggest club in the country, and then the world, Hardman's old-school ways ultimately drove him into the arms of a man who shared his vision and would do everything he could to help him fulfil it. Which brings us right back to Matt's lap-dog, Louis 'the Meat King' Edwards.

*   *   *

THE DIRECTORS STRESSED THAT promotion was their main priority for 24/25 but the prospect of financial meltdown meant that winning back the springtime deserters came a close second. Encouragingly, the summer break appeared to have acted as an interest stimulant. The smell of meat pies and freshly cut grass, the sound of leather on leather – or in Barson's case, leather on bone – and the prospect of strangers urinating on their shoes (such was the standard of the gents) must have had a Bisto effect in enticing people back to the ground – the demand for season tickets was heavy while the crowd on the opening day numbered a respectable 22,000. But early-season anticipation can soon wear off if a new dawn turns into a false one. In August 1988, for example, it lasted barely half an hour of the moribund opening day stalemate with QPR. In 1989 the Knighton effect had vanished within a fortnight as United followed their famous thumping of champions Arsenal by staggering along the road that eventually led to Moss Side and a score that escapes me. Chapman's Reds badly needed a good start to keep the punters on-side. Not even the Pop Side's wildest optimist could have envisaged how well they would rise to the challenge.

A difficult opening week gave few clues of the fun to come, United stumbling through an awkward fixture-list with a stolen 1-0 in the Leicester opener, a messy draw at Stoke and another embarrassment at Edgeley Park. It wasn't until the visit of Barnsley on September 8, and the most comprehensive 1-0 win that anyone could remember, that the team shrugged off their early-season lethargy but once they had done so, they were nigh on irresistible. Divisional weaklings Coventry were swamped 5-1 on the 13th, then came a three-goal romp at cash-strapped Oldham before September ended with a home canter against Sheffield Wednesday. Aggregate score: United 10, their Victims 1.

Perversely, it was the loss of the side's likeliest goalscorer, Goldthorpe[1], that sparked the September goal flow, Scottish misfit Willie Henderson making the most of the chance handed him by Ernie's knackered knee – and Bain's transfer – to knock in a single, double and treble against Barnsley, Coventry and Oldham and, in the space of twelve days, resuscitate a career that had all but flat-lined. But the real story of the month was the midfield revamp that the selectors undertook before the Coventry game. In the opening matches, the half-back line had erred on the side of defensive solidity rather than attacking flair. Once the selectors had replaced the grinding defensive contributions of Bennion and Hilditch with the added offensive threat of Grimwood and Mann, they got the mix just right. Jack's best work

---

1.   Goldthorpe, who hadn't played competitively since the previous September, made a goalscoring return to the first team against Leicester (on August 30) but broke down again almost immediately and never played for United again.

---

often went unnoticed but he could tackle, pass and dribble with the best of them. Frank's rapid transformation from forward caterpillar to half-back butterfly, meanwhile, made him the phenomenon of the season. Whereas Henderson's second coming soon fizzled out, 'Daddy' Mann[2] established a reputation for calm efficiency that lasted not just for the rest of the year but for the rest of the decade.

It wasn't just the midfield rejuvenation that made the Coventry 5-1 a milestone in United's campaign. Indeed, it was just one of a hat-trick of points that would snowball in significance as the season wore on. Even for the visit of a team with as little pizzazz as the Sky Blues, the crowd of just 12,000 was a disappointing one. However, instead of marking the onset of another financial migraine, that September afternoon marked the seasonal low. Despite a series of wet weekends which re-ignited the old debate about covering the Pop Side, attendances would not sink below the 18,000 mark again (in fact, the average crowd for the rest of the season was over 29,000). For now, at least, the battle for the hearts – and shillings – of the supporters had been won.

The other point of future interest was the visitors' consolation, an apparently meaningless goal that became more and more meaningful as the weeks passed without United conceding another. Coventry found the Old Trafford net at roughly 3-15pm on September 13. Alf Steward would not be beaten again until shortly after 4pm on November 8, more than twelve playing hours later. For much of that time – in fact for much of the season – the fight between the Reds' back three and the opponent's attack was as even as that between the Christians and the lions. Steward had shown glimpses of his true quality the season before without ever truly emerging from the giant shadow of Jack Mew. Now he was coming into his own, his bouts of nervousness a thing of the past. 'Steward has gained as much confidence this season as Spence has gained speed,' wrote the Wanderer approvingly. In front of him, the Silcock and Moore partnership, on ice since 1920/21 because of the remarkable

2.   *In retrospect, it should have been obvious that a move back to midfield would suit the veteran forward. He had not scored nearly enough goals in his eighteen months at Old Trafford, which is why he had lost his place to springtime signing Tommy Smith, but his back-tracking and probing had always been top drawer. The switch to wing-half played on his strengths, camouflaged his weaknesses, disappointed the obituary writers and gave hope to ageing spamheads everywhere. Bald men, as Stuart Hall used to say in the ads, really could set the pace.*

catalogue of injuries affecting both men, was proving as good if not better than ever. They had been one of the best full-back pairings in the first division. They were in a class of their own in the second. No wonder Alf had gained confidence – he was getting better protection than Osama Bin Laden.

Steward and his defence were on course to set a new divisional record for the lowest number of goals conceded in a season. Now that a goal was virtually a guarantee of maximum points, the Reds were in football nirvana. Only three times all year did they score and lose. The events of October, in particular, demonstrated how easy it is to win matches when the other team are not allowed to score. Despite netting just four goals in their four games, United picked up seven points, beating Clapton and Palace 1-0 and then running off with Southampton's unbeaten record at The Dell. Morally, they claimed a full-house eight. In the second half of the goalless scrap at Molineux, Henderson had a perfectly good 'goal' ruled out, the referee (a forebear of Brian Hill?) deciding that his shot hadn't crossed the line even though the ball was virtually in the crowd.

Lochhead, who had previously been left in the shadows as big Willie hogged the forward headlines, contributed all four of the (official) October goals to earn a place among the *Athletic News*' 'Eight Men of the Moment in League Football'. But most of the plaudits were magnetically drawn to Barson. Frank was on fire, by common consent the centre half-back of the season and the player that every supporter in the country loved to hate but deep down would love to have. 'The thing that impressed me was the fact that the United had a real leader,' one of the Southampton directors swooned. 'It was obvious that the team would do anything he wanted, and it was equally obvious that he was a great positional player. His head was always in the way, and he found time to instruct his men. I have not seen captaincy like if for years.' Even the London critic of the *Daily Express* contracted a dose of Barson fever. Lending his pen to the Frank-for-England campaign, he wrote: 'Barson is probably playing better than at any other stage of his career. His defence is superb, his attack most deadly and it is difficult to see how he can be kept out of the England team. Certainly he is much better on this season's form than George Wilson, or Healless, of Blackburn, who was the pivot in the recent game against Ireland.'

An eighteen-point haul from their opening eleven matches

represented United's best start to a season since 1913/14[3]. Remarkably, their form hadn't yet been good enough to take them to the top of the table – Derby, who had led the division from day one, had always managed to hold them at bay. But those Reds who had been dying to break into a 'top of the league' chant for eleven years did not have much longer to wait. On November 1, Fulham were swept aside at Old Trafford, Derby lost at Palace and United took a one-point lead at the top. Two goals either side of the break sealed their elevation. The first was a classic, Spence's lightning breakaway setting up Lochhead's sumptuous volley. The second almost as good, Henderson ending his six-week drought by smashing in McPherson's centre.

It had taken United two years and sixty-seven days and close on one hundred matches to climb to the divisional summit. Annoyingly, it took them just seven days and one match to get a nosebleed, an outbreak of carelessness at Fratton Park allowing Portsmouth to scramble a scrappy equaliser and in the process bring Steward's seven-match invincible streak to an inglorious end. Derby's instant return to winning ways put them back on top on goal average but the Rams seemed just as eager as the Reds to indulge in a game of top-of-the-table leapfrog. On November 15, United beat Hull, Derby drew at Chelsea and the Reds were back in pole position. A week later, United were held at Blackpool, the Rams beat Stockport and Derby were back on top. In neither match did the Reds recapture their early autumn cohesion. Just about the only moments of significance were the two goals, both of which were rammed home by Jimmy Hanson, the Mancunian wonder boy now given his first mini-run in the side in place of the hero-turned-scapegoat, Henderson. But if the players had seemed distracted, they had good reason to be. The rest of November had been a mere appetiser to the main event, the United-Derby match on the 29th.

As so often happens when the stakes are high, the game never reached any great heights as a spectacle but few among the huge, 60,000 crowd left Old Trafford feeling they had been short-changed. For an hour, the bad blood and tension bubbled under the surface. In

---

3.   *Only twice in their history had United started a season more impressively. In 1907/8, Mangnall's side won thirteen and lost one of their opening fourteen matches en route to the club's first ever championship. Six years later, J.J.Bentley's outfit won nine and lost one of their opening ten matches but then suffered a spectacular collapse which saw them win just six more times all season. They eventually limped home in fourteenth place.*

that time the visitors had just about the better of things and probably deserved the lead given them on nineteen by giant Scouse centre-forward Albert Fairclough. It wasn't a moment that Alf Steward could look back on with any pride, Fairclough's admittedly clever shot on the turn dribbling past him at Harry Leonard pace. But as United threw everything forward in the desperate search for an equaliser, the mood grew appreciably darker. In the end, the descent into shadiness worked in the Reds favour. With ten minutes remaining, Fairclough, who had already been cautioned, lunged wildly into a tackle and was sent off. Two minutes later, United finally drew level with a goal that probably best summed up the match; an almighty scramble from a set-piece. Olney, the Derby keeper, failed to deal with McPherson's vicious in-swinger, punching the ball straight up into the air rather than sending it out of his area. In the moments that followed he was given a taste of what Emily Davison went through when she stepped out in front of the King's horse. Six or seven Red shirts descended on him, Barson barged him out of the way and Hanson scrambled the ball over the line. Derby lined up in a furious protest, Olney displaying his bruised ribs to all and sundry. Perhaps wondering how he was going to beat sixty thousand Reds to the station, the ref did the sensible thing and pointed to the centre spot.

The press dubbed the game the Battle of Old Trafford and the FA set up a commission to look into it. Fairclough was banned for fourteen days, half the normal suspension for a sending-off, the commission accepting his argument that his second foul hadn't been deliberate. Then again, the prime target of the FA had always been their old adversary Barson. Why else would he have been dragged before them on the ludicrous charge of using improper language? (As if Frank was the only player in the game of the masses whose choice of words would have made Billy Meredith's parrot blush). Thankfully, the charges were soon dropped due to insufficient evidence but it would have been ironic if the commission had been able to make them stick. Imagine bringing down the most fearsome bone-crusher in the game on the back of some souped-up bad language charge. It would have been as ludicrous as putting Jack the Ripper away for kerb-crawling - or Al Capone for fiddling the taxman.

Barson survived but the Derby battle did leave one casualty; the goalscorer, Hanson, who was replaced by Henderson for the following week's trip to South Shields. Having scored three goals in as many matches, Jimmy was entitled to wonder what more he could have done to hang on to his place but this time the selectors' logic was incontestable. Events at Old Trafford had provided clear signs that his lack of experience and bulk were catching up with him. When Jacques wrote that the rookie had been 'lost in the swirl of tempestuous seas', what he really meant was that he had been powerless to save himself being booted around the park by the Rams' hatchet men (likewise, when Jacques described United's equaliser as 'suspicious', what he was really saying was that the Reds couldn't have committed a more obvious foul on the keeper had they rammed a corner flag up his arse). The general policy of easing Hanson into senior football made sense; he had only just turned twenty and the club were looking forward to him leading the forward line for years to come, not months. But the selectors perhaps erred too far on the side of caution when they wrapped him in cotton wool in December – and did not unwrap him until the following September. Even when United's striking problems turned chronic in the new year, the selectors refused to bring him back into the side – they were as reluctant to go for a Jimmy as someone with gonorrhoea.

For a fortnight, it looked like the Old Trafford furore had tilted the promotion race in the Reds' favour. Whereas Derby won just one point from their next two matches, United, with Henderson netting a three-goal haul, won both of theirs to open up a two-point gap at the top and extend their advantage over third-placed Chelsea to five. But then, after three months striding imperiously through the fixture list like a latter-day Goliath, the Reds met their David; little Port Vale at Hanley. For the sling and the stone, read a mix of overconfidence, dreadful finishing and Steward's second Leighton moment in three weeks. United were coasting 1-0 and creating – and wasting – a flurry of chances when Alf went down on a half-hit daisy-cutter like an arthritic prostitute going down… to pull up her fishnets. He missed it, the ball rolled in and Vale made the most of the gift by claiming the winner seven minutes from time.

The Hanley horror sparked off an away wobble that would last until spring. It shouldn't have lasted a week, United squandering enough chances on their Christmas Day trip to Ayresome to have won half-a-dozen matches. By gifting Middlesbrough a point that day, the Reds missed what would be their best chance to nip their away-day neurosis in the bud. By the time emerging rivals Leicester had given them their only good slapping of the season, 3-0 at Filbert Street on the 27th, the pattern for the next three months had already been set.

The consolation was that Old Trafford remained a Red fortress. On Boxing Day, Boro received the smacked bottom they should have been given twenty-four hours earlier. On New Year's Day, Chelsea were knocked out by one of Grimwood's occasional net-breakers; two days later, Henderson was too hot for Stoke. Mann of the match that afternoon was right-half Frank who, as a sanitised version of the old Brian McClair song would put it, was here, there and everywhere. In the build-up to the second part of Willie's double he even remembered his former existence as a jinking inside-forward, slicing his way through the Stoke defence before pulling the ball back for the big centre-forward to do the rest. Marking Mann could be an off-putting experience; he looked like a candidate for a stairlift but there was pace enough in those legs yet and because of his size and strength it was never easy to overhaul him once he got ahead.

Their holiday experiences had yo-yoed between the good and bad but, for all that, Reds returned to work with their team still on top. Most observers fancied them to stay there, particularly if Barson could maintain his autumnal excellence. 'Manchester United have their most accomplished side since the war,' Bill Bennion wrote in the *Telegraph*. 'I have seen cleverer teams but none better equipped for the battle for promotion. Every man is a fighter, a last ditcher, and Barson at centre half-back, probably without a superior in the position. He gets through a tremendous amount of work. Not a ceremonious player by any means, Barson, but wonderfully effective.' The same pundit would not have been so free with his compliments, mind, had he seen much of United over the next couple of months. The wheels on the promotion bandwagon did not quite come off but the hubcaps were nicked and a Stanley knife rammed into the tyres. And, yes, Scousers were involved along the way, though they were wearing Everton blue rather than Liverpool red.

January was a bad time for Reds all round. United were on the verge of a crisis; Labour were already consumed in one, having been toppled in Parliament and then blown away at the polls (though not so completely as the Liberals who had been left with a skinny rump of just forty seats). What sealed the government's fate was a combination of their own naivety, Tory cunning and *Daily Mail* fuelled rumours concerning 'Red Scare' stories. What almost did for United were injuries, an outbreak of lunacy in the boardroom and play from the forwards that plunged from second to third-rate and, at times, threatened to sink even lower. Henderson's second against Stoke was the side's final goal of the month. As the clean sheets momentarily dried up as well, it does not take much brainpower to work out how the next three matches turned out.

At least the 2-0 cup defeat at Hillsborough on the 10th was relatively painless. Unlike the previous season, the competition was an unwanted distraction rather than the only thing left to play for. There were echoes of 2001's Cardiff Hotel story in the rumours that the club had booked 500 seats for the Cup Final and that immediately after their exit they had phoned the FA to cancel them but few people doubted the directors when they insisted there was no truth in them. Like Villa and City in modern times, United's only involvement in the latter stages of the Cup tended to be when they hosted one of the semi-finals. Only a mad man would have taken the gamble of booking so many seats before the competition had even got going.

So it could easily have been true, then. Only a mad man would have reacted to a goal drought by selling the club's only sound, experienced centre-forward. But that was exactly what the directors did in the aftermath of the twin 0-1 disasters against Coventry and Oldham, lowlife that United had swamped back in September. Henderson had recently started flowing again, providing seven of the side's last dozen goals, but his admittedly horrific display against the Latics, when he had lumbered around the pitch in the style of the living dead, was his final contribution to the Red cause. The following week, he was packed off to Preston.

The Wanderer's postbag groaned with complaints. The transfer failed to make sense on so many levels. If, like Bain and Meredith before him, Willie was not good enough for United, why was he considered good enough for a club in the division above? On his bad days he might have been a one-man disaster zone but when he blew hot he was much too hot for the second division – his fourteen goals had come at the quick-fire rate of two every three games. Where were United going to find firepower like that at a price they could afford? If Goldthorpe was past it, and Hanson was being kept for the future, who was going to fill the centre-forward role in the present? There was an argument, too, that Henderson's off days had been a symptom of deep-lying attacking problems rather than the cause. The selectors had undermined the combination play across the line by their knee-jerk reaction to the Hanley disaster. The introduction of another talented youngster, Fred Kennedy, at inside-left had been a marked success, so much so that he was already being touted as one of the finds of the season. But moving Lochhead to the opposite flank and thus breaking up the Spence-Smith axis had been an undoubted own goal; Arthur had rarely looked as comfortable on the right and the service to flying Joe had suffered as a result.

Most galling of all was the club's perceived lack of ambition. When promotion rivals Leicester had recently lost a centre-forward, they had immediately gone out and bought another one. Reds were still waiting for the attacking reinforcements they had desperately needed the season before. Now the club had cashed in on Henderson, their net expenditure in six seasons was down to just three grand. In 1925, lumbering full-backs were going for more than that. To stand a chance of snapping up a top-class goalscorer you were talking nearer £6,000. Peeved, Pop Side grumblers were suggesting a change of motto. Their suggestion? 'We get the crowds, why worry?'

The Henderson storm wasn't the only problem rocking United's boat, either. By the end of January, the club were in the grip of a full-blown injury and illness crisis as well. McPherson was laid low with quinseys, Mann was confined to bed with 'an unpleasant trouble in the shape of a particularly perfect specimen of the boil species' (he was all glamour, our Frank) and Hilditch was surgery-bound after damaging a leg. Worst of all were the serious mishaps that befell the side's twin colossi, Silcock and Barson. The former's fractured cheekbone eventually sidelined him for twelve vital matches in the promotion run-in, Barson's ruptured groin for eight.

Here was a test of United's defensive resources. The Radford tragedy had left the club with no experienced cover for either Silcock or Moore. So, if the directors had been asked, pre-season, to compile a list of situations they most wanted to avoid, injury to one or both of them would have featured, alongside wet Saturdays and increased gin prices, somewhere near the top. But cometh the hour, cometh the Welshman. Tom Jones, a tough-tackling rookie who had joined from Oswestry Town the previous May, emerged from the reserves to ensure that big Jack was barely missed. Believe the bare statistics, and the defence was even stronger with the new boy in it than it had been before. In the dozen games that Silcock missed, the back three of Steward, Jones and Moore kept a remarkable nine clean sheets.

If only the half-back puzzle had been as simple to solve. Grimwood, who picked up the pieces at centre-half (with Bennion brought in alongside him), was good but there was no one in the English game capable of taking up the slack left by Barson. When Frank limped out of the Oldham game, the side lost their leader, their midfield general – and their way. The skipper's groin strain probably cost him a recall to the England team. For most of the spring it looked like it would cost United their promotion.

Because of their premature cup exit, the Reds had two weeks before their next fixture, against Clapton Orient at Old Trafford. That gave Chapman an extra seven days to soothe the fans' tempers by filling the Henderson void. Normally, his instinct would have been to head back to Scotland but the United manager had a more original coup in mind. Whether it was a calculated manoeuvre, a moment of inspiration or one of utter desperation, Chapman at least earned himself full marks for originality by waiting until Clapton turned up in Manchester and then pinching their centre-forward, Albert Pape.

The popular version of the cheekiest transfer United had been involved in since the Herbert Burgess deal in 1906 (when Mangnall, in a desperate attempt to prevent any other club negotiating for City's much sought-after defensive pillar, had virtually taken him hostage) involves Chapman strolling into the visiting dressing-room a few minutes before kick-off, tossing a bundle of tenners on the table and telling Pape to say his goodbyes. In reality he hadn't been quite so brazen. The rumours that Orient hadn't known about any deal until they arrived in town were false. What actually happened was that Chapman phoned his Clapton counterpart before he left London and arranged to meet up at Piccadilly. A fee of £1,070 was agreed, the player, who had relatives in the Bolton area, eagerly accepted United's terms and the FA rushed through his registration in time for him to make his debut against his old team-mates that afternoon. Yes, the Orient directors really were that dumb. By allowing the deal to go through so swiftly they set themselves up for what happened next; Pape played well, scored a goal and United cruised to a 4-2 win.

The Reds' first victory in a month was a relief but it did not convince; the demoralising effect of losing their centre-forward had made Clapton easy meat. And if Pape's arrival lifted spirits, it did not take long for the effects to wear off. United eased to a 3-0 victory against Wolves at Old Trafford but continued to drop points outside of Manchester. Falling to a late winner at Palace cost the club their place in the top two, Leicester sneaking ahead of them on goal average. There was more passion and drive on show in the 1-1 at Hillsborough but Pape's equaliser was overshadowed by Silcock's bad break. Then, a week after the Wolves stroll, Fulham extended United's winless away run to eight games by taking them down at Craven Cottage. With eleven matches remaining, the team's fall from promotion favourites to promotion outsiders was more or less complete. On March 12, Leicester beat Palace to move a point clear of the Reds with a game in hand. Derby, who had played the same number of matches, were a further four points ahead.

With deadline day approaching, United needed Chapman to have a Cantona moment. Instead, he – or the directors – had a Howard Wilkinson one; they sold rising star Kennedy to Everton for £2,000 and replaced him with another Clapton forward, Charlie Rennox. The outgoing half of the double deal sent both press and punters into apoplexy. The *Football Chron* raged that it was 'an astonishing and bad piece of business' while the supporters, who had yet to calm down after the Henderson shock, staged a noisy protest meeting before the Portsmouth game on the 14th and turned the ensuing ninety minutes into one long catcall.

The club conceded that the 22-year-old Kennedy was a terrific prospect but argued that they needed a bigger and more experienced forward at that time. That may have been so but Fred, undisputedly the inside-forward of the season, was far too good a player to let go, particularly for such a low fee. The deal seemed to confirm the fans' worst fears that United were turning into a selling club. In the *Football News*, one of them raged: 'Have the directors of United no regard or responsibility for the spectators who travel to Old Trafford to support the team, or are they working as a business concern only, so much so that whenever another official of a wealthy club comes along with an open cheque they shake his arm off, grab his money, and say "Take your pick"?'

Similar gripes found their outlet in the rumours that the directors, happy with the crowds they were getting anyway, were not bothered about winning promotion. As ever, Barson's name was thrown into the mix to add to the intrigue. Depending on which Barson theory you heard, he was either fit enough to play but the directors did not want him to, he was fit enough to play but he did not want to, he was one of the most popular players United had ever had and was desperate to win promotion or he was at loggerheads with the management and was desperate to move on (any guesses as to which theory emanated from within Old Trafford?).

What a nightmarish scenario, then, for Rennox to walk into. He was a marked man even before he tried on his kit, like Lee Harvey Oswald forever saddled, rightly or wrongly, with the tag of the man who did for Kennedy. It would have helped if he had not made such an obvious patsy. With a bigger name, the directors may have been able to ride out the storm. After a career spent in the footballing backwaters of Dykehead, Wishaw and Clapton, Charlie was simply not big-time enough. As all corny [Red] uncles used to tell you, only one star has ever arrived at Old Trafford from the Orient and that was the Chinese international Young Lee Sharpe.

Despite the bowel-loosening experience of being greeted with boos on his debut, Rennox did all right against Pompey. Predictably, though, he soon sank like a stone. Flash-forward a month and he had been deposited alongside Jimmy Hanson in a time capsule labelled 'do not open till August'. At that stage, the club's promotion chances looked doomed too. United beat Portsmouth and then ended their away jinx by scraping a 1-0 at Hull but in the next fortnight they dropped a point against third-from-bottom Blackpool at home and, worst of all, lost to Derby in their promotion four-pointer at the Baseball Ground. In front of 400 travelling Reds (an almost unprecedented number for a non-derby), the normally impeccable Steward re-enacted his Old Trafford calamity, misjudging the flight of a hopeful garryowen and allowing the ball to drop tamely behind him into the goal. At the other end, the forwards, in their worst barn-door-missing mode, fluffed four open goals and twice hit the bar.

United seemed set for a meaningless bronze but two shafts of light did at least split the post-Derby gloom. Barson was back fit and Smith was restored, in place of Rennox, alongside Spence. Now that most of the pieces of the pre-Christmas jigsaw were back in place, there was hope that the Reds would force themselves back into the promotion picture. But was there time? With only seven games remaining there was a five point gap to be made up.

United were in the market for miracles. Fittingly enough, the

Easter fixtures started cooking one up. On Good Friday, Pape was too hot for outclassed Stockport at Old Trafford. A defence that had conceded just two goals in its last seven outings then shut out South Shields and Chelsea. The water of Lochhead's early strike against the former had been turned into the wine of three points. It could have been October all over again.

As ever, the form of the forwards was a worry but if the Reds were finding scoring difficult, it was nothing to the constipation affecting both Leicester and Derby. Neither of them were able to squeeze out a single goal over the holiday period, a combined total of six matches that included their top-of-the-table stalemate on Easter Saturday. Derby, in particular, were ripe for a Devon Loch; their fortuitous victory over the Reds apart, they had been in free-fall since early March when they had been five points clear. Since then, they had dropped eleven points out of a possible eighteen and scored just three goals.

With Derby sliding and United grinding out results, a momentous Saturday approached. Both sides were away; Derby at Stoke, United at Bradford. The Rams lost again. The Reds, meanwhile, dug deep for another 1-0. If the performance was ordinary, the winning strike was anything but. Under the heading 'A brilliant inspiration and a new hope!' Jacques reported: 'The fortunes of this momentous game at Valley Parade turned entirely on a magnificent effort by Smith, the Manchester United inside-right, a quarter of an hour before the finish.'

Up to that point, the game had looked to be drifting inexorably towards stalemate. Then... 'Smith was discovered, not in his own position, but at inside-left. Practically in midfield he fastened on the ball, forged ahead, and deftly evaded the challenge of a desperate adversary. A heavily-built, big-limbed fellow, with a rolling gait, he went steadily ahead, and soon it was realised that no one could catch him. McClaren was tempted to dash out of goal, but, as he did, so Smith, keeping a cool head, drove the ball past him and into the net. It was an electric shock, and what that goal may mean to the United team, time alone can tell. The immediate effect was to place them above Derby County in the table and to brighten their outlook immensely.' Leicester remained odds-on for the second division title but United were now favourites to join them in the top league. They were back in second place, level on points with the Rams but with a superior goal average and a game in hand. Barring a Derby goal rush, two wins from their next two games, both of them at home, would be enough for promotion.

The outlook clouded slightly as the Reds wasted some of their advantage with a sloppy display against Southampton. Pape's first-half opener should have been the first of many. Instead, another crop of chances went unharvested, the Saints equalised and only the agility of Steward averted a damaging defeat. But what a difference three days later as Port Vale were swept aside at Old Trafford. After just ten minutes the 34,000 Reds who had staggered from the midweek nail-biter in need of some beta-blockers were able to relax and focus on what was happening at Coventry, where Derby were the visitors. Three minutes in, Spence cut back a centre from the goal line and Lochhead, though falling, swivelled to turn the ball past the keeper. Seven minutes later, Joe made sure there would be no repeat of the Hanley giant-killing with a thrilling, mid-jump volley from Smith's curling delivery. In the second half, a second from Spence and a long-range fluke from McPherson completed United's biggest win since September. Or, depending how you look at it, since the last championship season, 1910/11.

Radio had been around since 1922 but the BBC (then a privately-owned affair; the public corporation wasn't born until 1927) hadn't yet set up a comprehensive results service and, even if they had, fans would have needed a small crane to get their set down to the ground so they could to listen to it. Deprived of the faithful trannie of later years, the crowd had to wait until after the final whistle before the telegraph wires delivered the news that Derby had been held once again. Cue a mass of delirium on the pitch and the most enthusiastic scenes that Old Trafford had yet witnessed. Jacques, who had covered the best and worst of the Reds, was moved to write: 'It was all a picture in League history to be long remembered and often to be recalled when the embers burn low and the last pipe is smoked.'

Mathematically, promotion was not yet guaranteed. Realistically, United's three year wait was over. Because of their inferior goal average, Derby had to win their final match – at home to Blackpool – by something like four clear goals and hope that United lost at Barnsley by at least as many. As it turned out, it did not matter what the Reds got up to with the Tykes. The Rams assured themselves of a third placed finish in a two horse race by drawing 2-2 while

Leicester thumped Coventry to end any hopes of United taking the pot (what did that matter? Lower division titles should be a source of embarrassment rather than celebration). In fact, the Reds bade farewell to their poor relations with a goalless draw replete with the obligatory ropy finishing. Only a 1-0 could have summed up their season better. There had been moments, particularly in the autumn, when the side, even the forwards, reached peaks of flowing football that the club had not seen since the days of the Outcasts. For most of the time, though, they had relied on the excellence of their half-backs and record-breaking defence and their mastery of the art of doing just about enough.

As the Red Army gathered in Manchester to celebrate, the qualms and questions about the team's style and shortcomings could wait. Heaving crowds welcomed the promotion-winners at Central Station and thronged their path as they made their way to the celebratory dinner the directors were throwing at the Queen's Hotel. The choice of location was surely no accident. The Queen's Hotel, you will remember, was incontrovertibly linked with the rise of the club under Mangnall, the auction of City's cup-winning side providing the moment when the balance of power in the city swung dramatically from Blue to Red. The hope that night was that history was about to repeat itself. United had just made it back into the 'Magic Circle'. City, meanwhile, had just stumbled to a mid-table finish, they had financial headaches of their own following the expensive move to Maine Road and were already ruing the previous summer's shock decision to part with Mangnall.

Over dinner, an emotional John Henry Davies took the opportunity to congratulate the team on the great efforts they had made and also – rather unnecessarily – to nail to the counter 'the statement that the club had not been anxious to secure promotion'. Other speakers complimented the players and the trainer, Jack Pullar, and a fitting tribute was made to John Chapman for the important part he had played in the success of the side. Captain Barson then took the stand and said: 'It's a far better thing that we have done than we have ever done, it is a far better...' Sorry, no he didn't, that's enough messing with the boy Dickens (why do football people talk like that?). In fact, Frank congratulated every player for giving of his best and then came up with the crowd-pleasing – if, admittedly, difficult to substantiate – pledge that 'if they did not win the First

Division championship next season they would try to secure the English Cup.'

With that, Barson was off to claim his pub although he didn't stay there for long. Within a few minutes of opening the doors he got sick of all the attention and fawning from Red well-wishers. When he heard that scores more were on the way he threw the keys on the table, told the Head Waiter the place was his, and walked out for good. Impulsiveness and class laced with single-minded lunacy – it was classic Frank.

ROLL OF HONOUR

CHAMPIONS: HUDDERSFIELD

FA CUP WINNERS: SHEFFIELD UNITED

UNITED: DIVISION 2 (2ND) FA CUP (1ST ROUND) SHEFFIELD WED

WILLIAM HENDERSON

CENTRE-FORWARD, NOV 1921 – JAN 1925, 36 APPS 17 GLS

AFTER TOPPING THE Scottish scoring charts in his one season with Airdrieonians, most pundits north of the border were amazed when William Henderson was unable to match his exploits in the English game. A strapping lad who did not mind throwing his weight around, he seemed tailor-made for the Sassenach style of football. However, while Willie's physical attributes and gift for opportunism were never in question, his ball control and general play undoubtedly were. In many ways he was as classy as a night out in Burnley.

That Henderson's first season at Old Trafford fell short of expectations was perhaps predictable. Young (he was 23) and inexperienced*, the Scot was ill-prepared for such a big move. By the time he had adapted to life as a full-time pro in Manchester, the Reds were in serious relegation trouble and the time for patience had passed. Ten games into his new career, Willie was dropped, the selectors opting, sensibly enough, for the greater experience of Joe Spence.

The accepted wisdom in the summer of '22 was that, his teething problems over, Henderson would emerge as a genuine force in the second division in the season to come. In fact, a couple of serious injuries and an even more serious dip in form restricted him to just two appearances and one goal. The following season was even worse as Willie failed to score in any of his five appearances. If Ernie Goldthorpe had stayed fit, that might have been the end of his United story. Instead, Goldthorpe's knees broke down again, Big Willie was readmitted into the last chance saloon and this time he threatened to drink the place dry, rattling in fourteen goals in twenty-two appearances to set the club up for eventual promotion.

It was typical of the directors' logic that the Scot was not around to see it. Perhaps worried that his scoring spree was a one-off, United flogged him to Preston at the end of January for an undisclosed four-figure fee. Reds exploded into uproar when the news filtered through of Henderson's transfer. Such a scenario would have been inconceivable just five months earlier when those supporters who were aware that he was still on the books would have gladly coughed up for a taxi to take him out of town, preferably one driven by Don Brennan.

Willie's stunning debut season with Airdrie was his first in senior football; even then, he had been a part-time pro, combining playing with a civvy job in Edinburgh

BILLY SARVIS

FORWARD, MAY 1922 – MAY 1925, 1 APP 0 GLS

BILLY SARVIS WAS a professional footballer for five years but nothing he did on the pitch ever came close to giving him the exposure that his brush with death did. One run-out for United (in the 2-0 defeat at Coventry a couple of months before his horrific accident) and a handful of games for Bradford City and Walsall were all that he managed in League football. Would he have achieved more had the 'well-known Manchester gent' who knocked him down on Chester Road ever been made to take a driving test? Probably not, but then again...

ERNIE GOLDTHORPE

CENTRE-FORWARD, NOV 1922 – OCT 1925, 30 APPS 16 GLS

THE FIRST OF the decade's much mourned injury victims, Ernie Goldthorpe hinted at greatness for five injury-free months in 22/23 when he banged in four goals in the big promotion clash at Meadow Lane and fourteen goals in twenty-five games all told. It was a tragedy that his knees denied him the chance to make the mark on United's history that his talent demanded. Fortunately, the 27-year-old Tyke had plenty to fall back on when he hobbled back across the Pennines as his family owned more farms than the kulaks.

FRED KENNEDY

INSIDE-LEFT, MAY 1923 – MAR 1925, 18 APPS 4 GLS

A TRICKY LEFT-WINGER for his first club, Rossendale United, Fred Kennedy did all his best work at United in Arthur Lochhead's old number ten shirt. The directors' decision to sell him in the midst of the promotion push, particularly for a derisory £2,000, was further evidence of their inability to differentiate between their arses and their elbows. Their argument that they needed a bigger and more experienced forward to galvanise the team's promotion bid did not wash with the many pundits who had raved about Fred since his emergence as a first team regular just three months earlier. The consensus was that Kennedy, even as a 22-year-old novice, was 'the cleverest inside-forward at Old Trafford and one of the sturdiest' and that the decision to cash in on him was the club's worst bit of business since the sale of Tommy Meehan. Fred's subsequent career did not quite live up to his early billing but he was always comfortable in the upper echelons of the game and undoubtedly belongs in the lengthy list of Reds who should never have been allowed to get away.

SIDNEY EVANS

RIGHT-WINGER, MAY 1923 – AUG 1925, 6 APPS 2 GLS

THE PERENNIAL UNDERSTUDY (or mug?), Sidney Evans had already spent three frustrating seasons as the back-up right-winger at Cardiff City when he signed up for the identical job at Old Trafford. Eleven months of reserve-team anonymity later, Sid finally got his chance to emerge from Joe Spence's shadow and in a run of six consecutive appearances at the back end of the 23/24 season, he did well enough for one pundit to write: 'Evans has apparently been wasting his time in the Central League'. Sadly, Sid never got the chance to prove that pundit right and after wasting another season in the reserves he signed for Pontypridd.

WEMBLEY FEVER

EVEN IN THE midst of the promotion party, the critics had expressed doubts about United's ability to survive in the top flight. In his valedictory report from 24/25, Jacques warned: 'Defence is the prevailing factor so far. Now the objective is reached, the officials must do more than ponder on the forward deficiencies. It is easier to slide than to climb.' Three months of pondering later, the experts were more convinced than ever that the Reds would not score the goals they needed to stay up. The list of arrivals contained just one player of note – Bill Inglis from Sheffield Wednesday – and he was a full-back; Albert Pape, the anticipated first-choice centre-forward, looked like he had spent the summer on the eat-all-you-can buffet circuit while the pre-season form of the line can best be gauged by the outcome of their public practice match against the reserves. Embarrassingly, the seniors were comfortably outscored. Little wonder that the sceptics and scoffers were queuing up to get on the forwards' case. Even their team-mates had lost confidence in them. Speaking some years later, one unnamed United defender confessed: 'When we were a goal down, we knew we had had it.'

But these were surreal and illusory times in which the sceptics found themselves and in such times the prediction-making business is a particularly risky one to get involved with. Innovations, for example, were coming at a head-spinning rush. The wireless had only been around for what seemed like a couple of minutes but John Logie Baird had already produced the first, faint television pictures, using a cathode ray tube and a pair of dummies (Poborsky and Cruyff?). Medicine had taken the equivalent of a walk on the moon. Surgeons successfully operated on damaged heart valves at London's St Barts; a pair of Canadian scientists, Charles Best and Frederick Banting isolated insulin and ensured that diabetes no longer carried an automatic death sentence; Alexander Fleming, meanwhile, was about to provide the biggest breakthrough of all, his discovery of penicillin – courtesy of a Eureka moment and a mouldy slice of bread

- saving the lives of millions.

In the realm of international relations, the so-called Locarno effect created an illusion of tranquillity. The 1925 pact of that name, in which everyone basically promised to stop picking on each other (cross their hearts and hope to die) supposedly marked Germany's rehabilitation as a member of the international community. In fact it proved the ultimate triumph of image over reality. While the politicians were getting frothed up over the prospect of a lasting peace, the wheels of war were already starting to turn; a Red born in 25/26 would easily be old enough to see action in World War II. It was a similar story on the home front. The Twenties were supposedly Roaring but the image of cool cats and kittens dancing the Charleston did not often tally with the experiences of the working-class masses. Two days after the season ended, the miners would be leading British workers on their first General Strike.

Fittingly enough, surrealism as an intellectual movement took its first obscure steps in the twenties. Presumably, some of the fashion designers were keen supporters. Certainly there were some dodgy threads knocking around, none more bizarre than the baggy tents that passed for trousers amongst fashion-conscious flappers. With a decent pair of Oxford Bags on, you could keep your whole family dry in the rain; they were less handy in the wind, mind. While gents' outfits were getting baggier and baggier, women's dresses were getting shorter and thinner. The pressure of fitting in with 'flapper style' had started to take its toll on female ravers. Now their spare tyres were no longer hidden under a melee of bloomers, corsets and skirts, crash diets were becoming the in-thing. So was popping pills, smoking and knocking back booze. Young women were making the most of their new-found freedom in time-honoured style – by getting wrecked.

Even more drastic than the changes in fashion were the changes in football. In an effort to combat the growing negativity in the game, the FA took an axe to the old offside law. Previously, three defenders had governed the application of the law. Now it was down to two. Amidst the arguments and counter-arguments about the change that raged all summer, one thing seemed set in stone; it was going to be the least predictable football season since the League competition began. So the doom'n'gloom merchants were perhaps asking for it when they wrote United off before a ball had even been kicked. Like Michael Fish when he laughed off reports of a hurricane in '87, the alecs and arses in the press were just too smart for their own good. Unlikely as it seemed, a Red storm was on its way.

*   *   *

FOR THE BEST PART OF TWO months, football struggled to adjust to the most drastic law change of the century. Tactics that had succeeded before were now rendered obsolete. The dire one-back game, for example, had gone the way of the string crossbar and Frank Mann's hair. Under the three defender rule, one of the backs could, theoretically, have spent the entire ninety minutes giving his goalie a rub down without playing any of the forwards onside. Now, if one of the backs dropped back to act as cover, the attackers could legally go back with him. The new rule set the forwards free, gave the backs migraines and doubled the workload of the half-backs. The centre-half was perhaps affected the most. Traditionally, the best number fives had played well up the field and supported the attack. Now there was pressure on them to act as a third defender instead of an extra attacker. In turn, the wing half-backs had to be prepared to move into the centre to support the pivot and inside-forwards to move back to cover the wing-halves. As a result of the changes, the deeper 'W' attacking formation came storming into fashion. Instead of pushing up together as a line, the inside-right and inside-left – the low points of the 'W' – often played well behind the three out-and-out attackers – the centre-forward and the two wingers.

With the game in tactical meltdown, goals and freak results flowed freely. The opening weeks of the season were marked by somersaults in form whereby teams would win by a landslide one week and lose by one the next. United's form may have been as up and down – or down and up – as a bulimic's dinner but, compared to some, their early season performances were the measure of consistency. They got hammered a couple of times and creamed one team themselves but otherwise the goal frenzy largely passed them by. So, while Aston Villa were leading the opening day avalanche with a ten-goal romp against Burnley, the Reds were playing themselves back into the first division with a low-key, single goal defeat at West Ham. The setback was easily excused. The heatwave, the uneasiness caused by the offside change and inexperience were all alibis for a United side containing five players who were making their top flight debuts.

No such excuses were needed four days later as the Reds bounced back with a surprise win against Villa in their first home game back. After their demolition of Burnley, the visitors must have arrived in Manchester expecting another walkover. Instead, it was they who proved easy prey. Nineteen minutes in and United were one-up, the Villa keeper, Spires, allowing one of the worst shots of the season, a mishit pea-roller from Spence, to squirm through his fingers. Moments later, Pape was tripped in the area and Lochhead stroked in the penalty. Lochhead then missed a second spot-kick before Barson rounded off the rout with, remarkably, his first United goal – a shot through the crowd from close range. You could say that Frank had been up for it in his first match against his old club, the Villa forwards in particular paying the price for the inimical nature of his departure. After suffering what Jacques nicely described as a ninety-minute 'shaking', they limped home sporting 'Barson tattoos' on their ribs and their legs. At least their skin matched the colour of their strip.

The 3-0 thrashing of Villa set United up nicely for a September schedule that rammed home the glamour gap between the divisions. A year earlier, they had just flopped at Stockport and were about to meet more C and D-listers in Stoke, Barnsley, Oldham and Coventry. This time around, they were about to go on sexy dates with Arsenal, Villa (again), City, Liverpool, Burnley and fellow promotion-winners Leicester. And with more of the same to come, it did not matter so much that their points haul for the month was a modest eight. For now, at least, it was just good to be back.

Admittedly, Arsenal at home wasn't quite the lip-licking prospect then that it is today. Flying the flag for football in London in the game's early days as well as the backdoor manner in which they had sneaked into the top division after the war (helped on their way, of course, by the Red-led match-fixing affair) was just about all the Gunners were known for. The 'boring, boring' tag had yet to be coined; they were a club to be pitied, not abused. 'Of the East London club whose team came to Old Trafford on Saturday, one had long thought and spoken in terms of "Poor old Arsenal"', led *The Manchester Guardian's* match report. But the old image had already started to fade. The Gunners had just taken a major stride forward by enticing managerial legend Herbert Chapman away from champions Huddersfield. Under Chapman, the club would undergo an image change as drastic as David Icke's when he swapped V-necks and snooker for shell-suits and aliens. A hat-trick of championships lay just around the corner.

And what did the manager get in return? A fatal infection, a poxy bust and a purgatorial afterlife spent pacing Highbury's marble halls. And things could get even worse for poor old Bert – Arsene Wenger could eventually join him.

As well as pulling off the managerial coup of the decade, Arsenal had also figured in the transfer sensation of the summer when they snapped up Charlie Buchan from Sunderland. The deal captured the imagination in more ways than one. Buchan was a football genius, by common consent the most inventive English forward of his day. His transfer showed an innovative streak too. Originally, the two clubs had been unable to agree terms. As a negotiation-enema, the Gunners came up with the novel idea of paying Sunderland £100 for every goal Buchan scored. It was a freak deal for a freak season and became the talk of the sporting world, particularly the *Athletic News*: 'For some time the public yearned for a particular hundred from Hobbs [in 1923, Surrey's Jack became just the third batsman after W.G. Grace and Tom Hayward to knock up a century of centuries]. There was considerable delay. Now the man in the street has centred his attention on Charles Buchan and the £100 goal.'

Buchan hadn't found the net in either of Arsenal's opening two matches. Now the £100 goal side-show moved on to Old Trafford. Steward managed to prevent him from scoring (Sunderland would not receive their first instalment until Liverpool visited Highbury the following Saturday) but Buchan did wriggle free long enough to set up the Gunners' third-minute winner. The way the Reds played, though, you would have thought that Sunderland had promised them a cut from any goals Charlie tucked away. They were abject shadows of the Villa beaters and deserved a good thumping.

Given the vast potential for foul play (imagine the farcical possibilities when Buchan played against his former club...), it will come as no surprise that the £100 deal made the football authorities extremely nervous. As no rules had been broken, they had no choice but to let it stand but they did move swiftly to rule out similar deals in the future. There would be no more transfers on a pounds-for-goals basis. Which was a pity for United; Birtles, Gibson, Davenport and the rest would have been far less expensive mistakes had their transfer fees been linked to their strike-rates.

The Arsenal surrender soured what had been a decent opening week but it did not take long for the Reds to redeem themselves. On the 7th, a stubborn performance and fine goals from Rennox and Hanson – in their first run-outs of the season – earned them a solid 2-2 at Villa Park. Five days later, the team rode the twin blows of losing Hanson to an early injury and their lead to a joke goal (City centre-half Cowan's admittedly clever header should have been disallowed for three different reasons: pushing, the ball was out, it wasn't a corner in the first place...) to claim another good point in the inaugural Maine Road derby. All the usual suspects rose to the occasion, particularly the 'glorious' Steward, but the undisputed man of the match was Rennox whose brilliant opening goal lent a 'blood-tingling battle' its most memorable moment. Picking up the ball in midfield, the rugged Scot brushed aside two Blues before launching a dipping howitzer past City keeper Mitchell.

Before the Villa match, Rennox had been considered a dirty word on the Pop Side. Two screamers in a week was a powerful challenge to the accepted view that he was no more than a poor man's Fred Kennedy. Soon the argument would be academic. A blast of five goals in United's next two home matches – a brace in the 3-2 thriller against Leicester and a hat-trick in the six-goal demolition of hapless Burnley – converted more people than Stork and when Charlie reached double figures before Christmas and ended the season as the club's top league scorer, the furore that surrounded his arrival and Fred's exit was all but forgotten.

But if Rennox's star was in the ascendancy, the career of the other Clapton old boy, Pape, was heading in the opposite direction. Just about the only rolls chunky Albert had been associated with in his time in Manchester were cheese and pickle ones and it was no real surprise when, after misfiring in his only two top-flight appearances for the club, he was packed off to Fulham in October.

Given the bizarre circumstances surrounding his arrival and the inherent difficulties in bedding into a new team mid-season, Pape could justifiably claim that he had been robbed of a proper opportunity to shine. But if his bottom was raw from the metaphorical shafting the directors had given him, it had nothing on the anal trauma awaiting Arthur Lochhead and his many admirers. For three years the club had peddled the line that lower division football did not really suit the silky Scotsman and that the fans would not see the very best of him until he reached the top flight (if people thought he was good before, they hadn't seen anything yet). Now, after just five first division appearances, two of them in his bogey position, centre-forward, they sold him to Leicester. Forgetting the maxim about the swallow and the summer, the management reasoned that Rennox was now the better long-term bet at inside-left. The thousands of Reds who had been left swooning by Arthur's skilled footwork, beautiful body swerve and bulging bag of tricks – notably his Meredithian backheel – begged to differ. As far as they were concerned, letting Lochhead go, particularly for as little as £3,300, was nothing less than a crime.

Lochhead's United swansong, at Anfield on the 19th, was a horrible experience all round, Liverpool capitalising on a rare Barson shocker to score four goals in the second half and, in the process, make a mockery of the early stages when the points had looked set for a trip down the East Lancs. The only, slight, consolation was that United were by no means the only team who got stung that day. With the first rain of the season adding to the existing imbalance between attack and defence, it had been freaky September's freakiest Saturday. Spurs and Huddersfield shared ten goals at White Hart Lane, City and Everton eight at Maine Road. At St James's, Blackburn smashed seven past Newcastle. A couple of days earlier, Newcastle had beaten Notts County 6-3 while Blackburn had been blitzed 6-2 by Sunderland. Form remained consistently and spectacularly inconsistent. The uncertainty proved too much for some people. After the first month's trial, the critics of the new law were ahead on points. The 'offside nuisance' had been checked but the balance of play seemed to have been transferred too emphatically in favour of the forwards. With the scoring rate up from 2.5 per match the previous season to 3.8 this, goals were coming too cheaply.

There were many in the game, including Barson, who would have preferred it had the FA plumped for the more cautious alternative of splitting the pitch into three equal areas and leaving the middle third free from the operation of the old, three defender offside law. Frank's suspicions about the new law were slightly surprising as, the Anfield disaster apart, he was thriving under it. The key, as he saw it, was to carry on playing the traditional centre half-back game, mixing both defence and attack. The national selectors had taken note and, for the first time in five years, Barson received a letter from the FA containing something other than the arrangements for a disciplinary hearing. Frank's call-up, alongside the in-form Spence, for the representative match between an FA XI and the Birmingham FA was viewed as a stepping-stone to a place in the full England team. Unfortunately, an ill-timed strain robbed him of his chance.

If the FA had not been such committed Mancophobes, the squad would surely have included at least one member of the 'resourceful and cool' defence as well. Barson's determination to keep on going forward had left the back-line with a tactical conundrum – stay back and allow a fatal chasm to open up between themselves and the rest of the team, or push up and risk being caught out by the long ball over the top. The mobility and positional nous of Silcock and Moore – plus Steward's flair for charging out of his area like the Great Dane on heat – had enabled them to do what was right for the team without leaving themselves open to a mugging. Even with the Anfield stain on their record, United boasted the second best defensive stats in the division and even though there would be other major spillages to come, the rearguard ended the season ranked, statistically, an honourable fifth.

There was nothing even this defence could do, though, to save the Reds from another painful experience at the hands of another northern rival on their next away-day. Guess the ground from the following quote from 'H.P.R': 'It is a long time since I was present at a match when so much bitterness was shown towards a visiting side.' That's right, it was Elland Road. One of the drawbacks of winning promotion was that United were back in the same division as their knuckle-dragging cousins. On their three previous visits to the Pen, the Reds had won twice and drawn the other. This time they were a yard too slow and deservedly went down 2-0.

Newcastle were given an almost identical write-up when they were swept aside by the same score-line at Old Trafford the following week. The manner in which both matches were won and lost brought the press out in another rash of lectures about how the game was going to the dogs, or at least turning into a greyhound race. 'This is the day of science subservient and speed predominant,' groaned 'the Impressionist' in the *Athletic News*. But if the scaremongers were convinced that the game was heading for an Ice Age that only the kick-'n'-rushers would be able to survive, the chances are that the Pop Side had more faith in football's brave new world. Already, it was clear that the fare they were watching was better than it had been before the rule change. Soon the quality dial at Old Trafford would reach a notch it had not touched for years. And it was a season-defining change in the forward line that ultimately made all the difference.

After a stinker of a nil-nil at home to Spurs, the music restarted on the selectors' game of pass-the-number-nine-shirt. So far they had tried out four different players at centre-forward. Two of them – Pape and Lochhead – had made such an impression that they were now picking up their pay packets elsewhere, the first one to have a go – the novice, Richard Iddon – was last seen having his confidence massaged in the reserves while the latest, Hanson, had merely convinced everyone that, at this stage of his development, he was a far better bet at eight or ten. By the time the music stopped this time, the shirt had landed in the lap of left-winger Frank McPherson. Had Reds been chewing on their teas when they heard the news, walls would have been redecorated across the city. Needless to say, Frank was considered an unlikely saviour. To his harshest critics he was a football airhead, his right foot was as redundant as Cliff Richards' wedding tackle, he had not pulled up any trees when he had been experimented with before and he was out of form. At the time he was not even in the side in his specialist position – after an early-season slump in form, his place on the wing had been taken by the speedy journeyman Harry Thomas.

In hindsight, though, the switch made just as much sense as Mann's the season before. McPherson was just about the quickest man in the game and despite having just about the smallest feet as well (dinky size 4s), he could lamp the ball as hard as anyone. The centre-forward position was now tailor-made for players who could sprint and shoot. Previously, the archetypal number nine had been built like a bouncer and had boasted a mentality to match. His raison d'être had been to fight for possession, barge defenders out of the way and then set himself or a team-mate up for a shot on goal. The offside change had cleared the way for a more subtle approach. Because of the likelihood of being caught offside, centre-forwards had traditionally played in front of the opposition backs. Now that they had licence to roam, there was a marked trend toward the lighter, pacier raider – like McPherson – who could nip in-between, and behind, his markers and get them turned. A new football term was coined, too; forwards could now play 'on the shoulder of the last man'.

It did not take long for the Bullet to make headlines in his new role, a brace against Cardiff in his first outing there earning United their first away win at the sixth attempt. The toughest examination of the season so far – Huddersfield at home – perhaps came too soon for the novice centre-forward and sure enough he, like the rest of the attack, flunked it (fortunately, the defence sailed to an A-plus and the champions were held 1-1). But it was a momentary stutter rather than the start of a slump. In the weeks to come, the Reds would find a consistency in front of goal that had eluded them for years. Pre-McPherson, they had failed to score in five of their eleven games. Now the Bullet was spearheading the attack, United would find the net in each of their next sixteen, sixteen games in which they came closer than ever to making their supporters' most rabid footballing fantasies come true.

November, in particular, was an unmitigated triumph, the Reds banging out four wins out of four. At Goodison, they even hinted at life after Barson by putting on a show while their one-man team was confined to bed with ptomaine poisoning (the book was open on what unlikely illness jinxed Frank would pick up next – Rabies? Foot and Mouth? Wembley fever?). In front of 42,000, United won 3-1. Over the next fortnight, both Birmingham and Bury were swatted aside by identical scores. Despite a nasty pea-souper, another crowd in excess of 40,000 were inside Old Trafford to witness the fit-again Barson dismantle the Brummies. Impressed, the Impressionist wrote: 'Beyond doubt the United have captured the imagination of the populace for the way they have acquitted themselves as a promoted club, else there would not have been such a fine attendance with so doubtful a prospect.'

Before the Gigg Lane derby, the crowd and the players paid their respects to Queen Alexandra, the wife of George V, who had died during the week. Flags flew at half-mast, the national anthem was played and the players wore black armlets. Other than that it was a typical United-Bury encounter; dripping with controversy. It was a curious anomaly that most United-City games at the time were comparatively orderly affairs. Put the Reds and the Shakers together, on the other hand, and a bad smell was all but guaranteed. This time the touch-paper was lit when, with the scores tied at one apiece midway through the second half, Moore launched himself superman-style at a goal-bound shot. Instant Bury penalty appeals were amusingly waved away and while several home players were still arguing the toss with the referee, the Reds burst away down the right, Spence centred and McPherson bundled it in. Then, as the understated Tim Bobbin put it, 'the bubble burst'. Players from both sides jostled around the officials, the referee, slightly losing the plot, consulted his linesman even though there was nothing he could do to bale him out and, after checking out the possible escape routes, made the only decision he could and awarded the goal. Thereafter, Bury lost their heads, United buckled down and Spence's late header made the points safe.

By the time Blackburn were brushed aside at Old Trafford on November 28, Chapman's men had risen to a barely believable third. If pushed, most Reds would have freely admitted they were in a false position – 'We're gonna win the League' was yet to feature heavily on the Pop Side play list. But the reluctance of the press to afford them any sort of respect was still a source of frustration and annoyance. Most pundits dismissed United as 'rush & tumble' specialists and inferred that they were the undeserving beneficiaries of a bad rule change. And the mud might have stuck had the general consensus on the new offside law not begun to shift from thumbs down to thumbs up.

Now that teams had had the opportunity to adjust their tactics, the vast majority were in favour of the change. The defensive bogey that had recently blighted the game had been nullified but not at the cost of the sport's finer arts. Reassuringly, the old, scientific methods still served and the threat of kick 'n' rush had not materialised – the long ball brigade had not taken over. For the most part, the top – and bottom – of the table had a reassuringly predictable feel about it. Logically, that meant that the Reds owed their revival to something more than the big boot up the field. Admittedly, they were not exponents of total football, preferring instead to play fast and direct, but there was some subtlety and science to go with their spirit, the defence was without a peer in the division, the half-backs better than most and the forwards under-rated, at least individually. There lay the secret of United's success, not the rules.

In time-honoured British style, the Reds received their best reviews when their unbeaten run came to an end. At a snow-bound Roker Park on December 5, Sunderland just held off a gallant United fight-back to edge the duel between the sides in second and third. According to Jacques: 'Two of the strongest teams in the league gave a wonderful exhibition of football' and 'United attacked with tremendous vigour and much skill.' When the Reds were then tripped up by Sheffield United at home, and thumped 5-1 at West Brom, it looked like December would break them but things did not pan out that way. Hanson's last-gasp winner on Christmas Day was the perfect way for the side to clamber out of their Advent rut. Even better, it was local rivals Bolton who filled the role of turkey's bottom to United's stuffing. McPherson's hat-trick at Filbert Street clinched the club's first away win since Gigg Lane five weeks earlier; the same player's free-kick then set up Rennox for a late winner against West Ham in the first match of the new year. By then, United had moved back up to fourth.

'Crisis? What Crisis?' summed up the Red attitude. Still, a more ambitious board would have chosen that moment to let their manager loose in the transfer market, particularly as Barson would be ruled out for another couple of months, this time with a combination of tonsillitis and flu. United had the funds – they had cleared a £10,000 profit during the promotion season – but the directors were focused instead on bringing down the club's debts and then obtaining the freehold to Old Trafford. The spiralling transfer market unnerved them. Only recently, Sunderland had taken the transfer record past the £6,500 mark by signing Robert Kelly from Burnley. Although he was a regular England international, Kelly was 31 years old. Elsewhere, clubs were spending big to entice the cream of the all-conquering Scottish XI across the border. Alec Jackson, the brilliant Tartan wingman, moved to Huddersfield; left-back Phil McCloy was already at City while promising forward Willie Russell was about to lead £20,000 worth of Scottish talent to second division Preston.

The Reds had been down the Scottish route before and had got their fingers burned. Chapman desperately wanted to return to his old club to sign the biggest jewel in his country's crown but he could not persuade the board to take a punt on another expensive 'foreigner'. The United manager later described missing out on Hughie Gallacher, who went on to join Newcastle for £6,000 (and thousands more, if the rumours are to be believed), as his biggest regret. Cheap even at that price, Gallacher was one of the few stars of his day whose name lived on past his retirement, albeit not always for the right reasons. A magnet for bad publicity as well as good, Hughie's career was a charismatic combination of goals, suspensions and strops. His life, meanwhile, ended in tragic and degrading circumstances (in 1957) when he threw himself in front of a train just days before he was due in court to answer charges of assault, ill-treatment and neglect of his teenaged son.

The board's reluctance to join in the transfer merry-go-round cost Chapman the prize forward who might have made the difference later in the season. Instead, the United manager had to settle for beefing up his wing division with the purchase of Charlie Hannaford from Clapton. Following, as it did, so soon after the deals for Pape and Rennox, the deal begs the question whether Chapman had a reward card for the Orient – or a mistress in Hackney.

A CUP STROLL AT PORT VALE kept the Reds rolling and set them up nicely for their top-of-the-table clash at Highbury on January 16. With United trailing just three points behind the league-leading Gunners, Barson's post-promotion pledge that they would go for it in both league and cup no longer felt like the biggest eruption of hot air since Henry VIII lit one of his farts. But unfortunate defeat brought the unwelcome whiff of reality to the nostrils of Red dreamers. In the first half, the latest instalment of Chapman versus Chapman appeared to be heading John's way. Arsenal led after 26 but United, a persuasive mix of penetrating attack and neutralising defence, stormed back first to equalise and then to edge ahead with contrasting strikes from McPherson and Spence. Frank provided the cutting edge to a rapier thrust down the left by Thomas; Joe the bludgeon from thirty yards. But a £100 moment from Buchan seconds before the break changed the game. Slowed by the snow-bound conditions, United lost their vibrancy and virility in the second half and when Steward was beaten again they had to settle for honourable defeat.

But if Highbury was the definition of defeat with honour, the derby disaster the following Saturday was the epitome of lily-livered capitulation. Losing 6-1 (yes, SIX) to City surely ranks in the top three of Old Trafford's darkest afternoons. It was the record winning margin for a Manchester derby, surpassing Newton Heath's 5-1 success in the first of the sequence – and the 4-0 for City in 1898. It was the first time that the Blues had scored even two goals in an away derby and it was the most shocking result of a shock-packed season. What made the defeat even harder to swallow was that, for the first time in years, United had gone into the match as overwhelming favourites. Some Reds were still dreaming of the championship; City, hamstrung by a defence that was as safe as the rhythm method, were fretting about the drop. Only recently they had been bottom of the pile.

It did not take long for the game to deviate alarmingly from the anticipated script. The Blues made – and wasted – four excellent chances in the opening quarter of an hour, stuck three goals away in the first half, three more in the second and were denied by the woodwork on another three occasions. By the time Rennox had slotted in his late consolation, most of the 49,000 crowd were already halfway down their third pint of home-brew – or halfway in the oven. Suicidal was the word that best covered United's display. All season they had been tactically sound, particularly in defence. For some reason, Chapman – or perhaps an interfering director – had chosen the derby to try out the old one-back game under the new rules. So, instead of lining up in his normal position of left-back, Silcock started the game pushed up amongst the half-backs. The predictable result was that City merely had to drop the ball into the space that Jack had vacated for their right flankers (aren't all Blues?) to have a clear run on goal.

Tactics weren't the only problem. With Barson still recuperating, the team lacked a leader and, more disturbingly, several of the players appeared to lack heart. Even when Silcock was belatedly pushed back into defence, the Reds were still badly overrun. According to Jacques: 'Bad tactics started the "rot" and temperament produced the collapse.' Though no Red, apart, perhaps, from Mann, emerged from the rout with the same reputation they had taken into it, the selectorial bullets were aimed exclusively at Steward. A touch unfair, perhaps, given the limited protection he had been given, but Alf had slumped badly after a brave opening and allowed his head to drop lower than any of his team-mates'. So, just three months after being touted for the England job, Steward was back in the reserves – and Jack Mew was back in the big time.

At least the Cup offered a quick route back into the supporters' good books. Tottenham at White Hart Lane also provided the opportunity for United to avenge their 4-0 humiliation at the same stage three years earlier. Home and away sizzlers ensued, the London leg in particular being the very antithesis of the autumn's soulless nil-nil. Two up after fifteen minutes through Thomas and Spence, the Reds conceded twice in the next fifteen, held on courtesy of a couple of Mew miracles before half-time (his keeper's jumper had gone up an X or two but Jack's agility still belied his frame) and then shared the plaudits in an absorbing, if goalless, second half. Four days later, 45,000 Mancunians observed the coup de grâce. A poor technical spectacle, but another immensely enthralling battle, was settled by a goal in each half, the second, from Spence, the more remarkable as he had spent most of the game hobbling around on one leg. If only for that one moment, his strained hamstring worked in his favour. Like the uncoordinated fat kid in the playground who always gets picked last, nobbled Joe was left unmarked as McPherson's deflected drive fell to his feet; unlike the last-picked numpty at our school, he banged the chance into the net and not the bike-sheds.

United were now in recently uncharted territory. Not since 1911 had they made it as far as the fifth round. Most critics were convinced that this was where their cup story would peter out. A bastard of a run with the balls had handed them another away tie, this time at second-placed Sunderland. The manner in which Spurs had been despatched had left the critics, including *The Guardian*, cold: 'It was blunderball rather than football with more bad play than would seem credible. United won but gave the fans little encouragement for the "battle tomorrow". In fact if Sunderland fail to win on February 20 no other unexpected result of that day would better merit the cherished word "sensation".' How quickly the press had forgotten the excellence of United's display in the original tie. Aided by the emergence of an unexpected cup hero, the Reds were about to make them choke on their words.

If the White Hart Lane clash had been a thriller, the Roker one was even better; 'one of the greatest cup ties ever fought on the ground' was an opinion expressed in one form or another in every report. Two down since the eighteenth minute and being completely outplayed, the Reds got themselves out of jail with two goals in five minutes either side of half-time. McPherson bagged the first, improvising nicely to steer in a loose ball from close range; Tommy Smith, who had not scored for five months and hadn't even been in the team for two, got the second with a clever shot from a narrow angle. The afternoon got its latest twist when Sunderland forward Death (terrible name – surely a bachelor) conjured up a stunning solo on the hour but just when the Reds looked to be heading for another 'glorious' Roker defeat, that man Smith muscled in for another equaliser. United's cup run had found its Mark Robins.

At the very least, the club had secured a place in the hat for the quarter-finals draw. When it took place that Monday, second division was paired with first division in every case. The road to Wembley – or the semi-finals at least – had now opened up for the surviving top-flight outfits, City and Bolton included. As if the replay wasn't saddled with enough tension and pressure already. Sixty thousand Reds raced out of work (or bunked off early) to make it to the game. At half-time they were burning with the full flush of cup fever. This time it was United, maintaining their impetus from the weekend and playing the brighter, pacier football, who established a two-goal first half lead, McPherson motoring and dribbling for a goal that rivalled Death's effort from the weekend and Smith – who else? – bundling in the second at the far post.

If anything, the Reds' interval position should have been even stronger. Enough chances had been made and missed to have seen off all the remaining cup teams. When the script from Roker started to reverse itself in the second half, it looked like United would suffer for their wastefulness. Five minutes after the break, Sunderland secured a foothold; ten minutes later, with the ball nestling in United's net, it seemed that the tie was level once more. Outrageously, according to the visitors and press, the 'goal' was not given, the referee, who had initially pointed to the centre, ruling it out on the word of his linesman. It was the lucky escape that Chapman's men needed. Sunderland dominated the final third but never looked like beating the incomparable Mew again. Their lone souvenir from the tie would be the wave of sympathy arising from the season's biggest refereeing controversy but even that was lost when they initiated an infantile attempt to get the game replayed. Quite rightly, the authorities did not want to know. For only the third time in their history, the Reds were through to the last eight.

Three days later, Chapman's battlers brought February to a close with another powerful performance at White Hart Lane. It had been quite a month. Despite resting several regulars, United had welded three league wins to their cup exploits. Understudies Haslam, Sweeney, Hall and Jones had all impressed in rare run-outs, particularly Jones who would have been a fixture at almost any other club. But the Spurs 1-0 was to be the side's final league hurrah. Six points behind the leaders Huddersfield but with two games in hand, the Reds entered March as perhaps the best placed of the championship outsiders. Once they had cleared another obstacle on the road to Wembley, their league campaign veered wildly off track. The Cup was now their sole obsession.

FULHAM AT CRAVEN COTTAGE might have been a kind draw for a quarter-final but their home record in the competition demanded respect; both sets of Scousers had already been knocked out there. Showing how much they had picked up en route, the Reds delivered the ultra-disciplined performance that the occasion demanded to restrict their host's big-name scalp collection to that pair of curly perms. United old boy Pape obeyed the 'law of the ex' by cancelling out Spence's quick-fire opener and, for some time afterwards, the Cottagers had their guests just where they wanted them – in the football equivalent of the park toilets. But the side's chin was too solid to be unduly disturbed by the unsubtleties of a lower league attack and though there were times when Fulham lived up to their potential as a banana skin, United never looked likely to slip. The Reds had too much power and know-how for their opponents; best of all, they had Tommy Smith and it was the talisman's goal, in the opening reels of the second half, that settled the tie. Their belief and spirit drained from them, the Cottagers never threatened from there on in.

Returning to the dressing-room, the victorious Reds must have hoped that the other ties had delivered shock results. Swansea, Forest or Clapton would have represented dream partners in the semi-final draw, particularly Clapton who, presumably, would have accepted any reasonable pre-match offers for their best players. In the end, only Swansea made it through, surprising Arsenal at the Vetch Field. Lucky Bolton bagged them in the last four. Which left United with a place in the showpiece tie at Bramall Lane alongside the side that had just triumphed 6-1 in the Orient – and by the same score at Old Trafford. If the Reds were going to make it to Wembley for the first time, they would have to get past City first.

Before January, the Blues would have been regarded as a plum draw. The Old Trafford embarrassment and City's cup-form had altered perceptions. In five matches they had banged in 28 goals. Champions Huddersfield had been demolished 4-0 in the fourth round, punch-bags Palace 8-3 in the fifth. The Blues were now well known as a team who could beat – and lose to – anyone on their day, a reputation the club carried with them right up to the modern era when the beat-anyone part was dropped. Their league form during the cup run had been abysmal. Seven days after thrashing Huddersfield in one competition, they had lost 5-1 to them in the other. No league wins in February had left them bottom of the pile. For most of the season, Mancunian double talk had been confined to Old Trafford. Now there was a strong possibility that City would manage a classically Blue version of the Double – winning the Cup and going down.

Enigmatic City versus United's archetypal cup-fighters; vibrant attack versus resilient defence. Most agreed that it was too close to call, most agreed that the outcome would depend on which City turned up. *The Manchester Guardian*, perhaps showing its true colours after years of negative United coverage, just edged towards the Blues: 'Manchester is entirely divided about the possible result at Sheffield. The United undoubtedly have the better defence, but the City have a forward line capable of great deeds when in their best form and of miserable failures in other hours. Everything depends on the mood of the City attackers. If they are at their best it is believed that the breaking-up ability of the United defenders will be of no avail, but about such a team as that wearing the City colours there can be no certainty.'

Thoughts now turned to securing a ticket for the biggest Mancunian tête-à-tête of the century. True to form, the FA were making it as difficult as possible. Between them, the two clubs were allocated just 1,700 seated tickets. By contrast, 10,000 stand tickets were set aside to be disposed of in Sheffield. 'Thus this all Manchester match is little better than a farce,' *The Guardian* thundered, 'and, unless they take their chance in the crowd, hundreds of people on whose week-on-week support the City and United rely and exist may be deprived of seeing an occasion that is almost unique in the history of the competition.' As great a source of frustration was the choice of venue. Compared with the super-stadiums in Manchester, Bramall Lane was viewed as a second rate ground. Plus it was in Yorkshire. Taking the game out of the county seemed unnecessary when Goodison Park provided a bigger and better Lancastrian alternative. But if Mancunians felt hard done by, they were urged to spare a thought for the followers of Bolton and Swansea who were faced with a trek to London (and double prices) for their semi-final tie. Presumably the FA's reasoning was that White Hart Lane is roughly equidistant from both towns – but if you go down that road, so is the

Maracana.

Cack-handed arrangements and gripes about locations and allocations were not the only cup themes that have survived to modern times. The future of Wembley stadium was another familiarly contentious issue. Just three years after the opening, White Horse, final, the press were convinced that the ground was about to host its last showpiece. The three previous Wembley occasions had cost the FA a small fortune – something like £10,000. Around half that figure had been refunded to ticket holders from the opening match who, because of the chronic overcrowding, had only been able to see a sea of caps, a policeman and a horse's butt-cheeks. The rest had gone to the ground's owners, the British Exhibition Authorities, in rent.

In their original agreement with the BEA, the FA had agreed to hand over 20% of the gross receipts and also provide a £1,000 guarantee. That was a steep enough price to pay for a stadium they used just once a year. Now that the Exhibition was being liquidated, the costs had shot up even more, to a level which convinced the football authorities that Wembley was a luxury they could do without. Nor were they interested in taking on the twenties answer to the Millennium Dome full-time. When the site was put up for auction that summer, the FA, worried about the £½ million cost and eager to maintain the accepted practice of spreading representative games around the provinces, opted out of the bidding. To the disappointment of many, Wembley passed into the hands of a private consortium instead.

As we all know, that did not mean the end of the stadium's ties with football. The sale went through subject to the consortium honouring the obligations of the original contract between the FA and the BEA which guaranteed the game a Wembley finale until 1943 at least. In all probability, the links between the sport and the stadium would have been preserved regardless. The new owners were a football friendly bunch as they later demonstrated by giving the FA the option to use the ground for replays and Internationals. Contrary to the press predictions, Wembley would soon be taking a giant stride down the road leading from national embarrassment to national stadium (and pride and joy). Little did anyone know that it would not be all that long before it began to retrace its steps.

The controversy surrounding ticketing and Wembley at least diverted attention away from United's pre-Sheffield form. After embarrassing January and perfect February came distracted and winless March. The only really good moment came early on as the Reds scored three times in the final quarter of an hour to salvage a point against Liverpool. In most other years it would have been the sensation of the season. In the Sky years, the tape of the match, complete with the sound of Andy ejaculating over Martin, would have been headed straight for the top of the video charts. With the semi looming, it barely got a mention. Four days later, United's lingering hopes of the championship were snuffed out by reigning champions – and champions-elect – Huddersfield at Leeds Road. An ego-bursting mauling dropped the Reds down to sixth, eleven points off the top albeit with three games in hand. After that, United coasted. A Bolton side packed with reserves were too good for them at Burnden; a United side packed with reserves somehow scraped a nil-nil with Everton. Encouragingly, most of the main players emerged unscathed. The exception was Mew who played himself out of the cup team with an uncharacteristically unsteady run of form. But taking it easy was a gamble, particularly for a side like United who relied so heavily on pace and tempo. There were no guarantees that the force would still be with them when they needed it most…

Bramall Lane, March 27 1926

It often seems inappropriate, particularly for Reds, to talk of sporting setbacks in terms of tragedy and disaster. Munich has given us all a bitter lesson in perspective. But every now and then a result comes along that thumps you so hard in the plums that it almost feels like there has been a death in the family. The FA semi-final provided one such moment. They say there is nothing worse than getting beat in a semi-final because no-one remembers the losers – the beaten finalists at least have their moment of shared glory on the day of the final. That isn't strictly true. Try getting hammered in a semi-final and by your fiercest rivals to boot. Then it becomes clear that the one thing worse than forgetting the beaten semi-finalists is remembering them. For years to come, Blues would be on hand to remind Reds of an afternoon which made January's 6-1 feel like a triumph. Just about the only, minor, consolation was that comparatively few United fans were inside Bramall Lane to witness it. As a result of the FA's bungling, a match that could comfortably have filled Old Trafford and Maine Road combined attracted a crowd of just 46,450 (roughly 20,000 below capacity) of whom only about 15,000 were from Manchester.

United's biggest game in the inter-war period demands maximum coverage. Given that it was also the most desperate ninety minutes of the era, you may want to skip the next bit. This is how Ivan Sharpe, the chief football writer for the *Athletic News*, saw United's 3-0 defeat:

CITY'S TRIUMPH IN GRIM MANCHESTER SEMI-FINAL

TALE OF SIX AND THREE; BARSON, A BUMP AND A SLUMP; HALF-BACKS HOLD THE KEY

THE BATTLE OF MANCHESTER was a battle of nerves. Nothing new or surprising in that. But how was is that Manchester United were most disturbed by the nerve-storm that swept over the teams as soon as the ball was set rolling?

They seemed to be more dour and less impressionable than mercurial Manchester City.

A week ago, in fact, I wrote that the United had little to lose in the trying atmosphere that would rob the semi-final of finesse and frill, because they had little pretension to class. But the Cup-ties deceived again. Manchester United seemed to shiver in their shoes. They never struck a winning gait. They sliced the ball and slipped and stumbled.

Like the cricketer of a Lancashire League eleven who was informed by a sportsman near the boundary that he could 'run hard but not fast', they played hard but not well – not smoothly, never convincingly.

Their dash and devil ran to waste so that their spirit was steadily sapped. The quite alarming energy that they had generated to the cost of the Spurs and Sunderland was never developed and hurled into a collective effort. It was all individual helter-skelter. Consequently the lack of individual skill and subtlety in the side came, at times, to be rather painfully exposed.

TWO VITAL MOMENTS

No doubt they suffered by reason of the fact that Manchester City got in the first blow. The initiative was priceless to the winners. Once in the grip of the United's determined defence, they would have remained there, one thought. But they scored the opening goal, and that was the first important factor in the day's proceedings.

Manchester United made quite a scene about it, but I deemed it a good goal. 'Twas said that someone was pushed, but I saw no such persuasion [many neutrals and all Reds begged to differ], and when BROWELL headed the goal from Hicks' corner-kick the referee was within three yards of the incident. The ball sailed to Browell and Browell headed in. It was forced out again, but there is no doubt that it had been just over the line [see the brackets above].

That was the first decisive factor, and, as it arrived in the fourteenth minute of the match, it was precisely the kind of send-off this mercurial Maine-road combination required.

THE SECOND FACTOR

Now let the story hustle along – marking, as the struggle sways, that, whereas Manchester United's best efforts were fast cross-shots from Rennox and Thomas that skimmed the bar, the City wasted chances when Johnson danced around the ball before the goal, and when Roberts ran right through and shot just wide when challenged instead of touching the ball to Browell on his right, and – after the interval – when Hicks sent a goal the way of Browell but the inside-right got his toes in a tangle and let the offer slip.

So the second vital moment of the match is reached, and it is an ugly one, for the imp of which I have written suddenly shouted into the ear of Barson, and Cowan was knocked flat-down and out. A merciless crash it was, and altogether too vigorous. Cowan lay flat; Barson crouched on his knees, and the crowd, suspecting 'the old soldier', roared the more.

Being a wise man, the referee had kept a tight hand, had started out that way and kept it up. Everyone wondered what would happen to the United captain, and it is sufficient to say that he escaped with an obviously plainly-worded caution. It was a vital moment because Barson thereafter was not the same man.

SECOND AND THIRD GOALS

Previously opponents had given him more elbow room than any player in the field. He had generally got the ball, and though not the masterful figure of days gone by, had been quite a power about the premises. Now he, too, was nervy – cautious and subdued. And when that happened the bottom fell out of the United's defence.

The City attack then touched a higher standard and romped ahead by playing free, open football. First Johnson offered Browell another goal. Again the inside-right muddled the pass – though it was rather to his rear – and allowed Silcock to save the situation. Then Austin struck the post. Next Barson missed the ball – fancy that! – and permitted Hicks to send one more gilt-edged offering to BROWELL.

This time the City forward had discovered that the ball was not to be trusted. He dashed at it venomously and shot hard. That was the second goal and there – at the end of half-an-hour on the second portion – the story really ends, for the match was clearly over.

But two minutes later Steward gave the City the third goal. When ROBERTS broke through and topped his drive, the ball spun along the ground towards the post – a harmless sort of shot from a matter of fifteen yards, which Steward, by throwing himself at full length, pushed against the post and into the net, so rounding off another City revel.

FLAWS IN UNITED DEFENCE

Of course, it was not a memorable match. When City rivals meet in a semi-final and one side suffers what it considers to be an injustice, the tone of the match may undergo a threat. So it was at Sheffield and Mr Bunnell handled a difficult duty firmly and well.

But an all-Manchester semi-final did not promise anything more than a rousing game. It realised expectations by providing one more match in which it was a case of excitement over all. The strange thing was that the United were the greater sufferers.

There were serious flaws, for example, in the defence. Steward and Silcock played the part well enough, but what was amiss with the right flank? Moore sliced the ball and was generally indecisive, while McCrae was nothing more than a toiler. What is more, he toiled in vain, for there was no plan of campaign between half-back and back, and Hicks, the opposing outside left, all too frequently was uncovered.

To Barson's slump I have referred, but he contributed to the failure by too frequently passing back, or to Moore, instead of getting the ball to the wings. I thought Steward, Silcock and Mann, the only satisfactory members in defence, and in attack the story is of the same disappointing display.

CITY HALF-BACKS' TRIUMPH

The forwards suffered a deal from the Cup-tie feeling, no doubt, but they suffered also from the effects of the only really solid and consistent line of the afternoon – the City half-backs. Here was the only approach to greatness in the day's grim duel. Pringle – a terrier – Cowan – tall, a man and a half when it comes to heading the ball – and McMullan, with a badly-cut and early-plastered eye, broke the shock tactics of the Old Trafford forwards, and cut the attack into ribbons.

These were the match-winners, though the forwards are the men who get the goals. They stabbed into the uprisings so decisively that not a man in the United attack achieved even prominence. Dash is of no avail when the other fellow is quicker on the ball.

Those half-backs were outstanding, and though Cowan, being of bonny build, caught the eye, the men on the flanks were every bit as successful. So was Cookson at right full-back – a bold challenger, fond of the shoulder charge and, if not polished, bad to beat. These were the men of the match, for McCloy was wayward and Goodchild not too quick in movement or certain in his handling of the ball.

SIXES AND THREES

There will be no club scolding of an attack that scores three times, and so paves the way for another appearance in the Final. But there is no doubt that the forwards sinned around the goal. As a line they were quick and elusive, but the inside play had that dangerous failing.

Browell was slow, yet managed to be there or thereabouts at the vital moment. Roberts did not really come to life until Barson's decline, and Johnson, though pertinent, did not round off his work in the way the season has promised. Still, it was a Cup-tie, and they won well, and so much can be excused.

The consistency, however, was on the wings, where Austin and Hicks played the game that told by adopting open methods and lobbing the ball between the backs, keeping them on the run.

At the end of it all the City earned very thoroughly the victory. That no one can deny.

They travelled to Sheffield in a charabanc whose number consisted of sixes and three. Six chances they had, and three they seized.

MANCHESTER CITY – *Goodchild: Cookson, McCloy : Pringle, Cowan, McMullan : Austin, Browell, Roberts, Johnson and Hicks.*

MANCHESTER UNITED – *Steward : Moore, Silcock : McCrae, Barson, Mann :*

Spence, Smith, McPherson, Rennox and Thomas.

OTHER REPORTS, POINTING to the spell in the second half when a Red equaliser had appeared far likelier than a Blue second, were slightly kinder to the Reds. All were agreed, though, that Barson's indiscretion was the decisive factor in how the game panned out once City had sneaked their dubious-looking opener. It would have longer-term consequences, too, once the FA, despite the absence of any footage, took it upon themselves to look at the incident again. The referee, who had been standing just a few yards away when Cowan collapsed, had seen fit to hand out a lengthy lecture and a caution rather than a dismissal. The gents of the FA, who had watched the incident from their plush seats in the stands, felt that Frank's crime deserved some time and upgraded his punishment to a two month suspension. A case of Wengervision in reverse, perhaps? More likely, another shot fired in the anti-Barson witch-hunt. Even if Frank deserved a carpeting (which he probably did if only for his crass lack of restraint in such a big game), there cannot have been many footballers who have been let off by the ref only to be tried and condemned by the crowd.

City had a Red Rose Final against Bolton to look forward to, the defeated and deflated Reds nothing but the meaningless remnants of their League campaign. That they failed to lift themselves for a ridiculous schedule featuring ten games in thirty days should have come as no surprise; they were physically and mentally shot. Of those ten matches, only four yielded any points. In the five game losing streak that followed their 3-0 trouncing of Notts County on April 2, United scored two goals and conceded fifteen, almost half of them to Blackburn in a club record 7-0 defeat. They did, though, manage to see out the season in some style, winning three of their last four to finish a respectable ninth. Only once since the second championship season in 1911 had the club done better and had it not been for the distraction of the Cup, and the resultant fixture pile-up, they would surely have finished in the top three or four (just four more points would have been good enough for third).

Despite the twin derby humiliations, Old Trafford wore a well-deserved air of self-satisfaction at the season's end. In terms of progress made on two fronts, it had been arguably the club's second-best campaign ever, lagging only behind 1907/8 when the peerless Mangnall side won the title and reached the cup quarter-finals.

Talented youngsters were emerging from the club's successful reserve side, none more dramatically than centre-forward Chris Taylor who netted hat-tricks against both Sunderland and West Brom in the final days of the season. Despite consistently poor weather – and the still uncovered Pop Side – the season had been another financial triumph, with another five figure profit winging its way into the club's coffers. More icing had been added to the cake in April when Old Trafford had successfully staged the home international between England and Scotland. And also when Spence and Silcock had been selected for representative honours.

But perhaps the greatest end-of-season satisfaction was derived from events on the other side of town where City were imploding. On April 26, they lost to a late Bolton winner in the Cup Final. Just seven days later, they completed the second half of a tremendous losing double by joining Notts County in the drop. Going into the final round of matches, the Blues led Leeds and Burnley by a point and, because of their superior goal average, needed just a draw from their trip to St James' to guarantee survival. What happened next was the most dramatic exit from the first division yet. City missed a penalty and lost 3-2 to Gallacher's hat-trick, Leeds thrashed Spurs 4-1 and Burnley hammered Cardiff by the same score. The headline in the *Athletic News* read: 'Bitter Experiences of Manchester City'. To the amusement of Reds everywhere, they would not be the last.

ROLL OF HONOUR

CHAMPIONS: HUDDERSFIELD TOWN

FA CUP WINNERS: BOLTON WANDERERS

UNITED: DIVISION 1 (9TH) FA CUP (SEMI-FINAL) MANCHESTER CITY

ARTHUR LOCHHEAD

INSIDE-LEFT, JULY 1921 – OCT 1925, 153 APPS 50 GLS

A PERPLEXED *Football Chron* put into words the feelings of the vast majority of Reds when they wrote of Arthur Lochhead's surprise transfer to Leicester in October 1925: 'His transfer will be something of a tragedy to the thousands who have delighted in the skilled footwork, long stride and beautiful body swerve of the young Scottish schoolmaster.' Mistakenly swayed into the belief that Charlie Rennox was the better bet at number ten, United's directors would be given ample opportunity to regret their decision. Whereas Rennox enjoyed one fine season in a Red shirt before embarking on a Lucanesque disappearing act, Lochhead turned on the style for the Foxes for nine years, knocking in a century of goals and winning himself an army of admirers in the process. 'The Analyst' of the *Topical Times* was one of the most fervent:

'A player of amazing dexterity and altogether the artistic temperament,' he gushed in September 1928, 'Lochhead reminds me of a ballet dancer, so perfect is his balance, able to change the action of his feet in a trice. Accordingly, he plays the ball from one to the other while still moving ahead, while the hook pass made with leg outstretched to the ball which you think he has overrun is a thing rare in the game as it is astonishing. Lochhead has no pleas to subtlety and ball carrying, and there comes in contrast to his dainty ways a shot like a rocket. However he should make it oftener. The drawback about Lochhead is that having brilliantly made the chance he wants to perfect it. As a result he many times misses his way, for there is always superiority of numbers against him who will over-elaborate. That is where Lochhead falls. So great a craftsman should strike a happy medium for the realisation of it both in opening up constructive play and in the shooting area.'

His reputation for always looking for the Hollywood finish combined with the fierce competition for attacking places deprived Lochhead of the Scottish cap his artistry deserved. The closest he came to the international stage was when he represented the Home Scots in 1920 and the Anglo Scots eight years later. As a club player, though, he belonged in the very highest echelon and it was a damning indictment on the United directors that they never realised what a special talent they had on the books. For Arthur was far more than a pretty ornament; he was a consistent source of inspiration who could set up play, bring the best out of his team-mates, make goals and score them. In his four full seasons at the club, the Busby-born Scot (making him the first Busby babe?) scored eight, thirteen, fourteen and thirteen league goals – not bad for someone who supposedly fannied around too much) and had a hand in perhaps fifty more. By selling him to Leicester, the directors had effectively kissed goodbye to twenty-five goals a season.

A brainy player whose IQ did not plunge when he changed into his civvies, Arthur was an engineering student when he arrived in Manchester but subsequently took up teaching and the post of assistant headmaster at a school in Salford (a position he gave up in the spring of '24 in order to concentrate solely on his football – getting hustled out of the door was the thanks he got for his commitment). His academic background, his Scottishness and also his apparent distaste for bad language, particularly Barson's, could have turned him into a dressing-room outsider as was the case with Wood and McBain. However, there was never any suggestion that Arthur met with a similar fate. A fine pianist and a soulful singer, he was an integral part of the music scene on away days, a position that guaranteed him a prominent place in the dressing-room hierarchy. In the absence of any evidence to the contrary, there is no reason to dispute the obvious conclusion that off the pitch, as well as on it, Arthur was, by a distance, the most successful Scottish signing of the decade.

ALBERT PAPE

CENTRE-FORWARD,
FEBRUARY – OCTOBER 1925
18 APPS 5 GLS

ALBERT PAPE
MANCHESTER UNITED

IN TERMS OF drama, at least, Albert Pape's move from Clapton Orient belongs in the top two or three United captures of the century, right up there with the deal which brought US international James Brown to the club in 1932 (while other interested parties were waiting for him in Dublin, United's representatives smuggled themselves onto Brown's ship and a deal was done in the mid-Atlantic). Eight months of plain bustle later, it was clear why the Orient management had been prepared to accept John Chapman's cheeky pre-match bid. Stocky, strong and game, Pape was a good man for heavy grounds and lower league hurly-burly but lacked the pace and panache to make the jump up to the highest level. In many ways he was a panic buy, the directors acting quickly to fill the gap left by their controversial decision to cash in on top scorer Willie Henderson. With five crucial goals to his name, Albert did his bit to get United up but he wasn't a runaway success even in the second division and most Reds would have gladly swapped him for the man he replaced.

That did not make it any less of a surprise when the chubby-cheeked 28-year-old was flogged to Fulham after making just two first division appearances. Not fancying a permanent return to the capital, Pape only agreed to the deal on the condition that he could continue to live in Bolton and train with United. A similar arrangement would never be countenanced today but in the twenties it wasn't that big a deal. Save for the weekly practice match between the first team and the reserves, most clubs skipped the technical and tactical stuff during the week and concentrated on fitness work instead. As long as the players kept up their physical training, it did not really matter where they did it.

The arrangement did present some problems, though, particularly when the club that paid the player's wages clashed with the club that trained him. United's cup quarter-final with Pape's Fulham in March '26 was one such occasion. Sneakier trainers than Jack Pullar would have run Albert into the ground in the build-up to the tie, or, at the very least, ordered someone to give him a sly kicking. As it turned out, Albert played well and grabbed a goal but could not prevent his old club from progressing to the semis. Given that a Barson-led reception committee was waiting for him at training the following Monday, it might well have been the best result all round.

James McCrae

RIGHT HALF-BACK, AUG 1925 – AUG 1926, 13 APPS 0 GLS

JAMES McCRAE DID not play many games for the club but what his United career lacked in quantity it certainly made up for in terms of prestige. An unused understudy during the first half of 25/26, Jimmy benefited from an injury to Lal Hilditch to clinch a run in the side just as the Reds' cup run was gaining momentum. A solid workhorse, he played in both Sunderland thrillers, the quarter-final tie at Craven Cottage and the semi against City. Like most Reds that afternoon, the ex-Shaker was a disappointment, the *Athletic News* describing him as 'slow and hesitant'. During the close season he was transferred to Watford. It said much that Jimmy was the only established player who was allowed to leave.

THE FA'S REVENGE

THE NINETIES PROVIDED multiple reminders of the human frailties of the rich, famous and powerful. The royal family, for instance, endured a royal nightmare, its stock dipping dramatically amid a series of sex and marital scandals. The Queen's eldest three children all got divorced (though arguably the biggest surprise came when her youngest got married); the Duchess of York became the first royal to feature topless in the tabloids, the Sun's front page headline of 'Fergie's top' contrasting nicely with the 'Fergie's bottom' line on the back (which celebrated United's pre-Cantona plunge to the foot of the table in August '92); the Princess of Wales swapped (rugby) shirts with the England captain and by the time she died, was well on her way to building a reputation as a man-eater par excellence; as for Charles, he was no longer viewed as the big-eared eccentric who talked to plants, he was now viewed as the big-eared weirdo who wanted to return to earth as Camilla's tampon.

The political terrain was also dominated by sleaze. Spitting Image may have caricatured John Major as a grey, pea-obsessed bore (little did we know then about his gruesome penchant for Currie) but the popular conception of your average Tory was of an overgrown public schoolboy with an overdeveloped interest in hanky-spanky. The image of David Mellor and his Chelsea-clad mistress Antonia de Sanchez was revolting enough but the thought of Stephen Milligan swinging half-naked from the ceiling with a Jaffa rammed in his mouth raised the bar to unprecedented heights. Tellingly, the line doing the rounds was that his family were most embarrassed by the fact he was a Conservative. After four successive election victories, the Tories finally drowned in this torrent of scandal. They should really have gone the election before but the country could not quite bring itself to vote in Kinnock. Ginger and bald was not a good start. Slipping into the sea at Brighton just about finished him off - not since the days of King Canute had a British public figure made such a knob of himself on a beach..

Elsewhere, Hugh Grant gave us - and her - something to chuckle about when he hooked up with Divine Brown; Gary Glitter got sent down once it became obvious what it really took to be a member of his gang; and the Guildford Five were reprieved after twenty years inside. The public's faith in the police and the justice system then took another battering as Deirdre Rashid was put away for a crime she did not commit. His smarmy hand forever on the public pulse, Tony Blair got involved in the campaign to free her. Unfortunately it paid off, paving the way for more Deirdre-Ken action on the couch at Number One - surely a sight as unattractive as any on the box, Gail and Phil Thompson excepted.

Football was hit by bungs and drugs; rugby by old farts and drugs; cricket by ball tampering and match-fixing. Skeletons were emerging from closets on an almost daily basis. And old timers who tut-tutted about the 'kids of today' and their 'lack of respect for authority' ([TM] moaning dodderers everywhere) still did not get it. No, not that they were retired so they no longer had to climb out of bed and straight into a shirt and tie but rather that there is less respect generally because there is generally less to respect. It is the media's fault of course. The more exposure public figures receive, the more the public find out about their warts and defects; the more blemishes we find, the more they seem like us; the more they seem like us, the less likely they are to inspire automatic awe and respect; the less we respect public figures, particularly those in positions of authority, the less we respect authority itself.

Charlie & co. chose the wrong era in which to misbehave. If they had been around seventy years earlier, when the media were that much less intrusive, they might well have got away with it. The public eye was so short-sighted back then that Charles could have pranced up and down the Mall in a man-sized tampon suit and still not made the papers. Likewise, if Mikhail Gorbachev's time had come at the other end of the century, few people would have ever known about the strawberry mark on his head (even in the eighties, the Soviets were airbrushing it out of official photos). Public figures could, quite literally, hide their blemishes under their hats.

So, despite the complete cock-up that upper-class buffoons had made of fighting the war, the establishment's hold on its subjects remained more or less watertight. But there were leaks, and there are no prizes for guessing where one of them had sprung. Even before the Meredith years the Reds had been firmly anti-establishment. The perception that the FA were still determined to get their own back for the Outcasts affair had strained the relationship between the club and the authorities even further. It was not just a case of innate Mancunian suspicion of authority either; there were compelling reasons for believing that the club had been made the targets of an FA witch-hunt. Red visits to Lancaster Gate always seemed to coincide with a reverse kind of Happy Hour in which all fines and suspensions were automatically doubled.

So, when United had fielded a weakened side for a league fixture in the run-up to the 1909 Cup Final, they were stung with a record fine. When they had given a trial to the son of legendary Outcast Dick Duckworth and made an innocent error regarding his registration, they were fined five guineas. Two other clubs who were found guilty of the identical offence were fined just two. Once the FA had declared an amnesty on all previous under-the-table payments, John Henry Davies was the only chairman who was forced to make his club's public. The supporters' conspiracy theories about the chances of United players earning international honours were not just paranoia talking either. Men like Barson and Roberts should have won bagfuls of caps; instead, Roberts won just three and Barson never added to the lone appearance he made during his Villa days. 'Unfortunately for the ex-Villa man,' wrote the Casual in '24, 'he is now playing for a Manchester club and this part of the map is largely unknown to the body of gentlemen who are able to grant honours in the game.'

Somehow Ernest Mangnall, who knew his way around the game's shadows better than anyone, had always proved too slippery for the FA. Unfortunately, they had not given up hope of making up for the one that got away. No one would have predicted it when the season started, but John Chapman was a dead man walking. Five months after the club's highest inter-war peak, the authorities were gleefully strapping him into their electric chair. And when Chapman fried, United's hopes of building on their recent success fried with him.

*   *   *

OCTOBER 8 1926 - THE DAY A SEASON DIED

THE COMMISSION APPOINTED by the FA in September to enquire into Red affairs announces: 'That for improper conduct in his position as

Secretary-Manager of the Manchester United Football Club, Mr J. A. Chapman be suspended from taking any part in football or football management during the present season.'

Manchester and the rest of the football world could not have been more gob-smacked if Frank Mann had run off with Dixie Dean. 'Mr Chapman suspended!' spluttered *The Football Chronicle*. 'It seems incredible. Never has such a cloud passed over United.' Here was one of football's good guys, a man known as 'Gentleman John' wherever he went, being ousted from his position as manager of one of the biggest clubs in the country over allegations of wrong-doing that he absolutely denied. It read like a bad joke and as none of the parties were prepared to reveal what 'improper conduct' Chapman had supposedly been guilty of, many football people refused to believe it; among the shoals of sympathetic letters the Scot received were many from his associates in the game. Reds were convinced that he had been made a patsy; the *Football News* tapped into their line of thought by rehashing the old gripe about the club not being forgiven for the Outcasts.

Frustratingly, there is more chance of finding out if Neil Armstrong really did make it to the moon, or if Marilyn Monroe voluntarily swallowed her final sleeping pills, than unravelling the Chapman mystery. The FA were sufficiently arrogant not to see the need to explain themselves to the public, United as a club took a similar view to public relations, categorising everything on a do-not-need-to-know basis while Chapman, who gave up football and went on to make a hefty fortune running a speedway and dog track, limited himself to a single interview with the *Topical Times* in which he said:

'It is putting it very mildly when I say that I was surprised to hear of the FA's decision to suspend me. I am suspended for what is described as improper conduct. That is, to say the least of it, a very vague and strong way of wording it. I can well understand that questions will be asked, and hasty conclusions formed which will be very wide of the mark.

'And yet I feel that I still have the full confidence of the big majority of the United Board, players, and countless friends I have made in the football world since I have been in England.

'"Improper conduct" may mean anything. Frankly, I am at an utter loss to know what it means in this case, and I say so very emphatically, in view of what transpired at the meetings of the

Commission and the evidence and statements made there.

'I cannot feel otherwise than upset about it all, and yet I am not worrying unduly. I have made one decision already, and that is to write to the FA to ask under what rule I have been suspended.

'I have nothing whatever on my conscience. I have worked conscientiously for Manchester United, and, apart from my salary, I can say honestly that I have never benefited a single penny piece in any shape or form.

'There are numerous occasions upon which I have, in the interests of the club, been out of pocket, but that is a mere detail. I cannot possibly discuss the matters which came before the Commission.

'But I will say this, that I considered them to be purely domestic, and merely concerned the club itself, and these dated back to more than a season ago.

'If I had been guilty of misconduct, should not the Board have dealt with me? In any event, what I do want to make very clear is that the matter brought before the Commission was reported by one of my own Directors, and I consider that any statement that has to be made should come from the Board [no chance, mate].

'It is quite possible that there will be some speculation as to my future movements. All I can say is that those who are wondering will just require to have a little patience, and wait.

'Reverting to the meetings of the Commission. I only attended with the members of the Board at the sitting in Manchester on September 20. I was perfectly frank with the Commission. I had no reason to be otherwise.

'Already I have received many sympathetic letters and telephonic messages from friends in all parts of the country. These have heartened me very much.'

It is frustratingly enigmatic stuff. At one stage, Chapman hints at a set-up cooked up between a United director and the FA. At another, he suggests that he does not understand what he has done wrong to warrant being suspended. Later on, however, he refers to 'domestic' events from a year or so earlier. Because John refused to expand on them, and no records of the Commission's investigation survive at Soho Square, the affair remains shrouded in mystery. Since then, only local journalist and Chapman confidant, Alf Clarke, has shed any real light on it. In 'Manchester United', his 1948 history of the club, he wrote: 'I know full well all the circumstances, and I know that had John come out into the open he would have cleared himself very easily. But a player was involved and John Chapman preferred the matter to rest at that.'

The Commission's ruling would have been a blow at the best of times. Its timing made it a disaster. If he had been hung out to dry a couple of years earlier, Chapman would have barely been missed. But his record in the two seasons just gone had been remarkable. Promotion, ninth place in the top division, semi-finalists in the Cup, a combined £21,000 profit... more of the same and many Reds would gladly have taken a bullet for him.

If the directors had been trapped in a burning boardroom, on the other hand, many would have thought twice about calling for help. The Chapman affair aggravated the existing rift between club and fans; the arrogant silence of the directors as big a turn-off as your average Reader's Wife. Chapman's suspension was a shock but in truth his departure was not. As far back as September 13, the *Athletic News* had 'exclusively' reported that John would be on his way when his contract expired at the end of October. In reality, it had not been quite as dramatic an exposé as the front page headlines had made it sound. Towards the back pages, nestled among the adverts for Chelsea Dubbin' ('How to stop that CODE FROB CUBBIN? Rub your boots with CHELSEA DUBBIN'!' Eat your heart out, Saatchis...), the 'Cup-winning' Manfield-Hotspur football boot (regularly worn, it was claimed, by 80% of British teams and, as they covered half the leg in leather, a steal at just 19/6), Cadbury's chocolate (1s for a half-pound block) and fags (1s for a pack of twenty) came the following:

'The Directors of the Manchester United Football Club Ltd are prepared to receive applications for the position of Manager of the Club as from November 1 next. Applicants must have the merit of previous success in similar positions. Must be an economical administrator and practically experienced. Applications, which will be treated in the strictest confidence, to be sent, with full particulars, to Mr J. H. Davies, marked "Personal" at Woodside House, Salford.'

Shamelessly, the United officials refused to confirm or deny the stories that they were advertising for a new manager. Their silence even extended to that month's Shareholders Meeting. 'Are you going to tell us that you refuse to give us any information why this advert appears in the paper?' queried one punter. The reply from the top table was a haughty 'yes'. The club had made their feelings clear.

Except when they were paying their money at the gate, the supporters were as welcome as shit in a snowball. All the shareholder-supporters could do was show their dissent by attempting, unsuccessfully once more, to unseat one of the members of the board – this time George Bedford – and by moving a vote of confidence in Chapman, one that was carried to hearty cheers. But if the directors felt smug after their latest 'victory', they should have known that a war with their own was one they could not possibly hope to win.

Presumably the applicants for the United job were not of a sufficiently high calibre; possibly the man they really wanted would not be available until the end of the season. Whatever the reason, the club opted against bringing in a new man from outside. Instead, they experimented for the first – and, so far, only – time with a player-manager. Faithful Lal Hilditch was their choice as manager

Lal Hilditch

and Walter Crickmer, an administrative legend-in-the-making, was brought in as the new secretary. As ever, the papers toed the party line, claiming that Hilditch was a 'very wise choice'. He may have had the respect and confidence of the players but wise choice? Not a chance. At best, Lal was an unnecessary risk. The second season in a new division is renowned for being the toughest. On top of that he had to cope with the inevitable backlash resulting from the shock departure of a manager who, according to *The Chron*, 'had endeared himself to the players as few other managers have done.' And they say that Wilf McGuinness, another managerial rookie, had problems when he inherited the 1969 European Cup semi-finalists from Sir Matt. In the circumstances Lal did fairly well just to hold on to his hair.

There were no guarantees that United would have avoided second-season syndrome even if Chapman had been spared. The Reds stumbled out of the blocks and straight into a bizarre run of results which suggested that those critics who had dismissed them as mere flash in the pans would avoid the previous autumn's experience of spewing on humble pie. Remarkably for a team that were renowned for not scoring many and for conceding even less, United scored two goals in each of their first eight outings but did not taste victory until the sixth of them. Having supplied the season's first seven goals, Frank McPherson in particular must have wondered whether he had been made the target of some elaborate practical joke; 2-2 draws against Sheffield United, Leeds and Arsenal and 4-2 defeats at Anfield and Newcastle were a lousy return on his red-hot streak. Then, when all the piss seemed to have been taken, the selectors sucked out some more by relieving the Bullet of his number nine shirt. Beadle could not have done it any better.

United's winless start, and particularly the events at St James's where they were torn apart by Hughie Gallacher, triggered a wave of neurotic predictions that they were doomed to the drop. Such a notion was met with scorn in *The Football Chron*: 'Nonsense! There are many teams in the upper circle at the moment immeasurably behind United.' An early-season injury crisis had to be taken into account, too. The side's unfamiliar defensive frailty was due in large part to their unfamiliar-looking defence. Steward was an ever-present but Moore had yet to feature while Silcock was just entering a spell in which he missed as many games as he played. Reds would have to wait until mid-December for the reunion of their defensive kingpins.

Hilditch, Barson, Thomas, Rennox and Taylor were all kept out for varying lengths of time as well. At least Barson's collection of knocks, particularly his nagging groin ('what did I tell you... I told you I needed stretching for longer'), did not sideline him for long. If beer was his weakness, Frank's ability to play with injuries that would have crippled other men was an undeniable strength – at Newcastle, his legs looked like they had just been through a machine but he was still United's most impressive performer. Exciting rookie, Chris Taylor, was the biggest worry. Just months after announcing his potential with a brace of hat-tricks, the 22-year-old was in hospital having a cartilage removed. Sadly, his was by no means a unique experience. Chris was just one of a clutch of bright young things from United's successful reserves who set off on the road to football stardom – and ended up on a ward at Salford Infirmary.

Fortunately, the squad had enough strength in depth, certainly in defence and midfield, to weather the injury storm. Chapman had taken some wrong turns in the past, most notably in his Airdrie and Clapton-obsessed phases, but his touch in the transfer market was improving. For every disaster like Wood, Ellis and Pape there was now a McPherson, Mann and Jones. This year's trading had offered further evidence, if not of a Midas touch, of the manager's burgeoning eye for a bargain. Two more talented players had been pocketed for next to nothing. Jack Wilson, a clever all-rounder who specialised at left-half, had arrived from Stockport; Billy Chapman, a right winger who had made no less a judge than Billy Meredith drool, from Sheffield Wednesday.

The competition to bookend Barson in midfield was now intense. For the time being, Wilson got the nod over Mann on the left while Bennion took advantage of Hilditch's on-going injury problems to cement a regular place for the first time on the right. Really, though, any combination of those four plus Barson's deputies, Grimwood and Haslam, would have done. The signing of Chapman, meanwhile, gave the selectors the option to move things around in the attack. Despite his goals, McPherson had never been considered the definitive answer in the centre. There were many who felt that Frank's strengths – his pace, shot and goal output – were outweighed by his defects – his poor link-up play and unimaginative distribution. Billy's arrival opened up the possibility of moving Spence back to his first love and shifting McPherson back to the left.

In retrospect, though, the extra attacking options were a handicap in disguise. Joe was no more a subtle leader of the line than was Frank while any team would have missed his work on the far right. Then there was the perennial problem of the selectors' addiction to tinkering. In 25/6, the dearth of alternatives had forced them to persevere with the same forward combination. As a result, the club had fielded their most consistently effective front five for years. A year on, it was impossible to predict how the attack would line up from one week to the next. Only once, in early winter, did the selectors pick the same combination more than three times in succession. On-pitch relationships – between forwards and also between forwards and half-backs – that had been built up over the past couple of years were badly affected as a result. Two of last season's heroes, Rennox and Smith, suffered the most. The breakdown of both men's relationship with their wing partners ended in a quickie divorce – with the club.

The home draw with Arsenal eventually represented the final moments of good sense before the meddling that blighted United's season kicked in. Initially, though, it seemed that the ends would justify the means. Eight-goal McPherson was bizarrely repatriated on the left for the visit of Burnley on September 22 but Spence came in and immediately fired the Reds to a 2-1 win, their first of the season. The changes played their part, as did the visitors' atrocious offside trap, but Red passion – on and off the park – was probably the difference between the sides. 'The United were not impressive,' wrote Jacques. 'Though victorious, they were ragged, possibly because they were so determined. But the spirit of the Manchester United men is just as amazing as it was a season back. The Old Trafford crowd has spirit too. No club, perhaps, can roar quite like it – none better, anyway. What a pity it grew so excited as to forget that no referee is quite so wicked as to deserve a boo!'

Booing crowds were a particular bugbear of the press. So was the growing tendency, or so the papers intimated, for players to dispute the decisions of the officials. 'Unless there is a change for the better,' Jacques added, 'the FA will have to take steps to protect the reputation of the game by dealing more drastically with players who dispute the referee's decision. Of itself it is sufficiently undignified and unsportsmanlike to inflict injury on the game and with the evil comes the further peril of crowd incitement.' Most reporters, their rose-tinted spectacles wrapped full-time around their faces, could not bring themselves to admit that behaviour on and off the field was no worse than it had been in the so-called golden age before the war. Respect for the officials had been so profound back then that they had needed to keep themselves in shape, not to keep up with play, but to give themselves a chance of beating the mob to the dressing-room, and afterwards the station. In Victorian times, in particular, many supporters felt that the right to molest the ref came with the ticket. And it would perhaps raise the standard of refereeing today if a similar fate awaited their ineptitude today. I'm not being serious, of course, but the image of hundreds of Reds chasing David Elleray down Chester Road unquestionably carries a certain appeal...

In the wake of the news that United were advertising for a new manager there were discernible signs that the players were 'doing it for the Gaffer'. The Burnley success kicked off what, in the context of a painful season, represented a mighty peak – three wins on the bounce. On successive weekends, Cardiff were steamrollered at Ninian Park and Villa outplayed at Old Trafford. The latter result sent the losers, if only momentarily, to the foot of the table. You can take it for granted that Barson's stint at the bar went into extra-time that night. For the second season running he had saved one of his rare goals – this time a thumping header – for his old team. Not only that but he had been the game's outstanding figure; along with his new accomplice, Wilson, the mastermind behind United's best work.

As the FA Commission delivered their verdict the following Friday, the Villa 2-1 brought down the curtain on the Chapman era. In positional terms it closed with the Reds in reasonable shape, down in thirteenth but just three points behind first-placed Sunderland with a game in hand. Mentally, though, the team were in a mess, still shell-shocked by the sensational departure of the popular Scot. If Hilditch was not already aware of what he had let himself in for, he soon would be. His first match in charge, away to cup-holders Bolton, was an eye-opener on a par with finding your dad in bed with the vicar. United were blitzed 4-0, the new regime saved from an even more ignominious start by the home side's wastefulness and Steward's brilliance.

Admittedly, the absence of two of the side's mainstays, Barson and Spence, had not helped the new manager's cause. Joe was away with the Football League XI, and played well enough in the 6-1 thrashing of the Irish League to earn his second England cap the following week. The curiosity of the same player being viewed as the best outside-right in the country and the best centre-forward at his club was not lost on observers (or, presumably, McPherson). Frank, meanwhile, missed out with an 'acute pain in the groin'. Ever hungry for Barson stories, there were those who were reluctant to believe that he was in fact injured. Had he had his nose put out by the club's decision to bring in Hilditch over his head?

Possibly. The potential for conflict with the dressing-room's most dominant personality was just one of a myriad of reasons why Lal was drinking from a poisoned chalice. The transformation from player to player-manager is a notoriously difficult one to negotiate at the best of times. As Gianluca Vialli discovered at Stamford Bridge, it basically requires a personality transplant – from one of the lads to potential bastard. What made Hilditch's task particularly arduous was that, while the selectors would carry on aiming the bullets, he would be the one doing the firing. As a player, Lal had commanded the respect of his team-mates but how long would that last once he started telling them they were out of the team or, even worse, that he was replacing them?

Another post-Burnden rumour suggested that the players, in a half-hearted protest against the FA's treatment of Chapman, had decided not to try. The papers dismissed it as absurd. In his farewell address to his players, the Scot had expressed his heartfelt wish that they should get behind the new regime. According to *The Football Chron*, he said that 'if the players wanted to remember him, and do him a kindly turn, they would play the game for all their worth during his suspension'. He then added that 'Clarence Hilditch was one of them and it was up to the team to support him in every way possible'. Despite their well-deserved reputation for gullibility, the press view was probably correct. Not trying did not fit in with the character of this team, nor the club. If they were honest, most of the 26/27 side would have admitted that they would never have made it as far as Old Trafford had they been anything but 100 per centers – few of them would have made it by skill alone. Even after the October revolution, United's main problem was not a lack of spirit but a lack of goals.

A week after Burnden, signs of Red solidarity were emblazoned all over Gigg Lane as United, with Spence back and helping himself to a double, pulled off a surprise 3-0. But their next goal did not arrive until the trip to Filbert Street, four games and four weeks later. In the interim, the reviews for the ever-changing front line lurched from the acerbic to the scathing. Not even the returning Barson could get anything out of them at St Andrews. 'Barson is the finest constructive centre half-back playing,' observed the Impressionist. 'I know what a real forward line would be like in front of Barson... generalising on this display, they are one of the poorest forward lines I have ever seen in senior football... the club ought to be thankful for serviceable wing half-backs, two fine backs, and a goalkeeper living up to the one saving grace – defence.' Another Saturday brought another defeat, this time a resounding 4-0 at Upton Park. Then came a soul-draining home stalemate with Wednesday to start November. The best action of the afternoon took place on the Pop Side where rival factions clashed in a rare terrace battle.

By then, United had slumped to sixteenth place, five places and just two points above the relegation places. Most Reds were bracing themselves for a winter of discontent. But if they were in need of some perspective, their luck was in. For most of the year, shafting the miners (a decent title for Graham Rix's autobiography?) had been a national sport. Now, after holding out for seven months, they had finally been forced to abandon the fight that had culminated in May's General Strike.

*　　　　　*　　　　　*

MINERS HAD LONG since earned a reputation for downing tools at the drop of a canary but since the 1921 strike which indirectly led to United's near miss on the Moors, they, like most workers, had tended to steer clear of industrial action. They would still have gladly used the pit owners for pick-swinging practice but the recession had taken the edge off union militancy – walking out was an unnecessary risk when there were so many people around who were desperate to inherit your clocking-in card. The partial cease-fire lasted close on four years, until the middle of '25. By then the industry was even deeper in crisis, knee-capped by the unlikely mix of then chancellor, Winston Churchill, the Germans and the Poles. Churchill made a fundamental economic cock-up, returning the pound to the Gold Standard at too high a rate and consequently making life even harder for British exporters. Meanwhile, the coal industry's main European competitors, Germany and Poland, had emerged from their post-war slump and were undercutting British prices. By July 1925, it was official government policy to enforce wage cuts. The pit owners went even further, increasing working hours and enforcing a local, rather than national, wage – bad news for miners who worked in struggling pits.

The miners would have walked out then had Baldwin's government not stumped up millions in wage subsidies and launched an enquiry. It was solely a means of buying time. The Samuel Report, which called for better working conditions and opposed an extension to the working day but supported wage cuts, raised heckles rather than the prospect of lasting peace. The owners could not have been less impressed had they found the chief trumpeter – or trumpet-polisher? – from the colliery band in bed with their missus; the unions if they had found Mr Samuel in bed with theirs. With the TUC pledging its full backing for the miners, the battle lines were drawn. When the owners put up lock-out notices in an attempt to force through the wage cuts, the TUC gave the go-ahead for the unprecedented General Strike.

Initially, the solidarity of the workers was impressive. Railwaymen, dockers and bus and tram drivers came together to offer united resistance to the notion that enforced wage cuts would solve the mining problem. In total, almost two million workers manned the pickets. But their solidarity dissolved in a matter of days. The contingency plans that the government had drawn up in the nine months it had taken to compile the Samuel Report worked well. Coal stocks were high; the weather was mild; an army of soldiers and volunteers kept the transport system, if not running, then at least moving. The government took the honours in the propaganda war too, branding the Strike unconstitutional and the strikers the enemies of the country. Recognising that they were on a hiding to nothing, the TUC backed down on the ninth day. But the miners pushed on, still chanting their mantra 'not an hour on the day, not a penny off the pay' until starvation and wintry misery finally drove them back. November 12 was a dark day both for the striking miners and for the trade union moment as a whole. The miners' seven month struggle had effectively been pointless; in the end, the owners got everything they wanted, including the dismantling of the treasured national wage.

The miners were left with skinny ribs and the deep-lying conviction that they had been betrayed – by the owners, the government, even by their fellow workers. As an unhappy season lurched into December, Reds were in a position to empathise. Disappointment and betrayal seemed to lurk round every corner. And that despite some respectable results which returned them to mid-table. United lost on an anarchic afternoon at Ewood Park (more of that later) and were humiliated 6-0 at Sunderland but also won back-to-back against Leicester and Everton and drew, commendably, with Huddersfield, the champions. But the best results were invariably the work of the defence. Their eyes opened by the team's trophy-chasing exploits the previous season, Reds now wanted more than spirit, organisation and a concrete rearguard. They had had their fill of missionary position football; now they were hungry to explore the Karma Sutra. Unfortunately, this forward line had little idea how to unbuckle their own belts, never mind locate the Pop Side's G-spot. Bland and often inept, they were a betrayal of the attacking ethos laid down for the club in the Mangnall era. And the supporters were letting them know about it with increasing vehemence. Spence was universally popular but Partridge, Rennox, Smith and McPherson (a permanent villain unless he was scoring) were all regular targets for the boo boys. It was no coincidence that three of the side's six wins so far had come on their travels – the forwards regularly played better when they were out of range of the sharp tongue of the Pop Side.

* * *

MOUTHY SPECTATORS HAVE been part of football ever since some bright spark blew up a pig's bladder but no matter how much a player deserves their abuse, there is nothing that will convince me they are doing the right thing. Slag the bastards off all week and boo at the end by all means, but 'get behind them for the ninety minutes' should be one of the commandments in the supporters' bible. Unfortunately for Partridge, McPherson and the rest, the Pop Side housed a noisy crew of agnostics who took the view that cutting off their nose would not spite their face. The lone consolation for those twenties scapegoats was that their experiences were by no means unique. Even now, during the (relatively) good times, Old Trafford is well-stocked with supporters who like to spend as much time on the players' backs as their numbers.

It is strange what gets the veins bulging at the ground today. Being crap and/or a waste of money used to be the yardstick by which potential victims were judged but in recent years a trend has emerged whereby players guilty of either of the above are given disproportionate levels of support. It is a sign of the siege mentality that has gripped all Reds from Fergie downwards that players who are targeted by the media stand a good chance of being fast-tracked to cult status. The more criticism Andy Cole received in the press, for example, the more popular he became with the crowd. To a lesser or greater extent the same phenomenon has done wonders for the image of May, Silvestre, Forlan and Blanc. Even Phil Neville had a song (admittedly a tongue-in-cheek number) dedicated to him.

Conversely, there was a time when home-grown talents were automatically backed to the hilt. Not any more. Reds still like nothing more than watching a latter-day Babe emerge from the ranks but there are plenty of grumblers around who think nothing of turning on them once they have made it. Red antipathy for anything to do with England – or Posh Spice? – helps explain why David Beckham's relationship with the support suffered in the wake of his elevation to the status of nation's darling. But what about Giggsy? On the face of it, he should have always enjoyed the unconditional backing of the fans no matter how severe any slumps in form – after all, he is a local lad, a genuine Red who shafted City as a kid, a loyal and successful servant and, for a decade, the first name on every England manager's wish list (bar Glenn Hoddle who, of course, would have wished for Glenn Hoddle). Instead, Giggs has torn his own support apart and, in the process, lumbered himself with his own devoted band of detractors.

Giggsy-grumbling provides a useful insight into the psychology of recent Red barracking. Envy plays its part. Young, rich, good-looking (and that's just his girlfriends); sometimes it is too much for gruff old Reds – whose only experience of knicker-wetting is putting their wives' in the washing machine – to bear.

The suspicion that he and other high-profile players are more committed to their social lives than to their football is another factor. Most Reds revel in the club's reputation for glamour but that does not prevent many of us being suspicious of it. Thus, when Giggsy became one of a number of mid-nineties stars to be snared by Dani Behr, it became common practice to ascribe mistakes he would have probably made anyway to the perception that they were spending more time in bed than John and Yoko. Funny, that. For all we knew, Ryan could have been the epitome of professionalism while a less sexy player, or at least one who managed to keep his private life out of the papers, could have been out all night drinking Canal Street dry (admittedly, not a pleasant thought). Likewise, Denis Irwin could have passed the time between matches by squeezing into a pair of leather lederhosen, clipping clamps to his nipples and getting a Steffen Effenburg look-alike to light him up.

Perhaps, though, the key point in the Giggs debate is that he has never quite delivered on the great expectations that have surrounded him since he was Ryan Wilson. Most Reds recognise that there will never be another George Best, if only because the nostalgia industry has elevated him to a god-like status that makes him untouchable. However, for a time, it really did seem that Ryan was capable of reaching Best-like greatness. In such a context, his enduring faults – his right foot, his crossing, the suspicion that he does not turn it on in the really big games – have taken on an unwarranted significance while his strengths have been relegated to the sidelines. Nor is Giggs alone in suffering from comparisons that he would never have asked for. Now that the Champions League is the benchmark by which United's seasons are judged, it is no longer acceptable for Reds just to turn it on in the Premiership. They have to cut the mustard in Europe too. Such is the price that the players have had to pay for the rising standards and expectations of the Ferguson years.

*   *   *

THE PSYCHOLOGY OF the barrackers was different in the twenties. Being a footballer was a sexy occupation but United's set of forwards were not; they were as glamorous as Grimsby. Their pay packets, restricted to a maximum of £8 a week, were not that sexy either. Certainly it was not out of the question for the man on the street to be earning more. Unlike today when criticism of a player's performance is invariably linked to the amount of money he earns ('£40,000 a week and he can't score a penalty...', '£50,000 a week and he can't kick with his left foot...' etc.), the players' wages and lifestyles could not be used as a stick to beat them with. The supporters were solely bothered about how committed they were and how well they could play. And the general consensus was that most of the forwards were not fit to pull on the shirt. The right to barrack them was one of the few perks of buying a ticket. The fans' ultimate hope was that their vocal demonstrations would galvanise the directors into spending some of Chapman's £21,000 legacy and thus fulfil the President's wish of building a forward line that matched the standards of the defence. Yet despite the club's protestations that they were scouring the country in search of attacking reinforcements, the money remained unspent.

Following so soon after the ostrich-like manner in which the club handled Chapman's departure, the lack of transfer activity further aggravated the rift between the public and the board. The relationship between the club and the FA, meanwhile, slumped again as the authorities reacted to November's Ewood anarchy by handing out another slice of rough justice. In the closing minutes of United's 2-1 defeat, Jack Wilson had lost his rag with Blackburn's international forward Sydney Puddefoot, kicking him to the floor. The incident had prompted a pitch invasion involving three or four thousand Rovers supporters which culminated in heights of disorder not seen in the town since they clamped down on sex between siblings. Before the police arrived on the scene to usher them to the dressing-rooms, several United players, Charlie Moore in particular, received a minor seeing-to.

With the safety of the players being paramount, you would have imagined that Blackburn would have had the book thrown at them. Instead, the FA banned Wilson, who had previous, for two months (that wasn't quite as harsh as it sounds; in the twenties, suspensions were much rarer but far more severe) and let Rovers off with the merest of slapped wrists; a warning that Ewood Park might be closed if the fans misbehaved again and an order to post warning notices at the ground and publish them in the programme. The Commission declared themselves satisfied 'that the conduct of the spectators at the conclusion of the match was consequent upon the action of Wilson'. Effectively, the FA had given the spectators carte blanche to seek retribution for sins committed against their team on the pitch. But what about the players? Should they not have the right, as Eric Cantona felt he did, to fight back; to seek retribution for abuse directed against them from the terraces? After all, if it was good enough for the goose...

The point that emerged from the furore surrounding Eric's Selhurst kung-fu was that any normal person who was subjected to a similar campaign of sustained, xenophobic abuse would have some recourse to the law. When they are out on the pitch, there is nothing to protect footballers from levels of abuse and slander that would otherwise land the perpetrators in court. Eric took the only course of action that was open to him at the time. But it is not beyond the realms of possibility, particularly in our increasingly litigious society, that players and managers will eventually take legal action against clubs whose fans slander them. In years to come, singing something along the lines of Wenger's 'cheeky smile' song may land United in court.

*   *   *

AFTER THE EWOOD riot and the Roker Park rodgering, the visit of rock bottom West Brom provided a welcome easy ride, the Reds strolling to victory with a Sweeney brace in the opening quarter. Their morale boosted, United then netted five points from their holiday foursome with Arsenal, Tottenham and Sheffield United, a reasonable return given that some foreskin in the League fixtures department had scheduled three matches at opposite ends of the country in the space of just four days. Steward took a starring role as the Reds battled to a Christmas Day draw at Spurs. In the rematch, three of the floundering forwards finally stepped up to the plate, Rennox and Partridge shining on either flank and McPherson scoring twice to underline the point that, on his day, he was as likely to find the back of the net as anyone. Few players in the country could have scored Frank's match-winning second. Almost scorching the Old Trafford mud with his pace, he cottoned on to a pitch-length defensive gump, sped past three defenders and embarrassed the 'keeper.

Arsenal took advantage of tired limbs to win at Highbury just twenty-four hours later but the players were clearly refreshed for the visit of Sheffield United on New Year's Day. Possibly inspired by the reappearance of Hilditch for only the second time as player-manager, certainly inspired by Barson, the Reds roasted the Blades by the tune of five second half goals to none. They created enough chances to have won by double that score. If it had been ten, Barson, who netted the goal of the game with a low-flying header, said he would have walked around all night with his hat off (how big a moment that would have been depended on what it was covering – after all, Frank did live in Full Monty country). For the first time under Hilditch, United had shaken off their club-in-crisis mantle – their home treble had lifted them well clear of the relegation places. Reds could now look to the future with some confidence. And then they met Reading in the Cup...

Losing to a lower division side is embarrassing enough in any circumstances. Losing to a lower division side after being outplayed in the original tie and two replays is the stuff that laughing stocks are made of. Every underdog can have their day. Reading, promoted from the third division only a season before, enjoyed three on the row and should have completed their giant-killing act long before they actually did so. The 1-1 score-line at Elm Park almost insulted them. In the final quarter they lost a player to a broken leg, took the lead, had a man sent off for making an offensive gesture at Barson in the subsequent celebrations and were only dragged back in the final minute when Bennion – a first teamer since '21- finally nodded in his first-ever senior goal.

The Old Trafford replay made for similarly painful viewing. As an attacking force the Reds were rewarded beyond their just desserts, a goalkeeping disaster handing them a lifeline after they had fallen behind on the half-hour and only the excellence of Steward keeping their noses above water once the visitors had equalised Sweeney's second. United's luck eventually ran out in the second replay, played in front of several thousand Barson-haters at a supposedly neutral Villa Park. Typically, it was the game they least deserved to lose.

Trailing to McPherson's sharp free-kick, Reading were beginning to run out of ideas when they were made the beneficiaries of the worst penalty decision outside of Escape to Victory. When the referee first blew his whistle, both sets of players, presuming that he had spotted an obvious foul on Moore, turned and headed for halfway. Instead, and despite United's lengthy protestations, the official placed the ball on the spot. Reading accepted the gift and, with confidence surging through them, scored again to progress to the fourth round. Damningly, *The Manchester Guardian* wrote: 'The better team won, and at times Manchester were made to look very small by their Second Division opponents.'

What a difference a year had made. The previous January, Reds had been dreaming of a double. This year they were already dreaming of August. With four months remaining, their season was effectively over. The only prospect they had of genuine excitement – and we are talking about something that would have tempted Frank to sacrifice more than his hat – was if United sank low enough to become involved in the relegation scrap. Fortunately, the stragglers were so far adrift that the Reds were nigh on safe already. Nonetheless, they made a good stab at joining them in the mire. Between January 8, the date of the original tie with Reading, and April 2, United played eleven league games and picked up just six points. For the second season in succession March was pointless (this time literally so). By then, even the defence, worn out by the continual strain of compensating for the shortcomings of the attack, had started to fall apart. On successive Saturdays towards the end of the month, the Reds lost to Birmingham, West Ham and Wednesday by scores of 4-0, 3-0 and 2-0.

The side's cup heroics had bought them some immunity from criticism the previous spring. That immunity had long since worn off – like Pacman once he stopped flashing, United were again vulnerable to attack. By now, the supporters' pre-Christmas disillusionment had developed into ranting apoplexy. The boo-boys had never been noisier; pre-match, the seats on the dressing-room toilets had never been warmer. As for the postman, he needed protective clothing so barbed were the letters that flooded into the offices of the football press. The criticism ranged from the standard of the half-time band to the old chestnut of covering the Pop Side. Most, though, focused on the main point, that unless the club spent money to improve the forward line there would be a supporter exodus of biblical proportions. And, in George Greenhough, the fans already had a leader who was capable of filling Moses's sandals.

What follows is just a taste of the bile that was spat in the direction of the board:

'I THINK IT is a disgrace to the United directorate that a poor club like Hull City can pay £4,000 for a forward. I think that every United supporter will agree with me when I say that had it not been for the magnificent defence of Steward, Moore and Silcock, the club would have been now keeping company with West Brom at the bottom of the league. If the club had had two good inside-forwards, they would still have been fighting for the cup.'

Disgusted from Ardwick.

'AT PRESENT THEY have only two forwards on the books who are worth their place – Chapman and Spence, same position. As for the rest they simply cannot do any better. This is shown every week, at Old Trafford or away.

'When will supporters make a proper move to show their views and make United part with a little of that £21,000 profit they made? Which is better, 35,000 people every home match going away satisfied at seeing tip-top play or 20,000 people going away grousing at the "lot of old women"? Have United acquired a first-class forward since their ascent into the First Division?'

G. E. Eaton

'ONE HAS SENTIMENTAL reasons for supporting United but sentiment dies too. The management will find this out if we are subjected to many more inept displays.'

'Old Trafford'

The directors, for their part, kept repeating the mantra that they were striving to bring in new talent but would not be held to ransom. They refused to pay the inflated prices they were being quoted by clubs who were well aware that they had cash to spend. The managerial situation at the club mustn't have helped the search for new blood, either. Unlike his predecessors, Hilditch had yet to compile a little black book packed with contact numbers. Also, potential targets may have been put off joining the Reds until they found out whether Lal was merely a stop-gap appointment or the long-term choice. My guess, though, is that the directors were never genuinely interested in flexing their muscles in the transfer market. They had other uses in mind for Chapman's profit; principally, owning the Old Trafford ground outright. This had been a deep-seated ambition of the United board. In February, they agreed terms with the Manchester Brewery Co. to buy the land for £10,150 while another £11,200 was set aside to cover the rent still owing up to March 1927. In June, the deal went through.

In a sense, you can see why the directors did not feel the need to act on the exodus threats. The supporters had undermined their own position by turning up in their droves all year. Considering the season the club were having, as well as the lingering belt-tightening effect of the General Strike, their loyalty had been exemplary. Championship-chasing Sunderland were attracting an average gate of 14,000. In mid-February, and in mid-decline, United pulled in twice that number for their messy 1-1 with lowly Cardiff. But it wasn't long afterwards that the fans began to vote with their feet. The derby games with Bolton and Bury would normally have generated a combined crowd of 80,000-plus; in the spring of '27, neither gate rose above 20,000. When transfer deadline day passed without any new signings, many regulars opted to spend their shillings elsewhere. Reports suggested that hundreds of Reds from the Swinton district were turning up at the rugby league instead. By early April, when United finally dragged themselves out of their two month winless streak with a hit-and-run 1-0 against Leicester, just about the only thing missing from the picture of desertion on the Pop Side was the tumbleweed.

The gaping holes in the terraces finally shook the management out of their complacency and into decisive action but, frustratingly, the only player they had in their sights was the caretaker, Hilditch. Two days after the Foxes win, the directors downgraded him from player-manager back to plain player. In truth, they should have put him out of his misery months earlier. Too nice, too inexperienced, too close to the players, perhaps betrayed by the board who refused to sanction much-needed spending, hamstrung by injuries, suspensions and the post-Chapman hangover, Lal had clearly been the wrong man at the wrong time. In the circumstances, he was probably more relieved than upset to have his title sawn in half. But the player-manager experiment he had been subjected to had not been a complete disaster. There were some good memories for him to take back to the ranks; that mid-season run of five wins in ten matches, plus two results that stood out like diamonds in the turdish new year decline – the 3-2 win at Leeds in late January which nudged the Tykes closer to eventual relegation and United's result of the season, February's wholly unexpected 3-1 trouncing of Newcastle, the champions-elect.

Lal's replacement was Herbert Sydney Bamlett, a stern-faced forty-something who had been lured from Middlesbrough just as he was on the verge of guiding them back to the top flight. Hopes were high that the club had found a worthy successor to Robson and Chapman. The media, at least, were confident that he was cut from the right cloth. Bamlett had built a reputation as an astute judge of a player, his teams were renowned for serving up

Herbert Bamlett

entertaining, attacking football, and he knew his way around the right half of the top division, having steered Oldham to the runners-up spot in his first season in management (in 1914/15). In his latest, his Boro outfit had feasted on the second division like no side before. By its end, they had banged in a league record 122 goals of which George Camsell, Bamlett's most talked-about discovery, contributed a record-breaking 59 (had Dixie Dean not outscored him by one goal the following season, Camsell would have become as fundamental a part of football anorakia as the score between Arbroath and Bon Accord and the winners of the first World Cup – 36-0 and Uruguay if you're interested).

Cut away the predictable excitement and optimism generated by his appointment, however, and there were stains on Bamlett's CV that needed explaining. In a sense he owed Middlesbrough their promotion as he had been the man who had taken them down in the first place. It was significant that the Boro directors had been prepared to let him go before he had finished the job at Ayresome. Did they suspect that he would struggle again in the top flight? Did they already have a better option lined up? In hindsight, the question that should have been bothering United fans was not whether Bamlett could find them a Camsell but whether the club had found themselves a one-season wonder.

As so often happens when there is a change of manager – and, most pertinently, a new man to impress – United's form picked up dramatically. Inspired by the goals of Spence, who netted seven times, the Reds ended the campaign with an unbeaten run of two wins and six

---

1. *'anyone but United'*

draws to finish a flattering fifteenth. But the mini-revival came too late to raise the spirits of the support. By waiting so long before taking any preventative action, the directors had effectively waited until the post-coital cigarettes were stubbed out before slipping on a condom. The Pop Side remained pregnant with discontent as 'Casual' of *The Chron* pointed out in his end-of-season review: 'The curtain is rung down on another season, and there can be little to create enthusiasm amongst the supporters of the United. It has, to my mind, been a season which will go down in the history of the club as one fraught with suspense, little enthusiasm, and numerous complaints.'

But if United fans were miserable, at least they could be miserable in the top flight. After another dose of last-day agony, Blues were facing another season in the shadows. Before the final round of matches, promotion-chasing City lay in third place, level on points with second placed Portsmouth but with a minutely inferior goal average. The Blues faced Bradford at Maine Road, scored five goals in the first hour and ended up with a thumping 8-0. A promotion place seemed guaranteed when the news flooded through that Portsmouth, who had kicked off fifteen minutes later, were being held 1-1 at half-time by Preston. But then Pompey launched an astonishing second half recovery, scoring four times to pip City by six thousandths of a goal, or one goal scored that afternoon. The *Athletic News* called it a brilliant failure. What they really meant, of course, was that City were brilliant at failure – which other club, when needing to win by a landslide to go up, would score eight and still end up one short?

Given the ABU[1]-ist abuse that United fans have copped in recent years, it may well be hypocritical for us to derive so much satisfaction from the goings-on across town at the Comedy Club or from other classic non-United moments, most memorably Michael Thomas's championship-stealing winner at Anfield in '89. What makes your typical ABU-brigade member a particularly unattractive piece of football lowlife, though, is that they seem to take more pleasure out of United doing badly than they do from their own club (if they have one, apart from 'Anyone But United', that is) doing well. As long as your main passion remains Red, I cannot see anything wrong in cherishing moments like this...

A Brilliant Failure

'...Immediately the whistle sounded the huge crowd [at Maine Road] surged across the playing pitch and it was only with difficulty and the assistance of the police that the players made their way to the dressing-room. Everyone was eager to congratulate them on the magnificent fight they had made and on 'getting back'.

'Meanwhile it had become known that Portsmouth had got the lead, but it was not until half an hour later that the tragedy was unfolded. Despite their brilliant effort the City had not succeeded. The band had played "Auld Lang Syne" but it was not good-bye to the Second Division. By some infinitesimal fraction of a goal they have to go through it all again.

'Joy was turned to disappointment that could be felt, but everyone's sympathy was extended to the players and the club. Never has there been such a cruel blow of fate in the history of the league.'

As the headline said: Brilliant.

Roll of Honour

Champions: Newcastle United

FA Cup Winners: Cardiff City

United: Division 1 (15th) FA Cup (3rd Round) Reading

DEPRESSION YEARS LEGEND

JOE SPENCE

CENTRE-FORWARD OR RIGHT-WINGER
MAR 1919 – JUNE 1933
490 APPS 160 GLS (TOTAL 510 APPS 168 GLS)
B. THROCKLEY, NORTHUMBERLAND 15TH
DECEMBER 1898
D. 31ST DECEMBER 1966
HEIGHT: 5' 8½" WEIGHT: 11ST.
DEBUT: DERBY COUNTY 1-1 UNITED 30/08/19

Career: *Blucher Juniors, Throckley Celtic, Army football, Newburn F.C., Scotswood, United Mar 1919, Bradford City June 1933, Chesterfield May 1933, retired 1938 close season*

International career *(for England)*:
2 apps (England 5-3 Belgium at Antwerp 24/05/26, England 3-3 Ireland at Anfield 20/10/26), 1 gl (v Ireland)

'TO MY MIND, Spence has been a fortunate person to obtain international honours. True, he has his international days, but also very much the opposite. I regard him as a most excellent club player, able to play at centre or on the wing, and there can be no doubt about his earnestness and grit. But I cannot place him among the leading school of wingers, for the reason that he is too stereotyped. We have seen him flying along the wing, unstoppable almost, for England and club, but there was something lacking in a defence which permitted this, for there is only one lane for Spence, full speed ahead, pushing the ball on, and bang into the centre with it. Sometimes he flies inside, and again will double back, but this is usually fatal. Like the rest of his forward-colleagues Spence is spontaneous enough with little guile. Quite on the contrary, a deal of his play is the obvious, and thus we have the occasions when he is quite easily held by the thinking half-back or back. But he can shoot, and comes with a crash into the ball crossed from the other wing. He knows the value of the 'first-timer', and though impetuosity makes many a miss, there is often a valuable billet from his foot.' ('The Analyst', writing in *The Topical Times,* October 13 1927).

In football, as in most walks of life during the Depression Years, there was a tendency to look back on the days before the war as some sort of golden era. In Edwardian times, or so the theory went, the sun never stopped shining, every minute seemed like hours, the ugliest women made Mary Pickford look like a saggy-faced trout and professional sport was an orgasmic mix of craft, guile and cap-launching entertainment.

OK, logic dictates that the monotonous majority who harped on about the good old days had a valid point. The four-year hiatus in League football had slammed the door shut on many great careers and it would inevitably take time for the next wave of stars to emerge. In general, however, talk of Edwardian football reaching some sort of stylistic perfection was so much romantic bunkum. United in particular had raised standards to new levels in the late noughties but they were ground-breaking freaks rather than representative of the general standard. The English game had always been based fundamentally on strength and aggression. Those pundits who were now sneering about 'modern' football's devotion to speed and power rather than skill and flair had either been brought up in Scotland or were writing in a dream-world. If the players appeared less skilful it was probably because they had less time to be so. The game quickened up after the war and then went mental after the change in the offside law. Football was evolving and the critics did not like it – and they would have liked it even less had they seen how quick it was going to become.

As a hard-running, hard-shooting ambassador for modern football, Joe Spence was one of the principle victims of the common perception that it sucked. In the national papers, no profile of Joe was complete without some condescending reference to his plain style, his occasionally suspect control and his limited bag of tricks. The Analyst wasn't alone in sneering that he had been fortunate to be capped twice by his country. In their blinkered pursuit of this idealised version of an international forward, the critics had missed the point; Spence would never have pretended to be another Meredith but he was brilliant nonetheless. He was not just the best forward that United had in the twenties, he was the club's best two forwards rolled into one, excelling both at centre-forward and in his international position of outside-right. Forget his plain style, the only fault that Pop Siders could find in him was that he could not play in both positions at once.

The obvious question then is which position was his best. Joe himself preferred life in the centre and no less a judge than Frank Barson raved about him in the role, nominating his team-mate as one of the most dangerous number nines in the game: 'I know I may be considered a little prejudiced,' he said, 'but that is neither here nor there. All I am concerned with is my opinion, and I say again that Joe Spence is a dangerous customer to handle.'

A stunning strike rate from the centre of roughly two in three made sense of Barson's commendation. However, it was as an outside-right that Joe truly excelled. The perceived weaknesses in his game as a centre-forward – the question marks over his control, distribution and size (he was a wiry 5ft 8in) – were not so relevant on the wing where he could showcase his lightning feet and crossing skills without unduly diluting his goal threat. His opponents rated him highly, even if some critics did not. Naming Spence as one of his 'best opponents' (in a 1925 article for the *Topical Times*), Everton's Harry Hardy wrote:

'Most of my readers will have seen this player, and will agree with me, I think, that he is a real top-notcher. Spence is a terrier-like player, and never knows when he is beaten. He is very speedy, even for a winger, and he has a partiality for cutting in towards goal, and delivering those nasty, oblique shots. And he gets some power behind them, too! Spence is very smart at placing his centres, and on occasions I have found that he can get an uncanny screwing power behind his crosses. This is especially noticeable when he is taking corner kicks.'

Whatever the critics felt about him as a footballer, all were agreed that, as an all-round footballing personality, Spence demanded a place among the sport's true greats. Most players have to wait until the end of their careers before they get to read their own eulogies. Joe was reading his when his career was still in its short-pants stage. In September '27, the Official Programme enthused: 'The nature of Joe Spence has become something of a historical fact at Old Trafford. Perhaps we can say we have never had a player who means so much to the club – is so popular with everyone and who is so versatile. Joe Spence, I believe, would play anywhere in the interests of the club. He has been a long time with us now, and we hope he will be with us for many, many more seasons. For without Joe Spence, the United team seems to be incomplete. A more wholehearted player there never was: a hard-working player to the end of the game and a popular figure with his colleagues, Joe Spence has won the esteem of all with whom he has come into contact.'

Outgoing and mischievous, Joe was the friendly face of the dressing-room directorship; together with his great friend Charlie

Moore, the unofficial 'Minister of Fun'. On away trips the pair formed a two-man variety act, a mix of songs and gags, and if Charlie had the richer voice it was Joe who had the better material. On one occasion, during a stop-over at Southampton, a well-known comedian, George Gregory, came down to the team hotel to entertain the troops. As it turned out, he needn't have bothered; Joe seized top billing for himself and wisecracked his way through a thirty minute turn.

If he was vital for team spirit, Spence was also a godsend for the directors who benefited from his willingness to play anywhere for the sake of the team. And if Frank McPherson and Teddy Partridge jostled for bottom place on the supporters' cigarette card wish-list, Joe was undoubtedly their number one pick. He had everything the Pop Side were looking for in a hero – he was loyal (numerous enquiries by other clubs were met with ridicule), he was hard-working, he was rattle-swingingly explosive, he created goals and he scored goals. Those Reds who were looking for a forward to worship had only one real choice in the Depression Years, the little north-easterner with the elusive swerve and the shock of curly hair.

When the Pop Side awarded him the ultimate accolade, his very own catchphrase, Spence's status as the team's most popular individual was beyond dispute. For almost a decade, no United match was complete without someone in the crowd shouting 'Give it to Joe!'. According to conventional wisdom and the player himself, the catchphrase had its first airing during the 1926 semi-final disaster when Joe was criminally neglected on the wing. You don't need to be Cagney and Lacey to realise that as several supporters on the Bramall Lane terraces that afternoon were waving 'Give it to Joe!' placards, it must have dated to before then.

What is inarguable is that the phrase took hold on the terraces and stayed there, lasting well beyond the club's shock decision to sell their talisman to Bradford City in June 1933. When Spence returned to Old Trafford for the first time as a visiting player the following November, the Supporters' Club demonstrated their appreciation of his record-breaking service by presenting him and his wife with a canteen of cutlery. As the Club's bigwigs prepared to hand over the gift, one wag in the audience shouted out – you've guessed it – 'Give it to Joe!' In comparison with the other 'rib-tickling' anecdotes from that time, believe me, it stands out as a comedy gem.

JOHN GRIMWOOD

HALF-BACK, MAY 1919 – JUNE 1927
205 APPS 8 GLS

JACK GRIMWOOD GAVE the Reds eight years of splendid service but, rather like Lal Hilditch, probably ended his career thinking he should have achieved so much more. Hyped as the new Roberts when he made his big breakthrough in 1920/21, Jack failed to sustain his early brilliance at centre-half and instead developed into an extremely useful utility man who could turn it on in every half-back position.

Jack's metamorphosis from leading light into unsung hero began almost before the pundits' drool had dried on their ties. Just four months after being hailed as the club's newest star, the young Geordie was out of the team, a victim of the selectors' chronic impatience and his own unsteady form. The arrival of Neil McBain and, later, Frank Barson pushed him out of contention for the central berth and precipitated a move to left-half, a position he occupied for most of the next four seasons. During that time, Grimwood rarely got the credit his smooth all-round play deserved (when Barson was around, Jack, like everyone else, tended to be shunted into his shadow) but he was an important cog in United's engine-room, a point recognised by the *Athletic News* in their pen pictures of the 1925 promotion-winners: 'Grimwood is a native of South Shields who has discovered one great secret: how to keep the ball down. Has rendered excellent service.'

Sadly, Jack's career was never quite the same again after the promotion campaign. Cartilage trouble restricted him to just eight appearances during the 25/26 adventure and by the time his knee had healed, Frank Mann had taken root on the left of midfield. Barson's injury nightmare did allow Jack a run of games in the centre in 26/27 but a part-time role did not appeal and the reluctant deputy left to join the fledgling Aldershot Town in the summer. If only he had bided his time. Jack was still in his twenties when Barson moved on in 1928 and there is every chance that he would have gone on to enjoy a lengthy Indian summer at Old Trafford like his half-back colleagues, Hilditch and Mann. Instead, he passed quickly between Aldershot, Blackpool and Altrincham and United splashed out £3,250 on Billy

Spencer. What a waste – on both counts.

TOM SMITH

INSIDE-RIGHT, JAN 1924 – JUNE 1927, 90 APPS 16 GLS

A £600 SIGNING from Leicester midway through 23/24, Tommy Smith took time to justify even his inconsiderable fee but eventually represented excellent value for money. The sort of bloke whose pint you would not want to spill, Tommy was well-endowed with weight and muscle (often over-endowed with the former), possessed a decent touch, a howitzer of a right foot and a work ethic that would have shamed Sir Alex. His ability to hold the ball up, his relish for the physical battle and his capacity for unremitting toil made him perfect shotgun material. Apart from Jimmy Hanson, and, presumably, his missus, he was the best partner that Joe Spence ever had.

The downside to Tommy was his lack of speed as well as his disappointing goal return. A tendency to shoot from hopeless range as well as his general unselfishness restricted him to just a dozen goals in eighty-three league appearances and placed him at a serious disadvantage when the free-scoring Hanson emerged as a genuine threat to his place. As the home-grown and clearly talented Mancunian was the darling of the crowd, it was not unusual for Smith to be barracked by his own supporters whenever he was chosen ahead of his young rival. The chunky north-easterner deserved better. In 24/25 his late-season return, alongside Barson, had provided the key that ultimately unlocked the door to the first division. And in 25/26 no one did more than Tommy to propel the Reds to the verge of the Cup Final.

His 'golden-balls' spell in the midst of United's epic cup run was undoubtedly Tommy's career high. When he played like he had concrete ones in 26/27, the directors, their thinking perhaps clouded by the anti-Smith feeling on the Pop Side, sold him to Northampton for just £250. Seven years and two low-grade clubs later, the hero of Roker Park died, aged just 33.

Clatworthy 'Charlie' Rennox
Inside-left, Mar 1925 – July 1927, 68 apps 25 gls

Tagged, by a sceptical public, as a poor man's Fred Kennedy, Charlie Rennox lived down to expectations with a sluggish start to his United career but recovered in spectacular fashion in 25/26, scoring seventeen goals in thirty-four league appearances to emerge as the surprise inspiration behind the club's finest inter-war season. Impressive upper body strength and a deceptive turn of pace made him a hard man to dispossess while his heading ability gave the attack a dimension it had previously lacked. Frustratingly, the sturdy Scot was unable to hit the same high notes in his second full season as a Red and by the spring of '27 the boo-boys were on his case again. In less than two years he had gone from the villain of the Kennedy affair to terrace hero and then back to villain again. He never recovered. Transferred to Grimsby that summer, Charlie disappeared without trace, failing to make even a single league appearance for his new club and then dropping out of league football altogether.

Jack Hall
Right-winger, May 1925 – May 1927, 3 apps 0 gls

Jack Hall had more reason than most to be pulling for United during their draining cup run in 25/26; the resultant fixture pile-up and Joe Spence's nagging muscle injury allowed him his only run of matches in the senior side. An ever-present in February ('26) when the under-strength Reds won all three of their league fixtures, the Bolton-born winger did well enough to earn another year's contract but the competition from the newly-arrived Billy Chapman as well as the consistent excellence of Spence denied him another taste of first team action. Released in the summer of '27, Jack was unable to get himself fixed up with another league club and was dumped on the football scrap heap aged just 22.

RICHARD IDDON

CENTRE-FORWARD, MAY 1925 – SUMMER 1927, 2 APPS 0 GLS

THROWN INTO THE first team for United's first game back in the top flight in 25/26, Richard Iddon never quite delivered on the promise he had shown pre-season when his speed and ability had been the eye-catching features of the practice games. His only other first team appearance for the Reds came at Burnley eighteen months later. The *Manchester Football News* summarised his performance thus: 'He is a keen, enthusiastic young player, and he almost ran his feet off but it is obvious that his day has not quite arrived.' It never did. Subsequent, goal-laden spells in the Lancs Combination with Chorley, Morecambe and Lancaster Town contrasted sharply with a barren period at third division New Brighton and served only to illustrate the point that, while Dick could score goals for fun in junior football, he was out of his depth in the proper stuff.

ALBERT SMITH

CENTRE-FORWARD, OCT 1925 – JULY 1927, 5 APPS 1 GL

ONE CLEVERLY-TAKEN goal in a 2-1 home defeat by Bury in March 1927 was as good as it got for Glaswegian forward Albert Smith during his short-lived United career. The *Manchester Football News* delivered a rare put-down when they summed up his impact thus: 'Smith occasionally showed glimpses of cleverness, but they were very occasional.' Meow.

CHARLES HANNAFORD

LEFT-WINGER, DEC 1925 – SUMMER 1927, 12 APPS 0 GLS

WHEN CHARLIE HANNAFORD joined United from Clapton, much was made of the fact that he had been a star as a schoolboy. As he was a month away from his 30th birthday when he followed in the footsteps of former team-mates Pape and Rennox, it was understandable that such a billing did not make Pop Siders giddy with excitement (not unless he had chronic learning difficulties). They were right not to be taken in. The Charlie Hannaford they saw before them still wore short pants but the days when he was thought capable of scaling the game's peaks had long gone. After playing second fiddle to Harry Thomas in his first season, Charlie slumped to fourth choice behind Thomas, McPherson and – the shame of it – Partridge the next and was back at Clapton for the start of 28/29.

RONALD HAWORTH

INSIDE-FORWARD, MAY 1926 – AUG 1927, 2 APPS 0 GLS

ONE-TIME BLACKBURN starlet Ron Haworth was only 25 when he joined United from Hull City in the '26 close season but his best days were already well behind him by then and he spent all but the opening three days of his Old Trafford career (when he was given two first-team run-outs in place of the injured Charlie Rennox) in the reserves. At the end of his only season with the club he was transferred to non-league Darwen.

*　　　　　*　　　　　*

UNITED IN THE NEWS

I - THE RETURN OF THE MAGNIFICENT SEVEN

IN 1927, BILLY Meredith hit the headlines again by starring, as himself, in a silent movie called The Ball of Fortune. No copies of the film survive today, so it was clearly no all-time classic, but the *Topical Times* film critic was impressed enough to give it a favourable review, writing in the February 12 edition of the paper: 'A British sporting picture which I think most people will like is "The Ball of Fortune". The somewhat complicated plot deals with the adventures of a young man who is swindled out of his money by relatives, and relates how in the course of his wanderings he makes friends with Billy Meredith, the international footballer, under whose guidance he becomes a popular favourite in the sporting world. James Knight is very good as the hero, and there is a capital football match, which is bound to arouse enthusiasm.'

The *Kinematograph Weekly* predicted that the film would be 'a winner' with 'popular sporting audiences' and praised Billy for a part 'well played'. The audiences in Chirk certainly liked it. According to Meredith's biography, they cheered every time he appeared on screen.

In March 1927 Jack Pullar cast aside his usual low profile to share some of his experiences as United trainer with the readers of the *Topical Times*. Admittedly, most of his tales belong in the 'had to be there' category but they do at least give some insight into life behind the dressing-room – or hotel room – door.

II – JACK PULLAR SPEAKS
JOYS AND SORROWS OF A TRAINER

THE BIG PART of a football trainer's duties is not to be found in massaging limbs and bodies. Nor is it to be found in deciding that this man needs five laps round the ground and that the other fellow can get along nicely with two. After a little experience these things become very simple. But the big problem is always with you; to see that the players are pleased with their lot and are kept in good spirits.

The players must have their jokes and the trainer encourages this sort of thing provided it is not carried too far. He must put his foot down very heavily when there is a chance of that happening.

The trainer must promote good feeling among the players. He must encourage fun in the dressing-room, but must frown on rowdiness. In doing so, the trainer himself gets a lot of amusement, at least that has been my experience at Old Trafford. Most of the players I have had through my hands have all been very keen on a joke. Stripped in their red and white jerseys they may have seemed otherwise to the spectators, but in their lighter moments some of them have proved a rare handful to me.

By Candle-light

I remember on one occasion we were drawn against Tottenham Hotspur in the Cup, the game to be played at White Hart Lane. To ensure that the players would be quite fresh we left Manchester the Friday afternoon and spent the night at Chingford, where Burnley did their special Cup training this season.

Chingford may now have become quite modernised, but at the time I speak of it was old-fashioned indeed. Our hotel was lighted by oil lamps, but when going off to bed a candle was provided for everyone.

The candles tickled the lads greatly, and I sensed that there would be trouble before I got them all safely to sleep. I have always made it my duty on these trips to see that all the players are safely bedded before I go away for the night. The reason for this is that I never know what trick they may be up to.

On this particular night I intimated that it was bedtime. The players went upstairs with their candles and half an hour later I went to have my tour of inspection. All seemed well, but on passing one bedroom I heard voices. I stood and listened. The voices continued and grew louder, so I thought I had better look into the matter.

The Shadow On The Wall

Opening the door quietly I found Frank Barson and Charlie Radford, who was unfortunately killed in a motorcycle smash some time ago, warmly arguing over something on the wall. They should have been safely in bed, as I told them quite seriously, but when I discovered what they were arguing about I found it very difficult to keep a straight face and be serious.

A candle placed on a table does not give much light, but it causes big shadows. These shadows, I discovered, were the cause of the discussion. Barson and Radford argued as to which of their noses cast the bigger shadow on the wall! Each of them in turn had stood sideways to the wall and had traced out the shadow of the other's nose with a pencil.

I was called upon to settle the dispute and decided in Barson's favour.

BILLY IN HIS BATH

I have been called upon to settle more serious arguments. One I remember well occurred in the visitors' dressing-room at Anfield, Liverpool's ground. One of the parties concerned was Billy Meredith, who argued while in the bath, the other side was represented by a famous football legislator, who is one of the leading lights of the Lancashire FA. He was assisted by Mr Dave Ashworth, then manager of Liverpool and by the ref in charge.

The occasion was the Final of the Lancashire Cup, in which United met Liverpool. It was May, but it was hot enough for July. Ninety minutes had been played without a goal being scored, which was a distinct compliment to us, for we had played most of the time with nine men and a crock.

Early in the game we had Forster so badly hurt that he had to leave the field. Soon afterwards Sapsford went lame. Still, we struggled on till time and were still on level terms. Half an hour extra was then played, but even in this extra-time Liverpool could not score a goal, and after two hours' gruelling in the heat our nine men and a crock were glad to leave the field.

THE ANTI-CLIMAX

Within a minute of entering the dressing-room Billy Meredith and Jack Silcock were in the bath, congratulating themselves, when in came a deputation wanting us to play another twenty minutes extra. Liverpool were very keen to do so, but our lads would not hear of it.

Some of them had been doing two men's work and their feet were worn raw by running about on the hard ground. The Liverpool deputation appealed to me to get the United out on to the field, but I said that the matter had better be decided by the players themselves as they were most affected.

It was a deadlock. Billy Meredith, up to the chin in water,

became the spokesman, being captain, and said he knew of no rule of the Lancashire FA that authorised a game being extended the way Liverpool wanted. He thought both clubs should be joint holders of the trophy until August when another game could be played. Billy's argument, I think, was perfectly right but in the end, after much persuasion, he was prevailed upon to leave the bath and play another twenty minutes.

Liverpool were very pleased, but they were amazed when we scored. With a minute to go we were still leading and the ball rolled gently towards our goal. Jack Mew made to pick it up, but Charlie Moore waved him aside. Charlie was going to boot that ball well and truly, and over the stand if possible, and so put the issue beyond doubt. But Charlie missed the ball and it rolled over the goal line for the equaliser!

What a scene in the dressing-room after the game.

JOE SPENCE AND HIS DOG

Joe Spence, as most people know, hails from Scotswood, and coming from a mining district, Joe has an eye for a dog, particularly a whippet. A whippet pup which Joe bought in Manchester, and was taking home with him when we went North to play Middlesbrough, once landed me in some trouble. The pup had cost Joe a price which, for the animal's size, seemed very expensive. Consequently he guarded it well and never let the pup out of his sight.

We spent the night before the game at Redcar, and there the animal was placed in Joe's bedroom and the door was locked. The other players were keen to play some trick on Joe, but it did not seem that they were going to get any chance.

Next forenoon Billy Meredith inquired quite casually where I had the bandages. I thought nothing of this at the time and told Billy. Lunch time came along and the first person to leave the table was Billy, taking with him some chicken bones. I thought he was going to give a treat to some poor dog. What he did was to make a raid on Joe Spence's bedroom and commandeer Joe's pup.

After lunch we made preparations to leave for Middlesbrough. Joe went for the dog, but the dog was not to be found. Everybody joined in the search, and at last the pup was discovered in a waste paper basket, wrapped round and round in my bandages and cotton wool.

It was doing its best to chew up the chicken bones, but about the only part of it visible was one eye. It did look comical – to everybody but Joe Spence. Joe was very wroth. He grabbed the pup and as he walked out of the hotel he was removing the last of the bandages. At Middlesbrough the dog was handed over to Joe's brother, none the worse for its adventures.

A Fruity Story

When he was with us, Billy Meredith was the chief mischief-maker, but when he left Old Trafford, the job became Frank Barson's. I have despaired of Frank mending his ways. On one particular occasion one of his tricks caused me to leave a warm bed to quell what promised to be a riot.

We were at Rhyl at the time in special training and all the players were very lively indeed. The cause of the trouble in this particular case was the 'eat more fruit' crusade.

One day Barson and Hilditch, sharing the one bedroom, had laid in a stock of grapes and bananas. That night, when I thought that everyone was fast asleep, they were wide awake, consuming the delicacies. In the next room were Joe Spence, Charlie Moore and Charlie Radford. They smelt a rat and proceeded to the next room. They would not leave until they had had a good whack of the fruit.

Next day Barson suggested to the trio in the next room that he could get the fruit very cheaply, having made a friend of the shopkeeper. The others liked the idea and handed Frank some money to get them a supply for a midnight repast, and Frank promised he would get them good value.

A Rough House

This was where the joke started. Barson handed over a big bag. On the top was a bunch of grapes, below that were several bananas, but underneath were potatoes. After going to their bedroom, the three victims had fallen on the 'fruit' and had made the discovery. They were annoyed. So much so that they raided the next room to have a rough house.

Much scraping on the floor and thudding on the wall wakened me, and I arrived on the scene to find nothing but whirling pillows and bolsters. After a struggle I succeeded in restoring peace.

It is little incidents like these that make all the difference. They cheer one up immensely. You can't always be winning, but you can always be cheery.

THE FOUNDING FATHER

T HERE IS NO need for a paternity test to determine the true father of Manchester United. Many men had contributed to the rise of the club from the ashes of the bankrupt Newton Heath outfit, Mangnall, Stafford, Meredith, Roberts and Robson among them. But John Henry Davies was the guiding light, the wealthy visionary whose drive and cash built a football empire.

Sadly, the Davies era was almost at an end. In May, John Henry watched his last match; in late October, after a three year struggle with ill-health, he died, aged 63. In a sense he had lived just long enough to see the job done. Under his presidency the club had won every possible honour in the game, swapped fume-ridden Clayton for swanky Stretford and, just a few months before, fulfilled their long-term aim of owning the Old Trafford ground. Which was no mean achievement for a man who had barely followed the game when he had first become involved with the Reds a quarter of a century

John Henry Davies

earlier. In another sense he had lived fifteen years too long. Others had allowed the giant Davies had built to fall asleep. By the time of his death, the years of stagnation had eaten away at his achievements – memories of the great Mangnall era were already sepia-tinted.

The stories (there are a few of them) of how Davies first became involved with the club in 1902 read like the Disney version of history but just in case you haven't heard them, here goes... At least they all end in the same way – and in the same place.

Days after the FA had given their consent to reform the now bankrupt and defunct Newton Heath club, the shareholders held a public meeting at the New Islington Hall in Ancoats. At that meeting, the Newton Heath President, Mr Palmer, indicated that it would take

£2,000 to save the club. As the crowd filled their collective breeches, Harry Stafford, the club captain and perennial showman (he was renowned for wearing a white hat and brilliantly coloured waistcoat, an outfit which would have made him stand out at a seventies pimps' convention never mind Edwardian Clayton) emerged from the back of the auditorium and revealed that he knew of four men who, along with himself, were prepared to invest that sum and more. The four men he spoke of were Messrs Taylor, Brown and Jones plus one John Henry Davies, chairman of Manchester brewery Walker & Homfray, husband of a Tate heiress and now a sugar daddy in the making. It was an offer that the old board, try as they might, could not refuse. For the start of the 1902/3 season, the club had a new name, a new chairman, a new board – and new purpose.

Where the stories differ is in their explanations of how Davies and Stafford first hooked up. The most romantic version – and the one that smells the most – stars Stafford's St Bernard dog, Major (I told you he was a showman – there was no chance of flash Harry owning a bog-standard whippet). With Newton Heath in serious danger of going belly up, the directors held a fund-raising bazaar at the town's St James' Hall. The attendances badly hit by rain, the bazaar turned out to be an expensive flop. Indirectly, though, it paved the way to financial salvation. Towards the end of the event, Harry's St Bernard, who had been one of its few star attractions, escaped the attentions of its keeper and wandered off, eventually turning up in a pub belonging to one of Davies's associates. Somehow the dog was then passed on to Davies, his daughter Elsie took an immediate shine to it and when her dad answered the advert that Stafford had put in the press for Major's safe return, the two men struck up an historic, if phoney-sounding, deal – Davies, who had been impressed by the potential of the club, would bankroll the revival and Elsie (the spoilt bitch) would keep the dog.

From the story about the shaggy dog to the one about the accountant and the badly driven horse and trap. One match-day, George Lawton, an accountant at Walker and Homfray and an avid Newton Heath fan (and future United chairman) who had the ear of Stafford and other Heathens, was cycling to the ground when he was knocked off his bike by a trap carrying none other than his boss. Picking himself up and no doubt doffing his cap and apologising for the bumpy ride, Lawton carried on his way. On his arrival at Bank

Street, he was shocked to find that bailiffs had positioned themselves on each of the three turnstiles to confiscate the gate money. The grimness of the situation prompted George and Harry to cycle to the Davies family home at Mosely Hall (Stafford no doubt arriving on a diamond-encrusted penny farthing), remind John Henry that he might owe them one and beg him for his help. The two of them supposedly put over such a case that the brewery chief, despite his confession that he had never seen a game of football in his life, agreed to go down to the ground and take a look around. He liked what he saw so much that he ended up doing a Victor Kiam and buying the company.

And from the tale of the horse and trap to the one about the brewery boss, the prostitute, the pair of dwarfs – and the photos of them slashing on him that Harry Stafford had stored in his safe. Facetious, perhaps, but only marginally less plausible than the other two. The relevant point, however, is not how Davies rose to the throne but what he did once he was sat on it. His philosophy was a simple one – 'if something is worth doing, it is worth doing well'. There would be no half measures. Within months of the boardroom coup, the new chairman had sanctioned a multi-thousand pound spending spree funded in the main by money from his own personal account. In the build-up to the club's first season as Manchester United, close on £4,000 was spent on the team and perhaps the same again on the enclosure at Clayton. In just one summer the Bank Street stand was transformed from an eyesore into one of the finest in the land, with covered accommodation for 8,000 people. For the rest of the decade, money was thrown at the team and the ground, both legally and illegally. City took a hiding from the FA for under-the-counter trading but the Reds broke the rules just as flagrantly, the only difference being that they never got caught.

The ends justified the means. Mangnall's team won the league, Cup and the inaugural Charity Shield and left the watching public wetter than the string quartet on the Titanic. But, for Davies, the move from Clayton to Old Trafford was the greater triumph, the fulfilment of his ambition to give the club and the public the stage he felt they deserved. Right from the start he had posed the question: 'Why should Manchester not have a ground second to none in the land, a place the club and the people can be proud of? Here is a great sporting population. The people are only waiting for someone to do it.' Many felt that Old Trafford would be his great folly, a testament only to one man's arrogance. Instead the ground remains as a lasting memorial to his name.

The success that the club enjoyed under Davies came at a price, personally. 'There is probably no quicker route to unpopularity than financing a great football club,' mused the United programme in their Davies retrospective. Having insisted on a controlling influence, the President was often the subject of bitter criticism. Not that he was bothered about winning popularity contests. In common with the fiercely driven everywhere, John Henry had no qualms about treading on people's toes and consequently picked up enemies like a tart picks up STDs. The football authorities, in particular, loathed him. They knew that he was splashing the cash under-the-table but were never able to prove it, at least not until after the 1909 amnesty. When Davies accepted the position of chairman of the Players Union, a relationship already bubbling with distrust deteriorated even further.

The gents at the FA were not the only ones who would have gladly used his bushy moustache for bog roll, either; many of Davies's business associates shared their antipathy for United's sugar daddy. A reputation for machiavellian ruthlessness made him one of the most feared names on the Manchester business scene. But it would be overly simplistic to write JH off as a bowler-hatted version of JR. A character that was pockmarked with contradictions had an attractive flip-side too. According to those who knew him, the ultra-cunning mogul was also prone to moments of 'wide-eyed and childlike simplicity'. He could also be amazingly generous and sympathetic. For instance, United's record for aiding charitable causes, and for rewarding players with benefit matches, was exemplary. As is often the case with larger-than-life figures, he was only really appreciated when he was gone. 'There was a time when I could not stand John Henry Davies,' wrote the editor of the Official Programme, 'but I am inclined to think that the truth was that he was too big a man for us to understand.'

The supporters understood all right. Davies, the wealthy magnate who lived in a stately home, was by no means one of them but he was as ambitious and, once he had caught the football bug, as passionate as any United fanatic. His business friends were often amazed by how excited he became when he was watching his team. Occasionally he would have to leave his seat before the final whistle because he could not stand the tension. And despite a preference for road over rail, the President's attendance record would have shamed the most ardent modern Red. In twenty years he and his wife (the archetypal great woman behind the great man and, like Lady Jean Busby in later years, a woman whose loveable nature did much to cultivate a real club spirit at Old Trafford) drove thousands of miles in the United cause.

Crucially, Davies' was a regime that the supporters could trust. When John Henry promised something, he invariably delivered. His style was fan-friendly too. It was not unusual, particularly in the Clayton days, for him to go and stand among the crowd on the Pop Side and listen to their views. He got a buzz out of hearing the rough and ready comments of the supporters, particularly the six penny – later, one shilling – merchants whom he always maintained were the heart and soul of the club. As for the shareholders, Davies had a happy knack of keeping them onside and in the dark all at the same time. Until the outbreak of the cold war between the board and the supporters, shareholders' meetings were usually convivial affairs, an excuse for plenty of leg pulling and, later on, a bit of a session. Shareholders would be invited to 'take wine with the club' and the booze would usually be accompanied with a top-quality Havana – unless it was his great lieutenant, Mangnall, there was no better judge of the weed than John Henry. Consequently, most of the shareholders would leave the AGMs having forgotten that they were none the wiser about the club's affairs than they had been before.

Clearly, it was no coincidence that United's golden period came when Davies and Mangnall both had a firm grip of the rudder. By the time the club were veering off course, the great manager had left for Hyde Road while the great benefactor had taken more of a back-seat role. In part, it was his own choice. Once you have climbed Everest once, there is never quite the same urge to do it all over again (not unless the photos don't come out). Possibly he felt that he had taken the club as far as he could and that it was up to someone else, someone perhaps younger and fitter, to write the next chapter in United's history. Possibly he felt that the golden tit had dripped enough. Davies had staked large amounts in the club without any security and without charging any interest. In the depressed economic climate of the time it made no sense to keep ploughing money into as notoriously unreliable a venture as a football club. In any case, it was imperative that the club learned to breathe on its own, to cope with financial dramas without having to run to its sugar-daddy for help.

Partly, the decision was made for him. In 1910 the FA at last got their teeth into the chairman and his team. In January that year, they appointed a commission to inquire into, and report on, the affairs of 'any club playing under the laws of the Association'. In theory that was a field stretching from Salford under-eights to the big boys of the top division. In reality it meant only one thing – an excuse to get at United, a club that just months earlier, at the height of the Outcasts affair, had been labelled 'the wreckers of the game'.

Even for the unbiased it smacked of a vendetta. What followed lost the authorities any benefit of the doubt. Arriving at High Holborn for the opening round of talks, United agreed to the request to drop their trousers but, when they learned that the information they provided would be passed straight on to the press, they initially refused to cough. The meeting had to be quickly adjourned as the directors stormed out. In the end, though, they had no choice but to return and comply. The FA were determined to hang the club's dirty washing out in public. So when the commission completed their investigations, their report was published in the papers in full. That included details of the money that United had paid out in illegal wages and bonuses – a total of £5,743 between 1903/4 and the cup-winning season, 1908/9. So much for the post-amnesty clean slate that the authorities had promised.

Never before had the FA taken the public into its confidence so completely. Or, for that matter, strayed so far out of their jurisdiction. One of the principal objections of the commission were the terms and conditions on which United had secured the land at Old Trafford from the owners, Walker & Homfray. In the opinion of the investigating team, the club had got themselves too good a deal. As a result they ordered that the terms be reconsidered and rearranged so they weren't quite as advantageous. It was a nonsense. The directors were guilty of nothing more than looking after their best interests while there was no precedent allowing the FA to order 'the rearrangement of terms of rent and fortune'. The Old Trafford deal had nothing to do with them – they had as much right to interfere as a school milk monitor has to hand out parking tickets. But that was how the football authorities were able to behave in their murky past; as a general rule, the only laws they bowed to were the ones they made themselves.

The main target of the commission, however, had always been the constitution of the club. For some time, the FA had not been satisfied that United were 'a genuine club', a definition of which was suggested in the *Athletic News*: 'That is to say that it was formed by the voluntary effort of a number of people resident in the locality of its headquarters and that there were many shareholders who, with separate interests, had the right to elect directors.' The FA did not allow 'the private proprietorship of clubs carried on for the purpose of speculation and profit' or at least they did not back then – the authorities were noticeable only for their silence when Murdoch and Glazer came knocking. To meet the requirements of the FA, United had apparently been remodelled two or three years earlier but the authorities had still not been appeased. They were unhappy that the club still did not make their balance sheet public – a legacy of the days when the figures, because of the stream of cash-stuffed envelopes flowing out of the secretary's office, did not add up. They examined the share list and found that one name, that of John Henry Davies, dominated far too much for their liking. The commission concluded that United should be floated as a limited liability company with 'a subscription open to the public at a price determined by an independent valuer'. Time had been called on Davies's Old Trafford dictatorship.

By the time of his death, then, it had been some years since John Henry had been the absolute power in the boardroom. In that time, United had grown used to coping with the slings and arrows of long-term economic depression. In most cases the end-of-year results had made for good reading. Despite the lingering effects of the General Strike, the early cup exit and the outbreak of absenteeism towards the end of the season, the club had still made a £4,400 profit in 26/27. There was now a belief that United, despite the added burden of paying for the Old Trafford freehold, could survive without the financial muscle of the Davies family. In their tribute to the dead President at December's AGM, the board referred to the club's 'present proud and secure financial position'. Meanwhile, the tribute in the Official Programme declared that 'today, Manchester United can go on and prosper without his support and guidance.'

Their confidence was misplaced. Many people had forgotten that the club's financial stability in the twenties had effectively been underpinned by Davies's interest-free loans. That safety net was no longer available to them now that the great man had signed his last cheque. Like many others across the country they had been lured into the mistaken belief that an economic corner had been turned since the General Strike. In fact, it was the lull before the storm. Within two years, both club and country would be hit by an economic crisis that made the depression of the early part of the decade seem like boom-time. Time would show that the death of the man who made Manchester United heralded the most desperate period in the history of the club.

WITH A NEW manager at the helm and that end-of-season unbeaten run still fresh in Red minds, United kicked off the 27/28 campaign confident of proving themselves a better side than the previous year's fifteenth place had suggested. Never mind that footballers always produce their best performances in the weeks immediately after the arrival of a new manager; or that the side had won only one of their seven games they had played under Bamlett; or that only two players (Hanson and Spence) had so far scored a goal for him; or that the directors had once again turned a deaf ear to the fans' pleas for major surgery; the Old Trafford spin doctors were determined to put the message across that United were on their way back. It made a good sound bite but, for the reasons outlined above and a stack of others, it was the sort of wishful thinking that makes a chubby minger invest in a pair of hotpants.

Since false bravado about the club's prospects – both playing and financial – was rapidly becoming an Old Trafford disease, the two wins and two draws with which the Reds started the season could only mean one thing – a false dawn. Within a couple of months of topping the season's first table, the side had begun a steady slide down the division that seemed certain to take them out of it. By April, they looked stonewall certainties for relegation; the biggest certs to go down until Jordan's G-string. But just when it seemed that there was no way out, the Reds found a chink of light. By May, the Great Escape was on. And, unlike the film (let's face it, as most of the cast ended up with bullets in them, it wasn't that great an escape), all the big names had at least a slim chance of making it. Except one.

Agonisingly, the one exception was Barson. For the second year running, the skipper struggled badly with injuries, appearing just eleven times. At the end of the season, the directors came to the conclusion that, at the age of 37, his injury problems were only going to get worse and released him on a free. The frustration with Frank was that he was still, by a distance, the club's most influential player. His long absences were the principal reason why United struggled so badly although the directors did a good job of turning a crisis into a disaster by inexplicably selling both his long-term deputies, Grimwood and Haslam. Eventually, Mann came in and did a good job as pivot but he was no Barson – nobody was. For five years Frank had been the sheet anchor of the side, the Captain Marvel whom the team could not do without. For long periods in the months that followed, the Reds were like a one-man band without the all-important one man. Often the only sound to break the silence at Old Trafford was the chorus of heckling from the Pop Side.

Admittedly, a winter of discontent seemed unlikely as United ushered in the new season in some style, thrashing Bamlett's old side Middlesbrough 3-0. 'If you can imagine fully 50% of a gathering of 45,000 people whistling "Bye, bye, blackbirds" as the band played the season in [OK, probably not], and then imagine the joy of the multitude when Manchester United scored, one, two, three goals in the second half against "the team of the season", you receive a mental picture of the piping send-off at Old Trafford, Manchester,' raved the excitable Ivan Sharpe. For half an hour 'Boro, passing and moving to good effect, provided a thrilling advert for Bamlett's preferred brand of football. Then they were swept aside by 'a burst of Old Traffordism that has come to be characteristic of the modern Manchester United.' Spence, who, because of his pace and at-the-throat style, was perhaps the symbol of this 'Old Traffordism' at its most effective, netted twice to wrest the headlines from his opposite number Camsell; his inside-right partner Hanson headed the third.

When the Reds then took three points from their trips to Hillsborough and St Andrews, they led the table for the first time in years. For the superstitious, it was immediate justification for the close-season decision to abandon the white-with-red-V abomination the team had worn since 1922 and return to the all-red jersey that, one disastrous season in the thirties apart (when the directors experimented with cherry and white hoops – the kit designer had clearly been experimenting with something else), has remained United's trademark ever since.

For the rest, it was a rare excuse to hit the town. Of course, it was far too early in the season for the league table to mean anything but success-starved Reds were determined to enjoy themselves while they could. It was obvious from the side's performance in the Wednesday return that they would not be stopping at the summit for long. In front of 20,000, a decent enough crowd for a September mid-week, United laboured to a 1-1. Pre-season hopes that the boo-boys would lay off their latest target, McPherson, were swiftly dashed when he missed what would have been a match-winning penalty. A pulled leg muscle completed a nightmarish afternoon for the flying scapegoat. Far worse than that, Barson, who jarred the base of his spine in a heavy fall, beat him to the treatment table. The injury would keep him out for five weeks, five weeks in which United faced some of their toughest examinations of the season. Even with their talismanic skipper, the Reds would have struggled to rustle up a pass from assignments at the champions-to-come and 'the team of the decade', a trip to the ultimate bogey ground, Ewood Park, and a visit from the champions. Without him, they might as well have not turned up.

Of the six autumnal fixtures that Frank missed, five were lost; three of them badly and one of them – the home game against Newcastle on September 10 – criminally. Some reporters were kind enough to argue that no side would have been able to live with the reigning champions in the mood they were in that day but their words would have been little consolation to the 50,000 who were left to look on, like bystanders at a car crash, as United collapsed to a 7-1 defeat, a record trouncing for a match at Old Trafford. Or, for that matter, to Alf Steward who suffered his greatest humiliation on the very afternoon that the England selectors, impressed by the reports of his early-season form, had come to Manchester to give him the once over. Needless to say, Alf did not get the call. Worse than that, he was dropped with almost indecent haste by his club. By the time Spurs arrived in town on the 24th, Lance Richardson, a cavalier keeper to Steward's normally reliable roundhead, was the man wearing the green roll-neck. Unlucky Alf spent most of the season in the reserves.

The following weekend, Huddersfield set aside the premature whispers that they were in decline by banging four past Steward inside an hour; two days later, Blackburn did something similar at Ewood. The 3-0 stroll against disappointing, ten-man Spurs was a welcome relief but miserable defeats at Filbert Street and Goodison soon got the Reds sliding again. Leicester, featuring one of the forwards of the season in former OT favourite Arthur Lochhead, cruised home by a deceptively comprehensive 1-0; Everton, featuring the forward of this and any other season in Dixie Dean[1], hammered United for five, Dixie buffing his legend by bagging the lot. On both occasions, the damage would have been far greater had it not been for the alertness and eccentric elasticity of the club's latest goalkeeping find. At Leicester, Richardson received the biggest ovation that any visitor had been given for years; at Goodison he was so good that Dean made a point of rushing over to him at the end to shake his hand.

Just eight days into October, the season's first table-toppers lay just two points clear of the table-proppers. Spirits on the Pop Side had slumped just as dramatically. It did not help the fans' mood that Everton were demonstrating what a club could achieve if they displayed genuine ambition in the transfer market. The Toffees' £20,000 spending spree would eventually transform last term's cannon fodder into this one's champions. Suggestions that the United board would follow suit were treated with disdain. In a letter to *The Football Chron*, 'Aitch Gee' described the constant gossip linking the club with new blood as nothing more than 'disgusting propaganda' and added: 'The only consolation the supporters get at Old Trafford is that a player is a big-hearted man and so on. I wonder if the management would give a navvy the job of covering the pop side because he was a big-hearted optimist.'

For once, though, disgruntled Reds scoffed too soon. In the wake of the Goodison rape, they were given a little of what they wanted; a good run of results, the return to fitness of Barson and, most welcome of all, the first heavyweight signings of the Bamlett regime. But first of all came an interesting reshuffle behind the scenes as the directors acted to dilute the spiralling workload now facing the manager of a club the size of United, resuscitating the old position of assistant manager and moving Louis Rocca, the club's legendary chief scout, across to fill it.

*   *   *

ROCCA, WHOSE NAME LAUNCHED a thousand stories, has become an almost mythical figure in United's history. Believe even half of them and you have yourself a Manc-Italian version of Forrest Gump, someone who was there or thereabouts when each crucial page was turned. One tale

---

1   *In 1927/28 Dean scored sixty goals in Division One, a Football League record*

claims that it was Rocca who should have been holding the lead when Stafford's St Bernard wandered off in 1902. Another that he was the inspiration behind the choice of Manchester United as the name of the re-formed organisation. At the time he was employed by the club as a 6d-a-week tea-boy. As the sceptics have pointed out, he must have been an extremely influential one.

What is beyond dispute is that Louis was a maniacally obsessed Red and a fine, long-serving clubman. Along with his elder brother, Joseph, he was perhaps the club's most celebrated fan – before the war, the so-called Rocca Brigade, with their 'uniform' of red and white umbrellas, were known on almost every ground. Having been part of the furniture at the club since the 1890s, Louis was arguably its most celebrated employee, too. During his thirty-plus years on the payroll (he would end up clocking up more than fifty), he had filled virtually every position from brew-boy to number two but none of his titles ever really came close to doing him justice. If anything, he was a bit of everything, the football equivalent of the POW-camp 'fixer' who could be relied on to rustle up passports for escapees, sherry and cranberry sauce at Christmas, the finest whisky and rolling baccy for the officers and pictures of Betty Grable for the privates.

But if his charm, passion and savvy made Rocca the man for every occasion, it is for his work as a scout – and the tales of how he got his men – that he is best remembered. A man with more contacts than a Hollywood madam, Louis' genius lay not in spotting new talent but in tapping into the football grapevine and making a move on good youngsters before anyone else did. His reputation as both a parasite and master of subterfuge often preceded him, making him *persona non grata* at several junior clubs. It was not unknown for Rocca to be approached by shadowy figures and informed that he would be better off leaving town. That was as likely as the Pope appearing in a porno. They sought him here, there and everywhere but Louis invariably managed to sneak in – and often to sneak out with the man he was after. Over the years, the Red Pimpernel found more good players than any other official then in the game. However, his best 'signing' for the club was not a player, but a manager – one Matt Busby.

The 1948 cup-winning side was Louis' great legacy. The team that Matt led to United's first Wembley triumph was built primarily on gems that Rocca had dug up. But his greatest contribution to the Red cause came much earlier, in the throes of the Depression, when he and fellow backstage hero Walter Crickmer helped pull off the miracle of keeping the club afloat whilst also laying the foundations for its post-war renaissance.

*   *   *

IF BRINGING IN Rocca as Bamlett's wing-man was one of the board's wisest decisions, the following week's £5,000 double move for Sheffield Wednesday's Rees Williams and Stockport's Billy Johnston was more of a mixed grill. Williams was the miss. The man whose chief claim to fame was ousting Meredith from the Welsh team found coping with his legend at club level far more difficult. His shambling inadequacy ensured that Old Trafford's reputation as a graveyard for imported right-wingers remained intact. Inside-left Johnston, by contrast, was a hit, a bona fide terrace-hero-in-the-making. When Billy was signed, there were many who felt that he was too much of an individualist to fit in at United. Those sceptics had missed the point. The Reds did not need a forward who would just fit in. Fit in to what – the worst attack in the division? Rather they needed an inspiration, a catalyst for change. Billy was that inspiration, not a prolific scorer perhaps but a player who could get the best out of the lesser lights around him. With Johnston settled in at number ten, McPherson rediscovered the form he had shown in his first season alongside Lochhead, and there were positive knock-on effects right across the line. And now that Barson was back to load the bullets for Billy & co to fire, United produced some of the best football that Old Trafford had seen since the promotion campaign. The frustration for both club and fans alike was that neither Barson nor the good times lasted long enough...

A frenzied 2-2 against Cardiff on October 15 stopped the rot and gave Joe Spence the platform to make history, his late equaliser making him the third member of the Reds' century club (the others being Sandy Turnbull and old Heathen Joe Cassidy, both of whom scored a round 100). A week later, quality was welded to effort as Derby were crushed by the finest display the Bamlett regime had yet produced. After a goalless and soulless opening half, the forwards scaled peaks that only their opponents had conquered in recent memory, scoring five times in a twenty-minute blur. Spence moved on to 103 (and first place in the all-time scoring chart) with a lob, drive and tickle; Johnston and McPherson bagged the others. The manner of Billy's first United strike – a Choccy-style scramble from a corner – was the antithesis of virtually everything else he had done during the ninety minutes. With his deft footwork, elusive swerve and eye-of-the-needle passing he could not have looked more like a conductor if he had taken to the field wearing tails and carrying a baton.

Unexpected success at Upton Park, a ground where Red experiences have always been bittersweet, maintained the momentum and ended a run of four consecutive defeats on the road. The side's match-winning rally from 0-1 to 2-1 was a fitting tribute to Davies, who had been buried the previous day. A solid home performance against bottom-placed Portsmouth was another. By then, United, the season's yo-yo club, were back in the top six, just four points off the lead.

Such was the quality of the Reds' football that for now, at least, the 4-1 defeat at Sunderland could be written off as a blip, the result of playing for 75 minutes with ten men (after Silcock tore a thigh muscle) rather than concrete evidence of deep-lying frailty. Back in Manchester, with a full compliment of players, United added more power to the optimists' elbow by thrashing Villa 5-1. Despite the rain which restricted the crowd to less then 30,000, Barson could not have chosen a better afternoon on which to take his benefit. As usual he had saved some of his best football for his old colleagues. But the side's hottest act remained Spence, whose early tap-in took his tally to thirteen goals in sixteen starts. In most other seasons, a similar ratio would have made him the talk of the game. But Camsell and now Dean had raised the bar to implausible levels. Overshadowed by the scoring feats elsewhere, Joe had to settle for a place as first reserve when the squad was chosen for England's autumn international.

From a Barson-inspired high to a Barson-caused low in seven short November days. For the second away game in succession, United lost a key player and conceded four. For Sunderland read Burnley; for Silcock read Barson. Frank's second serious injury of the campaign was the one that he and the club feared most; a recurrence of the ruptured groin that had blighted his season a year earlier (although some reports suggested his main problem remained his spine). In a sense it was a career-ending injury. Barson played on after he left Old Trafford but he had played his last full game in a Red shirt. He did make a short-lived return in March but, like Muhammad Ali's ill-advised bout against a young and hungry Larry Holmes in 1980 or any one of Bestie's 'final' flings after '72, it was one comeback too many.

Shorn of their sheet anchor, United stumbled, righted themselves and then slumped. For the first time that season they failed to score in successive matches as the Burnley disaster was trumped by another Lancastrian embarrassment, this time a home defeat by a Bury side that had previously lost every game they had played since October. The *Athletic News* spelled out the supporters' worst fears by posing the question: 'Shall we say there is no team without a Barson?' If nothing else, there was a chronic lack of control and style. With no one to pull the strings in the middle of the park, even Johnston's artistry became swamped. United were one of the fastest teams in the division but that did not count for much when they made headless chickens look like candidates for Mensa.

Drizzle-coated Bramall Lane was just as depressing, United being ripped apart by a blunt set of Blades. 'There is no disguising the pitifulness of Manchester United now,' groaned the Impressionist. But the strange thing about the class of 27/28 was that no matter how bad their play or results, a sublime performance or a thrilling goal fest was never that far away. Just a week later, give or take an interesting reshuffle of the forward line (with Hanson moving to centre-forward and Spence back to outside-right), the Reds destroyed a far superior side in Arsenal. Once Wilson's own-goal gaffe had gifted them an unlikely first-half equaliser, the smart money would have been on a Gunners triumph. Instead, United hit back with three more at the right end. The best of them was a goal-of-the-season certainty from McPherson who did the visitors' rearguard for pace and then crashed in from distance with his normally redundant right peg. That was one for Frank's Pop Side tormentors to put in their pipes and smoke. Frustratingly, he did not stay in credit for long; the next time the Reds played at Old Trafford, against Blackburn on Boxing Day, the Bullet's second penalty miss of the season cost his side a deserved win.

If there was such a thing as a Bamlett effect, then, it was that United were a more exciting proposition for the neutrals. But their tendency to switch suddenly from the ridiculous to the sublime and back again left them less well-equipped for the battle ahead. A team with the misfiring set of forwards that the Reds had could ill afford to lose the capacity to grind out 0-0s and 1-0s, particularly when the depressing days came around far more often than the happy ones. Three parts bad to one part good, as was the ratio for the next three and a bit months, was a recipe for only one thing and I am not talking about the Edwards' pies.

A trip to Anfield inevitably put an end to United's post-Arsenal high. A 2-0 defeat was just about par for the course at a ground where the Reds had not won since 1914. There was a ray of light amid the gloom, though; Mann won rave reviews for his work in the centre-half position vacated by Barson. Unlikely as it seemed to those critics who felt he should have been pensioned off, Frank would emerge as one of the saving graces of the season. To paraphrase one of the comments in the papers, the sceptics erred badly when they thought his football skill was falling with his hair. At Ayresome Park on New Year's Eve there were more signs that Frank was the man to guide the club towards survival. The veteran Red blotted out of the threat of Camsell at one end and Spence set up goals for Hanson and Johnston at the other as United ended the year by soiling Boro's unbeaten home record.

The holiday gains against Arsenal and Boro gave the Reds a five point lead over the bottom two but did nothing for the supporters' mood or absentee rate. For the home games against Blackburn and Birmingham, both of which ended, frustratingly, in draws, the Reds pulled in crowds of thirty-one and seventeen thousand when gates of fifty and thirty thousand were expected. Those who remained were getting agitated again. How quickly the atmosphere had changed since the late-October oasis of good play. Frustrated and angered by the side's inability to hit a consistently acceptable level of form, the crowd were a ticking bomb waiting to explode. It did not take much to set them off – seeing Partridge or McPherson warming up was enough for some. In the Birmingham game, the catalyst was the referee's decision to disallow Spence's decisive 'goal'. The reaction of the supporters prompted another of the Impressionist's peering-down-his-nose lectures in the *Athletic News*: 'The habitués of Old Trafford are becoming badly behaved. They are not helping their own team by execration, and it was scarcely palatable from the stand at the close to see and hear a premeditated demonstration against the referee because he would not permit a goal to win the match.'

As far as the Impressionist, and other football watchers of the old school, were concerned, crowds should maintain a stiff upper-lip at all times and generally deport themselves like sex slaves – taking the blows without complaint and still somehow getting off on it. In its early years, Old Trafford had been touted as a bastion of fair play but times they were a-changing. The Pop Side had been grumbling loudly for some time. Now there was evidence of an outbreak of Red attitude in the grandstand. In its editorial, the *Football News* lamented the outbreak of 'partisanship' in a stand that had previously been 'almost famous for its sportsmanship', reminiscing: 'The Old Trafford stand found accommodation for many of the city magnates, bank managers, merchants, barristers and the best type of citizen... The majority of the present occupants are still men held high in esteem and responsible businessmen. Unfortunately, however, in certain sections there has crept in the type of individual who must air his opinions, and who must make himself heard in directing the referee to conduct the game and the footballer how to play it. Some of the remarks are positively rude and the barracking of players ought to be unknown on all grounds. Very often you will hear a player loudly blamed for not taking a ball which he could not have gathered had he been travelling by aeroplane.'

The shift in atmosphere should have surprised no one. Lengthy exposure to the sort of dross that the players had been regularly serving up would have made a hooligan out of Gandhi. Also, the Old Trafford crowd had grown up. When the club upped sticks in 1910, the crowd dynamics changed dramatically. The old Clayton supporters still formed the bulk of the hard-core support but there was also a substantial influx of fans from the Stretford side of town who hadn't previously felt a strong affinity for the club. Initially, they had been interested bystanders rather than partisan supporters. Eighteen years on, they were genuine, dyed-in-the-wool Reds – and they had no qualms about telling the world about it. Which was a blow for anyone from the silence-is-golden school. For now, at least, the Old Trafford library was closed for business.

Supposedly your mum only nags you because she loves you. Likewise, supporters only moan because they care. Anyone who has ever been given a maternal earful over the state of their room or for using the house like a hotel, or their dad like a taxi service (or any other parental cliché) will appreciate that it does not feel like love at the time. That the supporters cared was little consolation to those United players who were the targets of their bile. I referred earlier to the self-defeating effect on individual players of systematic barracking. Now the papers were floating the theory that the crowd, by hammering the players, were also hampering their attempts to play a better style of football. A large percentage of United supporters had two stock expressions – 'Kick it' and 'Get rid'. Worried about the consequences of losing possession in a dangerous area, the supporters preferred to see the ball up the field and airborne than played slickly across the floor to feet. Concerned about the prospect of having the crowd on their backs, the players complied, sacrificing artistry for hard kicking and even harder running. Or so the theory went. 'The sooner the Manchester United players are given credit for the ability to manoeuvre and make the subtle ground transfer,' the Impressionist continued, 'the more readily will they justify themselves at home. Compare Duckworth, Roberts and Bell, Meredith, Halse and Sandy Turnbull – geniuses by comparison with modern football, but men who won by methods now discouraged.'

The argument had its merits but also a flaw the size of Dion Dublin's saveloy; if the abuse from the Pop Side really was holding the players back, how come their away displays made their home ones look like championship material? A week after spanking Brentford 7-1 at home in the Cup, the Reds got a hiding of their own at St James'. In their next league outing they lost by the same 4-1 score at Spurs but seven days later Old Trafford served up another delight, a 5-2 thumping of Leicester. Two of the Reds' goals that afternoon were supplied by George Nicol, a young centre-forward who had been playing for Glaswegian junior side Saltcoats just a few weeks earlier. His United career began like a fairy-tale; sadly, it ended like a snuff movie. When he failed to add to his debut-day tally in five subsequent starts, George was swiftly bumped off. After spending 28/29 in the reserves, the former butcher was sold to Brighton.

All season, United picked up just nine points on their travels. From New Years Eve to late April they did not win any. In that same period, the players turned Old Trafford into a fortress. Admittedly, the bare statistics do not show how many brainless draws the supporters had to suffer but Bury's triumph on December 4 wasn't repeated for another four and a half months. Blaming the barrackers was a nice try but pinpointing the real reason why the season was rapidly turning into a desperate scrap against relegation could not have been simpler.

It says much that the side's happiest away experience in the months after Ayresome was the cup draw they stole at Gigg Lane on the weekend after the Newcastle disaster. United were very much second best for long stretches of a muddy mediocrity of a match but Johnston's sensational half-volley, delivered at the end of an afternoon when he had played his worst game for the club (picture a hungover Ralphie Milne with his laces tied together), rescued a replay from the jaws of defeat. Four days later, another single blow, this time from Spence, finished the job at Old Trafford.

According to United's fifth round opponents, Birmingham, that was as good as their latest cup adventure was going to get. In the build-up to the tie, on February 18, the Brummies' secretary, Richards, crowed: 'We have a feeling that this is Birmingham's year in connection with the cup. We have been playing really well of late.' But if the visitors' name was on the trophy, it was badly misspelt. In front of 52,000, Mann gave his best Barson impression yet, Wilson and Bennion roared back to something approaching their best while Silcock and Jones were impeccable, obsessive cleaners, mopping up what little the half-backs missed. In the circumstances, a clean sheet was almost guaranteed. Which left United needing just one goal to secure their place in the last eight. Johnston provided it, hurling himself through the air to get his head on the end of Spence's drilled centre.

Having forgotten how to win 'scruffy' in the league, it was a pleasant surprise when the Reds remembered how to do so in the Cup. And with the side following the old Robson recipe of defensive solidity and the odd goal pinched here and there, it was possible to visualise them at least matching their semi-final achievement of two years earlier. Standing in their way, though, were Blackburn at Blackburn. It was precisely the draw that the club did not want. On this season's form, any away game would have provided a formidable test. Ewood, though, had built a particularly nasty reputation for quashing Red hopes. In six winless trips there since the war, United had conceded twenty-two goals and scored just one. They had caused as many riots. There was no question, then, that the Reds, the supposed dark horses for the Cup, were the undisputed underdogs going into their quarter-final. A nasty experience at Cardiff in the midst of the cup saga hardly helped their cause. Another away defeat left the club in range of the bottom two and deepened their neurosis about playing outside Stretford. To make matters worse, Silcock picked up another injury. United would go into their biggest game since the all-Mancunian semi without their key defender.

The directors made sure there would be no more mishaps by taking the players away for the week and spoiling them. Monday was spent in the brine baths at Northwich, Tuesday and Thursday on the golf course, Wednesday at Blackpool, Friday evening at the theatre. Meredith, who always felt that such pampering did more harm than good, would have been appalled. Treat them mean to keep them keen had always been his maxim.

There were no signs that the players had gone soft, mind, when the game kicked off. The Reds were the main aggressors as the match started like your average day on the Western Front – plenty of fight and effort, little meaningful progress. Grinding away at the home side, United gradually took control of the midfield and for most of the game looked the likelier of two tension-riddled teams to sneak a goal. But Hanson headed tamely at the keeper when well positioned and then missed his kick when Wilson and Johnston combined to present him with an even better opportunity. Still, with ten minutes remaining, the worst possible scenario for United appeared to be a replay at Old Trafford. Then Richardson, who was prone to the odd Dudek moment, spoiled a season's good work by racing out of his goal to meet a long throw-in. Needless to say, he did not make it. A Rovers player won the flick-on and Puddefoot nodded into the open net. Two minutes later the same player steered in a low shot and the Reds, despite dominating the play for most of the game, were out.

When a post-mortem was carried out at Old Trafford, the consensus was that Blackburn had got lucky. Jack Wilson, who had more reason than most never to set foot in Ewood again, argued: 'We lost the game because we had no luck and because unfortunately one or two chances were allowed to go by. I maintain that the United were the better team on the day's play: we were better than the Rovers in everything save the goals. They were secured luckily. At the same time praise to the winners.' There must be grave doubts whether that final sentiment would have passed a sincerity test. Not that Blackburn were fussed either way – having sneaked into the semi-finals, they went on to lift the trophy.

In the aftermath of their big cup disappointment in '26, the Reds had taken their ball home and sulked. They could not afford to do anything similar this year. As if the Ewood knockout wasn't painful enough, good results for their relegation rivals had pushed them even closer to the second division. Slightly superior goal average was all that saved them from splitting the Sheffield clubs in the bottom two. Another maddening, mournful March – the club's third in as many years – dictated that it would not save them for long.

Admittedly, the month got off to a reasonable start, results-wise, the Reds emerging unbeaten from a run of three matches at home. But the side's insipid form still gave the critics plenty to tut about. Most supporters would have settled for a nil-nil against double-chasing Huddersfield but United's failure to convert their marked territorial advantage into goals was a marked and disturbing negative. Another insipid draw, against West Ham, offered further evidence, if any were needed, of the team's attacking impotency. Given a choice between laughing and crying, it appears that many of the watching 22,000 had opted for the former. 'Sardonic laughter and epithet does not help,' warned the Impressionist, 'Manchester United, at any rate five of them – alleged to be a forward line – are bad enough but do not make them worse. Encouragement, I am sure, would mean a lot. I do not suggest that it would make them better footballers – perhaps less inferior.' Ouch.

A last-minute piece of robbery from Johnston rescued an undeserved point. By then, the directors had seen enough. Bamlett had been eyeing up Bill Rawlings, Southampton's former International centre-forward, for some time without ever getting past the winking stage. With the club's top-flight status in serious jeopardy, the time had come to make a move whatever the cost. The eventual £4,000 fee was a shade steep for a player in his early thirties (more evidence of the falseness of United's economy – had they invested in the market before it was common knowledge that they were desperate to do so, they would have avoided paying over the odds for a short-term fix) but it was money excellently spent. For a while there were fears that Bill's sword had got caught in its scabbard but it wasn't long before he emerged as the white knight the club needed to help tackle their relegation demons.

Rawlings' United career got off to a flier, a sumptuous header against the prospective champions, Everton, earning his new club a shock 1-0, but the initial, instant lift provided by his arrival soon evaporated, a run of four successive away games yielding no more points and two more serious injuries. The relegation four-pointer at Fratton Park on the 17th was particularly gruesome, Portsmouth pinching the points and Barson's final comeback ending in disaster. The match was just twenty minutes old when a freak collision with Billy Johnston left him with a smashed nose. After receiving treatment to stem the flow of blood, the old warrior returned and, with characteristic gallantry, soldiered on until the break, first at centre-back and then at outside-left. However, when the doctor confirmed that a snout that had taken more blows than the Sphinx's was again buggered, even Barson was forced to back down. In the end, the great champion retired on his stool. There could not have been a less fitting finale to the Barson era. Still, the irony of the King being killed by one of his own would not have been lost on the countless adversaries who had enjoyed the dubious privilege of meeting Frank at his prime.

When Wilson hobbled out of the following week's 5-0 Baseball Ground disaster with a torn leg muscle, United were down to the bare bones in midfield. Injuries and misguided sales had left the selectors with just two experienced men, Mann and Bennion, to choose from. In the circumstances, the emergence of Hughie McLenahan, a former Schoolboy International and the most exciting Red prospect for years, could not have been better timed. In the weeks to come he would deliver the most precocious piece of hole-filling since the Dutch boy and the dyke. Talk about throwing him in at the deep end, though. By the time McLenahan was summoned from the Central League, United had already broken Sheffield's steely hold on the bottom two. Miserable defeats at Villa and then Bolton, on Easter Friday (no Red could see anything Good about it), made certain they stayed there. The outrageous overhead kick that cost the club a useful draw at Burnden backed the hunch that the fates were using Old Trafford as a khazi. For some, the relevant Easter-time question was not whether the Reds would be relegated but whether they would finish last. A two-pronged Sheffield revival meant that bottom-placed Wednesday, who had almost been lapped earlier in the season, were now just two points adrift while the Blades, who had played two games less, were the same number of points ahead.

A run-in featuring five home games to two away was perhaps the only thing that United had going for them. A brace of holiday victories hinted at an Old Trafford-driven miracle, Rawlings blasting four goals as the Reds just edged out Burnley and Bolton. But successive defeats in mid-April appeared to have ended the club's survival dreams. Relegation-haunted teams are supposed to scrap and bore their way to 1-0s and 0-0s. In typical Bamlett style, the Reds shared seven goals at Gigg Lane and five goals with Sheffield United. Unfortunately, Bury netted four of them – and the Blades three. Old Trafford defeat against one of United's main rivals was particularly disastrous. The referee, a Mr Bowie, did not help their cause by disallowing a perfectly good goal by Rawlings but the Reds ultimately only had themselves to blame for failing to take numerous opportunities to extend the lead given them by Thomas's early opener. And then for switching off defensively during the twelve second half minutes in which Sheffield claimed all their goals.

The Old Trafford crowd gave a convincing demonstration of their enduring class – whatever the pundits sneered – by applauding two blinding strikes from Sheffield's England left-winger, Turnstall. Now that the club were rock-bottom, the United players could not expect comparable treatment. Still, there were signs that the boo boys were beginning to lay off their favourite forward targets. Supporters like 'J.R. of Weaste' were in no doubt where the blame for the club's slump really lay:

'The United are at long last in their rightful position. It had to come; it was inevitable. To many loyal supporters it is a relief similar to that afforded by the extraction of an aching tooth.

'The forwards have done their best, but they are just short of being good enough and that is not their fault. No blame attaches to any man who does his best. The pop side supporters have risked rheumatism, pneumonia and general ill-health on the most neglected ground that I know to give unstinted support to their beloved team.

'All have hoped against hope that the directors would see the writing on the wall ere it was too late. Everyone has known that failure was in sight, but we have hoped until the heart turned sick that the directors, who have the means, will do their minimum duty.

'Instead, they have sold the pass, the gallant defenders in the team, the traditions of the club, the spectators, and the Press, and not all the concentrated persuasive eloquence of the latter will now keep tens of thousands from turning away and giving up Old Trafford for good.

'Buying cheap, raw, unfurnished material and a 1923 model with which to win a 1928 high-speed race in the highest and most difficult competition, has brought the only possible result, and between now and the end of the season more will be lost than would have kept Manchester's senior team in their rightful position and relieved long-suffering supporters of all anxiety.

'The ostrich-like policy of the directors will have a boomerang effect from which they will not recover for years.'

*   *   *

WITH THREE MATCHES remaining, United lay at least two points adrift of their rivals, all of whom had games in hand, and a repeat of '22 seemed guaranteed. But the nine or ten teams who were also involved in the most competitive relegation scrap for years were about to discover that it was easier to finish off Rasputin. Sunderland were edged out on an afternoon when the Reds hurled themselves into battle like rabid clansmen. Hanson banged the first inside three minutes and even though Spence miskicked his first-half penalty so badly that he almost dislocated an ankle (shades of Gordon Strachan's stubbed-toe embarrassment in '85's Easter crunch with Everton), Johnston's second clinched the points. Three days later, the team took their 100% away record – eight league defeats out of eight since December – to Highbury for a match they could not afford to lose and really had to win. What a moment, then, for Bamlett to play a tactical joker. And what more appropriate place for his new offside ploy to pay off. The offside web spun by Moore and Jones, plus the determination and hunger flooding through Red veins, provided the key to eventual victory but two magic moments settled it. Seven minutes before the break, Rawlings picked up possession from Johnston's eye-of-the-needle through-ball and creamed a low shot past the keeper for his eighth goal in eleven starts. Two minutes from time, Steward, deputising for the injured Richardson, made a Banksian leap to turn an Arsenal header past the post. Ultimately, it was the save that defined his career – people were still talking and writing about it thirty years later.

The train journey back to Manchester was by all accounts a happy and boozy one. United were not safe yet but at least their fate was back in their own hands. They were still bottom but so tightly clustered were the teams in the lower half of the table that a home victory against Liverpool on the final day would guarantee survival. United, Wednesday, Sunderland and Middlesbrough all had 37 points; Sheffield United and Spurs, who had already played their last game, had 38. Because Sunderland and Boro were playing each other on the last day, even a draw would be good enough as long as Wednesday lost and the match at Ayresome Park did not end all square.

According to a story in the *Evening Chron*, Bamlett held the key to United's prospects. Not Herbert, mind, but his eight-year-old daughter Mary – or, more accurately, her little black doll. Bamlett junior had been given the doll in the midst of the Reds' bleak spring. For some reason she had convinced her dad to take it into the dressing-room before the Burnley win. The doll had also made an appearance for the 2-1 against Bolton but did not travel with the team for the Bury defeat and was booked in for a tea-party back at the Bamletts' when United lost to Sheffield. However, it had been at Old Trafford for the Sunderland success and went on its first away day when the Reds won at Highbury. Before he packed the doll in his suitcase, Bamlett was given strict instructions by his daughter to 'Tell Mr Wilson [now fit again and captaining the side in Barson's absence] to take hold of my doll and show it to the United players.' Her request had been carried out and now the doll was the team's unofficial mascot. And if Mary thought it was staying in on May 5, when Liverpool were in town, she had another thing coming.

Another thing in the Reds' favour was that they were facing de-motivated opponents. Today, the opportunity to send United down would arouse Scousers as much as the prospect of soaring prices in the used hubcap trade. In the twenties there was little or none of the United-Liverpool aggro that exists in modern times. Lancastrian solidarity remained resolutely strong. Both clubs would rather the other did well than teams from other parts of the country, particularly Yorkshire and the snooty south. The region as a whole took genuine pleasure from seeing Lancastrian sides prosper in league and cup.

Throw in the fact that Liverpool had hoisted themselves clear of their own relegation worries the previous week, that they had two former Reds on their books (Hopkin and McBain, though there was no love lost between United and the latter) and stir in memories of the previous occasion that the club had needed a helping hand from the Scousers to save them from the drop and you have the ingredients for a result of convenience. So it proved. Instead of ninety minutes of acid-rising tension, the game was over as a contest before half-time. Spence and Rawlings both bagged braces as the Reds established a 4-1 interval lead and Spence completed his hat-trick as United powered to a season's best 6-1 in the second.

Bearing in mind the match-fixing affair from 1915, the observation in *The Manchester Guardian* that 'Liverpool retired from the pitch at Old Trafford bearing with great cheerfulness the burden of a 6-1 defeat' may possibly have set alarm bells ringing at the FA. However, it was never seriously suggested that Liverpool had been induced to roll over. As FIFA found out in '82 when West Germany and Austria walked through a mutually convenient 1-1 draw, there is nothing they can do to make a team play well. Which was no consolation to Algeria, the team that was affected by the Aryan pact in the Spain World Cup, or to Boro and Spurs, the two sides that were stood over the relegation trapdoor when it opened in '28. Bamlett's old club lost at home to Sunderland to finish bottom while Spurs only found out their fate late that evening because they were in Amsterdam on a summer tour. As good a place as any to hear that sort of news? Today, perhaps. Before the hippies moved in there was no spacecake at hand to help ease the pain.

Back in Manchester, Reds were still wondering whether their pot was half-full or half-empty. United's end-of-season escape from relegation was an achievement that ranked with anything the club had managed since the war. Then again, it was a source of embarrassment that they had dug so deep a hole for themselves in the first place. Bamlett's attempts at developing a more attacking style were brave and honourable but the club could ill-afford to lose the defensive solidity that had been its only real strength in the post-war era. In his first full season in charge, the Reds had scored more goals (72) than in any campaign since the first championship year but they had conceded more (80) than any other side in United history. And even though Reds were desperate to see a return to the club's trademark dashing football, they would much rather have watched a defence-minded team re-establish itself in the top division than an attacking one go down in a blaze of goals, most of them in their own net. Bamlett's mistake had been to try too much, too soon. Anyone with the slightest football nous could have told him that United did not have the personnel to change overnight to a more scientific, classical style. The loss of Barson had made a bad situation even worse.

Replacing Frank – an impossible task, most would say – would be Bamlett's biggest test yet. Encouragingly, his three major buys, Johnston and Rawlings plus Mary's doll, had been unqualified successes. There were signs, then, that he was up to the demands of the job. But it was a job that was getting more difficult by the week. The club and their public were as disUnited as they had ever been, a gate of just 30,000 for the Liverpool decider being renewed and distressing evidence that, after two miserable seasons, many Reds had started not to care.

Roll of Honour

Champions: Everton

FA Cup Winners: Blackburn Rovers

United: Division 1 (18th) FA Cup (6th Round) Blackburn R

Depression Years Legend

Frank Barson

Centre-half-back Aug 1922 – May 1928
152 apps 4 gls
b. Grimethorpe, Barnsley 10th April 1891
d. Winson Green, Birmingham,
13th Sept 1968
Height: 6' 0" Weight: 12st.10lbs.
Debut: Wolves 0-1 United 09/09/22

FRANK BARSON
MANCHESTER UNITED

Career: *Albion F.C., Cammell Laird F.C., Barnsley Aug 1911, Aston Villa Oct 1919, United Aug 1922, Watford May 1928, Hartlepool United player-coach May 1929, Wigan Borough (am.) Oct 1929, (pro.) July 1930, Rhyl Athletic player-manager June 1931, Stourbridge manager July 1935, Aston Villa youth coach July 1935, senior coach and head trainer Oct 1935, Swansea Town trainer July 1947 – Feb 1954, Lye Town trainer July 1954, retired 1956*

International career *(for England):*
1 cap (England 1-2 Wales at Highbury 15/03/20) 0 gls

It was Sophia Loren, I think, who said that glamour is half what you have and half what other people think you have. Hardness is not so different. Possessing the tools is one thing but a tough guy only becomes truly fearsome when people start to believe the hype about what he might do with them. Mike Tyson was blessed with a punch like a hammer but the reason he dominated the heavyweight division in the manner he did in the eighties was the perception that he would not be unduly bothered if he separated his opponent from certain of his body parts – and I'm talking about something more vital than their ear lobes. Frank Barson carried a similar aura onto the field with him. A hefty back-catalogue of anecdotes, both true and apocryphal, placed him on a par with the horsemen of the apocalypse (as one observer memorably described him) as an opponent it would be best not to run into. His bladder-emptying reputation for dishing out pain won him many on-pitch battles before they had even begun but if it gave him a psychological edge over all but the toughest opponents, Frank's infamy also condemned him to a lifetime spent amongst the great misunderstood. Few outsiders, if any, ever came close to separating the myth of Barson from the reality.

The refereeing fraternity, in particular, swallowed the Barson myth whole. That Frank never got the rub of the green from officials was an undisputed fact both on the Pop Side and beyond. Collisions that merely emphasised his superiority in strength and speed inevitably resulted in opposition free-kicks; bad fouls on Frank were invariably allowed to pass. The mere mention of his name left some referees, including Stanley Rous, later President of FIFA, with an uncontrollable urge to point to the dressing-rooms. On one occasion, at Burnden Park, Frank was forced to stand down just before kick-off with an injury and was replaced by an unknown reserve. Early in the game his deputy floored an opponent and Rous rushed up and told him: 'Cut that stuff out, Barson, or you're off next time.' If it's true, the story not only raises doubts about Rous's impartiality but also his eyesight; Frank, with his huge frame, 30 degree nose and severe, greased-back hairstyle was one of the most recognisable figures in the game.

The FA and the bulk of the press corps were also unable – or unwilling – to see beyond the caricature of Barson as the devil's own although, in their defence, they had good reason to be wary of him. If Frank wasn't the red-eyed monster he was often built up to be (most of his work being [extremely] hard but fair), he was certainly no angel either. Percy Young, in his definitive 1968 history of the club, put it nicely when he wrote that the United skipper had 'an instinct for natural justice'. If his opponents played by the rules so, invariably, did Frank. As he himself said: 'I shirked no collision, and I got up with more respect for the man who had put me down.' If they did not, Frank had no qualms about taking an eye-for-an-eye. In fairness he tended to be open about it. In another famous anecdote, again arising from a league game in Lancashire, Barson was hacked down by the opposing centre-forward, an England international. When the referee came over to caution the culprit, Frank limped towards him and pleaded: 'Don't send him off ref, I'll kick him off in the second half!'

Predictably, the FA failed to recognise that there was an honourable side to Barson's instinct for retribution. It was an unspoken truth that his reputation for wildness deprived him of the mountain of caps he would otherwise have been awarded. Ivan Sharpe, the chief correspondent of the *Athletic News*, wrote in September 1925: 'A little red devil has settled at times on the shoulder of Frank Barson and sung into his ear: "Can you stand for that?" And that explains the international record.' Frank's supporters argued that the selectors had merely fallen for the Barson myth but then, just six months after Sharpe's article hit the newsstands, he gave his critics all the rope they needed to hang him with by launching his infamous, unprovoked attack on City's Sam Cowan in the cup semi. The 'little red devil' that Sharpe had talked about had reappeared at the worst possible time.

It is often misleading to talk of talent in terms of caps, anyway. If the size of a cap collection was a foolproof barometer of ability, Mickey Phelan would go down in history as a better player than Steve Bruce and not even Mickey's mother would stand for that. Frank's claim to greatness is based not on the number of caps and medals he collected (one of each) but on the adulation and admiration that he attracted not just from team-mates, Reds and local pressmen but also from football people across the country. It was not only Mancunians who confidently proclaimed him the finest centre half-back that Britain had produced since the war.

It may have sounded like heresy to those Reds whose memories stretched back as far as the Outcasts but there were many who considered Barson to be the equal even of Charlie Roberts. Their shared command of the centre-back position lifted them to a higher plane than the very good and their Churchillian leadership qualities left even the greats lagging behind them. Some captains lead by example, others by the sheer force of their personalities; the two Red legends led with both. Louis Rocca said of Frank, 'as a captain I never knew one who could get more out of his team' and made special reference to the delight he took in 'encouraging the younger element'. Endorsing Rocca's words, Hughie McLenahan recalled how Barson's persistence and patience helped transform him from an average header of the ball into a brilliant one and had no hesitation in nominating him as 'the greatest captain I know'.

Even when Old Trafford was packed, the sound of Frank exhorting his troops was one of the principal features of match-day in the mid-twenties. He inspired admiration for his passion and skill and affection for the manner in which he would put his body on the line both for his team and his team-mates. The famous Barson bruiser was by no means saved exclusively for those opponents who had been foolhardy enough to cross Frank personally. It was also used to deliver swift retribution against opponents who had taken liberties with Reds anywhere on the pitch. In the circumstances, and given that he rarely made an attempt to disguise his intentions, it was a minor miracle that Barson's record-breaking tally of a dozen career dismissals was not doubled.

But if Frank was the warrior and leader whom you would want to share a trench with, the Barson myth suggested he was not the type of person you would want to share a dressing-room with. His fall-out with Villa saddled him with a reputation as a troublemaker and his United career was dogged by rumours that he was at the centre of various rifts in the camp. It was an image that did not tally with many people's impression of the man. Alf Clarke, the United correspondent of the *Manchester Evening News*, raved about Frank both as a player and a personality. In 1922 the legendary ex-England defender, Jesse Pennington, launched a vigorous defence of him in the *Topical Times*: 'By the way, many people regard Barson as a kind of football bandit, a man whose hand is against everyone and everyone's hand against him. Never was there a greater mistake. He is one of the jolliest, nicest, most affable, good-hearted and genial men in football.'

'He is a bit dour on the field? Well, yes: but as a companion he is splendid, and is very popular among his fellow players. Perhaps silly people who talk as though he were a species of hooligan will kindly noted those remarks. They are made by one who enjoyed Barson's friendship.'

Like hundreds of other on-pitch assassins, Barson was a different person on the other side of the whitewash. Clarke talked favourably of Frank's wit and humour; Young called him a 'great soft lad' while *The Football Chron* described how he would dish out one-liners whilst helping out with the post-match rubdowns. Clearly the team's leader was also one of the lads. He was also an incorrigible practical joker, a worthy successor to Billy Meredith as the club's chief buffoon. The delight he took in winding up his team-mates was not the only Meredithian trait that Frank shared, either. When the Barsons eventually moved to Manchester, to live in Gorse Hill, Stretford, their home became one of the regular haunts of the United in-crowd. On their return from a long journey, or from a session at the nearby Gorse Hill pub, Frank and six or seven of the party would invariably go back to his place for one of his wife's hot-pots. There they would be entertained by Frank's parrot who, just like Billy's, had a mouth like a sewer.

Frank was as assiduous a trainer as Billy but there the comparisons end. The Welshman treated his body like a temple; the Yorkshireman was a graduate of the work-hard, play-hard school. The way Frank dealt with the after-effects of his liver-lacerating sessions was to train like a beast. Early morning runs and post-training walks were key elements in his routine and I'm not talking about a couple of times round the block either, it was more a case of going to Northwich and back. When Chris Taylor and Harry Thomas accepted an invitation to join Frank on one of his cross-country walks, he almost killed them. His pre-season routine was even more taxing. During the summer, when his supping moved up a gear, Frank would invariably pile on the pounds. His way of dragging himself back to his fighting weight was to join the other lads for training and then don four or five sweaters and 'toast' himself in front of the fire in the boiler house. None of his techniques would have gone down well with today's fitness gurus but they certainly seemed to work for Frank; not only did he play consistently brilliantly for the Reds, he played competitive football well into his forties. If he hadn't grown increasingly susceptible to injuries as he got older, it is by no means inconceivable that he would still have been turning it on for United even then.

The downside to Barson's personality only became clear to those who were not part of his inner circle, those who did not share his passion for playing and living and who refused to share a pint with him at the Gorse Hill. Rocca, for one, found him a difficult man to get on with. 'If you threatened or kidded him,' he said, 'Barson would not tolerate you for a moment. Neither was he the type of man who welcomed flattery.' That ties in with the legendary story about him tossing his pub away because he could not stomach the excessive back-slapping from the punters.

It is not difficult to see therefore where the rumours about bust-ups between Frank and certain of his team-mates, particularly Neil McBain, came from. The extrovert, witty and blunt Tyke and the reserved, home-loving Scot were a personality clash waiting to happen. It has often been said of Ian Botham, a similarly larger-than-life figure, that if he takes a dislike to anyone it is total but if he likes someone they are a friend for life. All this calls for speculation, of course, but Frank possibly had the same take on relationships. Undoubtedly he was fiercely loyal to his friends and the vast majority of his colleagues. In his Villa days, for example, he copped a suspension for standing up for the right of a mate of his – an Everton player, Fazackerley – to come into the away dressing-room for a chat. Years later, when he left United for Watford, Frank insisted on honouring a pledge he had made to Tommy Barnett, a young forward whom the club were releasing, to take him with him wherever he went (Watford reaped handsome dividends from the strength of Barson's word; Barnett developed so rapidly that within two years he was rated in the £5,000-plus class). A mountain of similar anecdotal evidence points inexorably to the conclusion that, when Frank left, the club not only lost a great player but, in many ways, a great man. If the McBains and Roccas would have begged to differ, at the very least they would have accepted that, in life as in football, it was far better to have Barson alongside you than against you.

*   *   *

GEORGE HASLAM

CENTRE HALF-BACK, MAY 1921- NOV 1927, 27 APPS 0 GLS

GEORGE 'TINY' HASLAM falls into the category of great United servants rather than great United players. A hefty 6ft-plus (thus the nickname 'Tiny' – get it?), he was superbly built for his position but lacked the footballing nous and touch to make it his own. Instead, he played most of his football for the Reds in the Central League where his strength, leadership and experience made him the perfect foil for the stream of talented juniors flowing through the ranks. Always ready to sacrifice himself in the interests of the club, Tiny had a devoted fan base among the regular reserve-team watchers but his greatest admirer was John Henry Davies, with whom he shared an umbilical relationship à la Ferguson and McClair. It was perhaps no coincidence that Tiny was sold to Portsmouth just days after the President's death.

FRANK MCPHERSON

LEFT-WINGER OR CENTRE-FORWARD
MAY 1922 – JULY 1928, 175 APPS 52 GLS

ARGUABLY THE GREATEST sprinter and shot that the club had ever had, Frank McPherson had the firepower to make an international but not the ball control, variety of method nor, it seems, the mental strength. 'Had McPherson not been too impetuous there was no other wing-man – or centre-forward – in the game at that period who could have come within measurable distance of him,' argued Alf Clarke. 'Frank, however, was inclined to be temperamental, and if he did anything wrong and earned the crowd's displeasure he took it so seriously that he was thrown completely off his game.'

In fairness to Frank, few players would have been able to block out the abuse he regularly received from his own fans. It was something of a mystery why the Barrow Bullet was so badly treated by the Pop Side. All right, when he was bad he was on the wrong side of embarrassing but when he was hot, he could scorch his way through any defence. Considering that Joe Spence was the only other Red who regularly turned opposing backs into quivering wrecks, you would have thought that the crowd would have overlooked those moments when Frank disappeared up his own colon. Moreover, not even Joe could match the Bullet's goal ratio from centre-forward, the position he filled for eleven palmy months following the change in the offside law. Frank netted 35 goals in 53 games in the centre at a lightning rate of 0.66 goals a game; Joe 84 in 138 at 0.61. The self-styled football purists in the press poured scorn on McPherson's gawkish attempts at leading the line but his goals should have been all that mattered to the supporters. After all, they were not exactly flooding in from the rest of the side. Instead, Frank was invariably made the terrace scapegoat unless he scored and was effectively driven out of Old Trafford by fan power. His scoring exploits for his next club, Watford (67 goals in just 94 league games), demonstrated what an own goal that had been. The directors rightly took the blame for the club's interminable decline in the late twenties but the Pop Side's collective conscience wasn't completely clear either.

JIMMY BAIN

LEFT HALF-BACK, OCT 1922 – JULY 1928,
4 APPS 0 GLS

JIMMY BAIN WAS at United three times longer than his older brother David but never came close to matching his impact. A cool but plodding half-back, he was classic Central League fodder and only saw the light of day in the first team in the midst of chronic injury crises. Despite making just four senior appearances and even fewer headlines, Jimmy's lengthy service qualified him for a benefit in 1927. The following winter, a transfer fee of £250 took him to Brentford where he remained for the next twenty-five years, six as a player and the rest as assistant manager and then manager.

JOE ASTLEY

FULL-BACK, AUG 1924 – JUNE 1928, 2 APPS 0 GLS

FOURTH, AT BEST, in a queue headed by Moore, Silcock and Jones, Joe Astley was always fighting a losing battle to make it as a Red. In the end he made only two senior appearances for the senior side, neither of which would have left him with much to tell the grandkids about. Joe's debut, in a losing cause at Burnden in March '26, was a disaster, his lack of experience and mobility being painfully exposed; his second appearance, at home to Sunderland the following spring, was even worse, Joe sustaining a knee injury which cost him eight months' football. The injury was the final straw for both club and player. Shortly after regaining fitness, he was transferred to Notts County.

TOM HARRIS

INSIDE-RIGHT, MAY 1926 – JULY 1928, 4 APPS 1 GL

A BIG FISH at Skelmersdale United, Tom Harris was never more than fish food at Manchester United. A promising start and a goal against Newcastle (in February '27) raised hopes that the Reds had found a superior alternative to Tommy Smith as Joe Spence's provider. Those hopes were never realised – Tom did his best work as a professional for Crewe Alexandra's reserves.

BILLY CHAPMAN

RIGHT-WINGER, MAY 1926 – JUNE 1928, 26 APPS 0 GLS

BROUGHT IN ORIGINALLY as cover for Joe Spence on the right-wing, Billy Chapman's lively performances towards the end of the 1926/27 season earned him a regular place in the side at the start of 27/28 and allowed the selectors the luxury of moving Spence across to the problem centre-forward position. The Official Programme were clearly impressed, writing, in late September: 'He is a very clever player, as we at Old Trafford know. He possesses a delightful "feint" movement which has deceived some of the best defenders in the First league.'

Unfortunately for the former Owl, the directors can't have been as taken with him; just a month after the programme printed their platitudes, they made their move on his old Hillsborough rival, Rees Williams. The Welshman's arrival effectively sounded the death knell on Chapman's United career. The 25-year-old only made two more appearances for the club before he joined the Barson-led exodus to Watford where, in a six-season spell, he played the best football of his career.

DANNY FERGUSON

INSIDE-RIGHT, MAR 1927 – MAY 1928, 4 APPS 0 GLS

DANNY FERGUSON ONLY played four times for United but he could at least claim some minor credit for helping the club escape from almost certain relegation in April 1928. Thrown into a side that had just lost four must-win games on the bounce, Danny justified his promotion with useful performances in the Easter wins against Bolton and Burnley. Unfortunately, he was unable to build on his assured start and when the team started losing again, the young Welshman was swiftly jettisoned. A free transfer to Reading followed that summer but he could not hack it in the second division either and it was only when Fergie dropped down another rung to join Accrington Stanley that he found his true level.

DARK HORSES

I F ANYTHING ILLUSTRATES the gulf in lifestyles between today's footballers and their late-twenties counterparts it is their choice of summertime pursuits. Believe everything you see and read in the tabloids and the modern-day stars do little in the close season other than hang out at celeb haunts, rub shoulders with the glitterati (all right, soap actors) and keep the paparazzi in business. It is a fair bet that the Barsons kept a lower profile when they nipped out for a fish supper and a swift pint. And while today's millionaires could spend the entire summer in a suitably glamorous playground if they so wished, the most the stars of yesteryear could hope for was a week or two somewhere truly exotic like Scarborough.

For the 1919-32 generation of footballers, those summer holidays were an opportunity to indulge in traditional seaside pleasures such as riding donkeys, eating ice cream and falling asleep around with a knotted handkerchief on your head. For the Club 18-30 generation, of course, they are an opportunity to indulge in traditional Mediterranean pleasures such as sticking beer labels to your genitals and having as much sex as is humanly possible. Viewed charitably, the summertime sexploits of famous young players represent an attempt to put their names to good use by giving something (their penises) back to the community (anything in a skirt). However, you would have thought they would have recognised by now the dangers of recording their selfless act for posterity. Seeing their bottoms splashed over five pages of the News of the Screws is no way for their grannies to start their Sundays.

The leap from football to porn star is not one you would have envisaged someone like Harry Williams making, if only because of the difficulties in fitting anything but his ears into shot. Sexual excess is not an image that sits comfortably with players from the cloth cap years. Nor is the drunken violence that seems to be en vogue among modern-day prima donnas, particularly those of a southern persuasion. Trashing take-away joints, bottling bouncers and smashing up taxis – if it ever happened in twenties Manchester, the police and papers missed it.

Now I am not suggesting that old-school Reds were each the paragon of virtue, just that their working-class pay packets ensured they remained close to their working-class roots. So Ray Bennion spent the summer back home in Wrexham flying his pigeons; Billy Johnston and Lance Richardson went trout fishing; Alf Steward played cricket in the Birmingham leagues; several of the others wound down by playing bowls. If the directors had learned from the death of Charlie Radford, though, they would have wrapped the players up in cotton wool. A simple game of tennis proved costly for Tommy Jones – the hernia he picked up on court sidelined him for the whole of the season. No sooner had Billy Spencer, the £3,250 centre-half signed from Newcastle to fill the Barson void and joined up with his new team-mates than he contracted malaria. Injuries and illness, like bad luck, rarely wash as an excuse but Bamlett perhaps deserved special dispensation to play the card. Barson's problems had scuppered the team's chances the previous season. Now the Reds had lost two important players before the new campaign had even begun. And their luck wasn't about to change. For McLenahan, Johnston and Wilson, in particular, 1928/29 was a bitter cocktail of pain and frustration.

The supporters were more interested in what the directors had been up to during the summer than what the players had. Frustratingly, it seemed that the answer was very little. Spencer was the only new arrival worth getting excited about. Otherwise, the principal movement was outward. Barson took his free transfer and moved to Watford. Frank McPherson left for a short stint at newly formed non-league outfit Manchester Central before joining his former captain at Vicarage Road. The boo-boys had finally got their man. Their success did not taste half as sweet, mind, when the club failed to land a replacement outside-left.

A clutch of squad players, Chapman, Ferguson and Jimmy Bain among them, were also disposed of, leaving the squad significantly weaker than the one that had escaped relegation by the skin of its teeth in May. When the criticism of their inactivity reached their ears, the directors responded with the same pair of bland arguments. That a] 'the club strongly disapproves of the policy of paying inflated prices for good players and will not be a party to the practice' (note that they didn't rule out paying inflated prices for bad players) and b] 'we are searching indefatigably for new men who will strengthen the side'. Most supporters did not believe them. The chance to build on the feel-good factor from the Great Escape had been lost.

By the end of August, it had faded completely. True, United had ground out good draws against two up-and-coming sides, Leicester and Aston Villa. But the two points gained were no compensation for the horror moment at Villa Park when Hughie McLenahan had his leg shattered by Villa hatchet man, Frank Moss. The sight of hard-nosed pros from both sides brushing away tears was a dead give-away that a Busstian tragedy was unfolding. When McLenahan was carried, motionless, from the field, it looked like the game had seen the last of a shining talent.

Happily, that wasn't the case. Thirteen months of hospital and recuperative care later, Hughie did return to pick up the pieces of his career. But it was not the one he had seemed assured of when he had first burst onto the scene. After Villa Park, McLenahan was never quite the same player again, the nip and swagger that had made him arguably the club's most exciting ever prospect had gone. Over the next eight years he made another hundred or so appearances for the Reds, captained the side on occasion and played the odd 'grand' game but to see him after the injury was to see Gazza after his – or a bloated Elvis after '72. At least Gazza had already had his World Cup; Hughie was not so fortunate. Potential greatness was snatched away from him before he had managed even a dozen games.

By all accounts, the post-match meal that was awaiting the players on their return to their Birmingham hotel remained uneaten. The whole club felt sick. Perhaps, then, the McLenahan tragedy played a part in the side's poor start to the season – no wins from their opening half-dozen fixtures. But the real reason why the Reds sprang out of the blocks like an obese pensioner from their bathtub was Bamlett. His offside tactics had saved the club at Highbury back in April; his worrying addiction to them lost the team a string of points this time around and ensured they would soon need saving again.

The die was cast early as first City and then Leeds – two of United's favourite catches – were allowed to wriggle off the hook. In the first derby since the Blues' belated re-elevation to the top flight, the Reds were 2-1 up and looking favourites to score next when Silcock and Moore rushed forward, needlessly, in a two-man hokey-cokey. When the linesman didn't flag, City's Johnson was given the freedom of Maine Road to advance and slip one between Steward's legs. Elland Road was even worse. Again leading 2-1, this time following a hooked shot from Johnston and a Spence tap-in, United retreated, loaded the offside trap and were left helpless and hopeless as the mechanism jammed. Leeds scored twice in the final half hour and by the time the Reds had started playing again, it was too late for them to prevent their first defeat of the season though Spence came close to salvaging a point when his big dipper crashed against the underside of the bar.

The following week's clash with Liverpool was perhaps the derby in negative, United making up for losing a point they should have won by winning one they should have lost. Much of the fare at Old Trafford was depressingly mediocre but the Reds' two equalisers – Silcock's forty-five yard wonder-strike (or fluke) and Hanson's late, late penalty – did at least offer the watching 24,000 some value for money. Unfortunately, the same could not be said of summer signing Spencer, who produced a debut performance belonging in the Bellion rather than Rooney category. As he had yet to fully shake off the debilitating effects of his illness, or come to terms with the side's depressing 'lack of system going forward', both press and punters alike backed off from giving the new boy the critical mauling he perhaps deserved. In retrospect, though, they would have been justified in giving him the bird. Taking an instant dislike to Billy Spencer would have saved them time.

Nine years of Charlie Roberts and six of Frank Barson had turned United watchers into connoisseurs of the centre-back art. Spencer, despite a pedigree that stretched to two England caps and a league and cup winners' medal, just did not measure up. His defensive play was invariably sound but his work with the ball was, at best, patchy. For their money, the Reds had secured not a second Barson but a third back. By the spring, it was clear that they would have been better off keeping their £3,250 and banking on Mann or Hilditch instead.

The lack of a playmaker in the pivotal position would not have been such a problem had Bamlett not persisted with his ambitious plans to convert United into an attacking team more in keeping with the image of his old Boro side (as in the one that had just gone down). In an interview with the local press in September, he pledged to push the inside-forwards further up the field and concentrate on attack over defence. After seventeen months in the job, the United manager had still not grasped the fact that he did not have the personnel to fulfil his ideals. You may want to feed the starving but unless you have messianic tendencies you are not going to get very far with a couple of slices of bread and half a haddock. Bamlett had some impressive talent at his disposal – Spence, Spencer, Rawlings, Silcock, Bennion, Hilditch and Jones had all won international recognition; Steward, Moore, Wilson, Johnston and Mann all could have done while Hanson was on the verge of converting youthful promise into senior achievement. But he did not have enough players with the constructive ability to satisfy his, and the supporters', hunger for attractive football. Take the captain, Wilson, out of a half-back line already deprived of McLenahan and there was not much left other than experience, hard work and tough tackling. Take Johnston and Spence out of the forward line and there was not much left other than hard work and even harder running.

At one end of the pitch Bamlett had the right tactics but the wrong players. At the other end he had the right players but the wrong tactics. Few could understand the manager's devotion to offside when United's defenders were comfortably good enough not to need to resort to it. Silcock was still a great back, Moore as reliable as ever and waiting in the wings alongside Jones was another fine prospect, ex-Sandbach Rambler Billy Dale. Bamlett was making a faux pas by attempting to fix something that wasn't broken. And also tying himself in tactical knots by attempting to combine an attacking philosophy with offside tactics. Admittedly, the two philosophies do not have to be mutually exclusive – attacking teams can push up and play offside – but as a mindset they are as contradictory as despising homosexuals but loving Erasure.

A reality check was required. Until he was given the funds to build the side that he wanted to (and that was as likely as a lesbian needing a condom) Bamlett had to accept that his role at Old Trafford was as a plasterer, filling in the cracks in the side as best he could, rather than as a plastic surgeon, seeking to turn the ugly into the attractive. By abandoning the defence-minded pragmatism that had kept the club out of the second division for much of the decade and instead pursuing some sort of attacking utopia, the United manager risked falling halfway between the twin stools of scrapping for points and entertaining the public. Doing neither was a recipe for losing games – and supporters. This season, for the first time in years, the attendance figures were a worry right from the off. There would have been far fewer than 20,000 inside OT for the Leicester game had it been common knowledge that Spencer was not well enough to make his debut. The 24,000 Liverpool gate was 10,000 short of respectability. More and more Reds were kicking the match-day habit. The competition from the dogs and the latest sporting craze, dirt-track racing (sensibly renamed speedway) at nearby White City threatened to make a bad situation even worse.

When United tamely surrendered at Upton Park on September 22, they were the only top-flight club still looking for their first win. What better time, then, for the fixture-list to throw up a dolly of a match against the season's surprise strugglers, Newcastle. In front of 25,000, United finally broke their winless diet with a five-goal binge, three of which came in a seven-minute blur early in the first half. Hanson, Rawlings and Spence all pitched in with sweet finishes but the best of the lot was Johnston's magical fifth. Receiving the ball from Spence forty yards from goal, the shimmying Scot slalomed through half the Toon, eased his way round the keeper and rolled the ball nonchalantly over the line.

The Official Programme nominated it as one of the finest goals Old Trafford had ever seen. It was a shame, then, that the bulk of the crowd had already made a move for the trams. Which is another of football's great unfathomables. Why is it that getting home early seems to be a priority for so many supporters? Would they leave a theatre before they found out who'd dunnit? Or a curry house before they got stuck into the free mints? If people are so desperate to get back to their armchairs, why do they bother climbing out of them in the first place? In extreme cases – the birth of a child, a fire, Kleberson coming on – it may be acceptable to leave before the end. Otherwise, I am a firm believer that supporters should stay until the final whistle, if only for the opportunity to boo the bastards off. Two words should be sufficient for those who feel that being first off the car park, or first in the boozer, is the better option than staying put: George Best. In football you just never know when the next Nou Camp moment will happen. For Bestie, who left the ground when the European Cup was still heading for Bavaria, it never did.

As humiliating defeat by Newcastle the previous September had supplied the Bamlett era with its first reverse, there was a neat symmetry in United's winless run coming to an end with a massacre of the Bar-codes. Since the 7-1 disaster had enveloped his career in crisis, the 5-0 revenge must have tasted particularly sweet for Alf Steward. In the circumstances, his second clean sheet since his summertime re-elevation to first choice could not have been better timed; in psycho-babble, I think they call it closure. There was satisfaction, too, for Spencer, playing against his old club for the first time. His mastery over Gallacher demonstrated what a powerful destructive force he could be.

For a few surreal weeks he may even have thought he had made the right move. Losing to Newcastle in September '27 had plunged the Reds into a mini-crisis. Beating them this year was the prelude to a triumphant rise up the table – from bottom five to top six. The performances in the home draw with Cardiff and the 1-0 against Birmingham were as guileless as any that September had thrown up but the victories at league leaders Burnley and also Huddersfield, where the Reds had never previously won, were both contenders for the accolade of 'best under Bamlett'. The Burnley upset probably just shaded it. United were too quick and, for once, too skilful for their hosts whose two penalties lent the final score a flattering feel. Spence rolled in a gift on five, Johnston set up Hanson for 2-1, Jimmy, emerging as the spot-kick specialist the team had sorely lacked, then converted the third penalty of the afternoon for 3-2 and Joe reacted quickest when his original shot cannoned off the post to push United out of reach. The Spence-Hanson axis again shared the goals in the 2-1 Huddersfield triumph. The latter's penalty winner, three minutes from time, was further proof both of his steel balls and of his graduation from player of the future to player for now.

But if the right flank provided the goals, the inspiration for the victories came from the left. For now, at least, the experiment of playing Rees Williams, a toothless right-winger the season before, on the opposite flank was paying off. The Welshman's discreet use of the ball, combined with the promptings of the Old Trafford intelligentsia, Wilson and Johnston, added another sharp point to the Reds' left-sided triangle. If Rawlings had shown anything like his springtime form, the forward line would have finally shaken off the chocolate teapot comparisons. Unfortunately, the centre-forward who could do no wrong in 27/28, was in the midst of a spell when he could do no right. Already, worried Pop Siders were whispering that last year's saviour was looking like this one's Harry Leonard.

Annoyingly, it wasn't long before the rest of the side joined Bill in the supporters' bad books. Turf Moor and Leeds Road were a brief flirtation with excellence rather than the start of a long-lasting relationship; the equivalent of getting off with the girl of your dreams and then watching her get run over by a bus. When injuries and loss of form snuffed out the team's October spark, the goal rush subsided into a steady dribble of one a match and the Reds entered a tailspin of record-breaking proportions. What no one could have predicted in the wake of the Huddersfield triumph was that it would be nine weeks before they next scored twice in a match and another seven before they kept a clean sheet. Worst of all, it would be three months before they next won, three shameful months in which they swapped top six for rock bottom.

Johnston was the first to follow McLenahan onto the list of long-term absentees, tweaking a knee ligament after stepping on the ball in training. It would have been a laughable way to get injured if anyone had been in the mood to smile. The original injury ruled Billy out for six weeks. Later, when he was rushed back too soon, he was ruled out for the season. The number of times that United players broke down after returning too quickly from injury begs the question whether the club's doctors had ever seen the inside of a medical college. In late November, Jones attempted a comeback in the reserves and immediately aggravated his injury. In previous years, Barson, in particular, had experienced more breakdowns than a rusty Trabant. A better programme for treating Frank's chronic groin problems might just have extended his United career. It was clear, even during the October renaissance, that the team were missing him badly. 'When Barson was at United,' mused the *Athletic News*, 'they had a personality in the pivotal position. His successor, Spencer, though useful in defence, lacks Barson's dominating influence over the opposing inside men while his attempts to construct attacks are crude and ineffective.'

Not long after one Red schemer was ruled out through injury, the other was ruled out with illness. Wilson had bravely played on despite an attack of quinsies (pus-filled swellings in the throat, not an obsession with seventies' medical sleuths), even turning out in a couple of matches wearing a scarf. By mid-November, though, it was obvious that he couldn't keep on putting his neck, quite literally, on the line. Later it became clear that he should never have been allowed to; Jack was plagued by ill-health all winter and he was never quite the same influence during his two attempted comebacks as he had been before.

Less then three months into the season, the club had lost a trio of half-backs and both playmakers. They were blows a weak squad could not possibly absorb. Shorn of their midfield heartbeat and their attacking brains, the Reds became football zombies, stumbling around with their arms outstretched and only catching out those teams who were too stupid or too slow to get out of their way. Admittedly, their decline was gradual at first. One point was ill-reward for United's efforts in the November treble with Bolton, Sheffield Wednesday and Derby, good teams one and all. Bolton were gifted an ill-deserved point by Bamlett's offside folly on the 3rd, second-placed Wednesday were spared by feeble finishing on the 10th while league leaders Derby were pushed all the way for their 1-0 on the 17th. It wasn't till the trip to Sunderland the following week that United copped a proper spanking – by five lashes to one – but once the floodgates opened, there was no shutting them; in the next month alone, they conceded no fewer than twenty goals.

The goal deluge jolted the boardroom tinkermen – who had shown admirable patience thus far – back into feverish action. Three changes for the Blackburn match on December 1 ushered in a two-month spell that featured more comings and goings than an Annabel Chong movie. In that time, Hilditch, Mann, Nicol, Thomas, Sweeney, Ramsden and Partridge all yo-yoed in and out of the side but the player who suffered most from the selectorial flailing was Rawlings who was dropped, and recalled, nine times in just seven weeks. Initially, his demotion caused a stir in the press-box, the pro-Rawlings lobby arguing that any striker would have dried up given the dismal support Bill was getting – Hanson's form was good but Spencer regularly gave the impression that he would struggle to pass wind, Spence had just entered his worst trough for years while Williams, a lost soul on the left without his injured partners, was in the process of playing himself out of the side and onto the transfer list.

The counter-argument from the Pop Side was that Rawlings would have struggled to hold up a pair of stockings, his touch was in the rapist class and the service he was getting was nowhere near as bad as he was making it look. Their case was strengthened when, on successive Saturdays, two opposing forwards gave entrancing demonstrations of what a £4,000 International should have been doing for the Reds. At Old Trafford, Blackburn's Bourton gave a master-class in poaching, scoring all four of his side's goals from no more than half a dozen chances. And when Rawlings was recalled for the trip to Highbury he was comprehensively outshone by David Jack, the game's first £10,000 man, who celebrated his ground-breaking transfer from Bolton by netting the Gunners' first and final goals in a comfortable 3-1.

A home draw with the struggling champions Everton on the 15th constituted a bright moment in United's nose-dive. Another point was pinched from the Christmas Day fixture against Sheffield United. Otherwise, the final month of the year was an even gloomier experience than one-point November. At least the Reds had lost to good teams then. Portsmouth had not beaten anyone at Fratton Park for weeks but romped home 3-0 against Bamlett's visitors. The reports said that United played football typical of the second division, a skill-and-subtlety-free combination of crash and dash. Fittingly, they took Pompey's place in the bottom two. Boxing Day at Bramall Lane was even worse; a 6-1 hammering by another potential relegation rival. When the Reds ended the year with another defeat and another injury (with Johnston breaking down in his comeback match), this time at Filbert Street, they were in depressing disarray, only kept off the bottom by the dreadful form of local rivals Bury. It was a bad time for Manchester all round – City were only two points and two places ahead.

That the 30,000 gate for the 2-2 draw with Villa on New Years Day was the biggest of the season so far said much about the team's fading pulling power. So did a derby crowd of just 45,000 the following Saturday. Amid rumours of supporters ripping up their season tickets, one letter, printed in *The Football Chron*, typified the Pop Side attitude: 'You have continually told us during the past three seasons of the efforts of the directors to secure talent. Weekly we are told of players being "watched" and of their unsuitability, and all the time the patient, loyal and long-suffering supporters have to watch the ridiculous efforts of the most inept team seen in post-war football....One cannot be blind to the fact that United are only about third division class and would not be prominent in that sphere.'

In terms of losing foot-soldiers, Napoleon's retreat from Moscow had nothing on the Red Army's experiences in 1928/29. Thousands of Reds resolved to stay away until some new talent was acquired. Those who remained were building on their reputation as some of the grouchiest supporters around. One or two players, with Rawlings odds on to have been one of them, had expressed their off-the-record amazement that the team never got any encouragement from their own fans. For their part, the press dusted down the previous year's lectures about a country getting the government it deserves. This time, the theory that the players struggled to express themselves in front of their terrace tormentors had some foundation in actual results. With just two wins at Old Trafford all season, United's home record was comfortably the worst in the division.

In different circumstances, four successive OT fixtures to kick off the year would have represented a golden opportunity to leg it up the table. Not for a team with United's home-ophobia. The home run made a bad situation even worse. As in September, glorious chances to defeat both City and Leeds were carelessly tossed aside. The Blues should have been buried once Rawlings, with his final contribution of the season, had opened the scoring early in the second half. But the Reds mistakenly opted to shut up shop rather than look for the killer punch and paid the price for their negativity when City stuck away two goals in the final six minutes. Despite having the better of both this season's derbies, revenge for the semi-final humiliation would have to wait.

A kind draw against regular third-round doormats Port Vale at least ended the club's search for any sort of success but a league maximum remained elusive. By losing to the Tykes on the 19th, the Reds set a new club record for the number of games without a league win, eclipsing the unlucky thirteen from 1913/14. This latest defeat was particularly embarrassing, coming as it did against a team that played three quarters of the match with nine outfield players and a part-time keeper so inept that he punched the first, harmless cross he faced (from Sweeney) into his own net. Again United sat back on their one goal lead, again they paid the price, Leeds repeating the lesson about attack being the best form of defence by scoring twice in the second half, the second again painfully late.

The club were now bottom of the table but they had not stopped sinking, not yet anyway. Bury edged the fourth-round cup battle between the division's bums on the 26th, scoring a late-ish winner after Spence had missed a penalty and Sweeney, Johnston's occasional replacement at ten, had fluffed two open goals. The watching Charlie Roberts was asked whether Sandy Turnbull would have failed with such opportunities: 'Not a bit of it,' he replied. '"Give me a receipt for that," he used to say to the goalkeeper.' The glory days of Turnbull, Roberts and the rest had rarely seemed so far away. Another home defeat, this time against West Ham, and a 5-0 collapse at Newcastle on February 9 extended United's winless league sequence to sixteen games and pushed them another step closer to the second division.

Almost unnoticed, though, the corner had been turned. What with the 'squared' 2-0 in 1915 and the previous May's 6-1, Liverpool already had a history of acting as accomplices in United's relegation getaways. The arrival of bulky centre-forward, Tommy Reid was to complete an unlikely hat-trick. Admittedly, a pig farmer's face and a frame to match did not exactly scream saviour-in-the-making, nor did the fact that Reid had spent most of his time at Anfield in the reserves. When he first joined, then, most supporters doubted Thomas. But those who had done their homework would have already seen signs that Bamlett had struck gold. Reid's goal record when he had been given a chance at Liverpool had been impressive – the previous season he had netted fifteen times in just twenty-five appearances. Also, his strength, pertinacity and general, no-frills style made him the perfect foil for the collection of lightweight semi-midgets that made up the rest of United's attack. Soon it would become clear that Tommy was not only the goalscorer the supporters had craved he was also the granite-hard leader that his team-mates had.

If Rawlings's arrival the previous spring had been that season's Cantona moment, the signing of Reid was this year's Rawlings moment. Tommy made a scoring debut in the Hammers defeat and was swamped, like the rest of the team, at Newcastle but that was it as far as bad news went at least for the next couple of months or so. Once Reid had made a triumphant return to Anfield, scoring twice as his new club broke their winless streak with a by-the-seat-of-their-pants 3-2 against his old, the Reds were transformed into the form team of the division. Before Liverpool, they had drawn four and lost fourteen of their last eighteen matches and had languished three points adrift of second-bottom Portsmouth and four behind Bury who had a game in hand. With Reid scoring goals and rampaging through defences, they launched into a stunning fifteen game sequence which yielded twenty-four points, seven more than they had previously managed in the whole of the season.

Three days after the Anfield turning-point, Tommy trampled his way through the visitors' keeper to lay on the winner against Burnley. A week later, both he and Hanson scored equalisers against Cardiff. The dropped point was annoying but it was obvious from the relegation battle at Ninian Park which side had the better chance of staying in the division (and it wasn't the hosts, who ended up taking the wooden spoon). That final week in February was the last the Reds would spend in the division's basement. By the time they had passed through most of March unbeaten, the road to Damascus (or at least twelfth place, an almost miraculous position given the hole the team had dug for themselves mid-season) had opened up before them.

As the catalyst for the side's transformation, Reid deserved the plaudits that came his way. But United's revival was by no means a one-man job. After going four months without one, the defence remembered how to keep clean sheets, the half-backs tightened up while, either side of Reid, the wings abandoned their dead pigeon impression and started flapping again. Spence's return to form alongside the excellent Hanson was welcome enough but the real pleasure came from watching the emergence of a dynamic new partnership on the left. Johnston's injury and Williams's disappearing act had given an unexpected opportunity to the reserve wing-pair of Thomas and ex-Shrewsbury inside-forward Harry Rowley. After four matches spent acclimatising, the two Harrys clicked in the Burnley 1-0 and never looked back. Rowley, in particular, took the eye, with several commentators writing that United had another Lochhead on their hands.

Within months they would be proved right though, annoyingly, for a 'wrong' as well as a 'right' reason. So confident were the directors that Rowley, like Rennox before him, was now the future at inside-left that they decided to play hardball in their end-of-season contract talks with Billy Johnston. Unsurprisingly, the talks broke down and when they did, Billy, the side's brains, was dumped on the transfer list. Four years on from the disastrous decision to get rid of Lochhead, the club had still not learned that lesson about the swallow and the summer. It got worse, too. When no one came in for the classy Scot at the inflated price the Reds were looking for, he was pushed into football purgatory at non-league Macclesfield where he remained for two seasons until the directors admitted what cocks they had been and re-signed him. Imagine that, the equivalent of United choosing the Ginger Prince ahead of King Eric in '95, dumping Eric on the list and then not even cashing in, instead letting him play for Hyde United for free.

That was a problem for the future. For now, Hanson and the backs were making sure that March extended the Red revival rather than ended it. While the rest of the attack temporarily ran dry, Jimmy hit three goals, one each against Birmingham, Huddersfield and Bolton. The reinvigorated defence picked up those slim pickings and converted them into a couple of draws and a win, results that maintained United's two point advantage over the bottom two. What made the back-line's resurgence even more creditable was that it was achieved without the services of Silcock, out injured since Anfield. Following the lead of Tom Jones from the promotion season, Billy Dale stepped out of the shadows to prevent Jack's injury being the catastrophe that was originally anticipated. Dale made such an impression that when Silcock was back fit he insisted, in typically selfless style, that his deputy be retained in the side. Invariably, the press reports on the cultured, gap-toothed Mancunian were soaked in drool. In one of them, the Wanderer orgasmed: 'There cannot be another young player so certain of future honours as Dale. He is brilliant in timing a tackle, and if he has a tendency to balloon the ball on occasions that is his only fault.'

After his three week sabbatical from the headlines, Reid was back among the goals as Wednesday were overpowered at Old Trafford on the 23rd. Both the result and its manner would assume more kudos at the end of the season when the Owls were crowned champions. The two vital Easter games with Bury were both won, convincingly, Reid's hat-trick at Gigg Lane and Thomas's looping header in the Old Trafford return pushing the Shakers even closer to their eventual relegation. In the circumstances it hardly mattered that United's unbeaten sequence had come to a crushing, 6-1 end at the Baseball Ground on Easter Saturday (Derby, who hadn't had a game on Good Friday, making the most of their unfair advantage). Now they had gained a double dose of revenge for their cup KO, the Reds, who had five games remaining to their rivals' six, were five points clear of danger. Not mathematically safe, perhaps, but not far off.

Now that the pressure had eased, the run-in became a month-long purple patch. In that time, the team put together their best sequence of results in the Bamlett era. Not until Buddy Holly boarded a plane with Ritchie Valens and the Big Bopper were so many big names brought down in such a short space of time. Four months earlier, consecutive fixtures against title-chasing Sunderland, Blackburn and Arsenal had ended 1-5, 1-4 and 1-3. In April, the same three sides were swept aside by a cumulative 10-1. No wonder the crowds were swarming back to Old Trafford. An impressive 35,000 looked on as the Reds slammed three past Sunderland before half-time. When Frank Mann, who had not bothered the scorers since November 1923, banged in the second from thirty yards, most must have suspected that their pre-match pint had been fiddled with. Another 3-1, at Blackburn the following Saturday, brought some much-thirsted recompense for all those Ewood nightmares, 4-1 against Arsenal more evidence both of Red and Reid irresistibility. Tommy's two goals against the Gunners took his tally to five in his last three appearances and thirteen in fifteen all told. Best of all, they guaranteed the Reds another year in the big league. Whatever Rawlings had done, Reid had now matched. Or possibly bettered. After all, when Bill arrived, United had been laid low with relegation sickness but had not actually been in the relegation zone. When Tommy followed suit, they had needed snookers.

By the time the Reds had chewed up the outgoing champions Everton, 4-2 at Goodison, they were being freely tipped as potential dark horses for next season's crown. For a team of their limited talents and recent pedigree (one top ten finish in sixteen years) it seemed nonsensical, the sort of talk that normally spews from the mouth of someone who spends too much time leaning on gates and chewing on straw. But Sheffield Wednesday's title success had set a precedent. Twelve months earlier, the Owls had needed a similarly brilliant revival to keep themselves out of the jaws of the second division. If the Reds could maintain their momentum as successfully, there would be no stopping them next time around. Then again, much the same had been said after the first Great Escape. And look how 1928/29 had turned out.

ROLL OF HONOUR

CHAMPIONS: SHEFFIELD WEDNESDAY

FA CUP WINNERS: BOLTON WANDERERS

UNITED: DIVISION 1 (12TH) FA CUP (4TH ROUND) BURY

EDWARD PARTRIDGE

LEFT-WINGER & INSIDE-LEFT
JUNE 1920 – MAY 1929, 160 APPS 18 GLS

LITHE, BOLD, FAST and plucky, Teddy Partridge was an instant hit at United when he was picked up for a song from Ebbw Vale in the summer of 1920. By December, his performances as one half of the fastest left-wing pairing in the division had impressed the *Football News* correspondent enough for him to write: 'I shall be greatly surprised if Partridge does not prove one of the club's best ever goal-scoring forwards.' That journalist must have been effin'
flabbergasted, then, when Teddy, who had scored eight goals in his debut season, knocked in just ten more in his next eight. During that time, his status slumped from hero to laughing stock and then carried on sliding. Long before his 1929 adios, Ted was as fashionable as the comb-over.

The fall and fall of Teddy Partridge can be traced back to the summer of '21 when he was evicted from his favoured inside-left berth and relocated in the left-wing position that had been made vacant by the controversial sale of Fred Hopkin. Ted did his best on the flank but lacked the tricks and build to prosper there and after two years of unspectacular graft he lost his place to Frank McPherson. With Arthur Lochhead and, later, Charlie Rennox blocking his route back into the side at ten, the then 32-year-old all but disappeared from the first-team radar, making just nine appearances in the next three years.

Possibly he should have stayed disappeared. Instead, Ted did a kind of Tracy Barlow in reverse. In the Street, 'our Tracy' famously spent her puberty playing 'terps' in her room before the writers did the decent thing and relaunched the character with a different actress playing the part. When Partridge was recalled to the team in the wake of McPherson's switch to centre-forward, he was the same ginger-haired midget he had always been but he was no longer the same player. The boo-boys did not take long to cotton on. In 26/27 he was the subject of light barracking from the Pop Side, by the following year it had been amplified and during his farewell season many supporters would gladly have mounted him in concrete and dropped him in the Irwell.

For much of that time, the press lined up resolutely behind the veteran forward. In March '28, the *Football News* argued: 'A mere featherweight and lacking in inches, Partridge always plays under a big handicap, but no one can say that his first interests are not those of the club. Give me the man of the type of Partridge, who is willing to chance his arm in any position rather than players who are only willing to turn out when the occasion suits him'. The following April they added: 'He is one of the oldest servants of the club, willing to stand down or play as ordered to, and he has certainly earned every copper he has been paid in wages.'

Eventually, though, even the press set aside their admiration for Partridge's spirit and longevity (he was 38 when he finally left United to join Halifax Town) and came round to the supporters' view that he was not in first league class and, quite probably, was the worst winger in the division. In fairness, they did not have to change their tune too much – praise for Teddy's footballing prowess had recently been noticeable for its absence, anyway. This line, in a match report from 26/27, was typical of the write-ups he received post-'23: '[Partridge] chased the ball and worried the opposing players of every rank with the spirit of a terrier let loose on the seashore.' The comparison could not have been more apt – after all, Teddy ran around a lot and ultimately produced shit, too.

LANCE RICHARDSON

GOALKEEPER, APRIL 1926 – MAY 1929, 42 APPS 0 GLS

THERE WAS ALWAYS something a little bit different about Lance Richardson. There was the name for a start. Amongst the Jacks, Toms, Johns and John Thomases (four of them played for United in the Depression Years – most Reds would have sworn they had seen far more than that) in the dressing-room, Lancelot (and his middle name, Holliday) stood out like a third ear. As someone whose education did not start and end down the pit or at the school of hard knocks, Lance would have stood apart from his peers anyway. His penchant for hugely baggy pants and spats made sure, just in case, and won him plenty of good-natured stick from the dressing-room wags. To the working-class majority in the squad, Lance must have come across as a Ginger/Biggles figure – the archetypal English toff who would be bashing the Bosch one minute and bombing around the country lanes with his silk scarf flying behind him the next.

Given Richardson's innate sense of style, it was perhaps inevitable that his goalkeeping veered towards the extravagant too. His technique was certainly sound enough but, judging from the frequency with which he came roaring out of goal to attack both man and ball, merely doing the basics did not get his juices flowing. On his more eccentric days he spent so much time charging between his area and the halfway-line that it was reasonable to speculate whether he had got his jockstrap caught on the dressing-room door.

Because of his all-risks approach, match reports tended to describe Lance as either brilliant or a reckless fool, little else. Recognising that there was a fine keeper lurking behind the eccentricity, many commentators urged him to find a cure for his wanderlust. Bearing in mind the old maxim about sporting mavericks – the one that warns: 'take away their wild side and you'll take away half the player' – it was probably just as well that Lance ignored their advice even though his failure to find a happy medium between enterprise and madness ultimately cost him a lengthy United career. He was a virtual ever-present in 27/28, a season in which his dashing exploits won him admirers throughout the game (none bigger than Dixie Dean who included Richardson's Goodison heroics in his memoirs), but he lost his place to the more reliable Alf Steward the season after and, not fancying another year on the sidelines, moved to Reading that summer. What Lance did when he eventually hung up his roll-neck (in 1932) fitted perfectly with the Richardson persona. While his erstwhile team-mates headed for the docks and factories, or took up positions as trainers or publicans, when they finished playing, Lance moved to Argentina to work on his dad's ranch.

REES WILLIAMS

WINGER, OCT 1927 – AUG 1929, 35 APPS 2 GLS

THE REPLACEMENT FOR Billy Meredith in the Welsh side, Rees Williams never came close to ousting him from the affections of the Red Army even if he did enjoy a four-month purple patch at the start of his second season when he was experimented with at outside-left. In the midst of that patch, the *Topical Times* gave an enthusiastic write-up of the qualities of the pacy Welshman, paying special tribute to his 'tact and steadiness', mean body-swerve and his knack of bringing 'the high ball to heel' (a useful skill given that the service to United's forwards regularly arrived at head height). Ultimately, though, Rees lacked the devil and goalscoring ability to make it as a Red and even though he remained a regular in the Wales team, he was jettisoned after less than two seasons with the club. Years later (in 1963), the Rees Williams story drew to a tragic end when worries about his health caused him to take his own life, a lead that another Welsh Red, 1983 Cup Final hero Alan Davies, sadly followed in 1992.

GEORGE NICOL

CENTRE-FORWARD, JAN 1928 – MAY 1929, 7 APPS 2 GLS

THERE CAN'T HAVE been many Glaswegian pork butchers who have gone on to conquer the English first division. For ninety minutes in February 1928, George Nicol looked like he might just have it in him. Nine goals in four reserve games following his turn-of-year move from Saltcoats Victoria won him a rapid call-up to the first team; two goals on his debut against Leicester raised hopes that Herbert Bamlett had uncovered a George Camsell for United. Unfortunately, an appetite for scoring goals and their Christian names were all that the two strikers had in common. Nicol's subsequent performances for the Reds put an end to the fairy tale. Cruder than a pub comedian, slower than the carcasses he used to hang up at work, George remained a prolific scorer in the Central League but was out of his depth in the top flight. It was only when he dropped down the divisions to join Brighton that he made an impression at League level.

THE CRASH

I N MAY 1929 Labour and Ramsay MacDonald were voted back
into office. According to some, they owed much of their success
to girl power. Since women between the ages of twenty-one and
thirty were voting for the first time, never before had the country
spoken with such a high pitched voice. And it appears that the idea
of voting for the government did little for them. Perhaps they sensed
that Tory notions on sexual equality were unlikely to extend beyond
giving one to all the domestics, rather than just one of them. As the
Conservatives rightly pointed out, your stereotypical ferret-breeding,
trade-union supporting Labour man was unlikely to lead womankind
on a bra-burning spree either. But those ferret-breeders had at least
made some token efforts to butter up the female electorate, principally
by showing a level of support for the suffragette movement. The in-
breeders had taken few positive steps to attract either the female or the
youthful vote. All the Tories had to offer was Baldwin's uninspiring
and ill-advised policy of 'Safety First'; as a result, they finished a
disappointing second.

When Labour had first risen to power, five years earlier, they had
entered Downing Street through the back door, the Tories falling on
their swords when they were denied a clear majority in parliament.
This, then, was Labour's first triumph at the polls, conclusive proof
that they, and not the Liberals (whose attempted comeback under
Lloyd George was derailed when they won a miserable 59 seats in the
election and then extinguished when the Welsh Wizard of politics
was diagnosed with cancer of the colon), were now the country's
'other' political party. It was momentous stuff and in almost any other
year it would have ranked as the outstanding moment. But the final
roar of the twenties delivered a story that relegated elections and
everything else to the small print; five months after Labour's finest
hour, Wall Street crashed.

After four years of buying mania, in which time Americans could
have floated businesses selling anything from second-hand bog roll

to flaxen wigs and false dreams (anyone see the connection?) and still sparked a mass scramble to snap up stock, financial panic set in. On October 19 the New York stock market recorded its biggest ever day of selling, in the process setting off a chain of events that would lead the States into their Great Depression and, on the basis that everyone else farts when the Yanks sneeze (a problem the likes of which is becoming endemic among our family's more senior citizens), also trigger depressions of varying severity throughout the world. In relative terms, Britain was fortunate. Other countries did not fully recover until after the second world war; the UK economy was back on track within five years. But the cold the country caught was still a filthy one. The collapse of international trade combined with reduced consumer spending put a squeeze on manufacturers, particularly those in the traditional export industries such as coal, shipbuilding and cotton textiles, all of which had endured a bad enough decade already. The bosses had no option but to cut output and jobs. Between 1929 and 1932, unemployment rose from 1.2 million to 2.8 million and nearly half of that increase came in those old export industries. Which was bad news for the regions where they were primarily located – south Wales, the north-east of England, central Scotland and, most relevantly, Lancashire.

The Ship Canal and Trafford Park offered Manchester some protection from economic meltdown. In effect, though, United had the depression right on their doorstep. Following so soon after the purchase of the Old Trafford freehold and the death of John Henry Davies it was a potentially crushing blow. Certainly it hastened the club's spiral towards financial crisis. Perhaps it is no coincidence that the Depression Years for both club and country hit their lowest point between '31 and '32. But the financial nadir that would soon envelop the Reds could not be blamed on a bunch of bankers in New York, no matter how hard the club tried. United had been a depression waiting to happen ever since 1927 when the attendances had first started to slide. And, for that, the directors had no one to blame but themselves.

Their failure to make any serious investment in the team, build on the breakthrough that Chapman had made in 25/26 or cover the Pop Side were the reasons why the support had dropped off. With the fans on their side, the club would have been depression-proof. City, who had thought, and bought, bigger than the Reds for years (a legacy of their Mangnall era?), were faced with the same economic pressures but were on the verge of the most successful period in their history. At Maine Road they recognised that, when money was tight, the supporters would not turn up unless the team was producing the goods – clubs could not afford to rely solely on the public's enduring loyalty. So, City invested in the team, had a genuine tilt at the title and were rewarded with an average gate of 33,000 in 29/30. United, who did neither and instead gave their supporters their fourth consecutive relegation scrap, pulled in just 18,000 and made a loss.

The Red Army, of course, had been advocating a policy of spending to accumulate for years. The amateur economists on the Pop Side could have taught the country a thing or two about coping with the economic crisis. Effectively, there were two options open to the government. The first was to cut expenditure, baton down the hatches and hope to weather the storm. This was the Old Trafford approach. The second was to spend their way out of trouble by investing in public works schemes which in turn would generate jobs and outlets for the manufacturing industries. This was the Maine Road approach. Labour opted for the former and, like United, ultimately paid the price; within two years, the economic crisis had dethroned MacDonald's administration. We shall never know, of course, but had they plumped for the latter, the political Reds may have gone on to dominate Westminster in the thirties as comprehensively as the football Blues bossed Manchester.

By the time another summer had passed without the directors responding to their demands for action, most Reds had abandoned hope that they ever would. They had grown disillusioned and disaffected by the board's insistence on repeating the tired old line that the search for new players was ongoing (so, apparently, is the search for alien life – and women who admit to strumming the banjo – but that's no reason to start holding your breath). Few believed the management when they said that new names were coming. Most doubted whether they had the money to complete any deals even if they had the will. As it turned out, they were right. The club were on the verge of being skint; the one substantial signing that Bamlett made in 29/30 was a present from Mrs Davies. Otherwise, the United manager had to do his shopping in the Lancs Combination.

The frustration was that, had they been put in the picture, the public could have been an asset to the club. There are few things that supporters relish more than having a desperate cause to rally around, witness the explosion of interest in clubs such as Brighton when they were hurtling towards the wall. By coming clean, the directors would also have opened up the possibility of bringing in new money from outside. Instead, they pushed on with their misguided policy of treating intrusive questions with zero tolerance and the supporters remained lions in their path. The bloody mauling that was coming their way was no less than they deserved.

*   *   *

REMEMBER THAT END-OF-SEASON talk of United doing a Sheffield Wednesday? The notion that they could convert their relegation-defying heroics from one season into championship-chasing form the next had sounded far-fetched enough at the time. When the Reds kicked off the season with eight defeats in their opening eleven matches, it sounded like the biggest pile of pants since Moll Flanders got behind on her ironing. In truth, the dream had died before the campaign was even three days old. For thirty minutes at St James', United knocked the ball around tidily, created chances and looked comfortably the better side. Then Hughie Gallacher banged in an illegal opener (he was 'offside from here to Piccadilly' as the Pop Siders used to shout), Reid fluffed a chance to claim an immediate equaliser and a familiar story unfolded, Gallacher helping himself to two more in the second half and walking off with an opening day hat-trick.

And if that was a testicle-tweaking experience, the following Monday's trip to Filbert Street was even worse. The Reds shipped another four goals, lost Rowley to concussion and had a man sent off. That Charlie Moore was the player dismissed lent the moment a surreal tinge. In a decade in the first team, Charlie had developed a Charlton-esque (as in saintly Bobby, not devilish Jack) reputation for fair play so for him to get sent off was as out of character as Jonathan King walking past a playground. His story was similar to that of the hen-pecked pensioner who bumps off his missus after fifty years of marriage. When Charlie was caught by an ugly lunge from Leicester forward, Carr, something inside him finally snapped. His retaliatory haymaker gave the referee no alternative but to point to the dressing-rooms but most on-lookers, recognising that Charlie was ' "Moore" sinned against than sinning', felt sympathy for him. The FA, having taken into account his years of good behaviour, concurred. For his first – and final – offence, 'cheerful' Charlie escaped with a caution rather than a ban.

The Bank Holiday maulings turned off many Reds before Old Trafford had even reopened its gates. Only 22,000 were inside the ground for the Blackburn opener on September 7 and fewer than 17,000 showed up for the Leicester return four days later. Missing out on the only good week of the autumn was perhaps a fitting punishment for the absent part-timers. Mann, now talked of everywhere as the Peter Pan of football (to the selectors' Tinkerbell), banged in a long-range screamer to clinch a well-deserved 1-0 against Rovers; Jack Ball, recently drafted in from non-league Chorley, marked himself down as one to watch with the decisive second as United came from behind to beat the Foxes while Rawlings, now relegated to third place in the centre-forward pecking order behind Reid and Ball, made the most of a rare call-up by single-handedly demolishing lucky opponents Middlesbrough at Ayresome. A hat-trick was an impressive way for the saviour from 27/28 to sign off. One month and no goals later, he was flogged to Port Vale.

But what of the saviour from 28/29, Tommy Reid? Frustratingly, he was already on the treatment table, having been nobbled in the Blackburn game. Reid had emulated Rawlings by enjoying a wet dream of a start to his United career. A nightmarish second season would be another shared experience. A run of niggling injuries plus a nasty virus restricted Tommy to just two appearances in the next five months and an unlucky thirteen all told. You can talk all you like about luck evening itself out in the long run but Bamlett could justifiably argue that the scales of fortune were weighted against him. The plan for the campaign had revolved around Reid continuing his springtime goal splurge. Before the season was a month old, the centre-forward position was up for grabs once again. Tommy was by no means the only high-profile victim of United's on-going injury jinx either. McLenahan, last year's biggest loss, was on the verge of a medicine-defying return but two of his young, home-reared colleagues were heading towards personal disaster. And for them there would be no miraculous comeback.

After the victory treble, the backlash; an epic run of defeats that was every bit as demoralising as the three-month winless streak the previous year. Considering what they had done for the Reds recently, it was more difficult than usual to begrudge the Scousers their victory at Old Trafford. As United scored first, dominated for lengthy stretches and had a cracking effort from Rowley wrongly ruled out though for offside, it still felt like a mugging. Defeat by the same 2-1 score-line at Upton Park offered a far more accurate reflection of the on-pitch balance of power. Apart from Spence, who had his usual outstanding game against the Hammers (his repeated brilliance against them over the years had earned him regular ovations from a mini Upton Park fan club – not something that many Reds have enjoyed in the land of banana throwing and effigy hanging), the forwards and half-backs were brain-numbingly ineffective. A late, fifteen-minute salvo, stuffed with tantrums and studs-up aggression, was the only genuine pressure United could muster all game and their lack of science served merely to bolster the club's reputation down south for poor football and rough play. The London press described the conduct of 'certain' United players as 'awful' and singled out Hanson, in particular, as a 'nuisance'. Watching Jimmy hurl himself into challenges, it was difficult to believe that only a couple of years earlier the selectors had not considered him tough enough to handle heavy grounds or heavy defenders. In truth – and despite his lack of inches – he revelled in the physical battle. No wonder he was one of Barson's favourite Reds.

Comprehensive defeat in the Old Trafford derby raised awkward questions – thankfully, soon answered – about the capacity of the old warhorses, Silcock and Moore, to keep churning out neck-saving performances. Depressingly, United's sixth derby without a win also emphasised what every Red knew – but was loathe to admit – which was that the two Manchester giants were headed in different directions. City, buoyant again after halting their post-Mangnall slide, were following the signs marked 'Success'; United the ones marked 'The Shite'.

Sheffield United pushed their noses further into it by strolling to a 3-1 at Bramall Lane. As the derby hangover had barely subsided, post-traumatic shock and fatigue may have handicapped the Reds' efforts to bounce back. There were no such excuses, though, as Grimsby pasted them 5-2 at Old Trafford. It was no consolation that the visitors played some of the best football seen in Manchester that year, not when there were clear signs that the side's spirit was on the wane. 'Bad as they have been playing,' observed the Wanderer, 'I have not seen Manchester United so demoralised as they were during the last twenty minutes.' Within a week he would have reason to revise that opinion. If United were poor against Grimsby, they were abysmal against Portsmouth. Another Fratton Park debacle – their third in as many years – against the side that had previously kept the Reds off the bottom of the table could only mean one thing. United, the laughable pre-season dark horses for the title (Mr Ed for the National, anyone?), were bottom of the pile.

An edgy victory against Arsenal on October 26 finally pulled the Reds out of their wretched sequence of defeats but neither Ball's winner nor the subsequent home win against Derby did much to dissipate the atmosphere of impending disaster. The standard of play remained poor. Football writers dubbed United's style 'cranium football' and they did not mean that the players were using their brains, only their foreheads. As a rule, the ball was launched long and high. Which would have been bad enough had the forward line boasted a genuine target man in the Tommy Reid mould. Now it was packed with slender whippets, the front five needed high and hopefuls like an agoraphobic needs a raincoat.

What was worse, the Reds were increasingly susceptible to taking a battering on their travels. Losing by just a single goal at Villa Park, in their sixth away defeat of the season, was hugely flattering. But for Steward, whose battered hands at the end of the game resembled something you'd scrape off the road, Villa would have racked up a tennis score. Sheffield Wednesday were not so careless at Hillsborough a fortnight later. After Ball had sped away to shoot United into a shock lead, the Owls roared back with four goals in the first half and another three in the second. The Reds were back propping up the rest. And if that wasn't depressing enough, City were twenty-one places above them. If the first division was a club sandwich, the two Manchester sides were the triangles of toast on either end.

With the ghosts of 21/22, United's relegation season, again looming over the club, the *Football News* published a three-point plan outlining a potential route to safety. All were old chestnuts really. Priority number one was a first-class, constructive centre-half with 'personality and generalship qualities' who could feed the wings and bring the side out of its defensive shell. In short, the team needed a Roberts or a Barson, not a Spencer. Number two was a forward with a killer instinct in front of goal and a really telling shot. If that was a bit harsh on Ball, who was hitting more high notes than anyone with his inexperience had any right to, and also on Reid, who had done nothing wrong except fall ill, it did not take a genius to see that the Reds would continue to struggle unless they started to bang in more goals.

The final prong in the plan was better support from the terraces. 'With encouragement from the crowd,' wrote 'C.J.C.', 'the United would be a different team. McPherson made mistakes and the crowd hooted him and drove him away. Other players such as Rawlings, Rennox, Lochhead and Henderson were turned away. What is the use of United buying new players if the crowd will not treat them in a sportsmanlike way?'

The editorial in the *Football News* took up the fight, pleading: 'Be fair to United! However much Manchester United may deserve the criticisms that are being levelled at them one thing is certain and that is that those fickle supporters who are deserting or threatening to desert the club are showing themselves to be unworthy to be called sportsmen.' Since United had rarely been fair to the fans, however, the pleas for the fans to be fair to United inevitably fell on deaf ears. The relationship between the club and its public had reached crisis point. For those who were still bothering to turn up, the Reds had become an object of derision, a source of gallows humour. And the number of those still bothered was diminishing by the week. For the Lancashire derby against Burnley on November 23, the gate did not even reach five figures. Barring meaningless midweek games, it was the emptiest Old Trafford had been for years.

The attendance crisis finally drew the management from behind their wall of silence. In the week leading up to the Burnley match, Bamlett launched an impassioned defence of the club's transfer policy in the *Football News*, saying:

'Nobody realises better than we do how serious the position is and I can assure you that by every means within our power we are endeavouring to cope with it.

'But we refuse to be stampeded. We are out to get new players, but the type of man we want is not so easy to get as many people seem to think...People point out to us the case of Rawlings, but the circumstances were not the same. We secured Rawlings for a definite purpose, and he served that purpose. He was obtained to meet the ends of the moment. So was Reid, but Reid's case is different. He is a comparative youth, but at present, unfortunately, he is ill in bed.

'Now, however, we do not want a man merely to serve an immediate purpose. Our quest is for a man round whom we can build a team, and we have negotiated and are negotiating to get the type of man we want…Before we get him we want to make certain beyond all reasonable doubt that he really will prove to be the man we want. We do not want to make a mistake. In football you can never tell. We cannot risk signing a player on his reputation – we have to watch and study. Manchester United have no money to throw away, and when we do buy we want to make sure we are buying wisely.

'As for the statements that the club is doing nothing, well, you won't find any of us here on Saturday. More than that I cannot say.'

It would have been handy for chip-wrapping, I suppose. Needless to say, United did not get the man they wanted, kyboshing any plans Bamlett had to shake up the side from outside the club. He was left with no option but to attempt to engineer a solution from within. Because of the lack of alternatives in the squad, the forward line would continue to pick itself with Spence and Hanson on the right, Thomas and Rowley on the left and Ball, who would have benefited from a spell out of the spotlight, in the centre. Instead, the selectorial finger pointed to the middle line. Time had run out for the engine room that had powered the springtime surge. Spencer was dropped after Villa Park, Mann and Bennion after Hillsborough. Neither Frank nor Billy would pull on a United shirt again. At 39, the years had finally caught up with Peter Pan though there were plenty of people who felt that the club had made a mistake when they granted him his end-of-season free. Spencer's mourners, by contrast, would have fitted comfortably into his coffin. Astonishingly, given that he had only just turned 30 and had commanded a £3,250 fee less than two seasons before, no league club was prepared to take a punt on Billy once the Reds accepted his springtime transfer request. In the end, Spencer, like Mann, drifted into non-league football. From England international and championship-winner to player-coach at Tunbridge Wells Rangers in three short years. Not even Gary Glitter managed a fall from grace as dramatic as that. It just goes to show the perils involved in following a legend – just ask Frank O'Farrell.

Bennion's place was taken by Ol' Faithful, Hilditch, Mann's by the fit-again Wilson. So far, so predictable. Spencer's successor was more of a left-field choice or at least it was to those Reds who hadn't been tuning in to his impressive shows in the reserves. The last time we heard of Chris Taylor was when he was being carted off to hospital to have his cartilage removed in the autumn of '26. Back then, he had been an immensely promising inside-forward who had banged in six goals in as many starts. In the meantime, despite making a full recovery he had been unable to force himself back into contention in the meantime and, with his career stuck in reverse, he had requested a change of role. It had been quite a makeover. When the talented Brummie emerged from two seasons spent learning his trade in the Central League he immediately looked like the midfield enforcer all Reds had been lusting after. Admittedly, he was not the finished product defensively – he had the tools for the job but had yet to work out the correct balance between pushing up and sitting back. But his constructive work was outstanding. Taylor had vision, a sumptuous pass, the energy and desire to get forward in support of the attack, he loved a dribble and he could shoot. Soon he was being touted as the best attacking centre-half United had had for years, Barson included – high praise indeed.

Whether the remodelled midfield was the result of a tactical brain-wave or another desperate throw of the dice, only Bamlett and the selectors would know. My money is on the latter. Fluke or not, it was the defining moment of the season, the reason, ultimately, why 29/30 did not turn out as disastrously as it perhaps ought to have done. Burnley were the first to be swept aside by the new broom, Rowley bundling in Thomas's centre to secure a comfortable 1-0 at Old Trafford. A week later, United scalped Sunderland at Roker, Spence supplying two goals and a virtuoso performance to silence the famous roar, such as it was. In truth, it was more like a whimper. United were by no means the only club whose pulling power had been badly hit by a combination of poor results, economic misery and consistently filthy weather. It was a similar story not just at Roker but across the north-east where the top-flight contingent were all struggling – on and off the pitch – as badly as the region's mines. The Reds at their October worst had clearly made Grimsby look much better than they actually were; the Mariners were now bottom of the pile. When United moved out of the drop zone with a good point against Bolton, it was Sunderland who took their place. Newcastle, for all their spending excesses, completed the bottom four.

The latter's plight in particular was manna for those myopic apologists who argued that the United directors had done the right thing in not throwing money at the transfer market. Actually, they would soon have a much better example to cling to. None of the midseason stragglers would walk the plank in May. Everton and Burnley went instead, the Spencer-like demise of the former providing the season with its biggest sensation. Like Newcastle, the Toffees had recently bought a championship. Now, just two seasons later, they were destined for bottom place. Mind you, if anyone had been asked during the Reds' visit to Goodison on December 14, which of the sides would be leaving the division that year, it is a fair bet they would have plumped for the visitors. Steward was brilliant, United were poor; the point was a steal.

When the points were all important, it did not really matter how they came. But if the revival had largely been devoid of genital-tingling moments thus far, all that changed when the club unwrapped George McLachlan, their early Christmas present from the Davies family. Strangely enough, most Reds would have swapped the Glaswegian outside-left for some vouchers when he first arrived from Cardiff. His reputation for having 'the Scotsman's slowness in movement' plus his involvement in Cardiff's relegation the previous season turned many people off. Was McLachlan a better bet, the Pop Side had queried, than Harry Thomas who had the makings of a dangerous player even if he all too often failed to deliver on his promise?

The holiday games nodded a definitive 'yes'. For all of Rowley's promise, the left arm of the attack had recently been as potent as a weightlifter's one minute and a stroke victim's the next. The effect was frustratingly short-lived but when George teamed up with Harry, the earth moved, just as it had for the two Harrys the previous spring. The new recruit added a degree of brawn and much-needed IQ to the flank. He could keep the ball and pass it on the floor, two basic attributes that had been singularly lacking in United's season so far. With McLachlan in the team, the Reds, who had previously scored consistently but not heavily, surfed through the rest of the month on a crimson tide of goals. The Scot set up the first of Ball's double as Leeds were shrugged aside on his debut. Good news from the turnstiles as well as the crowd nudged back over 20,000. Then, after three points were eked out of Birmingham in the Christmas/Boxing Day doubleheader, Newcastle were hit for five, McLachlan scoring his first United goal with a tapped-in third.

Their end-of-year form lifted the Reds into twelfth place, six points clear of trouble and just seven short of City in second spot. The *Football News* tagged their revival 'the most remarkable occurrence in the football world of recent weeks'. But United's march up the table had come at a cost they could not afford to pay. An innocuous-looking challenge during the home draw with Birmingham had left Jimmy Hanson with a fractured tibia and fibia in his left leg. The talk at the time was that Jimmy would make a full recovery but such optimism was badly misplaced. His attempted comeback that summer was less than one practice match old when, in the words of Alf Clarke: 'He burst through the defence with Silcock chasing him. Silcock could not catch him, and shouted to Hanson; "Hit it, Jimmy." Hanson brought all his force behind a right-foot shot, but kicked the ground in the procedure, and snap went the leg.' This time it did not mend.

Hanson was just 25 when he was tossed on the scrap heap. The obvious question, then, is how much more he could have gone on to achieve. This, remember, was a player who had been tipped for international honours as a teenaged prodigy and who, in the past eighteen months, had shown signs of transforming that youthful potential into reality. Had his early development not been hindered by the cotton-wool treatment he had received from the selectors and by their ill-considered policy of shunting him around the forward line, Jimmy could well have added to his schoolboy caps by now.

Already, he was a player who was almost indispensable at Old Trafford. Without his right-hand man, things would never be quite the same again for Spence. Tommy Boyle, who had been waiting in the wings since his transfer from Sheffield United nine months earlier, was drafted in at inside-right but never looked capable of pushing Joe's buttons. A feature of the rest of United's season was the number of games in which the side's biggest name was starved of possession. Spence's enforced hunger strike did not go unnoticed among his public. The occasions when he was finally plied with the ball were regularly marked with jeers or ironic applause. Meanwhile, 'Give it to Joe' returned, alongside 'Boot It' and 'Get Shut', to the top three of the Pop Side's pop parade.

*   *   *

THE NEWS ON HANSON, combined with the team's unbeaten sequence, made December the month of all the emotions. January threw up just one; Misery in the James Caan class. The *Football News* had erred with its ejaculation of praise. By the end of the month, confidence and performance levels had drooped again. What was worse, United suffered an injury blow every bit as grievous as Hanson's double fracture. In the Middlesbrough match on the 18th, Taylor limped off with a twisted knee. The original prognosis talked of a five to six week lay-off but it was more medical bollocks. His knees had already threatened to finish him off once; this time they completed the job.

In effect, Taylor had two careers – one as a forward, the other as a half-back – ended by injury. Perhaps, then, he was the unluckiest of the threesome of much-mourned injury victims. Perhaps, also, he was the one who was missed most at Old Trafford. Hilditch, now playing as consistently well as he ever had, was around to pick up the pieces at centre-half and, in fact, formed the backbone of the side for the rest of the season. But Lal was now 35 and was never going to be more than a stopgap. With Taylor finished and Hilditch creaking, the engine-room badly needed a refit but that would be easier said than done. As the club had shown with the dog's dinner they had made out of replacing Barson, inspirational half-backs were difficult to find and, unless Mrs Davies felt in a generous mood, even more difficult to afford.

After winning the Bamlett way over Christmas, United kicked off the new year by losing the Bamlett way at Blackburn. In front of an army of 4,000 Reds, half as many as had watched the home game against Burnley in November, United attacked with verve, scored four and still lost. The Reds' first defeat in nine was then followed by three more in quick succession, all of which made the McLachlan effect seem like a distant memory. Even if two of their goals came when United were a centre-back short, Middlesbrough were good value for their 3-0 win at Old Trafford on the 18th. 'A more feeble exhibition of football than the one they [United] served up cannot be imagined,' groaned the *Athletic News*. An equally feeble showing, and another Liverpool defeat, raised the question whether the Reds were on the slide once more. From looking safe, they were now only three points clear of the trapdoor.

But the worst moment of all came in the Cup. Never perhaps

in the club's history had a money-spinning run been more vital. Even during the Depression, the competition remained a magical force, capable of conjuring big crowds out of the least inspiring looking match-ups – witness the near 40,000 gate for the visit of third division Swindon. More gates like that could have made the difference between the club plunging into the red and them breaking even. What a time, then, for the supporters to be force-fed footballing excrement. In their farewell performance, the Wilson-Taylor-Hilditch midfield managed the equivalent of fluffing their lines whilst getting caught in the curtain. Losing 2-0 flattered the Reds, not the Robins.

The first weeks of the new decade, then, had been a catastrophe. Fortunately, the next few provided some much-needed relief. Spence, whose recent quiet spell had been attributed partly to Hanson's absence and partly to the burden of captaining a losing side, relinquished the armband and reacted in Bothamesque style, scoring all four goals – from right wing – as the Hammers were blitzed at Old Trafford. Then, in the following week's derby, the spotlight finally picked out forgotten man Tommy Reid. His bundled winner in front of 63,000 at Maine Road ended a miserable ten-month wait for his next goal. More significantly, it ended the Reds' 8½ year wait for a derby triumph and gave them an historic first win at Maine Road, a ground where United would eventually scale greater heights than City ever did (if that sounds an idle boast, just consider the facts: the Reds won three FA Cup semi-finals and three European Cup matches at Maine Road [to City's none], notched the biggest ever 'home' win when they beat Anderlecht 10-0 and attracted the stadium's record league attendance, 81,962 for the visit of Arsenal in 1948).

Just as deliciously, the result knocked City's season off course. In the build-up to the match, the Blues, particularly their captain, Jimmy McMullan, had been telling anyone who would listen that they were on course for the Double. United's 1-0 was the first of three setbacks in a week that killed the dream. Midweek defeat by Everton effectively knocked the Blues out of the title race; the following Saturday, mighty Hull City dumped them out of the Cup. That City's knock-out came as early as the fifth round offered yet more proof of the enduring capacity of easily-excited Blues to spout nonsense. Most clubs would have waited until the quarter-finals at least before contracting a full-blown dose of Wembley fever, or until they had closed a four point gap on the reigning champions (Sheffield Wednesday) before considering themselves title favourites. Not City though. In a sense there is something to admire in their perennial over-optimism. If you are a supporter of a club that only has a slim chance of challenging for honours, it must be better to follow one which aims for the stars – and falls flat on its face – than one that settles for mediocrity, or worse, and achieves it. But you would have thought that Blues would have learned by now that delusion and disappointment (and bitterness) are permanent bedfellows.

Reid quickly made up for lost time, scoring three more goals in the next fortnight as United drew with Grimsby and satisfyingly thumped their Fratton nemeses, Portsmouth. There were no marks for style on either occasion but that did not really matter. In eleventh place, eight points clear of the bottom two, the Reds had all but booked another season in the top flight. But United would not have been United had they finished the job off without a scare. Continuing a trend of reinventing themselves (from good to bad and vice versa) with every turn of the calendar, results in March were every bit as desperate as those in January. Bolton, Burnley and Arsenal all hit the travelling Reds for four while, back in Manchester, Villa stormed back from two down to take the points in stoppage time. United did at least scramble a 1-1 at the Baseball Ground on the 15th but, in truth, Derby should have romped it. The Reds were grateful that Silcock's anticipation and timing remained superb and that Hilditch, the heartbeat of the side in the absence of Taylor, was also rolling back the years. If Lal had always been this strong and this healthy, a long, but ultimately frustrating career would have been that much more rewarding. Instead, a combination of injuries and a weak constitution had saddled him with a reputation as a club man rather than a star one.

Mad March prolonged the agony but at least saved the club from the added slump in attendances that a dead season would have triggered. United were never in genuine danger, always maintaining a reasonable points buffer between themselves and the clubs in the relegation places. Mathematical safety was not reached until the fourth from final game but, in reality, they made their necks safe with a string of good results in early April.

In a season of sad farewells, the vibrant return made by McLenahan that month provided even more welcome good news. Thrust into the side as an emergency partner for Spence, Hughie worked out some of his pent-up frustration by banging in six goals in his first five matches back. A brace in the home win against Sunderland sparked his scoring flurry. He then scored a goal a game as the Reds drew, impressively, with champions-elect Sheffield Wednesday, took three points off Huddersfield and stormed back from 3-1 down to draw with Everton. United's fight-back that Easter afternoon effectively rubber-stamped the Toffees' demotion. It also guaranteed that the Reds would not share their fate. Yet again, the club had stared down the barrel and lived to tell the tale.

But a quick recap of Red experiences a decade earlier would have shown that they could not hope to keep it up forever. The backbone of the side was growing old; Steward, Spence, Hilditch and Silcock were rapidly closing in on their last hurrahs while Moore, who hung up his boots in the summer, had already had his. Injuries had decimated the next generation of home-grown talent; two of the bright young things who might have taken the club forward in the thirties were finished, another was damaged goods. Money problems ruled out the possibility of bringing in a ready-made team from outside; the spending power of a club like Chelsea, who celebrated their return to the top division by splashing out £19,000 on the two Scottish greats, Jackson and Gallacher, contrasted sharply with that of United who would soon have difficulty paying for the staff's Christmas turkeys. Solutions still had to be found for the two problem positions, centre-forward and centre half-back. And also for the breakdown in relations between the club and public. The new decade should have been an excuse for looking ahead, dreaming and rejoicing that the difficult twenties were over. Instead, the thirties kicked off with the United board in the same boat as the King, who, in a famous anecdote, turned to James Thomas, the Lord Privy Seal, and asked him: 'What state is my country in?' After a short pause, Thomas replied: 'If I were you, I'd put it in your wife's name.'

ROLL OF HONOUR

CHAMPIONS: SHEFFIELD WEDNESDAY

FA CUP WINNERS: ARSENAL

UNITED: DIVISION 1 (17TH) FA CUP (3RD ROUND) SWINDON TOWN

Frank Mann

Inside-right or Half-back, Mar 1923 – Aug 1930, 197 apps 5 gls

'Whatta man, whatta man, whatta man, whatta baldy Frank Mann.' I have my doubts whether that line would have caught on on the terraces even if Salt-n-Pepa and their popcorn rapping had been around in the twenties. However, the fact remains that fans and pundits alike were fascinated by Frank's shiny head or, more accurately, by his ability to run around like a puppy on speed despite looking like the referee's elderly uncle. One anecdote from his Huddersfield days suggests that the attention his bald patch received in turn got to Frank. After miscuing a header, a voice from the popular side at Leeds Road rang out: 'Eh, Frank, old chap, you'll have to chalk the tip a bit next time' (presumably the *Topical Times* cleaned the line up; I have problems believing that your match-going Tyke ever sounded like he had a plum in his mouth – unless it was attached to a ram, of course). On his return to the dressing room, Frank asked the trainer for some brilliantine (basically, Vaseline) and was told to go to the cupboard and help himself. A few minutes later, the trainer looked up and found Frank, in his desperation to get some control on his headers, plastering his head with chilli paste. Cue dressing-room bedlam and one burning scalp.

It was a rare occasion on which Frank made a fool of himself. As a Huddersfield player, his forté was making fools out of others. A goal-scoring and scheming inside-right, he played a key role in the club's transformation from lower league nobodies into the team of the decade. With Huddersfield on the verge of the first of their hat-trick of league titles in 1924, B. Bennison, the football correspondent of the *Topical Times*, wrote: 'I would say of Mann that, in my opinion, he had as much to do with the making of Huddersfield Town as the team is today as any other man who has worn the club's colours. A more conscientious footballer I have never known. He looked very old in this day with his pate ever so bald, but he was the forward whom the Villa had most to fear [in the 1920 Cup Final which Barson's Villa won 1-0]. Mann then was what Clem Stephenson is now to Huddersfield – the brains of the attack.'

Frank's misfortune was to be too old to enjoy the fruits of his labours. He was part of the Huddersfield side that were promoted in 1920 and won the Cup two years later but he was sold to United the season before the Terriers' ice-breaking championship triumph. At 32, Mann's best years, like those of his barber, were thought to be behind him when he moved to Manchester and there were many who felt that Huddersfield had done well to get as much as £1,750 for him.

For the best part of a year, Frank's indifferent form backed up that point of view. He worked hard enough and his experience made him an effective foil for United's youngsters but in thirty games at inside-right he scored just three goals. Then came his switch to a midfield role and a new lease of life that lasted for seven seasons and made him one of the top three United signings of the decade. Too slow for a forward, Frank's brain and legs were easily quick enough to cope in midfield. Moreover, two good feet, a dour defensive streak, the ability to pick a pass and, of course, that famous Mann stamina, enabled him to prosper in any position along the line. For the *Topical Times*, and the rest of the football press, 'Peter Pan' Mann was a wonder of the sporting world. In October 1928, the Analyst swooned:

'In this age for speed, it is significant that a veteran like Frank Mann can keep a place, and that with distinction. The standard of Manchester United half-back play is not high, but undoubtedly would be lower with Mann out of the line, for he supplies the deficiency, or part of it, in constructive method. The craftsmanship of his days as a forward count in that direction, and as he was always a player, able to see a move ahead, a student of men and their methods, he has fallen naturally into the defensive needs of a half-back. Good forwards do not necessarily become valuable half-backs in their veteran days because they have lost speed for the former purpose. It requires some adaptability, and Mann has any amount of it. He can be placed anywhere in the middle line because he can control the ball in a second, and uncover his forwards, and, if beaten in a challenge, falls back naturally into place where the attack can be met again. Altogether Mann is the complete footballer, and lasts because he has his heart in the game, and spares no effort from beginning to end of the game.'

CHRIS TAYLOR

CENTRE-FORWARD AND CENTRE HALF-BACK, FEB 1924 – SEPT 1931
30 APPS 7 GLS

IN MAY 1925, Frank Barson informed the *Topical Times* that, in free-scoring reserve forward Chris Taylor, United had uncovered a 'star of the future'. Two hat-tricks for the first team at the back end of 25/26 apparently backed Frank's words up and hinted that the star of the future would soon be a star of the present. But that was before fate slid in with a two-footed tackle that brought the ambitions of the precocious Red, like those of his manager and team, to a grinding halt. John Chapman was fingered by the FA for an unknown misdemeanour and lost his job, his semi-final side staggered backwards and Taylor succumbed to a serious knee injury. By the time he had recovered from an operation to remove his cartilage, his career had lost momentum – in the next three seasons he made just six first-team appearances. The lower leagues or the scrapheap beckoned but then came his inspired request for a change of role…

…Almost five years after his first coming, and over three years after his injury, the *Topical Times* included the reborn Taylor in their series on 'Young Players Worth Watching'. Now 25 and a centre half-back, he had been the chief catalyst in United's recovery from another mid-autumn slump. After just sixteen games in the position, the Analyst was impressed enough to write that 'young Taylor shows every sign of establishing a club link with such giants as Charlie Roberts and Frank Barson'.

In build and all-action style, Chris had something in common with Barson; his side-step to both sides was apparently reminiscent of Roberts. And if there were rough edges in his positional and defensive play that needed attention, no one was betting against them being smoothed out. After raving about Taylor's abundant natural ability and lightning-quick progress, the Analyst concluded: 'By persevering with the same size in hats, and realising there is always something to learn, Christopher will become not only a discovery of the present but a personality of the future.' Sadly, there would be no great future for the multi-talented Brummie. On the same January afternoon that the Analyst's words hit the news-stands, United's injury jinx struck again.

JAMES HANSON

INSIDE-RIGHT AND CENTRE-FORWARD, MAY 1924 – SUMMER 1931, 147 APPS 52 GLS

FROM THE MOMENT he emerged as a natural and prolific goalscorer in schoolboy football, Jimmy Hanson found himself at the centre of a string of debates: Was he best at centre-forward or inside-right? Should he be thrown straight into the first-team or given time to develop in the Central League? Would he be strong enough to prosper against big opponents and on heavy grounds? (the answers were a] unsure; he played his best football for United at inside-right but he was never really given the opportunities in the centre b] yes and no; the directors showed rare foresight in not flogging Jimmy to death early in his career but they rather overdid it when they left him out for nine months after he had scored three  goals in his first three games c] yes; an in-your-face terrier, Jimmy relished a dust-up and was easily tough enough to cope in the mud). In the autumn of '28, the *Topical Times* posed another question; would Hanson kick on and force himself into the England reckoning or was he destined to 'remain a useful club unit'? Twenty goals in 28/29 and a starring role, alongside Tommy Reid, in United's dramatic escape from relegation suggested that Jimmy was set on the international path. Frank Barson, for one, had no hesitation in backing his claims. 'Put him on my side every time,' Frank crowed, 'and I'll have in front of me a forward who knows the way to goal.'

Within a year, Jimmy's smashed tibia had brought the debate to a premature end. Aged just 25 when he sustained his injury on Christmas Day 1929, he spent what should have been his peak years working as a monumental mason in the family business at Southern Cemetery. His own epitaph could have read: 'A grand, whole-hearted player [Alf Clarke's words] whom cruel fate tripped up'.

Eric Sweeney
Inside-left, May 1925 – June 1930, 32 apps 7 gls

Touted as the next Arthur Lochhead when he enjoyed his only real run in the first team (thirteen games under three managers during the ill-fated 26/27 season), Eric Sweeney eventually had to settle for doing most of his scheming in the reserves. While he could certainly play, he never reached the standards of his rivals for the number ten shirt, lacking the terrier-like dash of a Ted Partridge and the sheer inspiration of a Billy Johnston or Harry Rowley. Like many of the forward experiments of the twenties, Eric eventually found his true level in the third division, enjoying himself at both Carlisle and Crewe before bowing out of the professional game aged just 28.

Bill Inglis
Right full-back, May 1925 – June 1930, 14 apps 1 gl
Assistant trainer: Aug 1934 – summer 1961

During his peak years with Raith Rovers, Bill Inglis was a good enough defender to be picked three times as reserve for Scotland and represent the Home Scots in their annual fixture against the Anglo Scots. By the time he signed for United, however, his legs had started to go and apart from a spell of twelve matches straddling the 25/26 adventure and the 26/27 disaster, he never enjoyed a sustained run in the first team. Instead, the former Owl settled into the role of reserve-team captain that became vacant when 'Tiny' Haslam moved to Portsmouth in November '27.

A move to Northampton a couple of seasons later returned Bill to the League ranks but, after a sixty-game swansong with the Cobblers, he was enticed back to Old Trafford as the assistant to the newly-appointed first-team trainer, Tom 'Tosher' Curry. In time, the pair, in their long white coats, would become legendary figures at the club, forming part of the famous boot-room family (also embracing Jimmy Murphy, coach Bert Whalley and youth-team trainer Arthur Powell) that reared the flock of talented youngsters on which the Busby miracle was built. If neither of them were great 'academic' trainers, both were 'great fellas' who juggled and massaged egos and ensured that the dressing-room environment remained, as far as possible, clique and poison free. Their paternal streak meant they were probably closer to the players than even Matt and Jimmy.

It follows that no one would have been stung by the tragedy of Munich more than Inglis who not only lost the Babes he had nurtured but also his great ally Curry who, as senior trainer, had travelled with the party to Belgrade and had perished, along with Whalley, in the German snow. Understandably, things were never the same for the old guard of Murphy, Powell and Inglis ever again. Jimmy soldiered on alongside the 'Boss' but Bill soon retired, his position being taken by the youthful Wilf McGuinness. Seven years later, the adopted Mancunian passed away, aged 73. Sadly, he missed, by just four months, the Wembley night against Benfica which provided the climax to the Red resurrection in which he had played such an integral, if rarely prominent, part.

Bill Rawlings

Centre-forward, Mar 1928 – Nov 1929, 36 apps 19 gls

Bill Rawlings could justifiably claim to have had a raw deal from the Old Trafford crowd. The ten goals he scored in no time following his £4,000 move from Southampton saved the club from the drop yet, within months, the supporters, frustrated by his inability to keep churning out the miracles, were clambering all over his back. Admittedly the two-time England international was not at his best in his only full season as a Red but, on the basis that the service to him

would not have looked out of place at Fawlty Towers, that was by no means all his own fault. Bill was at his best when he was fed subtle through-balls and snappy, slide-rule crosses and at his worst when he was forced to play with his back to goal and scrap for possession. He could not have found a worse showcase for his talents, then, than a United team which regarded anything that stayed on the pitch as a precision pass. A diet of guileless gumps would have tested the patience of a saint never mind a former one.

Rawlings could only rue the fact that his second season at the club coincided with injuries to the team's chief playmaker, Billy

Johnston, the worst run of form of Joe Spence's career and also Barson's departure. With a fit and in-form Johnston, Spence and Barson behind him, Bill may have ended up with more mentions in United folklore; instead, he ended up at Port Vale.

Charles 'Billy' Spencer

Centre half-back, July 1928 – May 1930, 48 apps 0 gls

Billy Spencer had a habit of dividing opinions throughout his career but the one opinion that was held unanimously was that he was the most disastrous signing the Reds made during the Depression Years. For £3,250, the fee United paid Newcastle, the Pop Side expected another Barson; instead, they got a player whose most notable achievement during his two-year slide into non-league obscurity was contracting malaria.

In retrospect, Bamlett should have known that Billy was no Barson. Whereas Frank was a master of both sides of the centre-half's art, Spencer only excelled in a defensive role. His constructive play was known to be plain at best. However, there weren't many people in the game who were willing to stick their necks out and say that the United manager had screwed up when he signed Billy in July 1928. On the contrary, the consensus was that the Reds had done a 'rare stroke of business' in beating off competition from six or seven other clubs to win the race for his signature. His credentials, after all, were impressive. In seven years at St James', he had won the league and cup as well as representative honours with both England and the Football League.

Some observers went as far as tipping United's latest recruit for a return to the England scene. In the *Topical Times* 'The Odd Man' wrote: 'Not a showy player, Spencer, but a workman to the finger tips. I am quite prepared to see him installed as England's pivot again. He would walk into his country's team were he endowed with more constructive ability.' He went on to argue that 'Spencer, to me, is one of those players who mature late. The odds are that Manchester United will get the best out of him.' It was one of those predictions that can haunt a pundit for years. The Odd Man looked even odder when the next stage of Spencer's career took him, not into the England team, but to Tunbridge Wells.

TOMMY BOYLE
INSIDE-FORWARD, MAR 1929 – MAY 1930, 17 APPS 6 GLS

A CUP-WINNER WITH Sheffield United in '25, Tommy Boyle had been an idle Blade for a couple of seasons when he was snapped up by Bamlett and, along with the other spring signing, Tommy Reid, handed the impossible mission of saving the Reds from relegation. Whereas one Tommy (Reid) jumped at the opportunity of taking the Ethan Hunt role, the other Tommy (Boyle) was frankly as much use as a Tommy (Tank). From mid-February to the end of the season, the resurgent Reds lost just once, 6-1 at Derby on Easter Saturday. You've guessed it; that was the only time that season that Boyle made the team.

Jimmy Hanson's injury handed the 32-year-old Tyke more opportunities in 29/30 but he was rarely impressive (on consecutive weekends in late January and early February he was given the following write-ups: 'Boyle foraged to no useful purpose', 'Boyle was a disappointment', 'Boyle was not much better than poor Reid') and it was no surprise when he was invited to leave Old Trafford in the summer. A gamble that did not pay off, Tommy played out the final years of his career with Macclesfield and Northampton Town.

JOHN BALL
CENTRE-FORWARD, MAY 1929 – JULY 1930 & DEC 1933 – SEPT 1934, 24 APPS 11 GLS (TOTAL 50 APPS 18 GLS)

IN THE SUMMER of 1930 United were heading irresistibly towards the second division anyway. The decision to sell Jack Ball to Sheffield Wednesday was probably the moment when the directors kissed goodbye to their chances of delaying the inevitable by another year. An impotent forward line could ill-afford to lose someone with the sharp eye for goal that Jack had revealed during the first half of his debut season when he had netted nine times in just eleven games. In truth, the 22-year-old had been nowhere near as effective in the spring but a short-term slump was only to be expected given his lack of experience, service, rest and support. It did not mean that he would not come again.

That much became clear when the former Southport fish-monger emerged as a great catch for his new club. In three and a half seasons at Hillsborough, he scored close on a century of goals and built a reputation as an all-round centre-forward who could lead the line and make chances as well as take them. In December '33, United made a stab at righting a wrong by bringing him back to Old Trafford but again the Owls enjoyed the better of the deal, Ball falling victim to the old adage about footballers not going back. Sold on to Huddersfield the following September, his move to Luton Town just a month later created a unique record as he played in all three divisions of the league within a six-week period. Despite his natural gifts – his goalscorer's instinct and his strong build which he 'carried with commendable speed' – Jack never escaped from the basement division again. When he hit the headlines for a final time, in April '36, it was because he wasn't fit enough to play in Luton's home fixture against Bristol Rovers. Jack's deputy that afternoon, Joe Payne, went on to make football history by scoring ten goals in the match.

CIVIL WAR

BEFORE HE TURNED his hand to football management, Herbert Bamlett was a highly respected referee who, in a top-notch career, officiated in five semi-finals, one Cup Final and several internationals (now that's a watching-your-granny-perform-fellatio type thought for you – imagine a Willis, Hill or, god forbid, an Elleray reinventing himself as a manager and walking into the top job at Old Trafford). Objectively, those showcase matches were Bamlett's career highs but, in Red eyes, his greatest moment as a whistler was when he saved Mangnall's champions from cup catastrophe at Turf Moor in March 1909. Unfancied Burnley were just twenty minutes away from converting a 1-0 lead into a shock semi-final place when the town suddenly turned into Murmansk on one of its wilder days. The home fans, ignoring the heavy snow, freezing temperatures and poor visibility, screamed for the match to go on; Bamlett, worried about the dangers of losing his fingers to frostbite, ignored the inevitable 'fix' jibes and called it to a halt. According to legend, he was so cold that he had to ask Charlie Roberts to get his whistle out of his pocket for him (not a request he could have got away with in junior football) before he could even do that.

The sight of the opposition skipper helping the referee blow his whistle (wahey!) only inflamed the locals' neurotic conviction that they had been stitched up. 'Call that snow?' you can imagine them muttering, Monty Python style, to their pigeons. When United then eased to victory in the replayed game and went on to lift the Cup, beating Bristol City in the final, the Clarets' frustration at coming so close to a famous success developed into a king-sized grudge. Showing a capacity for holding one that would shame even the Irish, Burnley folk would harp on about the abandonment for years. Even two decades after the event, no match against Bamlett's United was complete without someone shouting 'And it's not snowing now', 'Stop the game, it's snowing' or some other terrace rib-tickler. But if he had made an enemy of a town, the old referee had made a friend of a city. Previously, the Reds had disappointed in the FA Cup, a pair of quarter-final defeats, in 1897 and 1908, representing their best efforts so far. The Burnley escape lifted their quarter-final bogey and began the so-called love affair between the club and the competition, albeit one conducted from long distance over the next forty years.

By saving Mangnall's side at Turf Moor, Bamlett had inadvertently filled the role of Cupid in kick-starting that affair. After three seasons as manager, it was tempting to say that it was the best thing he had ever done for the club. In the first summer of the new decade, his United stood in depressing disarray. Admittedly, it was not all his own fault. There were a whole host of mitigating circumstances to refer to in his defence, none more persuasive than the economic shortages that had handicapped his efforts to replace the injured, crap and ageing. It also bears repeating that football managers in those days were often helpless stooges to the incompetence of the men who wielded the real power at the club – the selectors and the board. But Bamlett would have taken the United job in the full knowledge that, when the time came for bullet-biting, he, and not his bosses, would be the one doing the chewing. Ultimately, he would be accountable for the results and performances out on the pitch. Ultimately, he would have to take the flak if the wrong players were bought and sold, or the wrong teams selected. And in every area the old whistler had come up short. A hat-trick of relegation scraps and a club record winless streak already made him the leading candidate for the title of United's worst-ever manager. The events of 1930/31 killed the argument stone dead. Reds had been forced to endure some desperate campaigns in the past but no season before or since has plumbed the depths that this one did. The nine apocalyptic months that brought the Bamlett era to a close made Old Trafford the swearing capital of the western world.

*   *   *

WHEN THE SEASON started, football's List of Shame (first division section) was headed by two teams – the Liverpool outfit that lost their first eight matches in 1899/1900 and thus established themselves as the section's slowest ever starters and the Newton Heath side that compiled its worst ever losing streak, eleven straight defeats en route to runaway relegation in 1893/94. Before October was out, Bamlett's incompetents had relieved both sides of their embarrassing burden.

Everyone knew that the club would end up in the second division someday. What nobody could have foreseen was how quickly the class of 30/31 would make it happen. As collapses go, the Walls of Jericho had nothing on this.

Cracks that had been evident ever since the mid-twenties suddenly had dramatically opened up and a side that had held on to their top-flight status with a degree of comfort in the spring ended up buried beneath the rubble. But the season might just have taken a different course had it got off to the winning start that the Reds probably deserved. In their Old Trafford opener against Aston Villa, United dealt manfully with injuries to Spence and Jones to lead twice in the first half and then peg the visitors back to 3-3 in the second. But the nine Reds' heroics were wasted in the injury-time moment it took for the previously excellent Steward to come over all Scottish and spill a gentle back-pass at the feet of Villa danger-man, 'Pongo' Waring. Waring's inevitable match-winner (which took his tally for the match to four) was particularly difficult for Reds to take as he could conceivably have been lining up in United colours that afternoon. Bamlett had apparently 'popped the question' to the free-scoring centre-forward back in the summer although that did not necessarily mean a deal had ever been close. Like Spurs recently, the Reds were always keen to be linked with potential signings. Had they managed to bring in even half the big names whom they 'nearly' signed, Huddersfield, Herbert Chapman and the rest would never have had a look-in.

All right, an opening day point would probably not have repainted the season's picture – United would almost certainly have gone down anyway – but it would possibly have made it easier on the eye. For one thing, Liverpool's record would have been safe so the Reds would have been spared the morbid fascination of the media, at least until they started making inroads into the Heathens' landmark. It follows that the players' temperaments would not have received as severe an examination, their confidence would not have been dented so badly, their style not cramped as much. It cannot have been easy for the team, particularly the rookies, to cope with the knowledge that most people were looking for them to fall flat on their faces and the rest, including their own supporters, were expecting them to.

If nothing else, the Villa twist rewrote one Red's life. Steward's gaffe cost him his place for the midweek trip to Middlesbrough and plunged luckless Arthur Chesters, the club's latest back-up keeper, into a personal nightmare. They say that the key to success is grabbing your opportunities when they come along. Equally, though, it is vital that they arrive at the right time. The 20-year-old Chesters had the misfortune of getting his big break just as the fixture-list turned nasty and the defence started operating on a buffet (help yourself) basis. In terms of its timing, his call-up was in the Allenby Chilton class. Big Allenby, a Busby favourite in later years, made his first senior appearance for the Reds, away to Charlton, the day after Hitler invaded Poland. Because of the war, he had to wait another seven years to make his second.

Ayresome did at least leave the Salford boy with some pleasant memories. United, handicapped by an injury to another key man – this time Wilson – lost 3-1 but Chesters was excellent, probably his side's best performer. It wasn't until the trip to Stamford Bridge the following Saturday that his career started to seize up. Reid shot the Reds into an early lead and Spence poached a second in the closing minutes. The problem was the in-between, Chelsea, inspired by their tartan terrors, having a field day and scoring six. Four days later, Huddersfield banged another half-dozen past the sitting duck at Old Trafford. By then, Arthur was showing clear signs of overexposure and when Newcastle joined in the fun that weekend he looked punch-drunk, a diagnosis apparently confirmed when he fisted a last-minute corner into his own net. At least his blooper wasn't decisive. A hat-trick of appalling defensive errors had already settled a nutcase of a match that packed in eleven goals, a brilliant United comeback from 2-4 to 4-4, a panting crowd and enough bad defending to keep Alan Hansen in rants for the rest of his career.

In the space of eight days, Chesters had conceded nineteen goals; in less than three he had let in thirteen at Old Trafford. Until the Luftwaffe bombshell, it was the worst experience in the ground's history. At that point, the selectors moved in, sending out an SOS to Steward and sending Arthur back to the Central League. It was the beginning of the end for the young Manc. The next couple of seasons threw up just a handful of first-team chances and when he did not play at all in 32/33 he dropped down the divisions to join Exeter. For seven days following his Ayresome heroics, Chesters had seemingly been poised for a bright future. In just 180 minutes of football he had been consigned to the status of yesterday's man, forever to be remembered as the keeper who was beaten twenty-two times in eleven days. He deserved better. It was not his fault that his opportunity knocked when the Reds were at possibly their lowest ebb. Like Massimo Taibi, the ill-fated Italian who had to cope with a move to a new country, the language barrier, succeeding a legend, the post-Treble cold turkey and, worst of all, a Matt Le Tissier pea-roller, Arthur never really had a chance.

It is doubtful whether Steward, even with all his experience, could have done much better. In his first game back between the sticks, Huddersfield added another three goals to the half-dozen they had slammed past Chesters the week before. By then, Charlie Roberts, for one, had seen enough. In an article in the local press, the United legend launched a withering attack on the board and warned that the club were doomed unless they found nine new players. Now Charlie was no Bestie or Docherty, former Reds whose comments have to be taken with a pinch of salt, mainly because they remain convinced that no one else could possibly do things better than themselves. Nor was he a Meredith whose controversial style would have made perfect copy for the modern tabloids but whose views were all too often tainted by the chips he still carried on either shoulder. Charlie was the epitomé of reason, the voice of *The Guardian* not the sensationalist, so for him to come out with something so controversial was big news.

He wasn't being overly-dramatic when he said that United needed to bring in virtually a whole new team, either. Even the Wanderer, who needed to stay on the right side of the directors and was thus inclined to defend the status quo, admitted that the club needed a minimum of five new players (four forwards plus a centre-half) if the season was going to be saved. For years it had been obvious that there was a shortage of quality at Old Trafford. A new and pressing problem was the shortage of quantity. Years of getting rid of players who could still have done a job for the side were finally catching up with them. Another clutch of experienced men – Moore, Thomas, Spencer, Mann, Sweeney, Boyle among them – had left in the summer without being satisfactorily replaced. The number of professionals at the club was down to a bare-bones twenty-nine. Most other top-flight outfits could call on forty-plus. For a club with United's injury record, such cost-cutting measures were tantamount to professional suicide.

In the build-up to the season, the *Athletic News* had run a series of articles debating the effects on football of the depression. A quote from United director, Mr J. Yates, outlined the cash-conscious philosophy the club had adopted: 'I believe that the depression in industry will be reflected in the attendances at football games. Clubs that have paid exorbitant prices for players will regret it before the end of the season. I do not think football is in the same class as in the pre-war days, but I believe that, first of all, all clubs will find there is a scarcity of cash this season.'

The inference was that United had played a clever game in pruning their expenses and that those clubs who had carried on spending were headed for a big fall. From some quarters, there was praise for the directors' refusal to be dragged into a transfer market where unproven players were fetching as much £5,000. For others, it was a sign that they had given up the ghost. And, as ever, there could be no defence for the club's policy on outgoing transfers. In the summer, the name of Jack Ball had been added to the long list of baffling departures. Considering his inexperience, Jack had excelled as Tommy Reid's stand-in in 29/30 but just when he was hinting that he could be the best thing to come out of Chorley since its cake, he was sold to Sheffield Wednesday for a derisory £1,300.

When the deal went through, the champions paid peanuts but the only monkeys were United who had left themselves with no recognised backup for Reid; an oversight which became a major issue when Tommy flattered to deceive for much of the campaign. After his initial spree in 28/29 and his illness nightmare in 29/30, the Scot's true colours were about to emerge. When he was good, he was often very good but when he was bad, god he hummed. Tommy's twenty-goal haul for the season was almost miraculous given the rubbish around him but he was a heavy goalscorer rather than a consistent one. His hat-trick in the Newcastle extravaganza, for example, was followed by three months in which he scored just once.

By mid-September, even the directors had realised that they had dropped one by selling Ball. They then made a stab at making amends by snapping up Chesterfield's thirty-goal man, Jimmy Bullock, but it was a transfer made in hellish irrationality. For £1,250, effectively the money that Wednesday had paid for Jack, the management had acquired a player who had always been prolific at lower league level but who, at the age of twenty-eight (five years older than his predecessor), had surely missed his chance of making the step up to the top flight.

Hillsborough on the 20th provided an instant indictment of the club's latest transfer 'adventure', the comparison between the two centre-forwards being painful to note. Ball, who had surprised many by making a niche for himself in the champions' attack, bagged two of his new side's three goals. Bullock, given a debut in place of Reid, missed one glorious chance in the opening stages and gave the most convincing rabbit-in-headlights impression of any United front-man yet. Clearly, he would need time to adapt to top flight football but that was a luxury the selectors seemed strangely reluctant to give him. When Bullock failed to make an impression in Grimsby's waltz at Old Trafford, he was unceremoniously dumped from the team.

The papers seethed at his 'unjust treatment'. If the new boy had been good enough to bring to the club in the first place, they reasoned, he was good enough to be given a chance of showing it. Allowances had also to be made for the lack of service he had been getting: 'The present United forwards do not know what a through pass is...' groaned the *Football News*. Jimmy's treatment by the selectors was all the more perplexing as he was the only new arrival who cost any money. Later it became clear that the Bullock fee was the limit to the club's budget, in which case the management had blown all their cash on a player they clearly didn't fancy. Which meant there would be no money to spend later in the season on a saviour in the Reid and Rawlings mould, never mind on the half-dozen extra players that both the squad and the supporters were crying out for.

When United crossed town for the first derby of the season on October 4, Reid was back in the centre-forward shirt. As City had scraped together just four points themselves, the match seemed to offer the club their best chance yet to get off the mark. In fact, it gave Pop Siders their biggest reason yet to reach for the revolver. On a dismal afternoon, the Reds shipped four goals and picked up another batch of bad injuries, all of them to players they could not afford to lose. Jones, who had just been rushed back from the cracked collar-bone he had sustained on the opening day, fell awkwardly in the first half and finished the job off. His now broken collar-bone would keep him out for the next five months. Hilditch, the only player who had looked remotely capable of hacking it at centre-half, damaged an ankle and would not play again this side of Christmas while Bennion aggravated his own ankle problem but soldiered on. When Silcock was temporarily laid out in an aerial collision, United were reduced to just seven fit players.

By then, the match had degenerated into farce. City had lost two men to injury themselves so the final scenes were played out without five of the original cast. It was like visiting day at the hospital with the line of visitors being 42,000 strong. But the hospital metaphor no longer worked for both teams' seasons. Their first Maine Road derby triumph took City off the sick-list and began a run of form which would take them into the top eight. Manchester's football fraternity could now take the black band off one arm. But United, who had been lapsing in and out of a coma for years, showed no signs of coming round. Already, the record for the worst start to the season was theirs. Within three weeks they had out-crapped the Heathens too.

Nobody was pretending that United were anything but a poor side but that did not mean that the press and the public had no sympathy for their ongoing injury nightmare. 'Manchester United have become the football which the fates are kicking,' wrote Ivan Sharpe in his post-derby report. Equally true words from *The Football Chronicle*: 'Manchester United are the unluckiest team in the country as regards injuries to players and they are, perhaps, the worst team in senior football.' A wafer-thin squad could ill-afford the injury blows that had rained down on it in this and other campaigns. Bamlett had been banking on Hanson's continued development this season but Jimmy's re-broken leg had put an end to those hopes before a ball had even been kicked. Once again, the established members of the forward line would pick themselves (which was bad news for the team if not for last term's bright spark, George McLachlan – his form had slumped so dramatically that picking himself was just about the only chance he had of getting a game). The club had three experienced half-backs – Wilson, Bennion and Hilditch – on the books and all three were dogged by injury in the pre-Christmas programme. The midfield cupboard was so bare that, on several occasions, the selectors had to resort to using Billy Dale, a left-back, in the problem centre-half position. Like most of his team-mates, the verdict on Dale was that he did his best but was simply not good enough. There were defensive problems as well. Moore was now running a pub, Jones's shoulder restricted him to just five appearances all season while Silcock, a virtual ever-present before Christmas, hardly featured thereafter.

Consequently, Bamlett had little choice but to rape and pillage the reserves. The knock-on effects were felt throughout the club as all three United teams – the midweek eleven as well as the firsts and the stiffs – endured desperate seasons. Ignoring the risk of long-term career damage of the type already sustained by Chesters, the selectors rushed rookie right-back Jack Mellor and untried forwards Stan Gallimore, Arthur Warburton and Sam Hopkinson into first team action. All of them could have used another year or two in the finishing school of the Central League. Perhaps only Mellor, whose performances in Moore's old role made him one of the season's few successes, came through the experience unscathed. There was even talk of the young Oldhamer developing into an international but then much the same had been said about Dale and, in the last year or so, his career had taken a stride backwards. It remained a strange anomaly, though, that the club could find promising defenders almost at will but struggled to unearth half-backs and forwards of comparable quality.

In fairness to Rocca and the rest of the scouting team, the club's money problems forced them to recruit from the least promising of breeding grounds. Of the batch of inexperienced no-names who had been drafted in during the summer, the likeliest lad, Rosenfield, arrived from that well known football academy, the Grove House Jewish Club. What was worse, Tommy Parker, the selectors' latest stab at filling the gaping centre-back void, was brought in off a building site on Oxford Street where he had been working as a plumber. Thrown straight into senior action, he would now be expected to plug the leaks for the Reds.

Both Parker and Gallimore, the latest talent to be saddled with the tag of 'the best junior the club had produced for years', made their debuts at Upton Park on the weekend after the derby. Neither let the side down; neither looked capable of shaking the side out of their inferiority complex. Despite playing their best football for a month, the Reds were thumped 5-1. A fortnight later, amidst disturbing evidence of the players' growing tendency to throw in the towel after falling behind, United were mauled at Fratton Park. With more guts and guile, a point could easily have been theirs. Instead, after a twelfth straight defeat, the Heathens' record was.

The consolation was that, back in Manchester, there were finally signs that the Reds' losing run was losing momentum. Had the players not shocked themselves by taking an early lead, it would probably have drawn to a close against cup-holders Arsenal on the 18th. In a match that was completely overshadowed by the furore surrounding it (much more of that later), United went ahead through McLachlan's third minute toe-poke and dominated for the first quarter but had a second 'goal' unluckily chalked out for Reid's legal-looking charge on the keeper and then conceded an equaliser shortly afterwards. For the rest of the game, the side made the mistake of sitting back and playing for a point and were made to pay for their admittedly understandable lack of adventure when the Gunners sneaked the winner seven minutes from time.

Eleven days later, the team finally broke their season's duck with a home win against second division Oldham in the Lancashire Cup. In the circumstances it did not matter so much that United had fielded a full strength side in a competition that, like the League Cup today, had once been worth winning but was now viewed as a glorified reserve-team kickabout. However shallow their victory, the Reds' losing habit was a good one to break. The following Saturday, they finally kicked it in the league. In front of 12,000, a remarkable gate given the circumstances, the team that had been easier to scalp than a bald man with a badly taped toupee finally got a scalp of their own, beating Birmingham 2-0. The strange thing about United's long-awaited maiden success was how easily it was secured. As in the Arsenal match they scored early, Rowley applying the finish to a zigzag of perceptive passes, but this time they capitalised on their fast start by scoring again, Gallimore claiming his first senior goal with a firm header from Spence's corner. Led from the back by the impeccable Silcock and his eager apprentice Mellor, the Reds had little difficulty holding on to their advantage from then on. 197 days after their previous league victory, the wait for the next one was finally over.

*   *   *

ONE WIN AGAINST ORDINARY Birmingham could not camouflage the reality that it had been a disastrous and shameful couple of months. In recent weeks, however, the continuing spiral of defeats had become almost an irrelevance for many Reds. Increasingly, their attention had been focused not on the battle on the pitch but on the battle for the heart and soul of the club that was being waged on the Old Trafford terraces and also in pubs and meeting-halls across the city. The political wing of the Red Army had been ripe for revolt for years, their patience stretched ever thinner by the failure of the board to put the club back on track or even to recognise their existence. After three years of relegation battles, meagre investment in the transfer market, rumours of financial crises and more silence from the board, those supporters were on the verge of triggering the most extraordinary episode in United's history.

When the season started, there was a definite sense around town that the club were on trial. Perhaps the news had not filtered through the iron curtain that screened the boardroom dictatorship. Perhaps it had and the directors just did not care how the public felt. Whatever, the management made no move towards appeasing their accusers. If anything, they antagonised them even further. Despite the horrendous losing streak, no money was spent on new players bar the grand and a bit wasted on the hapless Bullock. And the salt in the wound? The board's decision to pay out the usual 7½% dividend despite end-of-year results which showed a £1,341 loss and a leap in the amount owed to sundry creditors to £11,222. The money paid out in divvies was not very much – just £82 – but it smacked of contempt for the plight of the club and also for the feelings of the supporters many of whom were now convinced that the money they were paying at the gate was going straight into the pockets of the shareholders. Imagine that, United being run for the benefit of people other than the fans...

Now the directors had failed their trial, the supporters, led as ever by George Greenhough, were ready to declare their sentence – off with their heads. It was the moment the supporters' and shareholders' groups had been half-planning for six years or more. Still, the manner and speed in which the public were mobilised was impressive, as impressive perhaps as anything achieved by the freedom-from-Murdoch fighters seventy years later. Meetings were arranged, votes taken and plans formed. Most of the Red dissidents would have preferred a bloody boardroom coup but there was no chance of them taking this Bastille by force. Instead, they had to work on more subtle means of getting their point across. Attempts were made to secure an interview with the board and also to get the FA to look at the inner workings of the club. When they failed, the supporters' groups took what was perhaps the only option left open to them bar doing nothing; they threatened to boycott matches. In classic, ground-breaking style the Red Army were preparing to go on strike.

The radical boycott plans grabbed the imagination of the local media like no other non-football, football story. Unlike today, football coverage was restricted to match previews and reports and the odd paragraph devoted to new signings or managerial changes. It would be an exaggeration to say that the boycott story dominated the broadsheets but, over the five weeks of the affair, the coverage was still unprecedentedly comprehensive. As a unique story developed, the papers were there at every turn.

*   *   *

UNITED SUPPORTERS' BOYCOTT - AUTUMN 1930

The first round of supporters' meetings kicked off at the Railwayman's Club, Collyhurst, on Wednesday, September 24. In the ten days that followed, seven more meetings were held at different locations across the city. At each meeting, a vote of no confidence in the board was passed and the resolution to boycott a match was upheld.

SEPTEMBER 25 – MANCHESTER EVENING CHRONICLE
UNITED SUPPORTERS' CLUB; TALK AT MEETING OF BOYCOTTING MATCH

Mr G. H. Greenhough, founder and secretary of the Supporters' Club, and founder of the Shareholders' Association of the Manchester United Football Club, informs the *Evening Chronicle* that another vote of 'No confidence' in the present board and management of the United club was passed last night at a meeting at the Railwaymen's Club, Rochdale Road, Collyhurst, attended by 250 people.

'It has been arranged,' he states, ' that on a given day the ground will be boycotted for one match to prove to the directors of the club our strength.'

Mr Greenhough also said that there will be a meeting of supporters of the club at the Milton Hall, Deansgate, some time in October.

The meetings arranged were, he said, open to the general public as well as the supporters' club.

A meeting will be held tonight at 7-45 at the Grove House Lads' Club, Elizabeth Street, Cheetham Hill. Tomorrow night there is a meeting at St Philips Church room, Chester Street, Oxford Road, and next week's meetings are as follows:-

Monday: Bradford Labour Hall, Grey Mare Lane, Bradford

Tuesday: Butter Hall, Newton Street, Stretford
Wednesday: Hyndman Hall, Liverpool Street, Salford
The meetings commence at 7-45 p.m.

*   *   *

SEPTEMBER 25 – MANCHESTER EVENING NEWS
UNITED SUPPORTERS VEXED: COLLYHURST CALLS
FOR MANAGEMENT CHANGE: NO CONFIDENCE VOTE

'We have no confidence in the Board of Directors and we consider that an immediate entire change in the management of the United is necessary.'

This was the resolution which has been passed unanimously at a public meeting of the supporters of Manchester United in the Collyhurst district.

*   *   *

SEPTEMBER 26 – MANCHESTER EVENING CHRONICLE

Support for Boycott Plan; 400 United Supporters in favour: Arsenal Match suggested BY CASUAL

At the meeting of United Supporters' Club at the Grove House Club, Elizabeth Street, Cheetham Hill, Manchester, last night, a solid vote of 'no confidence' in the directorate was passed, and the boycott suggestion received further unanimous support.

Mr G. H. Greenhough of the Shareholders' Association and the Supporters'' Club, who called the meeting, spoke at great length to an attentive body of listeners, the hall being filled to overflowing, and the doors being kept open so that about another 100 people in the vestibule, unable to gain entrance to the hall, could hear some of the speeches. Altogether there were about 400 people present.

'CLASHING OF CANS'

The meeting was conducted harmoniously. There was very little heckling: instead there were occasions when laughter swept the room, as for instance when reference was made to the forthcoming City-United game at Maine Road which one person described as 'the clashing of the cans' [don't worry, I don't get it either].

Mr Greenhough does not disguise his lack of faith in the directorate of the club, whom he accuses of not listening to the cries of the supporters to get new players. 'They say they have no money,' he said. 'Well, why don't they issue the non-issued shares totalling nearly £14,000?'

Referring to the boycott proposed – and the match with the Arsenal at Old Trafford on October 18 was mentioned, but this will be confirmed at a later date – Mr Greenhough appealed to those present not to be absent from other games.

PLAYERS' VIEW

He further mentioned that 17,000 handbills would be distributed tomorrow, calling the attention of all supporters of the club to his endeavours to secure a better team.

Mr Greenhough also suggested that there should be a representative of the Supporters" Club on the Board [this was later denied], who could attend meetings and then report to the supporters. He further pointed out that if the first boycott did not have the desired effect, a further meeting of the supporters would be called at the Milton Hall, Deansgate, at which a second boycott would be arranged.

*   *   *

It should not be too difficult to second-guess the board's immediate reaction to the threatened boycott but here's a clue anyway; it's supposed to be golden...

SEPTEMBER 27 – MANCHESTER EVENING NEWS
UNITED OFFICIALS SIT TIGHT

In reference to the suggested boycotting of the Manchester United-Arsenal match at Old Trafford on October 18, Mr W. Crickmer, the secretary of the club, told me (writes 'Navigator'): – 'We are doing nothing. We understand that members of the Supporters' Club at today's home match with Grimsby Town are distributing leaflets. What these leaflets urge we do not know.' I understand, however, that several officials of the United are in favour of trying to annul the boycott by an official appeal.

Mr Greenhough, the secretary of the Supporters' Club, who has been chiefly responsible for the organisation of the public meetings to demand an FA inquiry into the affairs of the United, told me that leaflets issued this afternoon do not urge, as has been stated, the boycotting of the Arsenal match.

Mr Greenhough assured me that the boycotting will be done quietly, and in an orderly manner, so as not to incur any breach of the peace.

*　　　　　*　　　　　*

The Athletic News *swings the first punch in the establishment's backlash against the boycott plan.*

SEPTEMBER 29 – ATHLETIC NEWS
ONSLAUGHT ON MANCHESTER UNITED:
MANCHESTER 'UNITED'

Manchester United have yet to win or draw a match, and some of their followers are going the right way to delay the happy day.

'No confidence' resolutions in the directors of the club, and suggestions of boycotting the match with the Arsenal on October 18, have been the result of recent meetings, of which there are three more down for this week.

Allegations that the control of the club is not on a satisfactory basis have been made by Mr G. H. Greenhough, who is connected with the Supporters' Club and also with the Shareholders Association.

SHAREHOLDERS TO MEET

It is stated that he wants an FA inquiry and that a petition signed by supporters of the club is to be presented, asking the FA 'to make an inquiry into the inner workings of the club'.

Meanwhile the *Athletic News* is able to announce that Mr Greenhough is calling a meeting of the Shareholders' Association this week – Thursday is the suggested evening – when the whole matter of what action to take is likely to be decided.

CALLING IN FA

So far Mr Greenhough has not shown his hand regarding the grounds upon which he would call in the FA. It is understood that he is seeking counsel's advice before doing so.

Whatever grievance he – or any other follower of the club – may nurse concerning the poor displays of the team that in itself would not constitute a reason for FA interference, and no doubt Mr Greenhough knows it. He vaguely hints at 'mismanagement'. He considers that, as there is nearly £14,000 in unissued shares still available this should be secured for new players; and he talks about capital debt and asks to whom are the club mostly indebted, and why.

Boycott and Inquiry

He also suggests that an 'independent' board of directors – whatever that means – should be in control of the club. But, whatever it all amounts to, there can be no doubting the earnestness with which Mr Greenhough is conducting the campaign.

A football club boycott by 'supporters' is detestable, but the object of this agitation seems to be to force an FA inquiry. If the disturbing din of recent days in Manchester is to be maintained, no doubt the United club will welcome it and so much sooner be ready to get on with the game.

* * *

The supporters decide to boycott United's match with cup-holders Arsenal. Many people were bemused by their choice. If the rebels' aim was to empty the Pop Side, they would surely have had a better chance of success if they had chosen a less glamorous fixture. Aside from derby and cup matches, no game carried more magnetism than the visit of the glamorous Gunners. Then again, if the supporters' priority was to make people sit up and take note of United's problems, they could not have chosen a better vehicle with which to get their message across.

Perhaps, though, we are reading too much into all this. There is an alternative explanation for the boycotters' choice; the Arsenal fixture was United's next home game.

* * *

September 30 – Manchester Evening Chronicle

Latest Moves in United Boycott;
Suggestions to the Board

The boycott declared against the Manchester United club by a section of its supporters will come into operation on October 18, the day of the Arsenal match.

The last meeting to be held by the Supporters' Club is arranged for Hulme Town Hall on October 17 – the eve of the Arsenal match.

Mr G. H. Greenhough, founder of the United Supporters" Club and the Shareholders' Association, said today: 'I know what will happen – there will probably be a few new players for the Arsenal match, but the boycott won't be ended that way.'

Suggestions To Board

'Even if the club turns out an entirely new team, the boycott will still be on. Our quarrel is not with the lads. It is with the directors.

At the meeting in Hulme Town Hall we shall suggest to the board:

'That they resign in a body, or

'That they co-opt four independent sportsmen on the board

'The board of directors, of course, will do everything in their power to counter the boycott, but only drastic action will satisfy us.

'Unless the directors meet our demands they will lose thousands of their supporters.'

*   *   *

Greenhough outlines the points he would make to the board should he be granted his interview. Over the next fortnight his five-point plan becomes the talk of the town's chattering classes.

October 2 – Manchester Evening News
New Demands from United: Boycott leaders seek an interview: Five Questions: Plea for Change in Directorate

Manchester United today received an application from Mr Greenhough, the leader of the threatened boycott, for the Board to give him an interview, arising out of the grievances of the supporters.

The five questions he will ask the directors are:

- realising the position of the club are the directors agreeable to co-opting five shareholders on the board?

- do the directors agree that there is need of a change in the policy of scouting for players?

- do the directors agree that there is a need for a new trainer?

- do the directors agree that there is an immediate need for several ready-made players?

- realising the financial position of the club, do the directors agree that there is a need for the issuing of the unissued share capital, and with the money obtained buy new players?

Mr Greenhough says that Charlie Roberts will speak at Hulme Town Hall on the embargo on him to become a director of the club.

*   *   *

I should explain that last bit. Roberts' legendary status, his sympathy for the supporters' cause and his forceful charisma made him the obvious candidate to deliver the kick up the backside that the directors so clearly needed. His initial application to join the board was refused because he did not own any shares and only a shareholder could become a director of a limited company like United. Greenhough's subsequent efforts to bypass the problem by giving Charlie some of his own shares were foiled by a clause in the 1925 'special resolutions' of the club which gave the directors the power to refuse the transfer of shares.

The directors' decision to turn Roberts aside was yet another PR own goal. Placing an embargo on him not only fanned the flames of fan dissent, it cost them an opportunity to strengthen their own position. Had Charlie been co-opted as a director, he would have given the club an acceptable public face. With the club's greatest captain on board, the directors would have enjoyed a ready means of defence against the swarm of accusations that they were businessmen rather than football men. Without him, they had none.

*   *   *

The first wave of rallies closes with a meeting at Hyndman Hall, Salford. Once again, the public turn up in their numbers to demonstrate their sympathy for the boycotters.

OCTOBER 3 – SALFORD REPORTER
UNITED BOYCOTT: SALFORD MEETING SUPPORTERS PROPOSAL BY 'TRAFFORD'

A meeting of the United supporters at the Hyndman Hall, Liverpool Street, Salford, on Wednesday evening expressed itself unanimously in favour of Mr Greenhough's proposal to boycott the Arsenal match on October 18. Addressing the meeting, Mr Greenhough, honorary secretary of the Supporters' Club, said that he was not blaming the players for United's failure; they did their best to win, but unfortunately they were not of a sufficiently high standard; the management ought to purchase new players. For five years, not one first class player has signed on for the team. The directors, he admitted, had not money to spare, but he could see no reason why the money required could not be borrowed from the bank.

Statements had appeared in the Press to the effect that the speaker had attempted to have two supporters placed on the board of management. Such statements, he added, were untrue, and made by men who knew nothing at all about football. He would like to do to reporters what he would like to have done to Germans during the war.

He (Mr Greenhough) had sent an eight-page letter to the FA complaining of the way in which United was managed but had received only an evasive answer. The purpose of this boycott was to compel that body to make an inquiry into the inner workings of the club with which Mr Greenhough was only too well acquainted.

There were so many people in the building wanting to hear Mr Greenhough that two meetings had to be held, and both were unanimously in favour of the boycott.

*   *   *

The Manchester Football News *speaks its mind on the boycott debate. The stance taken by the News was duplicated in the editorials of most papers. They were sympathetic to the plight of the supporters, anxious about the future of the club, critical of the silence of the board but utterly opposed to the notion of a boycott.*

OCTOBER 4 – FOOTBALL NEWS
MANCHESTER FOOTBALL VIEWS

No one who claims wholly and thoroughly to be a sportsman can for one moment pretend that the proposed boycott of the Old Trafford enclosure is the best way by which supporters of the club may voice, and, at the same time, remedy, their grievance.

The traditions of sport demand that a supporter shall stick to his club through thick and thin. If necessary, he should be prepared to pay his shilling to see his club lose week by week till they retain their place in the Third Division by re-election only. Then he should set about doing his little bit towards retrenchment and reform till the League Championship cup is on the directors' sideboard at the club headquarters. We speak generally now, not of Manchester United.

To particularise, and to speak of United: surely it is quite clear that if the poor form of the side continues, a boycott will not be necessary, because the support awarded the team will diminish by stages until it is meagre. For modern professional football, while it remains a sport, has also become a very efficiently organised business and a competent entertainment.

We feel that, while this proposed boycott is not the way in which supporters should have voiced their displeasure, the directors might have broken their silence. They might well have shown, without pandering to those who wish to take an unwarranted part in the club's affairs, that they acknowledge the existence of a large body of one-time loyal supporters who are not prepared to see the club lightly lose its status.

*   *   *

The people speak. Whether these views were representative of the majority or not it is impossible to say. Nor, as one opponent of the boycott pointed out, were there any guarantees that the pro-boycott supporters were representative of the Red Army as a whole.

First comes the anti-Greenhough point of view...

SEPTEMBER 27 – FOOTBALL NEWS

'MAY I PUT IN A WORD – A LONE WORD, I FEAR – FOR MANCHESTER UNITED PLAYERS AND OFFICIALS?

'Why should the directors, having laid down a principle, depart from it because of the howlings of the mob? Why should they be stampeded into paying absurdly high sums for ready-made players whose careers at Old Trafford must of necessity be brief?

'There are youngsters on the staff who, if they are kept in the background for a little while, will develop into stars. United have struck a bad patch, as will all clubs at different times, but if they can survive a little longer these young players will make good and found a fine team. Stop the "Supporters" meetings, and support the players instead.' – 'S.P', Heaton Park

OCTOBER 4 – FOOTBALL NEWS

'Those so-called supporters of United who want to boycott matches are meeting under rebel leaders. I suppose those so-called supporters are those who wait at Old Trafford until the matches are nearly over, when the gates are thrown open and they can walk in free? They are very poor sports.

'I myself am a Manchester man, and I support both teams – not one. I have been on the popular side for years, and I say that to boycott a club is an insult to the visiting side – especially such a side as the Arsenal.....Manchester City supporters should turn up in thousands at Old Trafford when the Arsenal are there and cheer our local team on.

'I say, let each crowd pack each other's ground week in, week out, and I am sure we shall see some of the finest play in the League and both teams soon in the top half of the table. The teams only want backing up by real supporters, not scandal-mongers.' – H.L. Richardson from New Moston

'May I join "S.P." in upholding the principles of the Manchester United officials. What is wanted at Old Trafford are some supporters who know how to give encouragement.

'Mr Lawton, the United chairman, said quite plainly that he does not believe in paying fancy prices for players.

'Everybody is flinging advice and warning at the United powers-that-be, but what would the Press and public do, say, if it was the Aston Villa chairman who made those remarks? Ah, the old sloppy sentiment would crop up, and everybody would be with them to a man.

'I cannot say how many supporters have turned up at other places, but the meeting held at Bradford last Monday evening was a complete farce. The hall was full, but I will gamble there were not twenty Manchester United supporters in the crowd. I know personally twenty or thirty of my neighbours alone who shot up their hands for the boycott who never see Warwick Road before and after the Christmas holidays in each year. In fact, what they pay to football at all would not keep any club in sponges' – 'W.L.' from Bradford, Manchester

...and then, letters in support of the fans' action.

'SP needs a word in season! He asks why the directors should depart from a principle because of the howlings of the mob. Does he call the loyal supporter of United a mob? I venture to say that he has not watched United as long as I have – for 23 years: can he beat that? He says there are some good youngsters on the staff; where are they? 6-0 and 8-1 [the results of two recent Central League fixtures] – some grand youngsters, I must say.

'United have been in a bad patch for five years and would be for another five years if we had such nice people as S.P. as the directors.

We want a new board of directors and new management – the present men are played out. Last Saturday [against Grimsby] the team played more like a Third Division side, and yet no good players are signed. No decent player has been signed since Barson. If the directors spent £10,000 on two players it would set the team up – a centre-half and an inside-right. It's a wonder to me there has not been a riot at Old Trafford before now. I have a very poor opinion of the way the club is carried on; the directors, not the supporters (who are mugs!) are the mob!' – Disgusted from Altrincham

'I have been attending the recent meetings, and we have certainly had our eyes opened. I am making it my business to see that no supporters will attend the Arsenal match. It will show the officials what we can do. The team at present is the weakest that has ever been known in the history of the club...we may have another new man for the City match, so I am told. Yes, and pigs might fly...' – 'J.W.'

*   *   *

The pressure grows on the club to break its silence.

OCTOBER 6 – MANCHESTER EVENING NEWS

UNITED MUST SPEAK: TO SECURE CONFIDENCE OF PUBLIC:
THE BOYCOTT: MIGHT BE AVERTED BY DIRECTORS' STATEMENT
– BY THE CAPTAIN

By losing to Manchester City at Maine Road on Saturday, Manchester United achieved the unenviable record of playing nine games in succession and losing them all.

Will the directors now realise that there is a large body of public opinion which expects them to break their silence and to take in a certain measure the club's supporters into their confidence?

For, grave as is this record in itself, worse still appears the future. We all know that one Saturday afternoon the ball will roll nicely for United, and a match will be won, but a glance at the immediate fixture shows how hopeless is the prospect with the present team in its present form.

October 11 – West Ham (away)
18 – Arsenal (home)
25 – Portsmouth (away)

The Boycott

As all the world knows, the Supporters" Club (the existence of which is not acknowledged by the United F.C.) has proposed a boycott of the ground for the day when the Arsenal (divisional leaders) visit Old Trafford.

While I do not agree with that step, I do think that the time has come when the directors should make a definite statement.

Will they take the public into their confidence and state clearly the financial position: the policy regarding the buying of crack players: and why, despite the extraordinary number of injured players on the books, only one new man (Bullock, a centre-forward) has been signed?

Statement Refused

I agree that there are times when the directors of a company must keep their own counsel but equally they must realise that there are times when a policy of silence is definitely the wrong one. In the present instance the United directors are making their supporters feel that they don't count.

My view is that the public will be more likely to support them in this time of distress if the public is taken into the directors' confidence than if the present policy of silence is continued.

As representing the *Manchester Evening News*, I have approached the chairman of the club, Mr G. H. Lawton, and the manager, Mr Herbert Bamlett.

Any sort of statement has been refused.

Not Only A Sport

Association football is still, in the minds of the great majority of Englishmen, the great sport, but it is also one of the most lucrative forms of entertainment. Like other entertainments, football can not expect to keep its public unless that public enjoys the confidence of those respect for its control.

I feel sure that the United directors have only to recognise the existence of their supporters for them to receive the public's co-operation and support.

The boycott would be called off and everybody would want to lend a hand towards helping United recover the ground they have lost.

*   *   *

Shock news – the club speaks. However, Greenhough already smells a delaying tactic.

October 8 – Manchester Evening News

Manchester United have officially acknowledged a letter sent to them by Mr Greenhough, secretary of the Supporters' Club, who is organising a boycott of the home match with the Arsenal on October 18 failing satisfactory reply to his well-known five points and an assurance it will be submitted to the Board at the next meeting.

It has been brought to the attention of the *Manchester Evening News* that ardent well-wishers of the club not associated with Mr Greenhough and deploring the step he proposes to take, have written to the FA on their own behalf, but obviously the replies and the expressions of opinion they contain must be treated as private and confidential.

One of these self-appointed correspondents wondered from the communication he had received whether Mr Greenhough had communicated with the FA and received a reply.

*   *   *

October 8 – Manchester Evening Chronicle

United Boycott; Directors reply to Mr Greenhough

Mr G. H. Greenhough, who last week wrote to the Manchester United club asking for an interview with the board to discuss certain matters, has received a reply stating that his letter will be submitted to the Board at the next meeting.

'My contention,' said Mr Greenhough to an *Evening Chronicle* reporter today, 'is that the questions which will be put to the Board are so important that an extraordinary meeting of the directors might have been called to discuss the situation straight away.'

Mr Greenhough stated that if the directors of the United were willing to interview him and two other representatives of the supporters, he would be prepared to ask the meeting on October 17 not to boycott the Arsenal match.

Mr Greenhough asks us to state that no tickets are being issued for the meeting in the Hulme Town Hall. He has had many applications and wishes to make this clear.

*   *   *

The players rally round the trainer. Other clubs rally round the United board.

OCTOBER 13 – MANCHESTER EVENING CHRONICLE

On the return journey to Manchester (from West Ham), 'Casual' was approached by one or two United players, who referred to statements made at the supporters meetings concerning the trainer, Jack Pullar.

'No club could have a better trainer than Jack Pullar,' they told me. 'Every player receives just the same attention from him, and there is not a member of the playing staff who does not feel that a great injury has been done to him by the suggestion that a new trainer is required. Pullar is one of the best in the country. For sixteen years he has been at Old Trafford and never has there been a complaint against him.'

In the West Ham programme on Saturday was the following: 'At the present time, not only have the Manchester United people to battle with the bogey of defeat, but to listen to the dictation of a supporters' club. Just when they most need co-operation and sympathy, they meet with the outrageous demands of an organisation which runs no financial risk whatever, and yet would dictate to those who have been responsible for the many successes of their favourite club...

It seems such a pity that these enthusiasts, bounded together in the name of supporters club, should behave in a time of misfortune so paradoxically; apart from forgetting that one of the first duty of a sportsman is to be as good a loser as winner.'

*   *   *

Greenhough's nostrils do not lie; the club announce that he remains persona non grata in the boardroom. He had guessed as much from the board's persistent refusal to recognise either the Supporters' Club or the Shareholders' Association. The news was probably as welcome as it was expected. As Greenhough admitted to the Navigator, his request for an interview had always been a means to an end rather than the end itself.

OCTOBER 14 – MANCHESTER EVENING NEWS

UNITED BOYCOTT PLANS; ONLY GENTLE PERSUASION WILL BE USED;
DIRECTORS' REPLY (BY NAVIGATOR)

What hope there was during the weekend that the boycott of the United-Arsenal match at Old Trafford on Saturday would be called off has died today on receipt by Mr G. H. Greenhough, the leader of the threatened boycott, of a letter from the United, refusing him an interview with the directors of the Club.

Mr Greenhough applied on October 1 for the interview : today's reply from Mr W. Crickmer, secretary to the club, reads:

'I placed your letter before the directors, and they instruct me to say that in view of all that has been and is being done by you they do not think an interview with you should be granted.'

No Loophole

I am not surprised at the action of the directors and neither is Mr Greenhough.

'I never for a moment thought they would give me an interview,' Mr Greenhough told me today.

'The supporters I represent have not faith in the directors, and in face of that it seems ridiculous to ask them for an interview, but it was done so that there could be no loophole for any section of the public to charge us with unfair play.'

On Friday at Hulme Town Hall there will be a mass meeting of the supporters of the United.

At this meeting Charles Roberts will speak on the embargo placed on his becoming a director of the club, and Mr Greenhough will formally make known the decision of the directors regarding his application for an interview.

Mr Greenhough assured me that the boycotting of the match will be done in as orderly a manner as possible, so as not to cause any breach of the peace.

'We shall make no attempt to force people to stay away from the match,' said Mr Greenhough.

'Only gentle persuasion will be used. We are enlisting the sympathy of the public in our fight, which will be carried on now to the bitter end.'

Attack On Players

Mr Greenhough is annoyed by the circulation of a handbill directed against the United.

The attack is poorly worded, and epithets are used against individual players. The name of the printer does not appear on the handbill.

Mr Greenhough characterised the circulation of the handbill as low and contemptible. 'I do not know who is responsible for this,' he said. 'I wish they could be discovered.'

THE CLUB TODAY

Nothing was forthcoming from the United headquarters today.

Mr Crickmer said: 'We have not yet made a statement and as yet we do not intend doing so.'

*   *   *

From the Evening Chronicle; a Red and a Blue view.

'BURNAGE' :- RE THE PROPOSED BOYCOTT AT OLD TRAFFORD NEXT SATURDAY

'What do the Supporters' (?) Club want? Surely the directors are acting wisely in not being 'pannicked' into buying players who may not blend. Take a glance at Everton last season

'Where are class players to be bought today – except at a king's ransom? The United team have been heavily handicapped by injuries so far, and if, instead of 'barracking', the Supporters' Club would stimulate the team by encouragement, it would do a great deal towards United securing some points.

'The Supporters' Club should play the game. Boycotting is not sport. May I point out that a few seasons ago the Villa won the Cup after being plumb at the foot of the table for half a season? Being a 'Cityite' myself (I sometimes get to Old Trafford), I venture to suggest that every other 'Cityite' and lover of the game that they should visit Old Trafford next Saturday.

'Wear own colours and next to it the United's red. Help to fill the ground to capacity; encourage the team to win, and [cue Dambusters music] help to break a movement which is not sport, foreign to Lancashire, and most certainly not British.'

'M.M' from Cheetham:-

'I have been a supporter of Manchester United for over twenty years. I am writing you because of the emphasis you place on the comments in the official programme issued by West Ham. I think they are wrong in their remarks because the team generally is being encouraged as much as possible by the loyal supporters.

'The supporters of the club are justly complaining about a directorate which offers no legitimate reason why the position of the club is not improved by the only means possible – the procuring of the new talent.

'The players have the deepest sympathy of the crowd, and every decent bit of work is warmly applauded. You cannot blame the supporters if they show sings of getting 'fed up' with stories about how difficult it is to get the new men so urgently needed.'

*   *   *

In the same paper the following day, Greenhough tells Bluenoses to keep out of a Red fight.

Mr Greenhough further mentioned the letter from 'Burnage', publicised in last night's Evening Chronicle, in which the writer asked for the support of City's supporters at the match. 'I want to ask the City supporters not to take any notice of it.' said Mr Greenhough. 'The City supporters have plenty to do to look after their club, and this is a fight of Manchester United followers.'

'We have been the laughing stock of the City supporters for years. Therefore I do not see why, when we are doing our best to put our house in order, the City supporters should enter into it at all. I hope their supporters will not be influenced by the letter from 'Burnage',' added Mr Greenhough.

*   *   *

Possibly there were some boycotters who would have relished the prospect of turning their fight into a dirty one. However, because the Red Army had no legal right either to strike or picket, the use of intimidatory tactics was never seriously considered. The boycott leaders had no choice but to announce that their protest would be a peaceful one. Admittedly he did not say so in as many words but Greenhough planned to spend the afternoon of the Arsenal match shacked up in bed with his Red soul-mates, smoking peace pipes and having flowers tied in his hair.

October 15 – Manchester Evening News

Anti-Rowdyism Move; Old Trafford Boycott Simmers Down: No Pickets: Leader's Action after Legal Advice

Mr G. H. Greenhough, the leader of the threatened boycotting of the Arsenal-United match at Old Trafford on Saturday, tells me today (writes the Navigator) that it has now been decided not to place pickets outside the ground, nor to instruct anyone to mingle with the spectators as they arrive to persuade them not to see the game.

This decision has been arrived at following Mr Greenhough consulting a prominent Manchester barrister who is one of his ardent supporters.

'We do not wish to incur the displeasure of the police, and the only way we may assure ourselves that there will be no element of rowdyism throughout the fight lies in leaving, at the last moment, the boycott in the hands of the public,' said Mr Greenhough.

ARSENAL MAN'S VIEWS

During the week Mr Greenhough has received scores of letters from Arsenal supporters.

One London correspondent doubts if the boycott will be successful seeing that it is planned with the Arsenal – a gate-drawing team – as visitors.

He asks whether the present agitation of the supporters is not making it extremely difficult for the United to obtain ready-made players.

Mr Greenhough says that the United supporters think it is better to boycott Old Trafford when there is a strong visiting team.

'We are appealing to all Manchester football enthusiasts who follow the United, and who may attend Saturday's match for the one reason of seeing the Arsenal, to stay away this once in the interest of our case,' said Mr Greenhough.

'They must realise that the future will provide them with opportunities to see the Arsenal.'

'I am not attending the match, nor am I going near the ground.'

*   *   *

Despite Greenhough's claims that the boycott was stronger than ever, there were definite signs that the weight of public opinion rested against it. Two days before the Arsenal match, the club were smugly claiming victory in United's civil war.

OCTOBER 16 – MANCHESTER EVENING NEWS

End Of The United Boycott: Club Preparing For 50,000 Gate; Arsenal's Visit

Manchester United officials believe that the last has been heard of the boycott.

Following the announcement that the Supporters' Club would not picket the ground, Mr W. Crickmer, secretary of the United, states that the club is preparing for a 50,000 gate.

Nearly all the bookable seating accommodation has been already reserved for Saturday's visit of the Arsenal

New Factors

Nobody would be surprised at a gate approaching the figure so optimistically forecast by the United officials for, apart from the drawing power of the Arsenal, new factors have arisen to increase the size of the crowd.

United beat Oldham yesterday in a cup-tie, and doubtless a good many people will turn up at Old Trafford to see what a boycott looks like.

*   *   *

October 17 – Manchester Evening News

It seems certain now that the boycott has failed, and only half a dozen people or so will be sorry.

It may be that the supporters' resolutions of no confidence in the United directorate were passed in good faith – it may even be that they were justified: I do not want to discuss that here – but the boycott was never the right way to do things.'

Possibly the failure of this move may have its effect on the players, who will perhaps play with greater confidence.

I anticipate a big crowd tomorrow for the visit of the Arsenal. I have said that all along – and now the management announce that they are preparing for a 50,000 gate.

This need not frighten anybody away, for we all know that Old Trafford will be equal to any demand Manchester is likely to impose upon it tomorrow.

*   *   *

THE FINAL STAND:

Roberts appeals for the boycott to be called off. The supporters vote to fight on. They were probably right, too. It was too late for them to claw back any popular support now. Also, if they had given in, they would have left themselves open to accusations that they were all bluster and no balls. A hostile press disagreed but there was something honourable in the rebels' determination to see out a fight they were almost certain to lose.

OCTOBER 18 – THE GUARDIAN

UNITED CLUB BOYCOTT; RESOLUTION TO STAY AWAY

At a public meeting of about 3,000 supporters of the Manchester United Football Club in the Hulme Town Hall last night it was decided by a large majority to boycott today's match between the United and the Arsenal and a vote of 'no confidence' in the Board of Management was passed. Except for one or two minor interruptions the meeting was carried through in an orderly manner.

The chairman (Mr S. Mason) pointed out that the quarrel was with the management not the players.

Mr Charlie Roberts, who seconded an unsuccessful resolution that the boycott be withdrawn, said the players had his deepest sympathy and he blamed the management for the present position at Old Trafford. The management had created their own trouble, and they could not say they had never had a warning.

Mr Roberts's sympathies, however, were not with a boycott, which would not have public opinion behind it. He could not understand why the management called themselves business man and yet were losing at least a large sum of money a week through lack of enterprise.

Mr G. H. Greenhough, who convened the meeting, gave details of the domestic affairs of the club and quoted figures from balance sheets. As a shareholder he was entitled to know where the money went, and the balance sheet did not show that.

The directors of the club had refused to interview him.

*   *   *

The countdown to the boycott. Like the rest of the papers, The Mail does not mince its words...

OCTOBER 18

'This is the match which the hotheads among the Manchester club's supporters have deceived should be boycotted. The threat is so stupid and unsporting that the effect may well be that there will be more people at Old Trafford than on any previous day this season.'

*   *   *

The press give their verdict…

OCTOBER 18 – MANCHESTER EVENING NEWS

NO SIGNS OF BOYCOTT AT OLD TRAFFORD; NORMAL ATTENDANCE FOR ARSENAL MATCH; WIRE TO CHAIRMAN.

All was quiet on the Old Trafford front this afternoon. Also at the back and sides. More than ten thousand of them went in. But not the twelve hundred.

That was the question. Where were those 1,200 spectators who at last night's protest meeting solemnly decided to boycott the ground? Were they sitting over their firesides gloating over the action or did a *Manchester Evening News* representative see some of them quietly slipping through the barriers, paying their admission fees without a murmur?

Inside the ground there was no suggestion of a boycott. Long before the match started people began flowing in, and there was every indication that by the time the match began there would be a normal Arsenal gate.

WIRE TO CHAIRMAN

Mr G. H. Lawton, the chairman of the Manchester United Football Club, on the eve of this afternoon's match received the following telegram from Southport Football Supporters' Club.

'Our committee wish you all success in today's match with the Arsenal, and hope that you will have a bumper gate.'

The boycotters apparently boycotted themselves for practically up to the time of the kick-off not a single incident occurred that made today's match different from those of previous weeks.

At some of the entrances small crowds assembled as though anticipating a surprise development.

'We have not seen a sign of a picket,' said a gate official. 'The crowd appears to be its normal size, and we have had to use no blandishments to get the people inside.'

POLICE POSTED

Extra policemen had been placed on duty outside the ground, but there was not the slightest need for their presence.

About 1,500 people attended the meeting at Hulme Town Hall last night, called by Mr G. H. Greenhough, the leader of the agitation for the boycott, and about 1,300 by a show of hands decided to boycott the match.

This decision was arrived at in face of an appeal by Mr Charles Roberts, the famous international and former captain and centre-half of United, to abandon the boycott.

*   *   *

OCTOBER 20 – ATHLETIC NEWS

AN END TO MOB LAW; LET MANCHESTER UNITED NOW PUSH ON WITH THEIR PLANS

The much-discussed boycott was 'on' but no one noticed it!

Did any of those 1,000 people who voted for this boycott of the Arsenal game at Manchester United's ground on Saturday go to the match? In any event the United's largest gate of the season – 30,000 – saw the game.

This was an effective answer as rain simply pelted down at the commencement of the match and must have kept thousands away.

WHAT NOW?

The boycotters have thrown a boomerang and hit only themselves for the whole country is now anxious to cheer on Manchester United.

And let me add this;

The club, despite their eleventh successive defeat, should have been encouraged by Saturday's play and the demonstration of public loyalty that completely obliterated all boycott talk to proceed in their plans for improving the outlook. They have not been idle.

*   *   *

OCTOBER 20 – MANCHESTER EVENING NEWS

So the boycott failed after all just as those who knew the crowd best said it would fail. The crowd was variously estimated at from

25,000 to 30,000 and that despite heavy rain just about the hour people should have been starting out to the game.

United did not get the 50,000 gate they were hoping for but a crowd of 23,406 in the rain was still viewed as a moral victory for the anti-boycott stance. The Evening News *scornfully suggested that some of the rebels had given their principles a Judas kiss by sneaking into the ground to watch the match. Their amazement at the non-existence of picketing or even 'abnormal' scenes suggested that they had not been paying attention to what had been written in their own paper. Greenhough had made it perfectly clear that the boycotters would refrain from using intimidation as a means of making the boycott work. If they had done, would the day have panned out differently?*

That was one of a number of questions concerning the boycott attempt that remained unanswered. How many of the 25,000 turned up just because United were playing a glamorous side? How many of them were attracted to the ground out of mere curiosity? How many were supporters of other clubs (several City umbrellas were spotted on the Pop Side)? How many Reds opted to stay away? Was the rain merely a convenient excuse to explain away the missing 25,000? Are you getting bored of questions yet? If not, why not?

*   *   *

The Sequel

Before the Arsenal game, the band played 'Happy days are here again' to loud cheers. For a few weeks the board may even have felt that was the case as messages of sympathy and support piled up at their door. For instance, when United played at Fratton Park, the Portsmouth directors wrote in their official notes: 'Anything more stupid from those styling themselves "supporters" cannot be imagined.' The home crowd, meanwhile, gave the Reds a reception 'fit for the winners of the FA Cup' and the band belted out 'Pack up all your troubles'.

While United were enjoying their short-lived spell as the country's favourite team, the rebel supporters were coming under pressure to fall at the directors' feet and repent their sins. In the *Evening News*, the Captain urged: 'Will Mr G. H. Greenhough and his fellow boycotters now realise that their effort has been a disastrous failure, admit it publicly, and rally round Manchester United?' Talk about wishful thinking. As the press themselves would soon admit, the situation at the club had not improved. The board had not done anything to suggest they were capable of turning things around, rather they had stayed silent and waited for the storm to pass them by. But if the supporters' groups remained resolutely anti-establishment, the protest movement had undoubtedly lost much of its momentum. Talk of further boycotts and FA inquiries rumbled on for the rest of the year but another supporters' rally, at Salford in early December, marked the end of the rebellion – for now.

*   *   *

THE MEDIA AND the football establishment were falling over themselves to dismiss the Red revolt as a failure. You can see their point. Instead of them staying away, more supporters had turned up for the Arsenal game than for any match all season. By any definition, that was a failed boycott. Nor had there been any progress made towards achieving the stated aims of the rebel fans. The board remained intact and silent while the FA, arguably for the first time, had shied away from the opportunity to get their claws into the club. Not even a 7,500-signature petition could get them to change their mind. Similar considerations had not stopped them before but it was difficult to see how the authorities could have justified an investigation on this occasion. If the FA had acted every time a club was accused of being badly managed, there would have been little time left for them to do anything else. Had Greenhough been able to pin anything fraudulent on the board then the situation would have been different. Unfortunately, doing nothing in the face of imminent sporting and financial disaster was stupid rather than illegal. The club were a privately-run company and the directors were entitled to run it as badly as they liked.

Fundamentally, the supporters' groups had lacked heavyweight backing. Had they attracted the support of local politicians or dignitaries, they might have prodded the FA or the board into action. Unfortunately, this was 1930, not 1998. Unlike the BSkyB affair, there was no political gain to be made from becoming embroiled in what was essentially a private, supporters-versus-club dispute. Charlie Roberts had backed the protest movement publicly but he was just about the only respected figure who did. In the circumstances, it had been all too easy for the establishment to dismiss the agitators, as the *Daily Mail* did, as stupid and unsporting 'hotheads' and for Greenhough to be caricatured as some kind of Hitler-figure. In hindsight, a boycott, a notion that inevitably alienated the conservatives, was perhaps the wrong move. But what were the alternatives? Reds could have campaigned quietly for years and got absolutely nowhere. They could, as the press advocated, have taken their medicine like gents and sportsmen and watched the club continue to sink into the mire. And in a sense that is what supporters should do – support their team through thick and thin. But there is a fine line between being a fine, loyal supporter and being a mug, and after close on twenty years of decline that line had been crossed. And which is the better supporter – the one who blindly follows their club to the edge of the cliff and mourns when it falls off it or the one who makes a stab at saving it while there is still a chance?

At least by going for broke with their boycott attempt, the rebels had made the city, and the football community at large, aware of the flawed policy and arrogant silence of the United board. They may have benefited from a short-term upsurge in public sympathy but the directors would not be the winners in this affair. Even before their Arsenal 'victory', they had been placed under attack for their refusal to communicate with the supporters. When the months passed without them taking any action to halt the club's slide towards the second division, they were subjected to unprecedented levels of criticism in the press. Those commentators who wrote the rebel movement off as a complete failure had written too soon. As important as making the boycott work was obtaining publicity for their cause. Why else would the activists have chosen as high-profile a match to boycott and then declined even to man the pickets?

The failure or otherwise of the protest wasn't the only assumption that needed challenging. So was the notion that the supporters were ignorant hotheads who were using the club's problems as an excuse to make trouble. That may have been the case for some. But it is difficult to sustain the theory that the protest leaders were anything other than concerned and devoted supporters who had been driven into a corner by the inertia of a bad board. Greenhough, in particular, demands as much Red respect – for his organisational skills, fervent commitment and bombastic oratory – as any of the leaders of the battle against Murdoch. Perhaps even more so, for while the battle against the Sky deal was one the fans had a slim chance of winning, Greenhough's battle with the directors was always going to be a losing one. The Sky deal had to negotiate a path past the DTI and the Monopolies and Mergers Commission whilst all the while being hamstrung by Murdoch's personal unpopularity; in 1930, the United directors were in the enviable position of not having to listen to anyone. Given the odds, there was something noble about Greenhough's campaign against the club. He should have listened to Roberts and others, though. It did not need a boycott to bring down the board, just a little more time.

*   *   *

IT HAS NEVER been absolutely ascertained whether off-field trauma has any impact on on-field performance. The general rule seems to be that if results are good it hasn't and if results are poor it has. The consensus among Old Trafford's dwindling band of optimists was that the boycott affair had been a factor in the side's losing extravaganza. The improvement in United's form in the Arsenal and Birmingham games, when the focus of the Pop Side had been back on the pitch, seemingly bore out the point. So did their performances in the rest of November. In most of their matches that month the Reds had the better of the play and created enough chances to take the points. So it was bordering on the scandalous that the Birmingham success remained their only win. Time and again, wretched finishing cost the side dear. So did their inability to finish teams off. United were the Bond villains of the first division, and not just because they always lost in the end.

Typically, the one afternoon the forwards fired – away to Leicester – the half-backs and defence fell apart. Bullock, given a second opportunity to make sense of his transfer, broke his duck in London-buses style, finding the net with a hat-trick of headers but the weighty contribution of United's newest recruit was overshadowed by that of a much-missed old boy, Arthur Lochhead, who stuck in a brace, gave Parker and Bennion a run-around they would need therapy to forget and, altogether, was the wily inspiration behind the Foxes' 5-4 victory. The score-line epitomised the fallibility of Bamlett's United. Under his predecessors, four goals would have come with a cast-iron, win guarantee. Now, the defence was almost as unreliable as the attack. The Birmingham 2-0 was one of only three or four matches all season when both units performed well simultaneously. Otherwise, the manager was like a one-armed fat woman who is surprised in the shower, permanently left with the dilemma of which part to cover up, top or bottom. And invariably failing to do either.

At Old Trafford the following week, she ignored her front and covered up her rear. Lowly Blackpool were blotted out by the division's youngest full-back pairing, Mellor and Dale, but chances went begging at the other end and the scrappiest match of the season ended goalless. Not for the first time, McLachlan was the worst offender – deep into injury-time, he embarrassed himself by shanking an open-goal sitter over the bar. The one saving grace about George's latest howler was that it came when most of the 15,000 crowd were already heading for the trams. His windows would be safe that night.

At least it was a point, only the third out of a possible thirty. United's reward for a far superior performance at Bramall Lane was a 3-1 defeat, for a similarly impressive showing against Sunderland it was 1-1. In both games the Reds had their opponents where they wanted them but, instead of a swift bullet to the head, they chose the Blofeld option – tying them up and leaving them on their own with a couple of sharks, one of Q's watches and a convenient escape route. Against Sheffield, United led early through Gallimore, stroked the ball around with consummate authority, created enough chances to have worn out the scoreboard operator and generally gave a passable impression of Arsenal, the flavour of this and the next three seasons. At half-time, one local pressman was overheard saying: 'This team is too good to be at the bottom of the league.' But the old failing of not scoring the second eventually scuppered them. The Blades scored an equaliser in that bad-time-to-concede period just after half-time and they were the sharper outfit from then on. They scored twice more in the final quarter and could have finished with six. As for the Sunderland frustration; take away that last sentence and it was almost a carbon copy.

In the wake of the Birmingham win on November 1, United had lagged six points behind the rest. Despite their vastly improved form, they ended the month even deeper in trouble, six points behind second-bottom Leeds and a yawning nine away from Blackpool and safety. Once desperate December had been and gone, they were in danger of being lapped. McLenahan, given a mini-run at centre-half, supplied a flash of what might have been to inspire the side to their second victory, at home to Derby, and Reid rescued a Boxing Day point against Bolton. Otherwise, the Reds were swept away in an avalanche of goals. The worst performance since the Fratton Park 4-1 condemned them to an identical helping of misery at Ewood. Amazingly, it was the high point of the club's December away-days. In thirty years as United, or so the papers alleged, they had never been as badly shown up as they were by trashy Leeds on the 20th. Then, a week after their 5-0 spanking in Yorkshire, Bamlett's losers were humiliated 7-0 at Villa Park. Amusingly, the management claimed that the first three Villa goals should not have been allowed. As an exercise in straw-clutching it takes some beating.

By then, the directors were back in the firing line, their short-lived surge in popularity in the wake of the boycott attempt long since forgotten. The demands for new faces continued to rain down on them but the emphasis had already started to change. No longer were they needed for this season. Most commentators were agreed that it was too late to save United now. Instead, an injection of fresh talent was required to put the club back on the football map and to assist in the rebuilding job that would be necessary if it was going to escape from the second division, or even survive in it. There were no guarantees that the present side would prosper at any level. For many Reds, the road to the third division north was opening up before them.

Surprisingly, the *Athletic News*, normally the strongest allies of the clubs and the status quo, led the market in anti-board angst, raging under the headline 'The Wrong Policy of Manchester':

'The position of Manchester United seems almost beyond hope, but what everyone interested in the club has been wondering is why the directors have not made some sort of effort to remedy the deplorable state of affairs.

'When the boycott was planned, and put into operation by a section of the supporters people in all parts of the country cried "Shame". But should not the directors have done something? Should they not have answered their critics, and proved that they were not allowing the ship to sink?

'They have done nothing, and more than that, they do not seem inclined to say what they are going to do in future.

'With the present team they cannot hope to have a chance of

avoiding the fate that has been threatening for some years. They have been hard hit by injuries, it is true, but where is their enterprise?

'Why is it that other clubs can secure new men and not the United? The chairman of the club, Mr G. H. Lawton, has stated that they will not pay big transfer fees for players: that, in his opinion, it is contrary to the sport, and that youngsters should be given a chance.

'That view is not shared by the supporters of the club in a crisis like the present one. Why is it that Manchester City have spent so freely even with a better side than the United?

'Can it be wondered that the gates at Old Trafford are dwindling to under 10,000? If there is no immediate change, they will probably be smaller than that.

'Bullock is the only new player, and he cost £1,250 when he was secured from Chesterfield. Money will have to be spent in bigger sums than that for better players if the United are to escape relegation.

'If the club does not possess the money, steps will have to be taken to get it. It can be obtained!

'The United have been on a decline for many years, but it is since Barson left at the end of 27-28 that the real trouble has set in. They have not had a dominating captain since his departure.

'The club have parted with players whom they might have retained. They allowed Ball to go to Sheffield Wednesday for £1,250 and now they cannot get a leader so effective for double the fee.

'Spencer, Johnston and Rawlings cost the club roughly £7,000 and while Rawlings' goals saved them from relegation the three players, now no longer with the club, were dear men.

'Mann and Thomas, like Spencer and Johnston, are out of League football, with transfer fees on their heads while McPherson left for a few hundred pounds and Barnett was given a free transfer after he had been developed from a youngster.

'Rees Williams is another player who cost about £2,000 and is now out of league football.

'Money has not been expended very wisely at Old Trafford in recent years, and perhaps, in an effort to retrieve the financial situation, the club has gone to the other extreme. In the last two seasons newcomers include: – Chesters, Mellor, Lydon, Williams, Howe, Kirkley, Reid, Rowley, Gallimore, McLachlan, Hopkinson, Bullock and Parker.

'Chesters, Mellor, Lydon, Williams, Rowley, Gallimore,

Hopkinson, and Parker cost nothing. Howe and Kirkley, from North Shields, were obtained at trivial cost. Reid's transfer fee from Liverpool was about £1,000. McLachlan cost something like £2,000 and Bullock £1,250.

'What is wrong now is that United are expecting too much from young and inexperienced players.

'Something must be done, and quickly, if the position is to be saved.'

*　　　*　　　*

THE QUESTION THE pundits were begging was whether, at the halfway stage of the season, there had ever been such certainties for relegation. They were probably right, too, but you did not necessarily have to be certifiable to raise the possibility that United, despite being ten points adrift, would find a way of digging themselves out of trouble. The examples of the three previous seasons offered some hope as did the number of points (38) still up for grabs. As in a relationship between two frisky hermaphrodites, anything could have happened. There were other, more substantial straws for Pop Side dreamers to cling to as well. The November bright spell had shown that, when the players hit their straps, they were capable of playing football of first division quality. And while their away form was nothing short of a disgrace, the Reds had recently been flying at home. In the two months since the Arsenal near miss, they had taken seven of the ten points available to them at Old Trafford. More of the same plus an overdue good run on their travels would at least have made things interesting.

Another sliver of hope; the team was finally showing signs of tightening up. The half-back line had been a problem all season but an imaginative new threesome featuring forward flop McLachlan on the left, Bennion on the right and fit-again Hilditch at its axis gave it a much-needed injection of experience, vision and beef. McLachlan was perhaps the greatest influence, his conversion the best since Frank Mann's. Meanwhile, in defence, the green team of Mellor and Dale were steadily negotiating the steepest learning curve of their careers. The Villa catastrophe had effectively been a slaughter of the innocents but United's youngsters would not be knocked around so easily in the months to come. Sure, the back line still endured their share of nightmares but the good days soon outnumbered the buffet ones. In the first 23 games of the season the club had conceded a lamentable 79 goals and kept just two clean sheets. In the final 23 they would concede 42, a quarter of which were shipped in the final two, meaningless fixtures.

Two clean sheets and three points in the space of two days was a promising way for United to start the new year, Leeds and Chelsea being blanked out at Old Trafford. A second (0-1) derby disappointment apart, the Reds continued to be a match for anyone at home. The champions and league leaders, Sheffield Wednesday, were dismissed 4-1 on January 28; West Ham were given a similar chasing a fortnight later. What scuppered the survival dream was that United were rarely as competitive once the team bus turned off Warwick Road. Anfield success in the third leg of the cup epic with second division Stoke raised hopes that the away bogey might get a flicking; so did a fine performance in a losing cause at St James' – after Newcastle had sneaked it 4-3, the home directors said that United had given the best display of football seen on the ground that season. But it did not take long for normal service to be resumed. Twice in the space of a week – once in the league, once in the Cup – the Reds were out-muscled by gormless Grimsby. When they next left Manchester, they were thumped 4-1 by Arsenal. It was now over a year since they had last won away in the league. It was ten months and seventeen games since they had even picked up a point.

Thank god, then, for Birmingham – and no, that's not a misprint. On March 7, the side that had passively ended the Reds' search for any point finally ended their wait for an away one, the teams grinding out a dismal nil-nil. But St Andrews had come too late to change United's season. With a nine point gap to bridge in just nine matches, the Reds were wobbling on the brink. Even a Rawlings or Reid would have struggled to turn this situation around. What irked the public was that the directors never had a real go at finding a saviour. This time there was no springtime transfer gamble, just an irritating acceptance of the club's fate. After fighting like tigers for three years, the Reds eventually went down like card-carrying pacifists. Held back by a forward line that consisted, if only for alliterative purposes, of spotty kids, spastics and Spence, March became a funereal month.

Two goals, and two points, from two bore draws – at home to Leicester as well as at St Andrews – were all that the team mustered. Three crucial, must-win games were lost. Most of the supporters had been already. Only 5,000 were inside Old Trafford to watch the latest Portsmouth flop, a dismal figure but still 2,000 more than the visit of the Foxes attracted the following week. Those prophecies that the supporters did not need to organise a boycott, that the team would do it themselves, were coming true. It was clear that few Reds would be hanging around for the last rites.

Defeat at Blackpool, one of the small band of clubs whom United could conceivably have caught, marked the point of no return. As was the case at Elland Road in December, the Reds did not just lose to a relegation rival, they got hammered, the Seasiders' 5-1 success offering further damning evidence that United were not just the worst team in the division, they were the worst by a street. Proving that blind optimism never dies, *The Football Chron* had worked out on the morning of the match that a United win plus victories in their remaining home fixtures would give them a chance of staying up. The one, major flaw in their calculations was that they required Blackpool to collect fewer than three points. One game against the division's bums had been a guarantee of two.

Almost from the first kick, Reds had been suffering in a form of football purgatory; the knowledge that they were leaving one division but were not yet allowed into the next. For many, it was a relief that the end came as quickly as it did. There were still seven matches remaining when Sheffield United arrived at Old Trafford on the 28th. Defeat by a team deprived of their goalkeeper for an hour cast the Reds twelve points adrift of a survival spot. The nit-pickers argued that United were not yet mathematically relegated but goal average was never going to save them; Sheffield's opener had taken their goals-against tally past three figures. Absolute confirmation came, both painfully and ironically, at Anfield where the Reds could only eke out a draw. Liverpool had done more than any other club to save United from relegation in the past. This year it fell to the Scousers to finally finish them off.

NOT RENEWING BAMLETT'S contract when it ran out the following week was one of the easier decisions the board ever had to make but before Bert boarded the train to Palookaville, or wherever managerial flops ended up before Sky and Super Sunday, he had one last stop to make; Roker Park on Easter Saturday. Annoyingly, the Reds chose that afternoon to finally break their away hoodoo. Perhaps Sunderland underestimated their demoted opponents. Perhaps the players were invigorated by the burden of battling against the inevitable being lifted. Quite possibly, it was a reaction to the news on their manager. Managerial changes get short-term results, there can be no doubt about that. Which begs the question why the board had not taken action when there was still a chance of it making a difference. In effect, they had ignored the two basic tenets in the fighting-against-relegation handbook – to throw money at the team and a P45 at the manager. No wonder the public and press viewed them as accomplices in United's relegation.

Admittedly, it would not have been easy to find someone who was willing to take the job on – with no money, no crowds and no hope, the club's pulling power was at an all-time low. The choice of Walter Crickmer as Bamlett's successor suggested as much though that could easily have been a cost-cutting measure – by combining the roles of secretary and manager, the club had saved themselves a salary. A glimpse of Bamlett should have been enough to put prospective managers off the job anyway. Their dour clothes and hairstyles as well as black and white photography invariably made the inter-war generation look older than they actually were. When Bamlett had arrived at the club, for instance, he had looked far too old to have a young family. Now, after a four year grilling on the Old Trafford hot seat, he looked like a walking skeleton. With his horn-rimmed spectacles and bowler hat, Bert had always resembled a middle-aged taxman. By the time his contract ran out, his gaunt face gave him the air of a pensioner who perpetually leaves his false teeth next to the bed.

In his final address to the players at Roker, Bamlett had said: 'I am leaving you but before I go I would like you to endeavour to beat one record. That is to secure at least 23 points this season and so pass the total of Boro [his Boro, he omitted to say] who were relegated with 22 points, the lowest on record.' At the time it sounded like wishful thinking but successive Easter wins – the Roker surprise plus a 4-1 thumping of Liverpool – lifted United's tally to 21 points and brought them within range. Thus the Bamlett regime seemed set to sidestep this one, final ignominy. However, defeat at home to Blackburn and another away drubbing, this time at Derby, sent them into the final game of the season still needing two points to avoid the record. The opposition just had to be Boro, didn't they? In front of another miserable crowd of just 4,000, United's top-flight swansong took the form of a breathless goal-fest. Camsell, the old referee's great discovery but also a great millstone round his neck (in the sense that he had been expected to uncover a Camsell-like goal machine for United), emulated Waring's opening-day feat by scoring all four of his side's goals. After trailing 3-1 and later 4-3, the Reds did well to claim a farewell point but that was not enough to grant Bamlett's final wish. He would now go down in history as the manager who had presided over the two worst sides that had ever worked their way through the colon of the top division.

As deep a stain on Bamlett's managerial record was the condition United were in when he left. If the future had looked bleak following the club's first relegation season nine years earlier, it had nothing on the outlook in May 1931. In '22, the club had at least been blessed with money, a sugar-daddy, turnstile-spinning crowds, a smattering of international-class players, a crop of hugely promising reserves and the best defence team that side of OJ's court case. Back then, the operative question had been whether the Reds would bounce straight back up. This time, it was whether they would avoid passing straight through the second division. The club's potential as footballing laxatives was plain for all to see. The squad was in ruins – the juniors were suffering from their premature exposure to the relegation scrap while the stalwarts, five of whom had featured in the first relegation season, were another year past their best. The support – boycott days apart – had slipped to pathetic levels, the debts were growing alarmingly and the board were still inactive. In short, the club was rotten from top to bottom. Unfair as it may be on Bamlett – an undoubted gentleman forced to drink from a poisoned chalice – to make the comparison but United after his departure were in as bad a state as Carthage after the Vandals. Or Elland Road after Ridsdale...

*   *   *

WHO WAS G. H. GREENHOUGH?

GEORGE HENRY GREENHOUGH was one of the most important figures in the Depression Years story. Unfortunately he seems destined to remain one of the least well known. A trawl of Manchester's libraries and numerous newspaper appeals has uncovered only the most basic details about the Supporters' Club leader. The Rusholme

Voters Register of October 1931 shows that George then lived at 175 Birchfields Road, Rusholme and worked as a taxicab proprietor. It also reveals that he had a wife called Nellie.

A much appreciated phone call from Mr Fred Adams (who answered an appeal for information in the Manchester Evening News) revealed that the two of them subsequently moved to Albert Grove, Longsight, where George ran the 'yellow and black' Supercab Association and Nellie ran a boarding-house where many of the Belle Vue performers, including Rudi de Vere (who starred in a famous ice show), used to stay. Mr Adams, who manned the phones at the taxi business for three years in the mid to late thirties, did not have particularly fond memories of his boss whom he remembers as 'grizzled' and 'gruff-looking', and very bad-tempered at times (he recalled how Greenhough used to put the fear of god up the Irish lads who drove the taxis). As far as Mr Adams could remember, Greenhough was of average build and height and was probably aged in his late forties in the mid thirties. That means he was probably in his mid-forties when he led the boycott attempt.

Walter Crickmer

ROLL OF HONOUR

CHAMPIONS: ARSENAL

FA CUP WINNERS: WEST BROMWICH ALBION

UNITED: DIVISION 1 (22ND) FA CUP (4TH ROUND) GRIMSBY TOWN

DEPRESSION YEARS LEGEND

JACK SILCOCK
LEFT FULL-BACK APR 1916 – AUG 1934
404 APPS 2 GLS (TOTAL 449 APPS 2 GLS)
B. NEW SPRINGS,
WIGAN, 15TH JANUARY 1898
D. ASHTON-UNDER-LYNE, LANCASHIRE
28TH JUNE 1966
HEIGHT: 5' 10" WEIGHT: 11ST.7LBS.
DEBUT: DERBY COUNTY 1-1 UNITED
30/08/19

Career: *Aspull Juniors, Atherton F.C., United (am.) Apr 1916, (pro.) 1917, Oldham Athletic Aug 1934 – Mar 1935, Droylsden United July 1936*

International career *(for England): 3 apps (England 0-0 Wales at Ninian Park 14/03/21, England 0-3 Scotland at Hampden Park 09/04/21, England 3-1 Sweden at Stockholm 21/05/23) 0 gls*

ONE WAS BORN in Dudley in the mid-thirties, the other in pie-eating

country almost fifty years earlier but judging from the photos of Jack Silcock and Duncan Edwards as young Reds you'd swear they'd been hewn from the same piece of genetic rock. Sculpted, muscle-bound torsos, trouser-splitting thighs and gentle-giant faces stare back from the team line-ups – if the two of them hadn't been so good with their feet they would surely have made a good living with their fists. The comparisons between Big Jack and Big Dunc extend beyond the merely physical too. Both had the football brains of a veteran, both were established as Red heroes before they had left their teens, both rose meteorically into the England team. A shy grin spread over their pen pictures gives a hint of a shared nature away from the game, too, both players being as quiet and unassuming off the pitch as they were boisterously dynamic on it. Backing away from a football battle would have been anathema to them. Being lit up by the modern-day media spotlight would have had much the same effect as an enema.

Silcock and Edwards were classic examples of footballers who let their feet do the talking. Duncan's, of course, were the more eloquent; the greatest Babe was a superstar long before his heart-rending death made him immortal. Jack's place in history is as a United great rather than an all-time one but his contribution as a pioneer of constructive defending undoubtedly deserves wider recognition. A unique combination of strength, speed, cool confidence, tackling and heading prowess, judgement and skill (good control, two excellent feet, the most-admired volley in the game...), he came close to reinventing the full-back genre. Traditionally, the role of a back had been to win the ball by any means possible and then get rid of it at the first available opportunity. Jack's ability to bring the ball down and drive his clearances to the feet of his inside-forwards pushed the evolution process along a notch or two. He was some way short of being a Franz Beckenbauer, admittedly, but if the 2-3-5 system had not shackled him to his own half, it is not beyond reason to imagine Jack galloping forward with the ball like an early day Gordon McQueen.

Did I mention he was tough as well? Jack Robson later revealed that he knew he had stumbled on something extra special when Silcock, then a teenager working down the mines, turned up for a wartime match with five stitches in his head, the result of an accident at work. Robson saw him and said something along the lines of: 'You cannot, of course, play today, Jack'. To which his great discovery replied: 'I've come to play and I've packed my cap with cotton wool.' Ignoring strong advice not to turn out, Jack arranged his cap on his head and by all accounts played a stormer, never ducking a header or a challenge.

Over the next decade and a half, Robson and his first five successors would have every reason to be grateful for Jack's bravery and immaculate defending. In his first season he was rated by his contemporaries as the best left-back in the country. A decade later, injuries and the passage of time had deprived him of a yard or two of pace but even then there were many, including the *Topical Times*' 'Analyst', who rated him among England's finest:

'One of the best in his position, and too quickly forgotten for honours after injury, he has a style all of his own, as, for instance, that swooping tackle which reminds one of the eagle coming down on its prey. There is certainly the impression of the defender coming down upon the opponent rather than up to him in a challenge. This is gathered from a long, graceful stride. On the track Silcock would be called a beautiful runner, symmetrical if not fast. You feel that he is not going to get to his man in time, but that is the deception both to the onlookers and the opposition. Silcock never retreats, therefore, and the wing forward who attempts to elude him along the touch-line is making a mistake. Not that he seeks refuge in touch, being, on the contrary, one of those backs the crowds like to see endeavouring to keep the ball in play. No forward line obtains more assistance from a back than does that of the United, for the reason that there are few of Silcock's classical methods in kicking. Whether he has the ball all to himself, which is often, or he has to take it on the move, he makes a lovely return of low flight and perfect length.'

In 1929 *The Football News* described big Jack as 'a man whose services to Old Trafford can never be adequately realised'. Arguably the finest full-back the club had ever possessed, his claim to Red immortality is persuasively strong.

*   *   *

DEPRESSION YEARS LEGEND

CHARLIE MOORE

RIGHT FULL-BACK
MAY 1919 – SUMMER 1930 – 328 APPS 0 GLS
B. CHESLYN HAY, STAFFORDSHIRE
3 JUNE 1898
D. UNKNOWN
HEIGHT: 5' 8" WEIGHT: 11ST. 8LBS.
DEBUT: DERBY COUNTY 1-1 UNITED
30/08/19

Career: *Hednesford Town, United May 1919 (released summer 1921, re-signed Sept 1922), retired 1930 close season*

AFTER 196 GAMES together at the heart of United's defence, their names went together like Bonnie and Clyde, Fred and Ginger, Sonny and Cher or even Dolly and Daisy. United were blessed with a clutch of talented backs in the Depression Years but the Blue Riband partnership was undoubtedly Jack Silcock and Charlie Moore. Had it not been for injuries to both men they could easily have set an appearance record that not even Steve Bruce and Gary Pallister, who played together a club record 316 times, would have been able to beat. A collection of

strains and fractures cost Silcock perhaps 100 outings, the ankle injury that Charlie picked up in a pre-season match at Northwich in 1921 cost him more than seventy.

As his subsequent comeback rivalled even Billy Sarvis's in the odds-defeating stakes, however, Charlie would have been the last to complain. The general feeling when he got injured was that his career was over – his ankle was so bad that he was actually awarded his insurance money. Amazingly, though, within twelve months he had recovered sufficiently to return to Old Trafford and successfully negotiate a trial. As the *Athletic News* put it in their pen pictures of the 24/25 promotion-winning side: 'He went out to try the foot and has been kicking hard ever since.'

In truth, Charlie's comeback wasn't quite as straightforward as that. In his first season back (22/23), he had to settle for scraps of senior action as his replacement, Charlie Radford, built on the strong start he had made the previous year. In his second, he was again regarded as no more than first-reserve though Silcock's injury nightmare did allow him to play in the majority of matches. It wasn't until Radford's tragic accident the following summer that Charlie managed to make himself indispensable again. The reluctant beneficiary of his rival's death, he stepped back into the right-back berth and stayed there for the next six years, until his retirement in 1930.

Cheerful Charlie was the first of the great wartime discoveries to call it a day. Like Billy Meredith a decade earlier, he baled out at just the right time, avoiding the boycott season and the twelve straight defeats by a matter of months. As Charlie was also missing from the 21/22 disaster, he alone of the Depression Year stalwarts ended his career without it being tainted by relegation. The obvious question, then, is whether history would have been altered if he had been around for either of the relegation campaigns. Unlikely. Radford did a fine job of making sure that Charlie wasn't missed during relegation number one while there was nothing he nor any other player could have done to save the team in Number Two; even Moses would have been hard pushed to conjure up an escape that year.

Missing out on the agony of United's first-ever relegation wasn't the only positive side-effect of Charlie's injury break, either. His time on the sidelines also allowed him to complete an education that, in footballing terms, had been cut short before the eleven-plus (before his League debut, Moore had played just one sectional match for United; by contrast, Silcock had already been a regular for three years). Admittedly, it is possible that he would have developed into the same player regardless. What is undeniable is that the back who emerged from a season spent learning his trade in the Central League was a far more accomplished performer than the one who had limped off at Northwich. Timing, judgement and an understated style had been added to the bare bones of heart, commitment and power to create a player who would have stood out as an England candidate had it not been for the brilliance of the big man who played alongside him.

Like Steve Bruce in years to come, it was both Moore's fortune and misfortune to partner someone who was so eye-catchingly good. Like Brucie, he was perhaps an averagely-gifted player who, by the sheer force of his personality, had turned himself into the best uncapped defender in the country. Criminally underrated by the national selectors, at least both had their abilities acknowledged by their club. Herbert Bamlett described Charlie as 'one of the outstanding defenders in the game', adding: 'He does things in such a quiet way that the finer points of his play may be passed unnoticed. But I would rather Charlie Moore be on my side than against me.'

And if both men had to play second-fiddle to their defensive partners on the field, their ebullient personalities guaranteed them the lion's share of the limelight off it. In partnership with his great mate, Joe Spence, and with the backing of Alf Steward's musical skills, 'laughing Moore', the voice and joker of the party, was chiefly responsible for entertaining the troops. His retirement, and subsequent reinvention as the cheeriest mine host in Manchester (he took a pub in Whalley Range), was met with deep regret on the terraces, in the dressing-room and even in a normally bland and emotionless programme, the editorial reflecting: 'Though he [Charlie] has given up football entirely, he leaves behind him happy memories of some great games that he played for the club. His cheery face and happy disposition will most certainly be missed by all the other players. Certain it is that Joe Spence will feel lonely without him!'

The tribute ended with the editor recalling an occasion when Charlie and Joe bet their team-mates that they could earn over 1s by singing a duet in the street: 'By the way, did you ever hear the story about Charlie and his "old china" (as he familiarly termed Joe Spence) singing in the street in Portsmouth, and being rewarded for their efforts with the munificent sum of 1½s? Whether they were worthy of so princely a reward I hesitate to say, but I do know that one of the directors was responsible for 3d of it. Perhaps a feeling of pity – one cannot say!' Unlikely. Charlie Moore, a swirl of charisma, class and congeniality, needed pity like Frank Barson, the man who gave away a pub, needed praise.

*　　　　*　　　　*

DEPRESSION YEARS LEGEND

CLARENCE 'LAL' HILDITCH

HALF-BACK

JAN 1916 – SUMMER 1932

322 APPS 7 GLS

B. HARTFORD, CHESHIRE 2ND JUNE 1894

D. UNKNOWN

HEIGHT: 5' 10" WEIGHT: 11ST.3LBS.

DEBUT:

DERBY COUNTY 1-1 UNITED 30/08/19

Career: Hartford, Witton Albion, Altrincham, United Jan 1916 (player-manager Oct 1926-Apr 1927), retired 1932 close season

International career *(for England): 1 unofficial app (England 1-2 Wales at Ninian Park 11/10/19) 0 gls*

ALL WOULD HAVE preferred their United careers to have coincided with a more glamorous and successful period in the club's history. Most had just cause to complain about the treatment they received from the national selectors. Only one of the holy quintet of long-lasting Robson discoveries ended his playing days pondering seriously what might have been. In his 1951 history of the club, Alf Clarke wrote of Lal Hilditch: 'I think he always had something to regret about his professional career. I don't  think he got out of the game all he should have done.' The start and end of Lal's career were undoubted triumphs. After just six weeks of

League football, the lanky centre-half was named in the England team for the Victory International against Wales. The following summer he was one of the trio of United players who were picked for the FA tour of South Africa. A decade later, a veteran Hilditch was winning acclaim for his heroism in a losing battle against relegation. The filling was the problem, the years in between the highs being a sour mix of good and bad, pain and frustration.

In many ways Hilditch was living proof of the perils of giving a young player too much, too soon. Launched as England's new half-back star, he spent what should have been the best years of his career saddled, through no fault of his own, with a reputation as the man who did not quite deliver. In truth, Lal was always miscast as a star in the making. He had the brains, positional sense, elegance and timing required of an international centre-half but there were question marks over his stamina, he lacked the burst of pace that often separates the good from the great and his constructive play was, at best, average. When it was bad, he could uncharitably have been billed as a player who was adept at breaking up attacks at both ends of the pitch.

5ft 10in tall and skinny, Lal was also short of beef and muscle for a centre half-back. He did not flinch from encounters with bigger and stronger opponents but he had to be at his best physically to really compete and that was a luxury he was frequently denied. Injuries were regular stains on his career but a weak constitution which made him a magnet for wintry ailments was his Achilles Heel (remarkably for a professional footballer, Lal had been passed over for active duty on medical grounds; instead, in another demonstration of his precocious positional sense, he spent the war working in an office as a clerk). To his immense credit, Lal never made an excuse of his handicap and invariably soldiered on regardless. Any criticism of his play, then, must be balanced by the probability that, in many of his 322 appearances, the real Hilditch was not on the pitch.

By the middle of his second League season, Lal's on-going struggle with his health, game and new-found fame had cost him his place. The arrival of Frank Barson, the archetypal all-round, dominant centre-back eighteen months later showed just what was missing from his locker and it was because of Frank, and to a lesser extent, the likes of Jack Grimwood, Billy Spencer and Neil McBain, that Lal never played another full season in his favourite position. The rest of his career was spent in a multi-player scrap for one of the wing-half berths.

Typically, he accepted his ever-changing role without complaint. A versatile performer, a loyal and consummate professional, the complete gentleman... in many ways he was a manager's dream. But Lal's selfless devotion to the cause came at a stiff price personally when he agreed to fill in for John Chapman in 26/27. His six-month nightmare in his dual role acted like ballast on his playing career (it was surely no coincidence that Lal's least productive seasons as a player came in the wake of his stint as player-manager) and strangled any thoughts of a full-time move into management (it was noticeable that, apart from one season in charge of United's colts, Hilditch opted for a clean break from the game when he finally hung up his boots). He didn't even receive adequate recompense for his sacrifice. Whereas Chapman had taken home a cool £1,000 a year, Lal was prevented by some obscure FA rule from picking up more than £25 for his time in charge. All that stress, so little cash...

For most pros it would have been dummy-spitting time but Hilditch was far too nice a bloke to make a scene. 'I ranked him amongst the kindliest persons I have ever met in the game,' Chapman eulogised and there were plenty of other people who were prepared to say the same. However, Lal's heart-winning personality may have been one more reason why his career fell short of his own expectations. Incapable of making the leap from off-pitch Hyde to on-pitch Jekyll, he played the game as he lived his life; nicely. 'If all players were as clean in their tactics as Hilditch there would be no such things as free-kicks for fouls, and no injured players, except for pure accidents,' one famous, but unnamed footballer told Clarke. Lal's Corinthian values may have won him the admiration of the FA (the one thing that Hilditch had and Barson, who won fewer representative honours, did not) but they left him at a disadvantage in the real world. Professional football was a hard-nosed business. Players thought nothing of trampling on the game's niceties to secure their all-important win-bonus. Hilditch did not finish last, as nice guys are supposed to, but his tactics held him back in the same way that staying drug-free handicaps competitors in sports where pill-popping is the accepted norm.

But it was not all bad news. Consumed by his own regrets, Lal would never have envisaged that his name would live on. My guess is that more modern Reds will have heard of him than any other inter-war player with the exception of Joe Spence. His long service, his unusual name and, if we're being honest, the lack of alternatives all played their part but it is Lal's enduring reputation as one of the game's true gents that best explains the apparent anomaly of a good club player going down in history as a United great. Most Reds are irresistibly drawn to Red Devils; Lal Hilditch, Johnny Carey and Bobby Charlton among others have shown that we also love our Saints.

*   *   *

HENRY THOMAS

LEFT-WINGER, APR 1922 – OCT 1930, 135 APPS 13 GLS

HARRY THOMAS WAS a United player for eight years following his move from Welsh side Porth but never quite did enough to nail down a permanent place in the side. A mix of the good and the grotesque, as the *Athletic News* memorably described him, Harry suffered from the fierce competition for the number eleven shirt, losing out, at various times, to Teddy Partridge, Frank McPherson, Charlie Hannaford, Rees Williams and, finally, to George McLachlan. The Welshman's most rewarding season was 1925/26 when he benefited from McPherson's move to centre-forward to emerge as an important member of the team that reached the cup semi-final. Despite United's testicle-mangling defeat that afternoon, it was one of the twin peaks of Harry's career, the other being his lone appearance for Wales, in the 3-3 draw with England in '27. That there were not more highlights to the Harry Thomas story was primarily down to a shortage of class (the *Football News*, for one, dismissed him as 'a forward of average ability with any amount of pluck') but a shortage of goals did not help his cause either. Thirteen goals in eight years was an abysmal return for a wing-man although it was an improvement on Harry's first four seasons (or thirty-three games) as a Red when he did not bother the scorers at all.

ARTHUR THOMSON

FORWARD, MAY 1928 – AUG 1931, 5 APPS 1 GL

TRIED OUT A couple of times at centre-forward and three times more at inside-forward, Arthur Thomson showed glimpses of first-team potential but never made a watertight case for a regular run in the side and spent most of his three seasons at Old Trafford in the reserves. Released in the summer of '31, the former Morecambe man went on to endure frustrating spells at Southend and Coventry before ending his career at the drop-in centre for washed-up former Reds, aka Prenton Park. At times during the Depression Years it must have seemed that United were acting as Tranmere's feeder club such was the exodus of Red rejects to the Wirral. Unfortunately for Rovers supporters, a diet of Thomson, Robinson, Prentice and the rest was as likely to make them puke as it was to get them promoted (the only time Tranmere looked like getting out of the Third Division during the Depression Years was when they finished in the re-election places in 24/25).

Frank Williams

Half-back, May 1928 – unknown (amateur from Sept 1929)
3 apps 0 gls

At some stage of his career, Frank Williams left United to join Altrincham. As his move never made the papers, and no other record of it exists, it is probably fair to say that he wasn't missed. Another virgin soldier who was violated by exposure to United's dirty dozen (defeats) in 30/31, Frank replaced the injured Ray Bennion in the Newcastle, Huddersfield and Wednesday disasters but was never called upon again. It was probably a good thing all round.

James Bullock

Centre-forward, Sept 1930 – June 1931, 10 apps 3 gls

A Gorton lad and a United fan, Jimmy Bullock scored well for enthusiasm and heading ability but less well for skill and speed and would probably have struggled at Old Trafford even if he hadn't had his confidence destroyed by the bizarre and insensitive treatment he received from the selectors. A horrible miss in the opening minutes of his debut at Hillsborough (think Andy Cole's wild slice against Blackburn in '95) did not help his cause either and, apart from a memorable afternoon at Filbert Street when he scored all three of his United goals, he never looked like translating his Chesterfield form to the first division stage. At the end of his only season as a Red he was put up for sale at £1,000 but there were no takers and he eventually disappeared into celtic football, first with Irish side Dundalk and, later, with Welsh outfit Llanelly.

OLD TRAFFORD MEMORIES

MR HUBERT STEWART of Wilmslow (formerly of Old Trafford) remembers what life was like for a young Red at the back end of the Depression Years.

"My earliest recollection of United was going with my dad, which was a great treat, to the reserve matches when I was about ten years of age, around 1927/28. At the time United were still getting good crowds and my father used to say, 'It's too crowded for you lad' so he took me to watch the reserves.

"We went to the reserve matches and then came the great time when my dad said, 'I'll take you to a first division match' and my first one was Newcastle United. I remember it so well, it is crystal clear. United were playing Newcastle and they won 5-0. Hughie Gallacher was playing centre-forward. That was around Christmas 1929. The team I remember, the one that stands out because I thought it was such a good one, was Steward, Moore, Dale, Bennion, Spencer, Mann, Spence, Hanson, Reid, Rowley and Thomas. Dale was transferred to City and that caused a lot of trouble. He played on City's team when they won the Cup. In return, United got a fellow called Ridding who became Bolton Wanderers manager and then, I think, he was a bus driver.

"At Old Trafford, there was no stand on the Popular Side. It was all terracing. Halfway down, there was a wall and a barrier against it and on the other side of the wall was a pathway and then it went down again to the level of the pitch. My father used to stand me on the front of this barrier and then lean on it so I couldn't get crushed and yet I had a clear view because I was that much higher than the people on the passageway.

"By the time I was eleven or twelve I was hooked. We used to come home – we lived in a terrace house with bay windows – and I can see it now. My mother used to be behind the curtains. As we came down the street, if I was jumping about, she knew we'd won so we'd have a nice high tea, a Saturday high tea with pineapple chunks, polony and fairy cake and all that. If I was walking with drooped shoulders, and my dad was saying, 'Come on, come on', it ruined it. We often laughed about that as a family.

"The time that stands in my memory from those early years as a supporter is season 1930/31. United lost twelve matches on the trot, I think it was a record. I saw all those games at home and I saw the one they won. I didn't stop going even though they were so rubbish. There were all sorts of corny jokes going round Manchester like they signed two Chinese internationals – We Won Once and How Long Since. All that sort of joke was going round. The attendances were below 4,000 sometimes at that period. You thought they'd never win.

"I remember the boycott match so well. 'Don't attend, Don't attend' they said all round the ground. And they had the best support they'd had for any match all season! They all came along to see the boycott. My father was on the committee of the Official Supporters' Club but because I was so young he never discussed anything about the boycott with me. The Supporters' Club used to do their bit to help the club financially and at one time my mother took to washing the jerseys. All the women used to take it in turns to wash the jerseys to save the club's laundry bill. I can't remember how long it lasted but I can remember my mother complaining that it wasn't her turn to do them.

"The only time we stopped watching United was when speedway first came to Manchester. It was called dirt track racing in those days. Stadiums opened up all over; there was one at White City, one at Belle Vue and one in Salford. My father, being Red Cross, used to be on duty because the riders were always falling over and getting injured. He got in free and he got me and a couple of pals in free. So we watched speedway for a time but after about twelve months we got bored of it and went back to watch the football. The racing was very popular for a time, though; it really took a hold and became quite big. White City got big crowds – fifteen to twenty thousand. The meetings used to be on Saturday afternoons and Wednesday evenings, so it was real competition for the football.

"Unless they were playing locally, you never followed United away. It just wasn't done; people couldn't afford it. When there was no home game, me and my father would go to watch City but I never used to support them. In fact, I got a kick out of it when they got beaten. At that time City always seemed to give us a tanking. I can only remember us beating them once; Jack Silcock played out of his skin and United won 1-0 and that was a marvellous thing.

"In those days there weren't many teams that you'd look forward to seeing especially. A lot of teams were, I suppose, averagely good. City was the big match, of course, but Arsenal were the really crack team of that time. Arsenal used to figure in glossy pictures in the football papers and in cigarette cards in particular. I used to collect them. I'd have whole teams in boxes. There was a magazine called the *Topical Times* which used to have long photographs of players. My father used to let me have this, I think it cost tuppence. I'd cut the pictures out and pin them on my bedroom wall. I had practically no United because they weren't famous enough. United did not have many stars. They never used to have the money to buy anybody big.

"My favourite player in those days was Joe Spence because he had been capped. He had fuzzy hair. I can remember going to Oldham one famous time when we won 5-1 and Spence scored three. And I thought he was the greatest thing since sliced bread. There was also a fellow called Mann. He was bald-headed. As a kid I thought he was a very old man. They used to call him Daddy Mann.

"When we were kids, we used to go and collect autographs after the match. We used to take a ball and play football while the players got showered and then when they came out, go across. We had a book full of nonentities like Chesterfield. Some of the players would walk to the tram or the bus and the kids would follow them, asking for autographs. I remember one fellow called Tommy Reid, who was a bit of a bastard actually. I remember my friend asking him for a signature and he said right and he signed it and then dropped my book in a puddle. He was known as a pig but he was quite a good player. He was a bit tubby but he used to knock the goals in.

"The players were just ordinary people then. They used to mix, no problem, with the fans. Years later, when I had a car, I used to give Jack Rowley a lift to the match. He'd be waiting for a bus and I'd say to him, 'Haven't you got the car today, Jack?' and he'd say, 'No, the wife's gone shopping' and I used to look out for him and he'd look out for me. And he was an international, a crack player.

"Most people couldn't afford to go seated at the football – that was for the snobs. There wasn't all that much seating accommodation and there was plenty vacant. Unless it was a cup-tie you didn't have to buy a ticket beforehand. You could walk up to the turnstile and pay there.

When I couldn't afford to pay, I would go and wait for three-quarter time. They opened all the gates then. Quite a few people would hang around. I've done that many times. It was better to see some of the match than none at all.

"There was massive unemployment in those days and no one had much money. I lived in a street (Dudley Street) where my parents said, 'You're lucky, your dad's got a job'. In that street, nine out of ten families were out of work. And it wasn't the poorest area in Manchester, it was Old Trafford, a lot of terrace houses. My dad worked for a firm called Robert Gibson & Son in Hulme which manufactured aspirin tablets, cough tablets and sulphur tablets for chemists. He was the manager. I can remember him coming home one Friday with his wages in a brown bag. My mother emptied all the money into her apron and said, 'Robert, you're three shillings short' and he said, 'I know, it's the cuts'. That was government policy. Things were so bad that they brought in a reduction in wages for all public employees and asked for private businesses to follow suit. Can you imagine a situation where you'd ask people to take a reduction and they'd take it? A job was a job, there was no choice. There'd be someone else to take their place if they refused. That's how bad it was.

"I had an uncle who was a victim of what they called the tally system. He worked on the docks. He had been badly wounded in the First World War; he got a big lump in his head in the Dardanelles. He was a docker and he used to have to report to the docks each day. The foreman used to stand on a big box and say, 'I'll have you, you, you and you and the rest come back tomorrow' and he'd give the men he didn't pick a tally to come back the next day. My uncle lived in Broughton and he'd walk to the docks and then to our house in Old Trafford. My mother would give him a meal and my father would give him some coppers to get the tram back to Broughton and then it started again the next day.

"When I got a little bit older I used to go to Old Trafford on my own. In those days you didn't have to meet your pals early, you just used to meet up inside the ground. You knew where they were standing, in our case behind the goal at the Stretford End. Then, at half-time, we all moved round to the other end and the away spectators moved the other way but there was no animosity, no fighting. I can't remember any fights. There were very few police at football because there was never any problem. And swearing, there was very little of that especially if there were women around. 'Hey you, I'll stick one on you. There's a lady here, don't you realise,' someone would say.

"You never got dressed up to go to the football because if it rained you'd get drenched (working men didn't carry umbrellas – you'd get looked at!). Most people wore hats, either cloth caps or trilbies. Some went in their working clothes. You didn't see that many rosettes unless you went away and only a few people wore colours. Wearing your team's colours came in after the war. So did all the chanting and singing. The atmosphere at football was very different back then. There was shouting and cheering and booing and catcalling but it was all very, very spontaneous.

"Outside the ground, people used to sell football cough drops in triangular bags. The idea was that all the shouting would make you hoarse. Plenty of those were sold. At half-time the only thing you could get was Bovril. I don't recall people selling pies. People couldn't spend money on pies. The toilets were OK if the ground was not full.

"The only entertainment was a brass band, the Beswick Prize Band. They used to play in the centre of the pitch and play all sorts of songs at half-time. There was nobody with a loud hailer, or a microphone or anything. At full-time people used to wait for the other scores to be phoned through and put up on the scoreboard. That was quite a ritual.

"Most people went to the match by tramcar; there were very few cars. Afterwards, the trams would all be lined up by the side of Lancs county cricket ground, probably about thirty or forty of them. A tram took about seventy or eighty people and they were all there when you came out and you'd go along and get on your nearest one. It was quite efficient really. The football might sometimes have been rubbish but at least it was easy to get home!"

ON THE BRINK

I F THERE IS such a thing as a good election to lose, the general election of May 1929 was one such occasion. Global depression lingered just around the corner and the new Labour government walked right into the eye of the storm. Fast forward two years and it was clear that they did not have it in them to survive it. A crisis situation had called for a government with flexibility, vision and guts. Instead, the nation had been saddled with one whose only policy seemed to be to cross their fingers and hope for the best. Believe it or not, the economy would have been no worse off if MacDonald's mob had job-swapped with G.H. Lawton's.

The beginning of the end for Labour arrived with the publication of the May financial report in July. Its gloomy findings, notably the prediction that Britain would soon have a budget deficit of £120 million, convinced foreign bankers that the country was on the verge of going bust. Like rats fleeing a sinking ship, they rushed to dump the pound, the flip side of which was that more gold left these shores than at any time before Big Ron took the Atletico Madrid job. In order to drag the economy back from the precipice, the financial doctors urged the government to make drastic cuts in benefit handouts, particularly the dole, but a powerful minority in the cabinet refused to sanction measures that would betray 'their people'. The scale of their resistance made it impossible for the government to continue and on August 23 MacDonald handed in their resignation.

Most people assumed that a Conservative-Liberal coalition would take Labour's place. Instead, an all-party National Government was formed with MacDonald staying on as leader. The arrangement was a controversial one, not least because MacDonald never got round to telling his old team-mates about it, but it was tailor-made to deal with the economic emergency. Previously, the government had backed away from making the tough policy decisions that were needed to turn the economy around because of the negative impact they might have on their election chances. Now that the load of unpopularity was being spread around the parties, they could afford to be that much bolder. Within a fortnight of its formation, the new government had introduced all the cuts that the old one had bottled out of making. Days later, when it became clear that something more was needed to stabilise the pound, they took the radical decision to come off the gold standard, the economic comfort blanket that had previously been regarded as the country's main defence against hyper-inflation. It was a huge success. The move halted more gold withdrawals from British assets, deterred foreign speculators and, crucially, knocked 30% off the value of sterling. For the first time in years, British exporters could enter the market-place without their hands tied behind their backs.

The gold standard wasn't the only financial tradition to get the boot, either. When MacDonald was given a 'doctor's mandate' to do whatever was necessary to cure the country's economic cold, the long-cherished principle of free trade was finished too. Protectionism was the new creed. 10% tariffs were imposed on most exports, excluding those from the empire. The measures stimulated the sales of British goods at home and made them more competitive abroad. The depression was too well set for the revival to kick in immediately but in effect the financial crisis was over. In the short-term, the unemployment figures continued to rise, topping three million during the winter of 32/33. By '35, though, the number of people out of work was down to two million and by '37 most of the country had completed a strong economic recovery. Only the areas reliant on the out-dated staple industries, most famously Jarrow, the home of the marchers, continued to struggle.

There ends the mini-lecture on economic history. Simplistic perhaps but the message is obvious. There had been options open to Labour other than allowing the country to drift. Likewise, there had been options open to the United board other than sticking their heads in the sand. But in the wake of the relegation debacle it was too late for them to take positive steps to get the club's finances back in order. The only straw worth clutching at was that the team would find some winning form in the second division and the crowds would flock to Old Trafford to watch a successful side. But no one truly believed that the record-breaking losers from one season would be transformed into Pied Pipers the next – not even the directors. At the AGM they preached pragmatics, not promotion. Amid talk of stabilisation and reorganisation, it was stressed that 'the United's first business and one more important than securing promotion is to build up an efficient side from youth'. You can imagine how well that must have gone down on the Pop Side. It had been bad enough when the club had seemingly settled for first division survival. Now they seemed happy to bide their time in the second division. For many Reds it was the greatest betrayal yet.

Events of the autumn continued their torment. Despite the dramatic drop in standards between the top divisions, United's form was even less impressive than it had been at the back end of 30/31. In their opening fourteen matches, they picked up just three wins and ten points. When November began with the club in the midst of yet another relegation battle, their descent into laughingstock was complete. Stage comedians had long regarded them as obvious joke material. Now even the football press, normally the epitome of broadsheet seriousness, were getting in on the act. Witness 'Marcus', reporting on September's home draw with Spurs in the Umpire: 'If the goals 'ad bin about 27 yards wide instead of 12 p'raps Manchester United 'ad 'ave scored twice...As for the United, in the first 'arf they was just about as united as the TUC is about the new Government... the United forwards tried to score a goal in Albert Square and the linesman 'ad to get the ball back from the Ship Canal... Orl I knows is that if either the Spurs or the United ever gets back inter the first division, it'll be after they've found out that a goal is twelve yards wide and that when they've remembered that somebody ought ter tell 'em the idea of the game ain't ter kick the ball inter the hands of the goalkeeper.' 'Ilarious.

*　　　　　*　　　　　*

LOSING TO CITY, watching your parents dance, dropping one in a packed lift, shouting the wrong name in bed, Old Trafford DJs; embarrassing they may all be, but unless it was the opening weeks of 30/31, it is difficult to think of anything that could match the cringe factor of the opening weeks of 31/32. Opening day hara-kiri at Bradford PA kicked off a chain linking desperate defeats by Southampton and Stoke, 1-1 draws both in the Stoke return and also against Spurs, and then a flattering 2-1 defeat at Nottingham Forest. Reid and Hopkinson both scored late goals as United came from behind to beat unlucky Swansea Town on September 5 while Chesterfield, newly promoted from the third division and seemingly set for a swift return, were kind enough to roll over in the month's final fling but the respite was brief. A week later, United slumped to a 2-0 defeat at Turf Moor, a spineless surrender that dropped them to third from bottom, the worst league position in their history. Not even the hapless Heathens had sunk so low.

The following weekend, the *Football News* posed the question whether the standard of football at Old Trafford had ever been lower. Presumably, it was a rhetorical one. They also warned that the club needed to find a new centre-forward before it was too late. They might have added that it was about time they got themselves a new manager, too. Almost six months after the departure of Bamlett[1], the directors were no nearer to relieving Walter Crickmer of his dual burden. In fact, managing United was in danger of becoming the job the rest of football had forgotten. When the directors had advertised the post in the summer, they had received applications from cotton men, furniture removers, builders and shopkeepers – in fact pretty much anyone bar genuine managers. Since then, they had pursued a 'well-known name' from the East Midlands area and also J.J. Commins from third division Barrow but in both cases negotiations had broken down. Clearly, Commins and the nameless other weren't naïve enough to expose themselves to the roasting that awaited the next man to lower his buttocks onto the United hot seat. Still, it had come to something when the pull of Old Trafford wasn't strong enough even to tempt the manager of Barrow.

Admittedly, there wasn't much talent on the books, the veterans excepted, for a prospective manager to get excited about. The summer intake, which amounted to another oddball collection of freebie journeymen and never-will-be amateurs, had added quantity rather than quality to an already poor squad. At least Billy Johnston was back from his ridiculous two-year exile at Macclesfield but even his return

---

1.   *Talking of Bamlett, news had just emerged that he had lost the sight in one eye following an operation. Looking back, it is clear that taking on the United job during the Depression Years was as bad for your health as chasing the Blair Witch. Of the five men who managed the club between 1919 and 1932, only Hilditch emerged unscathed. Bamlett lost an eye, Robson lost his life, Chapman was nailed by the FA and driven out of football for good while the last of the five, Crickmer, was sadly killed at Munich.*

had its negative side as it cost the club the services of last season's brightest star, Harry Rowley. As neither man was comfortable in any position bar inside-left, a ludicrous situation developed whereby Rowley was relegated to a back-up role while some of the most forgettable names ever to stumble around Old Trafford – other clubs' rejects such as the new wing pair of Bert Mann and John Ferguson and unproven hopefuls like Gallimore, Hopkinson and Robinson – enjoyed lengthy runs in the team. It was a problem that was mirrored at the back where four good players – Dale and Jones as well as the first choice partnership of Silcock and Mellor – were fighting for two places (and also in midfield where McLachlan and Wilson were scrapping it out for the left-half spot). Somewhere along the line, the Reds had developed a Noah complex whereby they picked up talented players two by two. But that was nothing compared to the Andrex complex that had left them irresistibly drawn to picking up crap.

It screamed volumes for the lack of quality in the squad, and the forward-line in particular, that the player who finally got the team moving in the right direction that autumn was a 33-year-old veteran with twelve years' service under his belt. The selectors' decision to move Spence, who had previously been struggling for fitness and form, into the centre for the visit of Preston on October 10 was a godsend, Joe cashing in with a rush of eleven goals in just ten games. But even with its sharp new/old cutting edge, the team still mixed enough bad days in with the good to limit their climb up the table to a pre-Christmas sixteenth. Preston (3-2), Port Vale (2-1), Millwall (2-0) and, most emphatically, Oldham (5-1) had no answer to the Spence-inspired Reds. Unfortunately, Plymouth (1-3), Bury (1-2) and Bradford City (3-4) all did. And the worst moment of all? There can be no doubt – the 5-2 home demolition by promotion favourites Leeds on November 7.

For years, the supporters had been told that they were getting the team they deserved. This team was undoubtedly getting the crowds it deserved. The Leeds match attracted fewer than 10,000 fans to Old Trafford; the local 'derbies' against Preston and Bury pulled in just 20,000 between them. If a game against United was still viewed by the rest of the second division as a cup final, it was clear that a trip to Old Trafford was no longer a guarantee of cup-final-sized receipts. In their three most recent seasons outside the top flight, United had enjoyed average gates of 22,955, 21,125 and 27,995 and had regularly played in front of crowds in excess of 30,000. So far this year, their biggest crowd was 11,745 and their average gate was down to an embarrassing 6,500.

The chronic lack of interest finally persuaded the directors to take positive steps aimed at buttering up the support and getting them back into the match-day habit. In early September, Billy Meredith, who had lusted after a role at the club as much as his old supporters had, was brought in as reserve team coach. Spectator comfort and admission prices also got the populist touch. At last, covered standing accommodation was provided in the Main Stand and prices brought into line with people's circumstances. The cost of admission for the covered terracing and the cheap seats at the back of the stand was fixed at 1s 6d while in bad weather Pop Siders could transfer for an extra 6d. It was, apparently, the cheapest covered and seated area in the country.

More good news followed when the directors introduced a new unemployed charge of just 6d (annoyingly, the FA scuppered the plan by refusing to countenance a minimum ticket price of under a shilling) and then when they froze prices despite the entertainment tax on the 1s man being increased to a crippling 2½d. But the reality was that this board had lost the fight for the hearts of the supporters months earlier. The gangs of lads who had previously followed the club Rocca-style were either saving their shillings or putting them to a different use. Many would rather watch the other set of Reds, Salford rugby league, at the Willows. At least then they were guaranteed of seeing their team get some points.

It was an open secret that the club were walking a financial tightrope. Only later did it emerge how close they already were to falling off. September's announced deficit of £2,509 did not sound so calamitous when compared with the losses made by other clubs, including Newcastle (£9,878) and Bolton (£5,168) as well as free-spending Chelsea (£3,340). What the figures did not indicate was the amount of money United had borrowed. That summer alone they had needed a £5,000 advance from Mrs Davies just to cover the wages. The list of creditors was ever-expanding, the overdraft at the bank had risen to over £2,000 and the amount of cash in hand was down to a pitiful £12 12s 1d. The balance sheet claimed that United had excess assets over liabilities of £38,000 but that figure was based on a tissue of wishful thinking and lies. According to the board, the land and buildings were worth £64,000. Later estimates slashed that figure and concluded that the club were in debt to a minimum of £26,000.

It was generally accepted that United needed gates of 15,000 just to break even. They were not coming close to that figure. Nor were they getting as large a cut from away games as they had in the first division. Recognising that they were bleeding to death, the board made a desperate attempt at sandbagging. The Brewery Company were asked to allow payment of the mortgage interest to stand over, an application was made to the Stretford Urban District Council for permission to pay road charges in instalments and efforts were made to get the Inland Revenue to relent on the schedule for the repayment of the club's income tax arrears. Later, the directors sent out a circular informing clubs that they were open to offers for their players, particularly their talented defensive reserves. Eventually, though, the situation deteriorated to such an extent that the board had to take really drastic action – they had to come clean.

At November's Annual Shareholders' Meeting, the chairman, Lawton, finally put the supporters in the picture about the club's financial position. He made it known that they needed money and were no longer in a position to buy new players, and made an appeal for influential gentleman to come to the financial assistance of the club, announcing: 'I want it to be known that myself and my colleagues on the board of directors will certainly retire if there is someone who will come forward with cash and help the club.' Lawton also made a stab at quashing the rumours that he and his fellow directors were not interested in either the team or the fans, only the money. Stressing his desire and commitment to making United 'a power in the land again', he appealed to the supporters to support the club and help it pass through these troubled times. Which was precisely what they had wanted to hear...a couple of years earlier.

Now they were perhaps more interested in what the chairman did not say. Questions such as how the directors had been able to breathe with their heads rammed between their bum cheeks and how a business that, over the past decade, had posted cumulative profits in excess of £60,000 was now heading for the wall, remained unanswered. Apologies, regret, admissions of culpability and guilt were left unsaid. Instead, the supporters were given another clutch of sob stories and excuses. In his attempts to explain why gate receipts had slumped by more than £7,000 in 30/31, Lawton blamed the trade depression (fair enough, but United were by no means the only club struggling with the depression), bad weather (the club's own fault – the Pop Side should have been covered years ago. Also a red herring – Old Trafford had covered accommodation for 10,000 people but on most weekends the covered stand was only half full), accidents and injuries to players (all clubs should be prepared for this – United's squad was much too weak and the selectors were often guilty of sending out patched-up players despite the risk of them breaking down) and unsatisfactory results (Bingo! No longer would the supporters turn up, as their fathers had, out of loyalty alone. The public now demanded value for their shilling and only good football and results would bring the crowds flooding back). Nowhere was there mention of the role played by the board – the bad selection decisions, the lack of investment in the side, the habit of buying players who either crashed and burned or flickered only for a short time and the failure to maintain a healthy relationship with the support.

Lawton's excuses did not wash with the watching Greenhough. Showing a level of perseverance that would have embarrassed Robert the Bruce's spider, the supporters' leader made another failed attempt to engineer a vote of no confidence in the status quo while his bid to submit a 6,000-signature anti-board petition was also ruled out of order. At times, Greenhough must have felt like a Red Cassandra, forever saddled with the knowledge that the board were killing the club but unable to make others believe. Soon, everyone would realise that he had been right all along. Financial first aid from outside was not immediately forthcoming, leaving the directors helpless to resist the whirlpool that was dragging them under. Nemesis approached for the current regime. On Friday, December 18, Crickmer was informed by United's bank, the National Provincial in Manchester's Spring Gardens, that they would not be given any more credit. There was no money to pay the players' wages or even to buy the staff's Christmas turkeys. If nobody had come in at that point, the club would probably have collapsed during the weekend. Just as in 1902, though, when the hour came, it produced the man.

*   *   *

James Gibson

LIKE JOHN HENRY DAVIES before him, 54-year-old businessman James W. Gibson made an unlikely football club saviour and sugar daddy. He was rich all right. The uniform-manufacturing game in which his firm had specialised had been a good one to be involved in during the war years. Since then, the business had expanded and diversified and even in a period of economic depression, Briggs, Jones & Gibson, now fully owned by the latter, was a thriving concern. But Gibson had never previously shown any great interest in football, never mind United. So why did he answer their call when the directors, in their desperation, shouted mayday?

According to Stacey Lintott, a football writer and regular Gibson lunch partner who acted as go-between (the Forrest Gump history of the club claims that Rocca was involved – once again – at the crucial moment but the Gibson family always backed Lintott's claims as kingmaker), it had a little to do with Gibson's weakness for taking over failing businesses and restoring them to solvency and a lot to do with his inflamed sense of civic pride. United, even then, were one of Manchester's biggest assets and Gibson wasn't prepared to sit back and do nothing while the economic maelstrom claimed another victim. 'Manchester is suffering enough today through depression without it being known that she cannot afford to keep a famous club,' he said. 'I do not think it would help Manchester business and Lancashire trade in general if such a famous club as United was allowed to drop out without some definite stand being made to resurrect it.'

Davies' take-over had been fanned by similarly fierce opinions on the importance of the club to its city and at times it would seem that Gibson was Davies incarnate. Both men thought big, both were winners, both were non-football people who were bitten by the football bug and were then unable to shake it off and both were prepared to spend heavily to convert their words into action. For now, though, Gibson was only willing to dip his toe into the water rather than jump in with two feet and risk getting them both burned, Princess Margaret-style. Initially, he undertook to take control of the club for just one month, from December 16 to January 9. He ensured that the staff received their wages and turkeys and immediately placed £2,000, the amount he estimated the business would lose during the month, at the club's disposal. But Gibson made it clear that that would be the limit of his investment and involvement in United unless he was given a clear indication that the Red-loving public were behind him. If the supporters gave him their mandate by turning up in force for the holiday fixtures, he would take any steps necessary to restore United to their pre-war eminence. If they did not, he would simply walk away and leave the club to its fate.

In an interview rehashed, at varying lengths, in all the local rags, Gibson declared:

'I have long been interested in Manchester United. But of recent years I have been very sorry to find that things have not been going with the success desired. My only concern is that the public will respond to my appeal. I stand to lose £2,000, I don't mind that. For a month I am at the disposal of Manchester United and during that time I want to see if the public of Manchester desire football at Old Trafford. If in the course of that month I find them coming down to the ground I will redouble my efforts.

'Although I have undertaken to see United through the coming month, I am not going to be a milch cow. If the public do not show sufficient interest in the club during the coming month I shall wipe my hands of the whole affair and I am afraid United will immediately wind up if no one steps into my place.

'I am at the head of the United now and if the public will back me up and give me any justification for carrying on I will assure them that the United will not fail. Manchester is sufficiently large and surrounded with large towns to support two first-class teams. It will be some time before anyone can establish a winning team, and I do not intend to try immediately. What I first require is some indication from the public that they are willing to give me support. I want to discuss whether the spectators who have drifted away are merely annoyed with what has been occurring during the last few years or if they are disgusted to such an extent that it will be a long time before their interest may be revived.'

The message was unmissable. If the public responded to his challenge to turn up at Old Trafford, Gibson guaranteed that money would be invested in all directions – on the team, a new manager and also on the ground. 'I want to place Manchester United, if possible, on a level with the great teams in the country, such as Arsenal,' he continued, 'and I also want to see the Pop Side people at Old Trafford afforded some protection from the bad weather. When I have been down at Old Trafford and have seen the shilling supporters standing in the wet I have felt heartily sorry for them. I want to get covered accommodation at Old Trafford. Of course, this cannot be done in a twinkling, but if the public will come forward then I will do my best; and I will also see that the United have a manager who will be one of the best in the country and will be paid accordingly...I shall then look at the first team. United want a good centre-half, a centre-forward and two wingers. Money ranging anywhere from £12,000 to £20,000 must be expected to be spent in securing players.'

It was dubbed the Gibson guarantee. It could just as easily have been called the Gibson gauntlet, the response to which would decide how the next pages in the club's history were filled. But if the responsibility for United's future lay with the public, Gibson was in no doubt that the responsibility for their crisis-riddled past and present lay with the board. A hotchpotch of hard-hitting quotes confirmed as much: 'Mrs Davies cannot be expected to keep on forking out money. The directors had done nothing to keep alive to the public the powerless position the club is in.'... 'In my opinion, unaccountable inertia was responsible for United's downfall'...'I do not blame the public in the least for staying away from Old Trafford. The United board of management have never taken the public into their confidence and they could not be expected to keep on rolling up at Old Trafford while a hush-hush policy was being adhered to.'

As a rule, the directorship had taken to criticism like a precocious three-year old and in any other circumstances Gibson's comments would have been viewed as an excommunication offence. But Lawton and his co-directors had no option but to accept the rescue package that had been placed before them. On December 21 the members of the board informed Gibson that they would resign whenever he so desired after January 9. In the days that followed, the FA gave the take-over their blessing and – more worryingly – Gibson was given the green light by the club and the authorities to start picking the side. As if they weren't in a tight enough corner already, the team's immediate fate now lay in the hands of a self-confessed footballing ignoramus.

Fortunately, Gibson's was not the 'my way or the highway' type of approach. In a move that spoke volumes for his grasp of PR, the club's new tsar straightaway sought guidance on team selection from the arch-revolutionary, Greenhough, and then took him up on his suggestion that he would be best served by a combination of Crickmer, Jack Pullar and Navigator. As a result, the responsibility for the playing side of the club passed from an under-informed entrepreneur to the secretary, the trainer and the bloke from the local paper. Apparently the tea-lady and the groundsman were unable to commit themselves to the job full-time. Sarcasm aside, at least all three were football men which was a considerable bonus in an era when selection issues were often left to people whose knowledge of the game, as Len Shackleton famously observed, ran to an empty page.

Whilst passing an olive branch to the supporters' leader, Gibson also gave him a taste of the direction he wanted the club to take, Greenhough revealing that 'he [Gibson] would be looking for the sort of manager to whom he would give full control, and allow to reorganise the club'. What he certainly wasn't interested in was a businessman-manager in the Herbert Chapman mould. Reasoning that the chairman and the secretary should look after the business side of the club, Gibson talked instead of bringing in an 'ex-player of skill and experience' who, when players made mistakes out on the field, 'could take a ball out and show them what they were doing wrong'. United's saviour had been in the game for all of two minutes but he was already years ahead of his time. The division of responsibilities between the playing side and the business side of a football club, as well as the idea of a tracksuit manager, belonged in the distant future along with the European Cup, 4-4-2 and streakers. Thanks to Gibson, the modern-style football manager (a genuine Boss rather than cap-doffing stooge) was born at Old Trafford. And there are no prizes for guessing the identity of the first one out of the womb.

Both in retrospect and at the time there was a feeling that Gibson was too good to be true. However, there was nothing in his words or actions that gave credence to the cynics' attempts to portray him as an egoistical dictator figure. Gibson had already democratised selection meetings. Next he stressed his desire for the club's shares to be distributed widely enough so that no man, least of all himself, would have a controlling interest. Even so, *The Manchester Guardian*, taking the attitude that not all that glitters is gold, still had reservations about the turn-up-now, get-rewarded-later pact he had made with the supporters, they warned: 'We should not be particularly hopeful of the future, say, of a theatre whose management announced that if the public would give it good houses for three possibly poor performances by a company that had fallen into disfavour, they could have a "star" cast afterwards. It is too much like "jam tomorrow".' But even if Gibson broke his guarantee, what was there to lose by taking him up on his challenge? And there were two thousand reasons, the amount of money he had already sunk into the club, which suggested he would be honouring it.

During the trial month from December 16 onwards, United played three matches at Old Trafford. The first of them, against bottom club Bristol City, fell on the same day that Gibson's gauntlet hit the papers, giving the supporters little or no chance to respond. The crowd numbered 4,000, a pitiful figure even for the last shopping Saturday before Christmas. That left Reds with just two opportunities to pass Gibson's test – the visit of Wolves on Christmas Day and the Park Avenue rematch on January 2. As it turned out, they needed only one attempt to prove they still cared as 33,312 of them, over 20,000 more than the season's previous best, flocked to Old Trafford for the Wolves match. Gibson was so moved by the fans' show of strength that he went down to the Pop Side at half-time to thank them for coming and tell them that 'the United club will go on'. Just fourteen months after they had tried to bring down the old board by missing a match, the Red Army had won themselves a new chairman, and a new start, by turning up for one. It was not confirmed for another month but in effect the Gibson era had begun.

At the board meeting on January 5, Gibson, now co-opted as a director, conditionally agreed to take over the liabilities of the club, an amount in excess of £40,000. As for the cost of the planned rebuild, his initial hope was that the public would shoulder the burden. At a press conference the following day, he launched an appeal to raise £20,000, the proceeds of which would be placed in trust and earmarked solely for transfer fees. Gibson's plan was to introduce a new breed of tickets – patrons' tickets – that would secure admission to the ground until the end of the 34/35 season. He asked for one thousand 'sportsmen' to come forward and pay £10 for patrons' tickets for the 4s seats and a further two thousand to subscribe £6 6s for tickets for the 3s section. Part of his pitch was that a flourishing United would be 'a decided social asset'. He also suggested that firms would benefit from taking out patrons' tickets for use by friends, business acquaintances and staff. They were the words of a visionary. Unfortunately, Gibson's concept of corporate supporters was the right idea at the wrong time. Even though the patrons' tickets offered good value for money (providing a saving of around a third over the three and a bit years), the response to the appeal was poor. In total, the scheme raised something like £500, well down on its original target.

Gibson was privately disappointed but publicly phlegmatic. He accepted that the timing of the appeal could have been better. Wallets were still recovering from the Christmas period, income tax payments were due and, of course, there was still the depression to consider. Nor was the failure of the scheme a reflection on the attitude of the mainstay of the club, the 1s supporter, as the patrons' tickets were out of his price range. Though disappointed, Gibson was not so disheartened that he no longer had faith in the public wanting football at Old Trafford. He admitted that he had been 'deeply touched by a postal order for one shilling from a working man who said he was never able to get to the matches on Saturdays, but hoped that his mite would help to keep the old club together'. With the Wolves attendance still fresh in his mind, Gibson pushed ahead with his take-over plans. On January 19, the old directors resigned en bloc and a new board was appointed. On January 20, the new board officially accepted their resignations and Gibson was elected to the chair. A week later, he became United President.

More than four years after his death, the Reds had at last found a worthy successor to John Henry Davies. But what of the men he replaced? George Lawton, who might or might not have been run over by Davies's trap in 1902, had been a key figure at the club ever since its re-formation. Between them, his fellow board members – Harold Hardman, George Bedford, Joseph Yates and Herbert Davies Jnr. – had served the Reds for almost sixty years. Clearly they had done great things for the club in its golden past. Ultimately, though, they would be remembered for their contribution to its turd-encrusted present and, most particularly, for their arrogance and silence while the business was taking its journey round the U-bend.

And lest anyone felt any lingering sympathy for them, the dying embers of the old regime provided one final reminder of why they did not deserve it. In a cost-cutting measure sanctioned before Gibson rode up on his white charger, Lawton's board swapped Rowley and Dale for City's inside-right, Bill Ridding, and a couple of grand. In principle, cashing in on a couple of underused assets and bringing in a desperately needed forward was not such a bad move. In reality, the deal was a give-away on the Cantona scale. Ridding had cost City £3,000 when he had moved from Tranmere two seasons earlier. Since then, he had failed, spectacularly, to live up to his billing as the next Dixie Dean, making just four appearances. On the off chance that the big-money flop had maintained his original value, the triple deal valued the two United lads at a bargain £5,000. As Ridding's stock had surely plummeted, City had got themselves two, potentially top-class players for a song.

The United directors had instigated the deal so City could justifiably claim that they had done their neighbours a favour. Reds would argue that by taking Dale and Rowley at below the going rate, City had taken advantage of their desperate financial position. A quarter of a century on, had the Blues finally gained their revenge for the Queen's Hotel steal? The first responsibility of the City directors had been to get the best deal available to them, there can be no argument there. But it stuck in the craw when the Blues, specifically their chairman, Albert Hughes, were then showered with praise for urging Mancunians to respond to Gibson's gauntlet and back the patrons' ticket scheme. If they were so bothered about United's welfare, why didn't they wire a couple of extra thousand across town? Or, even better, send Dale back. He had not wanted to go in the first place and had held out for as long as he could. Annoyingly, if Billy had kept City hanging on for just a couple more days he would never have had to leave. When he found out about the deal, Gibson was furious. For once, though, his timing was off; by the time he had dismounted his charger, the only innocents he could save from the desperate cost-cutting measures of his predecessors were the half-time band.

To restock the boardroom, the new chairman turned to a collection of business friends and long-standing acquaintances; Colonel George Westcott, an ex-Lord Mayor of Manchester and co-trustee of the transfer trust fund, Mr Hugh Shaw (yes I am), a director of a Stalybridge cotton mill, and two Manchester businessmen, Albert Thomson and Matthew Newton. The new directors had money behind them, a crucial factor since the public were clearly reluctant to take on their share of the burden. Gibson had now accepted that he would have to swallow most of the bill himself. Already, his commitment to the club had swelled far beyond his original intention. Later, he would admit that when he first became involved with United, his aim had been to oversee the recovery of the business and then pass the reins on to somebody else. He would not be the first to discover that once you fall victim to Red Fever, you remain a victim for life.

*   *   *

IT DID NOT take long for the new chairman to discover that the patience of your average football fan is anorexic-thin. By the end of January – a whole week after the boardroom version of musical chairs – there were already reports in the press that the public were growing impatient at the lack of transfer action. Two points had clearly passed them by. The first was that they themselves had failed to do their bit by responding to the patrons' tickets scheme – had the transfer fund not resembled a junkie's bank account, it would have been put to use by now. The second was that Gibson could not be expected to sink any more money into the club until he got his name above the door. Still, he would have been the first to admit that remedial action was needed, and quick. The previous six weeks had been great for the club but disastrous for the team. Since Gibson made his guarantee, United had played seven games and won just once. They were out of the Cup and were just a point ahead of second-bottom Charlton who had played a game fewer. The post-relegation laxatives were working; the basement division clearly beckoned.

Thanks to the fans, Christmas Day had been a double-decked triumph; the size of the crowd had given Gibson his mandate while the manner in which they had got behind the team had inspired them to a thrilling 3-2 win. 'It was wonderful to see the packed terraces at Old Trafford on Christmas Day,' the Official Programme raved, 'and the enthusiasm displayed was of such a whole-hearted nature that our players were forced to almost superhuman efforts by the very value of the cheering.' But the contrast between the Wolves match and United's other outings during the take-over period could not have been starker. Bristol City, the worst side in the division by a distance, rode their luck to pinch the points in the first 'gauntlet' game – Mann's third minute fractured collarbone was merely the afternoon's first bad break, the second being the referee's crass failure to spot that

Bristol's winner had been effectively slam-dunked into the net. Then, on Boxing Day, the lack of depth in Crickmer's squad was ruthlessly exposed in the Wolves return. At least four players who had picked up injuries the day before were patched up and forced to play. Against limping opponents, Wanderers created openings at will and scored as many goals as there were fit Reds. In another award-meriting piece of understatement, *The Manchester Guardian* announced that 'the events at Wolverhampton knocked some of the gilt off the [previous day's] gingerbread'. A year minus a day since United had equalled their record 7-0 defeat at Villa Park, they had done it again.

Confidence and ill-fortune remained a problem from then on. A surging late rally, replete with woodwork-rocking near-misses, could not save the Reds against Park Avenue in front of a rain-affected crowd of just 6,000. Thank god Gibson had seen enough against Wolves, otherwise the 2-0 defeat and gaping holes on the Pop Side might have persuaded him to retreat to his mansion in Hale and never return. The last time United had played at Plymouth in the Cup (in 1913), Dick Duckworth had knocked himself out by diving into a bath that was nowhere near as full as he had thought. This time, the players embarrassed themselves only on the pitch, Argyle romping it 4-1. Then, on consecutive weekends in mid-January, the Reds gave two contrasting demonstrations of how to piss points away. On their first-ever trip to Swansea, they conceded three goals in the last three minutes to lose a game they had led for an hour. On their reacquaintance with White Hart Lane, they collapsed early, the three goals they conceded before half-time lubricating their slide to an eventual 1-4.

By then, the fretters' wing of the Red Army (later to be renamed H stand) had started clucking that Gibson was a paper saviour, an early-day Michael Knighton. They needn't have worried. Once he got his hands on the tiller, the new chairman immediately demolished the theory that he was all talk and no trousers. He had pledged that a figure between £12,000 and £20,000 would be invested in new signings; in the final three months of the season alone, nine new players joined the club for a combined fee of £13,000. The old board had not spent that sort of money in six years. Forwards Dick Black and William McDonald brought great expectations down with them from Scotland – ex-Airdrieonian McDonald was, according to *The Football Chron*, a 'schemer of class' while Black, a prolific scorer for Greenock

Morton, was tipped to be the next Hughie Gallacher. John Moody, a goalkeeper, and wing half-back Leslie Lievesley were captured from Doncaster and wing flier Andrew Mitchell from Darlington; Dai Jones and Ernest Vincent were also plucked from lower-league obscurity. Deadline day, meanwhile, brought a new left-wing partnership in Louis Page, Burnley's former England international winger, and George Fitton, formerly of West Brom.

On the face it, it was an intriguing mix of old and new. As it happened, the new boys worked better as a signal of intent than they did as part of the team. Most had vanished from the Old Trafford payroll within a couple of years. But the management had struck gold with their £1,000 move for Southport centre-back, Vincent. A copper-topped hard nut known everywhere as Ginger, Vincent had been an unemployed nobody when he had won himself a month's trial at the third division club two summers earlier. In just over eighteen months he had left the dole queue, helped the seasiders reach the quarter-finals of the Cup and now earned himself a move up the league. And in the next couple of months Ginger did more than any other Red to make sure that the next turn in his career path did not take him straight back down.

United had long required greater speed, strength and stamina across the half-back line, particularly in the centre. Vincent, who, at 24, was almost fourteen years younger than his predecessor, Hilditch, was the answer. He had no pretensions of being a football stylist nor had he mastered all the arts of constructive play but he was blessed with good all-round skill, sound judgement, a cool head and, above all, the most impressive tackle outside of Dirk Diggler's Y-fronts. Constructive centre-halves à la Barson were a dying breed anyway. Chapman's all-conquering Arsenal side had set a new fashion for employing the centre-half as a third full-back and using the inside-forwards as midfield play-makers. The signing of Vincent allowed United to update their style. With him as stopper, something like the Arsenal plan was worked out. The inside-forwards, Johnston and Ridding, would lie right back in midfield preparing the way for devastating breakaways on the wings by Spence, now restored to his usual position on the right, and his mini-me, Hopkinson, on the left.

The plan shifted some of the play-making responsibility away from the centre-forward which was good news for United whose number nines were all graduates of the bull-in-a-china-shop school. In particular, the tactics suited Reid who, though never a stylish or effective leader, could be relied on to bang in his share of goals given the right service. In a twelve-game springtime spell, starting with the 3-2 win against Nottingham Forest on January 30 which gave the Gibson regime its first victory, Tommy bounced back spectacularly from his tortuous autumn (when he had taken so much flak that the Programme had taken the unusual step of issuing an appeal for 'fair play' on his behalf) to score a dozen times. But even when he was flowing, the cumbersome Scot retained the ability to infuriate those critics who wrote him off as a 'hit and miss, miss, miss' sort of player. 'When he hits,' wrote *The Manchester Guardian*, 'goalkeepers are in physical danger. When he misses he at least makes his foozles thoroughly laughable – at least to disinterested spectators.'

In Manchester in the spring of '32, Vincent threatened to make ginger cool. With their new stopper installed in the centre, United surged from third from bottom to safety in a matter of weeks and played their best football of a dismal decade. The first six matches he played in yielded eleven precious points. Reid, fresh from his match-winning treble against Forest, fired in another couple as Chesterfield were swept aside on Ginger's debut on February 6. Eleven days later, Ridding bagged a late brace, his first goals since his cross-Manchester switch, to rub in the home victory against Burnley. As the visitors rarely saw Steward up close and United could have had ten, even the final 5-1 score-line flattered them. Preston brought the Reds' best winning run since September 1929 to an end by claiming the nil-nil they had set their stall out for at Deepdale, but February still closed on a high, another Vincent-inspired performance taking care of visitors Barnsley.

Three more victories followed in quick succession at the start of March. If winning at Meadow Lane was satisfying, and gaining revenge for the twin Plymouth drubbings even more so, the best moment of the sequence was the magnificent 4-1 triumph at Elland Road which knocked Leeds off top spot (though, unfortunately, not off their stride – the Sheep and the Wolves, an odd pairing admittedly, were headed for better pastures in 32/33). Roared on by a small army of travelling Mancs, United were two-up inside fourteen minutes, a Reid solo and a Ridding header doing the damage. A pre-interval reply offered the hosts hope but the new spine of Vincent, Jones, Silcock and Steward stemmed any thoughts of a comeback and late, late finishes from Reid and Johnston sealed the Reds' Roses victory. And all but banished the spectre of back-to-back relegations. With nine games to play, United were a healthy eight points clear of the bottom two.

The revival of the team wasn't the only good story knocking around Old Trafford that month, either. Accompanying it were clear signs that the club, which had been riddled with angst and in-fighting for large swathes of the Depression Years, had taken giant strides towards becoming re-United off the pitch, too. Gibson had set the peace process in motion by inviting Greenhough in for their Christmas summit and also by publicly absolving the supporters of any blame for the boycott affair (Gibson had always accepted that they had been forced into mutiny by the treatment they had received from the old board); Greenhough, who had been hugely impressed by the chairman's openness, ambition and actions, had since returned the favour by cancelling his organisation's campaign for boardroom representation and announcing a return to old values. The aim of the Supporters" Club, he said, was not to have a say in the management of the club but rather to serve it and the fans by organising trips to away games, endeavouring to silence the Pop Side barrackers and helping to improve facilities at the ground.

By the middle of March, Greenhough and his outlaws had been brought back into the fold. A new, officially-backed Supporters' Club (membership, 1s a year) was formed and by the end of the season, an office and a hut for its members had been erected near the tunnel on the Pop Side. Gibson – who else? – was on hand to hoist the Supporters' Club flag and officially open their new premises. Rapprochement was rubber-stamped when the players accepted the challenge of six-a-side billiards match with the supporters at the Dog & Partridge. The United team got their asses whupped. Fortunately for them, the time had passed when they could be accused of being better billiards players than they were footballers.

At times, the club and supporters were so loved-up that outsiders had to apply feel-good factor 25 to prevent them becoming nauseous. The board and the players had rarely been as close, either. The team appreciated the efforts that Gibson and the other directors were making to spend time with them (amazingly, it seems that the old selectors had rarely bothered). One player, who must have come close to straining his tongue, raved: 'Mr Gibson is the best manager we have had. He comes down to the ground, watches us practice and makes us all feel very much at home. A manager could do nothing better for us.' Gibson's stock must have soared even higher when he took the players on an end-of-season freebie to his holiday place at Bournemouth.

Rocketing crowd figures completed the picture of peace and good will. 7,000 for a United-Preston game would have been par for the course in the autumn; in February, as many people turned up to watch the same fixture in the Central League. Against Barnsley the gate nudged back over 20,000, a further eight thousand were in the ground for the Plymouth game and an impressive 37,000 watched the Good Friday fixture against second-from-bottom Charlton. Continuing a tradition of succumbing to stage-fright on big Old Trafford occasions, the team lost for the first time in nine weeks.

It wasn't just Manchester's menfolk who were cramming into the match-day trams, either. The female division of the Red Army was well-represented, too, though it was a surprise so many bothered given the sexist tripe that awaited them in the programme: 'We are glad that so many girls and women support the Manchester United,' led one editorial. 'A woman wields the greatest influence, whether she be sweetheart, wife or mother, when she shares the life of those around. Sport keeps men good-humoured in any way, and since men need the lesson that to be a sportsman is not to be too proud in victory, and not too downcast in defeat, but to love the game for the sake of the game – then perhaps women can profit by this idea, too!' At least the attitude of the Supporters' Club was less condescending. A Ladies Committee was swiftly formed and a campaign started for better ladies' conveniences. It cannot have been very successful. Even today, perhaps the chief requirement for female football fans is Olympic-standard bladder control.

The Charlton slip-up rather set the tone for the rest of the season. United thrashed Oldham again and picked up maximum points against Port Vale and Bradford City but slumped to another Charlton defeat, lost at bottom club Bristol City and drew with Bury, Millwall and Southampton. A flurry of debutants, though, kept the interest alive. Moody, Fitton and Page all made their first starts over the Easter weekend. The twin Tartan terrors, Black and McDonald, were signed after the transfer deadline but the club were given special dispensation by the FA to play them in the final three matches. Black, in particular, made an immediate impression, scoring a goal in each of those games to suggest, for the time being, that the Gallacher comparisons were not that far-fetched. Despite April showers, a noisy 20,000 turned up to watch the two Scots' debuts against Bradford. Not so long ago, a trip to Old Trafford had featured alongside one to the dentist – or Liverpool – at the bottom of many people's wish-list. That so many supporters were prepared to get soaked to watch a dead rubber showed just how far the club had come in a short time.

Rescuing the team from the jaws of the third division had been the first priority for the new regime. It had been a breeze – despite easing up before the line, the Reds still finished in twelfth place, an

A. STEWARD
MANCHESTER UNITED.

embarrassing performance in most seasons but an achievement in this. Now Gibson could turn his attention to the future. So far, the search for a manager had proved a frustratingly fruitless one. Jimmy McMullan, the City captain, applied for the job but was turned down and a drawn-out chase for a 'mystery' manager came to naught. Eventually, Gibson enticed Scott Duncan, a star player with Newcastle and Rangers and another managerial recruit who had built up a fine reputation in Scottish football, from Cowdenbeath. 'We have made a great capture,' Gibson enthused though, sadly, that was an assessment that would later need revising.

Far more auspicious was the board's decision to enter a junior team into the Manchester League under the stewardship of Lal Hilditch and, by so doing, take the first step towards the formation of an independent youth set-up. Previously, United had relied on a network of junior clubs to produce promising youngsters for them

FOOTNOTES

1. *Blackpool (125 goals conceded in 30/31), Ipswich (121 in 63/64) and Charlton (120 in 56/57).*

2. *Since United and Blackpool started the trend in 30/31, a total of twenty-one sides (from seventeen different clubs) have conceded a century of goals in the top flight. Blackpool, Burnley and Leicester have all done it twice. It might interest you to know that Manchester City are the only club to have done it three times (in 25/26, 57/58 and 62/63).*

and then on Louis Rocca to pinch them; there had been no A, B or youth teams. The new arrangement dammed the talent drain out of Manchester and allowed Gibson to verbally masturbate about the Utopia of an all-Mancunian eleven. It would be the best thing the new regime did for the club bar saving it. After the war, Matt Busby and Jimmy Murphy took the idea and ran with it, eventually developing the revolutionary scheme of building a team on a conveyor belt of young talent, but the emphasis on home-reared youth, one of the philosophies by which the club would be eventually defined, was born in the thirties, first with the Manchester League side and then with the Manchester United Junior Athletic Club (the MUJACs).

The new broom sweeping through Old Trafford was clearly Merlin-powered. The new regime's commitment to spending big on players for now and producing local stars for later was nothing less than football Fantasia. Promotion seemed United's for the taking. There was excited talk of the return of 50,000 crowds and trophy processions. In fact it did not work out quite like that. Like the country, the Reds' recovery from crisis was slow. Duncan spent Gibson's thousands poorly and, in his second season, came within ninety minutes of taking the club into the third division – United needed a final-day victory at Millwall to save their own necks and send the Londoners down in their place. It took fifteen years[2], two promotions (in '36 and '38 – guess what happened in '37) and, of course, the arrival of Busby for the Reds to be restored to their Edwardian pre-eminence. But Gibson was right when he told the audience at his inaugural AGM that 'it would be a wise thing to wipe out as a nasty dream the happenings of the club recently'. Whatever disappointments the future held, the club was back in safe hands. The team remained in depression but the Depression Years were in the past.

---

2.   In 1946/47, the first season after World War Two (and the first season under Busby), United finished runners-up in the first division, their highest league position for 36 years. The following season they finished second in the league again and won the FA Cup, beating Blackpool 4-2 in the club's first-ever Wembley final. Two more runners-up finishes followed in the next three years before Busby finally brought the championship back to Old Trafford in 1951/52.

ROLL OF HONOUR

CHAMPIONS: EVERTON

FA CUP WINNERS: NEWCASTLE UNITED

UNITED: DIVISION 2 (12TH) FA CUP (3RD ROUND) PLYMOUTH A

DEPRESSION YEARS LEGEND
ALF STEWARD

GOALKEEPER 1919 (AM) JAN 1920 (PRO)
JUNE 1932
326 APPS 0 GLS
B. MANCHESTER, CIRCA 1896
D. UNKNOWN
HEIGHT: 5' 11½" WEIGHT: 11ST.13LBS
DEBUT: UNITED 1-0 PRESTON 23/10/20

Career: *Army football, Stalybridge Celtic, United (am.) 1919, Heaton Park F.C., United (pro.) Jan 1920, Manchester North End player-manager June 1932, Altrincham player-manager May 1933, secretary-manager Sept 1936, Torquay United manager 1938-40*

ALF STEWARD TROD a haphazard path to Old Trafford stardom. Dumped by Stalybridge Celtic after just one season, he was working in a Manchester warehouse when he decided to chance his arm and write in for a trial. Getting one was as likely as Jim fixing it for you to sleep with a Bond girl but it just so happened that Alf's letter ended up at the top of the pile in Jack Robson's in-tray and the recently demobbed soldier  got lucky. When he was given his opportunity, ironically enough in a couple of reserve team matches against Stalybridge, Alf made enough of an impression to win himself a new career, though initially he opted to retain his amateur status. The jump to full-time professional followed some months later when his boss in his day job refused to give him time off to play in a weekend match at Wolves. 'Well, if that's the case,' Steward replied. 'I'll go to the people who pay me most money.'

That warehouse jobsworth did the Reds a great service – Alf's progress once he turned pro was spectacular. In his first season he established himself as the outstanding keeper in the Central League, in his second he helped the reserves win the championship and in his fourth he took advantage of Jack Mew's Gigg Lane indiscretion to clinch a first-team place. In hindsight, though, his rise from warehouse floor to the big time was perhaps a season too meteoric. Asking a novice to fill the boots of a legend was one thing, doing so when the legend in question still fancied wearing them himself was quite another. Alf's first taste of senior action fell some way short of turning sour but he was undeniably weighed down by nerves and the lingering presence of Jack the Cat. He was a different player second time around. If 23/24 came close to giving him the bends, the 24/25 season, when he was a leading light in the promotion-winning defence, made him a star.

By conceding just 23 goals and keeping 25 clean sheets that season, Alf and his defence set a record that will probably never be broken. Unfortunately, it was the last time that the statistics ever came close to representing how good a goalkeeper he actually was. The rest of his United career was spent – through no fault of his own – rewriting the record books for all the wrong reasons. By the time he left Old Trafford, Alf had played in three club-record 7-0 defeats and – along with Arthur Chesters – had let in 85-plus league goals in a season twice and 100-plus once (no previous United side had shipped more than eighty). The total of 115 goals the pair conceded in 30/31 was particularly embarrassing. Only three sides[1] in first division history have ever conceded more; before United did it, no team had even made it to a century[2].

Given the chaos that raged around him in the six years that separated his record high from his record low, it was remarkable that Alf maintained his high standards for as long as he did. Inevitably, though, there were occasions when the keeper suffered from the Reds' deterioration from an average team with a great defence into an awful team with an average defence. And when Alf endured his career low-point, at home to Newcastle in September '27, he chose the worst possible moment to do it. The jungle drums about his pre-Newcastle form had been loud enough to reach even the ears of the England selectors. When the top brass deigned to visit Old Trafford to see what all the fuss was about, Alf played like he had frostbite and was beaten seven times.

As England's production line of top-class goalkeepers had all but dried up, an opportunity had presented itself for Steward to go where no United keeper has ever gone, and establish himself in the national side. His errors deprived him of a deserved cap and shortly afterwards cost him his first-team place. Harshly dropped by selectors who had a habit of forgetting his preceding brilliance when he had an isolated bad game, Alf spent most of that season in the wilderness before fighting back in 28/29 to reclaim the jersey from Lance Richardson. Having picked himself up again, Alf held on to his place for another three and a half years before finally losing it for good when John Moody arrived from Doncaster in March '32. When the club then allowed their long-serving stalwart to move on, many were fiercely critical of the decision. Steward still had plenty in the tank as he had shown by keeping his head above water in his final two seasons despite regularly facing odds of tidal wave proportions. Moody was not such a great choice anyway. He only lasted a year and for the rest of the decade the United goal was never satisfactorily filled. In retrospect, Alf's passing marked the end of the club's first great goalkeeping era. Arguably, Old Trafford will not see as regal a succession as Moger, Beale, Mew and Steward ever again.

As Alf's playing career passed through two distinct phases, that last line should probably end with Mew, Steward and Steward. At a fraction under six foot, with a long reach and lean, agile frame, Steward undoubtedly had the classical goalkeeper's physique. Initially his style was classical too. He had all the essentials – a quick eye, good hands, judgement, anticipation, strength, bravery and so on – but few frills. As *The Football Chronicle* noted midway though 24/25: 'There is nothing of the showman about his work between the posts. He does not strive after picturesque effect. The clean catch and quick clearance is the motto he has placed in his shield.' In comparison to Jack Mew, who was squat, temperamental, charismatic and, in all probability, a bit of a poser, Alf must have seemed the epitomé of cold-blooded efficiency, his only nod to individuality being his habit of blowing out his cheeks before he made a clearance.

As his career progressed, however, Steward's style veered away from the classical and closer to his mentor's – albeit minus the punch-ups. A growing penchant for careering out of his goal earned him a reputation as a top-class but 'risky' keeper, rather than a top-class and unshowy one. The metamorphosis was triggered by the changing circumstances of the team and also by the alterations in the rule book. The new offside law signalled the end of the days when goalkeepers could stay on their line and rely on the defenders to do all the outfield defending. United's failure to properly replace Barson and other members of Chapman's successful side, as well as Bamlett's ill-advised infatuation with offside, left Steward with more outfield responsibility than most. The switch to a more aggressive and proactive style was his means of coping with it.

'Goalkeeping is a different business now from what it was when I started,' the veteran told the *Football News* in 1931. 'The change in the offside rule altered everything. Formerly you could stay at home and watch the player who you knew was bound to finish up the attack with the ball at his feet. Now we Aunt Sallys have a much livelier time. My view is that goalkeepers must take more risks than formerly, and I have modelled my play on that opinion. No keeper now should be afraid to spend much of his afternoon on the edge of the penalty area, for he may be able to get in a few kicks at the ball whereas by staying between the sticks he would be waiting to be shot at.'

A Mancunian born and bred who had served with the Manchester Pals during the war, Alf was popular enough with the crowd already. His conversion from conservative to mild lunatic strengthened his bond with the Pop Side. 'The crowd loves him because he has personality. There is something of the man himself in those daring interceptions five or six yards out of goal,' raved the *Football News*. An infectious laugh and boyish enthusiasm apparently made him a dressing-room favourite, too, although his popularity amongst his team-mates may have had something to do with his piano-playing skills. Apart from reading, the only self-made entertainment available to the players on their travels was the oldest one and music. Having someone like Alf who could bang out a good tune and lead the lads in a sing-song was invaluable for team morale. A man of many talents, Alf was also a gifted slow left-arm bowler and exceptional fielder who spent two seasons on the ground-staff with Lancashire. Despite topping the bowling averages in the Manchester League, he never made it into the county team. Making a lasting mark at the other Old Trafford must have been consolation enough.

SAMUEL 'RAY' BENNION

RIGHT HALF-BACK, APR 1921 – NOV 1932, 301 APPS 3 GLS

RAY BENNION WAS never going to appeal to the football purist but a decade's hard graft on the right side of the Reds' midfield made him a warm favourite with the Old Trafford crowd. The supporters always knew what they were going to get from the former miner – enthusiasm, non-stop tackling and sackfuls of effort. A ten-time Welsh international, he was also a better player than most people gave him credit for, mainly because he recognised his limitations and played within them. Ray was not blessed with the speed, skill or imagination to burst through a defence or carve one open with an extravagant pass so he did not bother trying. Instead, he preferred the short, sharp pass to the man in front and saved the tricky touch or flick – which bamboozled those opponents who did not think he was capable of such subtlety – for special occasions. Bennion goals were rationed even more strictly. It took him five and a half years to claim his first – a face-saving cup equaliser against Reading in January 1927 – and, overall, his three goals for the club came at a rate of one every 100 appearances.

Yet another loyal and long-lasting Robson discovery, Bennion was plucked from Cheshire League side Chrichton's Athletic in April 1921 when he was 24. He made his first-team debut in the midst of the 5-0 Goodison disaster on the opening day of 21/22 and spent most of the next two seasons as Lal Hilditch's understudy. His breakthrough came in 23/24 when he made 36 appearances at right-half and he was a regular in all but two of his final eight seasons at the club. Unfortunately, the two campaigns he spent as back-up were the two that he would most liked to have played a full part in. Ray was kept out of the side by Frank Mann for most of the promotion season and by a combination of Mann, Hilditch and injuries in the cup-chasing year. At least he had the satisfaction of making a significant contribution to the promotion run-in, in the process earning a pen portrait in the *Athletic News* that probably best summed him up: 'Better in defence than attack, blessed with fine physique and a tenacious style, Bennion has been a consistent source of strength.'

TOM JONES

FULL-BACK, MAY 1924 – JULY 1937
119 APPS 0 GLS
(TOTAL 200 APPS 0 GLS)

T. J. JONES

ENTICED ON A free transfer from the green, green grass of home (OK, Oswestry) in the summer of '24, Tom Jones was perhaps the difference between United winning promotion in 24/25 and them missing out. Precocious judgement as well as the ability to play with either foot and on either side of the defence ensured that the injured Jack Silcock was barely missed and marked the pint-sized Welshman (at 5ft 8in tall and just 10½ stone, he was one of the smallest defenders in the league) down as a potentially great back.

Despite winning four Welsh caps, Tom never quite delivered on that early promise. The longevity of the famous partnership of Silcock and Moore, the emergence of rival defensive talents, Jack Mellor and Billy Dale, and a succession of ill-timed injuries all held him back. The worst of them was the rupture he sustained on the tennis court in the summer after the 27/28 season, a campaign in which he had been a virtual ever-present. The injury put him out of the game for a year and effectively cost him his place in the side for the rest of the Depression Years. It wasn't until the 33/34 campaign, by which time he was in his mid-thirties, that he re-established himself at senior level.

According to my calculations (which are based on the assumption that a player's United career started when he first played for the first team or signed a professional contract with the club, whichever came first), Tom was one of fifty-four United players who have completed a decade or more's service at Old Trafford. The rest, in alphabetical order, are:

Albiston 74-88, Beckham 1992-03, Bell 1903-13, Bennion 21-32, Best 63-74, Blackmore 82-94, Brennan 55-70, Buchan 71-83, Butt 92-04, Carey 36-53, Charlton 54-73, Chilton 38-55, Cockburn 44-54, Crompton 45-56, Duckworth 1903-14, Dunne 60-73, Duxbury 76-90, Fred Erentz 1892-1902, Foulkes 51-70, Gaskell 57-69, Giggs 90-,

Gregg 57-67, Hanlon 35-48, Hilditch 16-32, Hughes 80-86 & 88-95, Irwin 1990-02, Tom Jones 24-37, Keane 93-05, Law 62-73, McClair 87-98, McIlroy 71-82, Macari 72-84, Meredith 1906-21, Mew 12-26, Moore 19-30, Moran 78-88, G. Neville 92-, P. Neville (94-05), Stan Pearson 37-54, Robson 81-94, Rowley 35-55, Sadler 63-74, Scholes 93- , Silcock 17-34, Solskjaer (96-), Spence 19-33, Stepney 66-78, Steward 20-32, Stiles 59-71, Viollet 50-62, Walsh 85-95, Arthur Whalley 1909-20, Bert Whalley 34-47, Wrigglesworth 37-47.

Of those players, only eight made fewer appearances for the club than Jones's 200. Five of them (Hanlon, Mew, Wrigglesworth and both Whalleys) would have played more matches or, alternatively, would have been transferred had it not been for either one of the wars while David Gaskell (118 apps) and Gary Walsh (63 apps) were basically back-up goalkeepers. What that means is that, of all the members of the United decade-plus club, Tom Jones was probably the hardest done to in terms of minutes on the pitch. A double-century of games was ill-reward not only for his loyalty but also for his talent, which was so often overlooked particularly when he entered the veteran stage of his career. The Official Programme made some amends with a knicker-throwing eulogy in March 1928: 'For his size, there is no better full-back in the game; international honours have come his way, and further honours are certain. There may be better full-backs in the game, but, personally, I should be quite content to have this little bundle of Welsh pluck and energy on my side in any match, however important.'

One final point about that long-servers' list; what the fuck is Sunbed doing on it ?!?

WILLIAM DALE

FULL-BACK, MAY 1926 – DEC 1931, 68 APPS 0 GLS

UNITED HAD TRADITIONALLY had the better of any transfer deals between Manchester's big two. Billy Dale bucked the trend. Sold, against his will, in another of the old regime's finger-in-the-dyke exercises, Billy would eventually fulfil all bar one of the lavish predictions that had been made about him when he burst spectacularly onto the first division scene in 28/29. The exception was the one about him being a certain international. A stylish back who could play on either side of the defence, Billy was undoubtedly good enough to play for his country but fell victim to the FA's blind spot about Manchester-based players, even Blue ones.

In none of his six seasons at Old Trafford, however, was the toothy Mancunian a regular in United's back-line and it was the wealth of talent in that area that eventually persuaded the directors to cash in on him. Reds would spend much of the next decade wishing they hadn't. While United were yo-yoing between the divisions, Billy was winning the league and Cup with City and emerging as the thirties answer to Freddie Hopkin – the former Red whose antics with a close rival were a constant irritant (or the hair shirt that Reds would have to wear as penance for the sins of a bad board).

JOHN WILSON

LEFT HALF-BACK, SEPT 1926 – JUNE 1932, 140 APPS 3 GLS

AS A YOUNG centre-forward with Newcastle United, Jack Wilson showed enough promise to be tipped for England honours but a succession of injuries, including two broken legs, slowed his progress to such an extent that he was shown the door after just a handful of first-team appearances. The pits were calling when the then 23-year-old accepted the job of player-manager of Leadgate United in his native Co. Durham in the summer of 1920. It was the small acorn from which a good, if ultimately frustrating, career grew. After two years of non-league rehab, Jack returned to League football with Durham City; eight games and five goals later he was on the move again, this time to Edgeley Park where he spent four seasons and was successfully converted from an inside-forward into a wing-half. A contract dispute that dragged right through the 1926 close season opened the door for United to steal in and bag County's star man for a bargain £500 at the start of 26/27. In a difficult season, it was by far the best thing that happened to the club. Writing in 1951, Alf Clarke had no hesitation in nominating Jack as 'one of the most dominating wing half-backs United ever had'. Certainly he was an intimidating physical presence in defence but he was also a potent attacking force whose ability to deal out clever passes, often along the ground and at unexpected angles, quicker than a Las Vegas croupier put him on a different plane to the standard United half-back.

Like Frank Barson before him, Jack was a curious mix of craftsman, charismatic general and general lunatic. 'When things are going wrong,' observed the Analyst in the *Topical Times*, 'he is inclined to get out of joint.' It was another line dripping in understatement. After all, this was a player who started a riot at Ewood Park, got himself sent off in a reserve team game just days into his United career and basked in the reputation as one of the spikiest characters in the game. All his admirers could see, however, was an all-consuming will to win. Chris Taylor thrilled the crowd for half a season, the veterans, Lal Hilditch and Frank Mann, were regarded almost reverentially by the Pop Side but Jack Wilson was the most popular middle-man in the immediate post-Barson era. One letter, published in *The Football Chron* in November 1928, cast some light on the reasons why: 'He [Wilson] is a great player and a captain whose efforts alone ought to inspire the rest of the team. A harder worker there never was; his passes never go astray whether they are crosses to the right wing or lobs or pushed down the middle or to the left wing – they all find their man.'

Considering the minefield of ill-fortune he had been asked to negotiate earlier in his career, it must have been deeply frustrating for Jack to line up in a United team that did not come close to matching his constructive standards, to pick up a series of debilitating injuries and illnesses (in two of his six seasons as a Red, he was badly affected by quinsies) and to play in front of crowd who, in the words of the Analyst: 'value the holding of the ball only if it comes off to the betterment of attack, thus missing the merit aimed at it' (I know, it doesn't make any sense to me either; what I think he was referring to were the 'Get rid' and 'Boot it' merchants in the crowd who hindered the players' attempts to play a passing game). In every case the inspirational Geordie deserved better.

CHARLIE RAMSDEN

RIGHT-WINGER, MAY 1927 – AUG 1932
(JAN-MAY 1928 ON LOAN AT STOCKPORT COUNTY)
16 APPS 3 GLS

THROUGHOUT THE TWENTIES United had a habit of buying right-wingers who were, for the want of a better description, a bit crap. Charlie Ramsden, the most notable of the new signings that Herbert Bamlett made during his first summer at the club, was no exception. Arriving from Rotherham with a reputation as a goalscoring winger, Charlie was given just a couple of starts in his debut season before he became the meat in a former-Owl sandwich consisting of Billy Chapman (whom Charlie replaced) and Rees Williams (who replaced Charlie). A loan spell at Edgeley Park in 1928 hinted at a swift exit but Charlie was back at Old Trafford for 28/29 and ended up stretching out his United career for another four years, most of which he spent in the reserves. Game but lacking in talent, Ramsden was perhaps symbolic of the entire Bamlett era, the start and finish of which coincided almost exactly with his own first and final senior appearances.

HUGH MCLENAHAN

HALF-BACK, MAY 1927 – DEC 1936, 54 APPS 8 GLS
(TOTAL 116 APPS 12 GLS)

ULTIMATELY, HUGHIE MCLENAHAN was remembered for three things; his immense potential, the horrific injury which prevented him fulfilling it and, well, ice-cream. Hughie had always been earmarked for Old Trafford but, for reasons that are not altogether clear, United allowed Stockport County to nip in and sign him up on amateur forms. Cue another [tall] story from the Louis Rocca archives. Knowing that County  were struggling financially and were planning a fund-raising bazaar,

Rocca, whose family were well-known ice-cream manufacturers, softened them up with a donation of three freezers of ice-cream. Then he went in for the kill, apparently saying to the Stockport directors: 'You have a young player named McLenahan. He does not want to play for you, but prefers to come to United'. The ice-cream must have been good because Stockport subsequently let him go. And if you believe that, you'll believe anything.

WILLIAM JOHNSTON

INSIDE-LEFT, OCT 1927 – JUNE 1929 & MAY 1931 – MAY 1932
77 APPS 27 GLS

By OCTOBER 1927, talk of United must have been as welcome in the Edgeley Park boardroom as a streaker at a funeral. Three times in the previous thirteen months, the club's officials had visited their near-neighbours and taken off with their brightest talents. Billy Johnston was the final straw in a trilogy which also included Jack Wilson and Hughie McLenahan. Like his predecessors, he quickly became a big favourite with the Old Trafford crowd, principally because he added a splash of class and colour to a squad overloaded with functional triers. Billy's vibrant performances at inside-forward demanded comparisons with football's first £10,000 man, David Jack, and an effusion of appreciation from his wing-partners. Rees Williams, in particular, had every reason to be thankful for Johnston's ability to make ordinary wingers look like internationals or, in Rees's case, an incompetent one look ordinary.

Considering his obvious talent, it is strange to think that the critics initially harboured doubts about the £3,000 Scot's capacity to fit in at Old Trafford. Many wanted to know why a player who had been widely touted as a superstar of the future during his early days with Huddersfield had spent most of his career in the second division with County. The likeliest explanation is that he was never given a proper opportunity in the great Huddersfield team and that no one else had been willing to take a punt on a maverick talent. Like his 90s equivalent, Matt Le Tissier, Billy's deceptive, loping style put many people off. So did the common perception that he was an individualist rather than a team player and that he would struggle to adjust to the change from big to little fish status. What the sceptics had not taken into account was that, while the pool had unquestionably grown larger, Billy the fish would remain just as influential. His dribbling prowess and vision ensured he continued in the tradition of fine United inside-lefts.

Unfortunately, the United directors had their own tradition when it came to dealing with talented inside-lefts; falling out with them and then getting rid. Where Woodcock, Sapsford, Lochhead and Kennedy had gone before him, Johnston followed in the summer of 1929 when he was transfer-listed after a disagreement over terms. When no club came in for him at the price United were quoting, Billy joined non-league Macclesfield. Admittedly he had endured a frustrating time with injuries, making just a dozen appearances in 28/29, and the club had unveiled a potential successor in the precocious Harry Rowley, but his departure remained a baffling kick in the plums for the Pop Side.

After two years in which the forwards would have killed for a supplier of Johnston's class, the directors acknowledged their mistake and brought him back from his non-league purgatory. The Scot promptly showed what the club had been missing by running away with the forward honours in 31/32. There was a certain predictability about what happened next as the management informed the supporters that Billy, though clever, was not the bustling, thrustful player they wanted for the following season and promptly sold him to Oldham. A change of heart and two years later, United started sniffing around him again. Wisely, both Oldham and Billy told them to clear off.

GEORGE LYDON

HALF-BACK, MAY 1928 – JAN 1933, 3 APPS 0 GLS

GIVEN THE INTENSE competition for defensive places at Old Trafford, George Lydon made a sensible decision when he switched from full-back to half-back following his arrival from Cheshire League side, Mossley, in May 1928. Even then he had to wait two and half years for his first taste of league action, making his debut in a losing cause at Bolton on Christmas Day 1930. Unlike dogs, the selectors felt that George was just for Christmas and it was not until the following year's Advent programme that he was given another run-out. His crisp tackling and raking passing against Millwall earned him decent reviews but an indifferent performance at Bradford used up all of his credit and he was dropped for the next match. His chance of starring in his own cigarette card now gone, George spent the rest of his United career as an honest foot-soldier in the reserves. After leaving the club, he spent five months at third division (north) strugglers Southport before dropping into non-league football with Burton Town.

HENRY ROWLEY

INSIDE-LEFT, MAY 1928 – DEC 1931 & DEC 1934 – JUL 1937
96 APPS 24 GLS (TOTAL 180 APPS 56 GLS)

IN THE TWENTIES, United possessed, quite literally, an embarrassment of riches at inside-left. As none of them were anywhere near as effective when they were asked to play elsewhere, only one of them could play in the side at any given time. Consequently, a situation arose where the selectors were forced to play inferior players in the problem forward positions – usually centre-forward and on the right – and leave good players on the sidelines. It was embarrassing, for example, to play a workhorse like Tommy Smith and leave out an artist such as Arthur Lochhead but there was little the selectors could do about it, bar finding themselves a better inside-right or, ridiculous as it sounds, selling the redundant inside-left.

Plumping for the latter option, as they usually did, would have been easier for the fans to take had the club re-invested the profits wisely or, at the very least, got the price and the timing right. They did not. Of the dynasty of classy inside-lefts that United were blessed with in the Depression Years, it is hard to think of one who was sold well. Fred Kennedy, George Sapsford and Lochhead were discarded at ludicrous times (Fred went in the midst of a promotion battle, George at the back end of a relegation season – as if the supporters weren't upset enough already – and Arthur before he had the chance to prove his class in the first division), Wilf Woodcock and Billy Johnston went for virtually nothing while Kennedy, Sapsford and Lochhead should all have gone for much, much more.

The last member of the dynasty, Harry Rowley, was also sold at a give-away price although it was only when he moved again, to Oldham (in early 1933), that it became clear what a bad deal United had struck when they swapped him and Billy Dale for Bill Ridding and a couple of grand. Harry's form with the Latics was so good that United eventually re-signed him in December 1934 but his second stint at the club was just as bittersweet as his first. A career-best haul of nineteen league goals in the 35/36 promotion campaign suggested that he would be an exception to the rule about players not going back but United's instant relegation brought his Old Trafford return to a familiarly anti-climactic end. That summer, the then 33-year-old left to take the player-manager's job at Burton Town.

When he was released for the first time, Rowley had just spent four months as the barely used understudy to the newly re-signed Billy Johnston. It was an unwitting piece of pay-back for Johnston whose two year non-league exile owed much to the revelatory form Harry had shown following his £100 move from Shrewsbury in 1928. In the interim, the young upstart had more than justified the club's faith in him, earning comparisons with Lochhead for his imperious dribbling, feinting and dummying as well as for his precocious scheming and reading of the game. Of course he wasn't yet the complete inside-forward – his right foot and shooting, in particular, needed work – but *The Football Chron* were still impressed enough to predict, in February 1929, that he was 'going to be one of United's best post-war players'.

It was mainly the club's fault that Harry never quite lived up to those great expectations. Ignoring the fable about the golden goose, the selectors flogged him to death, expecting him to fill, concurrently, the roles of fetcher, carrier, defender, prompter and scorer. Ultimately, Harry paid the price for being the one star in United's feeble attack. As the *Football News* concluded when he moved to Maine Road: 'If Rowley had been fortunate enough to have been secured when he was ready to start on his football career by a club which could have afforded to introduce him gradually into higher class football, he would have made a [real] name for himself by today.'

TOMMY REID

CENTRE-FORWARD, FEB 1929 – MAR 1933, 89 APPS 57 GLS
(TOTAL 101 APPS 67 GLS)

'STRONG, BURLY AND yet a veritable Powderhall sprinter over twenty yards', Tommy Reid was, according to Alf Clarke, 'a centre-forward with a terrific "wallop" in his left foot.' The Official Programme called him 'an opportunist of the first water' and his goal record backed up their claim. A scoring rate of two every three games would have been an impressive achievement in a good team, never mind one that was breaking all the wrong kind of records. But Tommy, like Frank  McPherson before him, was denied the respect that his goal record deserved. Instead of being the darling of the Pop Side, he was given so much stick that the Programme and local papers regularly felt the need to appeal for fair treatment on his behalf.

In many ways, the barrel-chested, extrovert Reid was the antithesis of the slender, sensitive McPherson. As players and Reds, though, they had much in common. Neither buttered the bread of the football intelligentsia, lacking the brains, ball control, vision and distribution that the purists looked for in a centre-forward. Both were chronically one-footed, carrying rockets in their left feet but nothing but mould on their right. Both scored prolifically but were barracked for their failure to live up to the club's glorious ball-playing traditions.

In Tommy's case, the backlash started within months of his relegation-busting heroics in the spring of '29. As he was handicapped for long stretches of the following campaign by a combination of illness, injury and, believe it or not, boils, the criticism was bitterly unfair. It was to his credit, then, that he stuck it out at Old Trafford for three more years, still being victimised by the Pop Side but still banging in the goals. In 30/31, the Scot scored twenty in thirty-three games; in 31/32, his ratio improved to eighteen in twenty-six; even in 32/33, when he was deemed surplus to requirements and farmed out to Oldham, he managed ten in twelve. In the circumstances, Tommy would have been entitled to ask his terrace tormentors what more he could possibly have done.

John Mellor

Right full-back, May 1929 – Jan 1937
73 apps 0 gls (total 122 apps 0 gls)

Unlike Tom Jones and Billy Dale, who burst dramatically onto the scene but subsequently had to settle for lengthy spells as back-up to Silcock and Moore, Jack Mellor timed his rise to senior status to perfection, arriving in the team shortly after cheerful Charlie hung up his boots. Looked at another way, though, and Jack could not have got his timing more awry if he had arrived at Old Trafford at the same time as the Luftwaffe bomb. His opportunity knocked at the outset of the tortuous relegation season when most Reds approached match-day with the same zestful optimism that a death row convict carries down the Mile.

It was to his immense credit, then, that while his more experienced team-mates were losing their heads, Jack was keeping his and his emergence as a defender of genuine quality provided a rare bright note in a dismal season. In March '31, the *Football News* wrote: 'Jack Mellor was, a few weeks ago, one of the most promising full-backs in first-class football. Now he has definitely arrived, and has made the right-back position at Old Trafford his own. Born at Oldham, Mellor played for a while with Witton Albion and gained useful experience in the Cheshire County League where a young player can learn much from the several veterans belonging to various teams. He started with United as a left-back, but has moved over to the other flank with conspicuous success. Ideally built for his position, Mellor marks his play by admirably timed and fearless tackling, with strong and brainy kicking. He is young yet, but only last Saturday achieved the unusual distinction of earning personal congratulations from the Birmingham directors.'

In time, though, Jack's United career would prove just as frustrating as that of Jones and Dale, both of whom had been the focus of similarly lavish predictions in their debut seasons. The competition between the threesome did none of them any favours. Happy days for one inevitably meant hard times for the others. Mellor rose above second-season syndrome to cement his partnership with Silcock and inadvertently push Dale into the grabbing hands of City in '31. Then, after a dip in form at the start of 33/34, Jack was replaced by Tom who, earlier in his career, had been kept out of the side by Billy. After being a virtual ever-present in the side, clocking up 114 appearances in his first three years as a senior player, Mellor hardly featured in his final four seasons as a Red, playing just eight times in that period before moving to Cardiff where he squeezed out one last season before retiring.

ARTHUR WARBURTON

INSIDE-RIGHT, MAY 1929 – DEC 1933,
31 APPS 9 GLS (TOTAL 39 APPS 10 GLS)

THE LEAST SUCCESSFUL of the trio of inexperienced forwards – Gallimore and Hopkinson were the others – who were thrown into the side during the ill-fated 30/31 season, Arthur Warburton was capable of neat footwork and intelligent probing but was frail in build and finishing power. Still, he was regarded as a good find until prolonged and premature exposure to United's plight effectively ended his chances of making it at Old Trafford. Transferred to Burnley in December 1933, and then Fulham ten months later, Arthur spent the rest of his career in the second and third divisions. Even at that level he was never anything special.

STANLEY GALLIMORE

FORWARD, DEC 1929 – SUMMER 1933 & FEB – JUNE 1934,
57 APPS 12 GLS (TOTAL 76 APPS 20 GLS)

A VERSATILE ATTACKER who was comfortable in both inside-wing berths and was also an effective emergency winger, Stan Gallimore was tagged the brightest prospect since Hughie McLenahan when he was thrown into senior action as Joe Spence's sidekick in October 1930. The *Football News*, for one, came over all peculiar as they drooled over the 20-year-old's ball control, tricks and football brain as well as his speciality – a googly of a reverse pass that sent defenders running one way and the ball the other – and predicted that Stan would be the Man for United for years to come.

They could not have got it more wrong. Flash forward five years and the 'next big thing' was trawling non-league football with Altrincham. A combination of Stan's lack of form, goals and muscle, the intense competition for forward places in the Scott Duncan era and, worst of all, the serious knee injury he sustained in November '32 prompted the club to release him on a free at the end of 32/33. After undergoing surgery to remove his damaged cartilage, Stan did bounce back to win a short-term contract the following year but his Old Trafford encore did not last long. After making seven appearances at the back end of 33/34, he was one of a number of players who were shown the door that summer.

SAMUEL HOPKINSON

LEFT-WINGER, MAY 1929 – MAY 1935,
38 APPS 11 GLS (TOTAL 57 APPS 12 GLS)

SAM HOPKINSON WAS undoubtedly the odd man out of the virginal forward threesome he formed with Stan Gallimore and Arthur Warburton in 1930/31. All three were described as young in the papers but while Stan was only just out of his teens when he made his United debut, Arthur was 26 and Sam nearly 29.

As his age suggests, Sam was the most experienced of the trio. A former schoolboy international, he had already done time with two League clubs – Rotherham County and Chesterfield – and three non-league outfits by the time he moved to United in May '29. In the season and a half that followed, Sam was regarded purely as a back-up player but when he was finally given his chance in the first team, as part of the reshuffle that pushed George McLachlan back into midfield (in January '31), he did well enough to be ranked, alongside Gallimore, as the attacking discovery of the season. The pundits compared him to Joe Spence; not particularly tricky, perhaps, but a winger with a 'keep-on-playing-till-I-drop attitude'. Hindsight suggests that Red watchers were so desperate to find positives to take from an appalling season that they would have showered praise on a stray dog if it had run across the pitch without dumping. None of Sam, Stan or Arthur were destined to enjoy successful careers at Old Trafford; Sam at least hung around longer than the others but he was only a bit-part player in 31/32 and had even fewer parts thereafter.

ARTHUR CHESTERS

GOALKEEPER, NOV 1929 – AUG 1933, 9 APPS 0 GLS

ARTHUR CHESTERS MADE his United debut in the 5-0 romp against Newcastle in the final match of 1929. As Graham Taylor might have said, was that not a sign of things to come. In eight more appearances as understudy to Alf Steward and John Moody, Arthur conceded thirty goals at an overall rate of 3.33 a game. If the statistics provide an accurate guide, that means that Arthur was twice as bad as the 70s goalkeeping anti-Christ, Paddy Roche, who let them in at a rate of roughly 1.7. Of course, the stats rarely tell the whole truth. Peter  Schmeichel's throbbing snout would have exploded had he been afforded as little protection as Chesters was in most of his matches. Even Alf Steward's career experienced a major wobble when he was forced to fill the role of sitting duck behind the class of 1930; Arthur's would have had more chance of surviving a firing squad.

George McLachlan

Left-winger & Left half-back Dec 1929 – June 1933, 99 apps 4 gls (total 116 apps 4 gls)

A Christmas present from Mrs Davies in 1929, George McLachlan was the football equivalent of a reindeer-design tank-top knitted by an uncoordinated auntie. Few Reds wanted him. George had won the Cup with Cardiff in '27 but had just been part of their relegation team and was known to be on the slow side for a winger. A bright start, however, trapped the expected taunts in the boo-boys' throats and for most of his first half-season as a Red, the powerfully-built Scot was an effective influence on the left flank. It did not last. In his first full campaign, his form fell away badly, he lost consistency and nerve, failing to beat his man, find his fellow forwards or even to compete in the tackle. In the midst of United's relegation season, George was jostling for the dishonour of most inept Red.

Then, an injury to Jack Wilson and a switch to left-half opened up the road to Red redemption. As Frank Mann discovered when he made a similar move in 1924, dropping back into midfield suited forwards who had lost their pace and goal threat but who had retained their footwork, attacking brain and appetite for the game. One advantage that gay lovers have over heterosexual ones is that both parties have a good idea of what the other really wants and how to deliver it. So it is with converted forwards who play in midfield; they know when and where their strikers want the ball. It was probably no coincidence that McLachlan and Wilson, another former attacker, were the only United half-backs at the turn of the decade who had the slightest idea about locating the forwards' collective G-spot.

Shrugging off his earlier timidity, McLachlan also adapted successfully to the defensive side of the half-back role. His emergence as an all-round wing-half was such that, by the end of the 30/31, he was being hailed as one of the season's best finds. This time he was able to sustain his good form, winning the battle with Wilson for the left-half slot in 31/2 and also replacing him as captain. When George left United to become player-coach at Chester in the summer of '33, the player that the supporters didn't want to come was one of the few that they didn't want to go.

THOMAS PARKER

CENTRE HALF-BACK, OCT 1930 – MAY 1932, 17 APPS 0 GLS

A DESPERATE SIGNING in the midst of United's abysmal start to 30/31, Tom Parker worked and tackled hard but was never going to be good enough for the first division. If his plumbing had been as hit-and-miss as his passing, Oxford Road would have been ankle-deep in water. Transfer-listed at the end of 31/32, he spent the rest of his five-year professional career in the lower reaches of the third divisions with Bristol City and Carlisle.

JOHN 'JOE' FERGUSON

RIGHT-WINGER, MAY – DEC 1931, 8 APPS 1 GL

THE FERGUSON NAME wasn't exactly a byword for excellence at Old Trafford before October '86 (or should that be '93?). It says much for the relative merits of Depression Years forwards, Danny and Joe, that Darren was by far the best of the three Fergusons who have worn a Red shirt in anger. Equally, it said much for the state that the club found themselves in 31/32 that Joe Ferguson, an unremarkable right-winger who had just done time at Burton Town, was the first choice number seven for the opening month of the season. He had speed and ball control but his crossing was as wild as a night out with the Supervixens – when Joe swung in a centre, the ball was as likely to end up coated in an unsuspecting fan's Bovril as it was to end up on a United head. Replaced in October by another summer signing,

Herbert Mann, Joe did not fancy hanging around in the Central League and instead jumped on a ferry and signed for Derry City. A multi-club journeyman with stints at Wolves, Grimsby, Workington and Watford already behind him by the time he joined United, the second Red Fergie bowed out of English League football with the modest career stats of thirty-five appearances and five goals.

TOM MANLEY

LEFT HALF-BACK AND LEFT-WINGER, MAY 1931- JULY 1939,
3 APPS 0 GLS (TOTAL 195 APPS 41 GLS)

A PLAY-ANYWHERE TYPE who became part of the furniture at Old Trafford in the 30s, Tom Manley's most significant contribution to Red history was scoring one of the goals that beat Millwall on the final afternoon of the 33/34 season, a result that kept United out of the third division. Too young to play a prominent role in the Depression Years, Tom nonetheless made his mark as a likely lad with a hat-trick of mature performances at left-half in the winter of '31. The *Athletic News* remarked, after Tom's debut (coincidentally enough, at home to Millwall), that the Northwich-born teenager 'tackled crisply, extricated himself from difficulties with coolness, and opened out the game with raking passes that rarely rose more than waist height'.

MATTHEW ROBINSON

LEFT-WINGER, SEPT 1931 – MAR 1932, 10 APPS 0 GLS

IN ORDINARY CIRCUMSTANCES, Matt Robinson would never have seen the light of day at Old Trafford but he did possess one quality that the club could not ignore in the midst of their financial problems; he was free. Released by Cardiff in the close season, Matt did enough in a month's trial to earn a contract for the rest of the season and filled the number eleven shirt in ten consecutive matches that autumn. It is fair to say that the sight of him filling the shirt did not cause many opponents to fill their shorts. He was capable of delivering a useful cross but he was too slow and too hesitant to justify a permanent place in the side. The autumn's weakest link, Matt was sent packing to Chester in the spring.

HERBERT MANN

RIGHT-WINGER, MAY 1931 – NOV 1933, 13 APPS 2 GLS

IF MATT ROBINSON was the weakest link in United's forward line in the autumn of '31 then Herbert Mann ran him extremely close. Together, the duo formed possibly the worst wing pairing in United's history. Whereas Matt could cross but could not run, Herbert could run but could not cross. It was no consolation to the few remaining match-going Reds that, together, they would have made a half-decent player. All they wanted to know was how a club that could leave a top-class forward like Harry Rowley in the reserves could find first-team places for two lemons like Robinson and Mann.

HAROLD DEAN

CENTRE-FORWARD, SEPT – DEC 1931 (AM), 2 APPS 0 GLS

A SURE SIGN of the desperate state of United's resources – both playing and financial – in the autumn of 1931 was the club's reliance on amateur players to fill the holes left in the senior and reserve teams by the mass exodus of professionals during the summer. Harry Dean was one of thirty-one amateurs who were registered by the club amidst the chaos of the post-relegation season. Recruited from the Old Trafford Amateur club in September, Harry was thrown into first-team action almost immediately only to be chewed up and spat out just as quickly. Reporting on his debut match against Chesterfield, The *Athletic News* wrote: 'The weakness of United remained in attack and the young amateur Dean if anything increased it… He is full of fearless dash and enthusiasm and a Chesterfield official remarked afterwards that his harrying of the visiting backs had influenced the game but before he is ready for the first team he must learn to trap and control the ball, appreciate the importance of positional tactics – the offside trap for example – and judge when a little thoughtful dribble will be better than sheer explosiveness.' As you might have gathered, Harry was no Dixie, and his swift departure to Mossley was probably a weight off everyone's minds.

WILLIAM RIDDING

CENTRE-FORWARD OR INSIDE-RIGHT, DEC 1931 – AUG 1934
15 APPS 3 GLS (TOTAL 44 APPS 14 GLS)

AN AMAZING SCORING rate as Tranmere's centre-forward inevitably saddled precocious teenager Bill Ridding with the tag of the next

Dixie Dean. A disastrous £3,000 move to City, where he played just four times in eighteen months, put an end to the comparisons and he was never able to realise his full potential at Old Trafford, either, although he did well enough in 32/33 when he top-scored with eleven goals in twenty-three appearances.

As the least popular signing since Charlie Rennox, Bill was always playing under a big handicap. Only by scoring like Dixie would he have made sense of the deal that cost United the services of two favourites, Harry Rowley and Billy Dale. Instead, he was neither a flop nor a success and the unavoidable conclusion was that the Reds would have been much better off had the transfer treble never taken place. If anyone remained unconvinced, the back-end of 33/34 provided incontestable proof; while Dale was inspiring City to FA Cup glory, Ridding was getting set for a move to Northampton Town.

Short spells at Tranmere and Oldham followed before persistent cartilage problems brought Bill's playing days to an end at the age of just 24. The hours spent on various treatment tables may possibly have influenced the direction his career took thereafter. A qualified physiotherapist and chiropodist, he was England's trainer in the 1950 World Cup and, in the late sixties, the physio at the other Old Trafford. A man of many talents, but not quite enough goals, Bill also enjoyed a long and successful stint as trainer and manager at Bolton.

JOHN WHITTLE

LEFT-WINGER, DEC 1931 – JUL 1932, 1 APP 0 GLS

'THE INTRODUCTION OF Whittle, making his first league appearance at outside-left for United was a failure, though he had a part in United's goal. His lack of experience, however, became more and more evident, and late in the match he was little more than a passenger.' The *Athletic News* clearly did not rate the chances of John Whittle making the leap from the Lancashire Alliance to the second division. They were right not to; within six months of his sole United appearance – in January's 3-1 defeat at Swansea Town – he was playing for Rossendale United.

ERNEST VINCENT

CENTRE HALF-BACK AND RIGHT-HALF, FEB 1932 – JUNE 1935
16 APPS 0 GLS (TOTAL 65 APPS 1 GL)

THE BIGGEST INFLUENCE in United's late-season recovery in 31/32 and a young, talented symbol of the club's bright new future under James Gibson, Ernie Vincent was, surprisingly, never given much of an opportunity to mould it. Harshly replaced at centre half-back after making just five appearances there at the start of 32/33, he spent the remainder of that season at right-half before dropping out of contention altogether in 33/34. The following summer, Ginger was deemed surplus to requirements and sold to QPR.

JOHN MOODY

GOALKEEPER, FEB 1932 – AUG 1933
8 APPS 0 GLS (TOTAL 51 APPS 0 GLS)

BLESSED WITH A strong, agile frame as well as impressive powers of judgement and anticipation, John Moody had the gifts to become United's next great keeper but, like Ginger Vincent, was blown out before he had the chance to really prove himself. A masterly eight-game spell following his arrival from Doncaster in February 1932 supported the widely-held view that the Reds had signed the best keeper in the second division and convinced the directors that they could do without long-serving legend Alf Steward. One year later, John was a Chesterfield player. As he had been an ever-present in 32/33, his swift exit was difficult to understand. If anyone was naïve enough to imagine that the management had cooked up a master-plan, the events of 33/34 showed them the error of their ways. That season, United fielded four different keepers, conceded more goals than any other side in the second division and finished one bad result away from dropping into the third.

LESLIE LIEVESLEY

WING HALF-BACK, FEB 1932 – MAR 1933, 2 APPS 0 GLS

LIKE HIS UNCLE Wilf, Leslie Lievesley made little impact during his short spell as a Red, playing just two matches before being written off as a one-paced journeyman and packed off to Chesterfield. In time, though, his name would spread further than that of any of his Old Trafford contemporaries. When his playing days ended, the Red reject embarked on a spectacular coaching career that turned him into a legend but ultimately cost him his life.

Lievesley's metamorphosis from journeyman to guru began immediately after the war when he accepted a position on the coaching staff of the Dutch national team. His impressive work with Holland soon caught the eye of Torino, then the superpower of the Italian game, who offered him the role of youth team trainer and then shortly afterwards promoted him to the first-team set-up. Leslie's innovative genius[1] made him a vital part of the 'Claret' machine that completed a hat-trick of Scudettos in 47/48 and was all set to clinch a fourth successive title when it was all but destroyed by tragedy on the mountain of Superga.

On 4 May, 1949, 'Il Grande Torino', as the all-conquering team were known, were returning from a prestige friendly against Benfica in Lisbon when the plane they were travelling in crashed in the mountains on the outskirts of Turin (it was a simple if horrific case of human error; in a misguided attempt to circumvent the appalling weather conditions, the pilot flew too low and crashed into the side of the Basilica that stood on top of the Superga peak). In all, the tragedy claimed thirty-one lives, a death toll which included eighteen players, two directors, three journalists, one technical coach, one masseur and the trainer, the honorary Italian, Leslie Lievesley. For the 37-year-old, the timing of the disaster was particularly savage as he had just accepted the position of Juventus coach for the 49/50 season. The position would have sated his thirst to emerge from the shadows of head coach Egri Erbstein and make a name for himself on his own. Instead, he would be forever associated with Juve's great rivals as they passed from the brightest period in their history into the darkest.

After Superga, things would never be the same again for 'Toro'. The club that dominated Italian football in the 1940s, winning five championships and providing the national side with up to ten players per game, has only won one title since (in 1976) and has long since played second fiddle to their city rivals, Juve. In 1959, ten years after the air disaster, they slipped into Serie B. By then, they had left their ground, the Filadelfia (where Il Grande Torino had not been beaten for six years), in order to share the Stadio Communale with their neighbours. For many Torinese, it was the final insult.

What a contrast to United after Munich. Ten years after the disaster, the Reds scaled their highest peak by capturing the European Cup. By then, they were well-established as the premier

---

1. *A pioneer in his field, Leslie laid down the foundations for modern training methods by introducing stretching and strength work as well as formulating specific programmes aimed at improving the players' agility and technique.*

force in England and while it would be wrong to overplay the impact of Munich in the making of United (quite apart from the fact that the club were well set already, does anyone really dispute that they would have been better off if the Babes, arguably the finest side ever to emerge out of English football, had been spared?), there is little doubt that the tragedy, and the wave of public sympathy and support that followed in its wake, played a significant role in the development of the Manchester United legend.

So what happened to Torino? In terms of numbers, at least, their loss was the greater (eighteen players perished at Superga; eight at Munich) but the destruction of the Babes as a football force was just as complete as that of Il Grande Torino. One vital difference between the two clubs was Busby. Whereas Ferrucio Novo, the wealthy president who had masterminded Torino's emergence from Juve's shadows (and had escaped Superga) could not summon up either the strength or the inspiration to do it all again, Matt took it as his life's mission to finish the job the Babes had started. Another was the scale of the threat that lurked on each club's doorstep. When the power vacuum in Turin opened up, Juventus, backed by the Agnelli family fortune, seized the opportunity to reassert their traditional stranglehold on football both in the city and nation-wide. When Manchester was plunged into darkness, City had already grown accustomed to being second best.

Juventus took the scudetto in the first season after Superga. Significantly, Toro had claimed it the previous year despite the devastation of the air crash. For that consolation they had to thank the magnanimity of their rivals who opted to field youth teams in their fixtures against the stricken champions. That gesture contrasts sharply with the experiences of United after Munich who were in a tight championship race with Wolves (they were due to play the midlanders that Saturday). Moreover, the Reds still had a smattering of experience to call on and there were three months remaining in their season rather than four weeks but it would have been a welcome touch had their opponents also taken their suffering into account. For AC Milan (who thrashed United in the European Cup semi-final that the Babes had sacrificed their lives to reach), in particular, no victory can ever have come laced with so much angst and regret.

Louis Page

Inside-left, Mar – Oct 1932, 9 apps 0 gls (total 12 apps 0 gls)

In his prime, Louis Page was the most dangerous goal-scoring winger in the game. By 1932, the year that United wasted £1,000 on him, he was a battle-hardened veteran who still had the brains but no longer had the speed. An England international at both football and, bizarrely, baseball, he was only given a dozen opportunities at Old Trafford before new manager Scott Duncan struck him out.

George Arthur Fitton

Outside-left, Mar – Dec 1932, 8 apps 1 gl (total 12 apps 2 gls)

Arriving, alongside left-wing partner Louis Page, on transfer deadline day, Arthur Fitton was, according to the *Athletic News*, a 'dynamic winger' with speed, ball control and 'pluck in plenty' who 'showed almost a juggler's art in his centres'. In his eight appearances for United in 31/32, the former Baggie generally lived up to his billing and he was one of many new signings of whom much was expected in 32/33. However, like many of the new faces that arrived in the first wave of Gibson-funded spending in the spring of '32, Arthur's did not fit with Scott Duncan. The left-wing 'dream-team' of Page and Fitton only played together once under the Scotsman and neither player hung around for long. In October, Louis moved to Port Vale; two months later, Arthur was sold to Preston North End.

Arthur Richard Black

Centre-forward, Apr 1932 – Nov 1934
3 apps 3 gls (total 8 apps 4 gls)

Scott Duncan mustn't have cottoned on to the fact that Dick Black was supposed to be the next Hughie Gallacher. Despite Dick's goal-a-game start to his United career and his 33 goals for the reserves in 32/33, Duncan only gave him one opportunity at centre-forward (and four at outside-left) before selling him to St Mirren.

WILLIAM McDONALD

INSIDE-FORWARD, APR 1932 – AUG 1934
2 APPS 0 GLS (TOTAL 27 APPS 4 GLS)

Duncan clearly did not rate the club's other great Scottish hope either although he did at least give Willie McDonald a decent run in the side before deciding that his feet were not quite as scheming or silky as they were purported to be. Like Dick Black, Willie was pushed out of the door in 1934. Unlike Dick, McDonald remained in England, enjoying moderate success with Tranmere and Coventry before the war intervened and he joined the RAF.

INDEX

APPENDICES

1. UNITED'S RESULTS SEASON BY SEASON 1919-32

LEAGUE RECORDS

SEASON	DIV	HOME							AWAY						TOTAL							GOAL Avg	%			SP	DP	POS
		P	W	D	L	F	A	Pts	W	D	L	F	A	Pts	P	W	D	L	F	A	Pts		W	D	L			
1919-20	1	42	6	8	7	20	17	20	7	6	8	34	33	20	42	13	14	15	54	50	40	1.08	31	33	36	17	4	12TH
1920-21	1	42	9	4	8	34	26	22	6	6	9	30	42	18	42	15	10	17	64	68	40	0.94	36	24	40	7	18	13TH
1921-22	1	42	7	7	7	25	26	21	1	5	15	16	47	7	42	8	12	22	41	73	28	0.56	19	29	52	20	22	22ND
1922-23	2	42	10	6	5	25	17	26	7	8	6	26	19	22	42	17	14	11	51	36	48	1.42	40	33	26	8	3	4TH
1923-24	2	42	10	7	4	37	15	27	3	7	11	15	29	13	42	13	14	15	52	44	40	1.18	31	33	36	9	7	14TH
1924-25	2	42	17	3	1	40	6	37	6	8	7	17	17	20	42	23	11	8	57	23	57	2.48	55	26	19	5	1	2ND
1925-26	1	42	12	4	5	40	26	28	7	2	12	26	47	16	42	19	6	17	66	73	44	0.90	45	14	40	16	5	9TH
1926-27	1	42	9	8	4	29	19	26	4	6	11	23	45	14	42	13	14	15	52	64	40	0.81	31	33	36	22	5	15TH
1927-28	1	42	12	6	3	51	27	30	4	1	16	21	53	9	42	16	7	19	72	80	39	0.9	38	17	45	19	11	18TH
1928-29	1	42	8	8	5	32	23	24	6	5	10	34	53	17	42	14	13	15	66	76	41	0.87	33	31	36	18	12	12TH
1929-30	1	42	11	4	6	39	34	26	4	4	13	28	54	12	42	15	8	19	67	88	38	0.76	36	19	45	18	15	17TH
1930-31	1	42	6	6	9	30	37	18	1	2	18	23	78	4	42	7	8	27	53	115	22	0.46	17	19	64	22	21	22ND
1931-32	2	42	12	3	6	44	31	27	5	5	11	27	41	15	42	17	8	17	71	72	42	0.99	40	19	40	11	10	12TH
Total		546	129	74	70	446	304	332	61	65	147	320	558	187	546	190	139	217	766	862	519	0.89	35	25	40			20TH

KEY:

SP - SCORING POSITION: UNITED'S 'GOALS FOR' RANKING IN THEIR DIVISION

DP - DEFENSIVE POSITION: UNITED'S 'GOALS AGAINST' RANKING IN THEIR DIVISION

POS - UNITED'S FINAL LEAGUE POSITION

FA Cup Records

Season	Round	Home						Away						Total						Goal Avg
		P	W	D	L	F	A	P	W	D	L	F	A	P	W	D	L	F	A	
1919-20	4	1	0	0	1	1	2	1	1	0	0	1	0	2	1	0	1	2	2	1
1920-21	3	1	0	0	1	1	2	1	0	1	0	1	1	2	0	1	1	2	3	0.67
1921-22	3	1	0	0	1	1	4	0	0	0	0	0	0	1	0	0	1	1	4	0.25
1922-23	4	1	1	0	0	2	0	2	0	1	1	1	5	3	1	1	1	3	5	0.6
1923-24	4	2	1	0	1	1	3	0	0	0	0	0	0	2	1	0	1	1	3	0.33
1924-25	3	0	0	0	0	0	0	1	0	0	1	0	2	1	0	0	1	0	2	0
1925-26	S/F	2	2	0	0	4	1	5	2	2	1	10	11	7	4	2	1	14	12	1.17
1926-27	3	1	0	1	0	2	2	2	0	1	1	2	3	3	0	2	1	4	5	0.8
1927-28	6	3	3	0	0	9	1	2	0	1	1	1	3	5	3	1	1	10	4	2.5
1928-29	4	1	0	0	1	0	1	1	1	0	0	3	0	2	1	0	1	3	1	3
1929-30	3	1	0	0	1	0	2	0	0	0	0	0	0	1	0	0	1	0	2	0
1930-31	4	1	0	1	0	0	0	3	1	1	1	7	6	4	1	2	1	7	6	1.17
1931-32	3	0	0	0	0	0	0	1	0	0	1	1	4	1	0	0	1	1	4	0.25
Total FA Cup		15	7	2	6	21	18	19	5	7	7	27	35	34	12	9	13	48	53	0.91
Lge & Cup		288	136	76	76	467	322	292	66	72	154	347	593	580	202	148	230	814	915	0.89

Managerial Records

Name & dates	Home						Away						Total						Goal Avg	%		
	P	W	D	L	F	A	P	W	D	L	F	A	P	W	D	L	F	A		W	D	L
Robson 1919-21	50	18	14	18	66	54	50	14	16	20	71	90	100	32	30	38	137	144	0.95	32	30	38
Chapman 1921-26	108	58	27	23	172	97	112	28	31	53	115	171	220	86	58	76	287	268	1.07	39	26	35
Hilditch 1926-27	15	6	5	4	19	13	15	3	2	10	13	36	30	9	7	14	32	49	0.65	30	23	47
Bamlett 1927-31	90	40	26	24	157	121	93	17	18	58	120	245	183	57	44	82	277	366	0.76	31	24	45
Crickmer 1931-32	24	13	4	7	52	37	23	5	5	13	29	51	47	18	9	20	81	88	0.92	38	19	43

2. UNITED'S RESULTS (CLUB BY CLUB) IN THE DEPRESSION YEARS

HOME SCORES ARE GIVEN ON THE TOP OF EACH ROW, AWAY SCORES ARE ON THE BOTTOM. CUP SCORES ARE IN ITALICS.
RESULTS OF CUP GAMES PLAYED ON NEUTRAL GROUNDS ARE UNDERLINED.

Season / Opponents	1919-20	1920-21	1921-22	1922-23	1923-24	1924-25	1925-26	1926-27	1927-28	1928-29	1929-30	1930-31	1931-32	P	W	D	L	F	A	P	W	D	L	F	A
ARSENAL	0-1	1-1	1-0				0-1	2-2	4-1	4-1	1-0	1-2		9	4	2	3	14	9	18	6	2	10	25	2
	3-0	0-2	1-3				2-3	0-1	1-0	1-3	2-4	1-4		9	2	0	7	11	20						
ASTON VILLA	1-2	1-3	1-0				3-0	2-1	5-1	2-2	2-3	3-4		10	4	1	5	21	18	19	5	3	11	29	4
	1-2																								
	0-2	4-3	1-3				2-2	0-2	1-3	0-0	0-1	0-7		9	1	2	6	8	23						
BARNSLEY				1-0	1-2	1-0							3-0	4	3	0	1	6	2	8	3	3	2	8	5
				2-2	0-1	0-0							0-0	4	0	3	1	2	3						
BIRMINGHAM			1-1				3-1	0-1	1-1 / 1-0	1-0	0-0	2-0		8	4	3	1	9	4	15	6	6	3	13	1
			1-0				1-2	0-4	0-0	1-1	1-0	0-0		7	2	3	2	4	7						
BLACKBURN	1-1	0-1	0-1				2-0	2-0	1-1	1-4	1-0	0-1		9	3	2	4	8	9	19	4	2	13	17	4
	0-5	0-2	0-3				0-7	1-2	0-2	3-0	4-5	1-4		10	1	0	9	9	33						
BLACKPOOL				2-1	0-0	0-0							0-0	4	1	3	0	2	1	8	1	4	3	4	9
				0-1	0-1	1-1							1-5	4	0	1	3	2	8						
BOLTON	1-1	2-3	0-1				2-1	0-0	2-1	1-1	1-1	1-1		9	2	5	2	10	10	18	3	7	8	22	3
	5-3	1-1	0-1				1-3	0-4	2-3	1-1	1-4	1-3		9	1	2	6	12	23						
BRADFORD	0-0	1-1	1-1	1-1 / 2-0	3-0	3-0							1-0	8	4	4	0	12	3	16	5	8	3	21	1
	1-2	1-1	1-2	1-1 / 1-1	0-0	1-0							3-4	8	1	4	3	9	11						
BRADFORD PA	0-1	5-1											0-2	3	1	0	2	5	4	6	3	0	3	14	1
	4-1	4-2											1-3	3	2	0	1	9	6						
BRENTFORD									7-1					1	1	0	0	7	1	1	1	0	0	7	1
														0	0	0	0	0	0						
BRISTOL CITY				2-1									0-1	2	1	0	1	2	2	4	2	0	2	5	5
				2-1									1-2	2	1	0	1	3	3						
BURNLEY	0-1	0-3	0-1				6-1	2-1	4-3	1-0	1-0		5-1	9	6	0	3	19	11	18	8	0	10	27	3
	1-2	0-1	2-4				1-0	0-1	0-4	4-3	0-4		0-2	9	2	0	7	8	11						
BURY				0-1	0-1		0-1	1-2	0-1 / 1-0	1-0			1-2	9	2	0	7	4	9	17	5	3	9	19	2
				2-2	0-2		3-1	3-0	3-4 / 1-1	3-1			0-0	8	3	3	2	15	11						
CARDIFF			1-1 / 1-4				1-0	1-1	2-2	1-1				6	1	4	1	7	9	11	3	5	3	14	1
			1-3				2-0	2-0	0-2	2-2				5	2	1	2	7	7						
CHARLTON													0-2	1	0	0	1	0	2	2	0	0	2	0	3
													0-1	1	0	0	1	0	1						
CHESTERFIELD													3-1	1	1	0	0	3	1	2	2	0	0	6	2
													3-1	1	1	0	0	3	1						
CHELSEA	0-2	3-1	0-0			1-0						1-0		5	3	1	1	5	3	10	4	3	3	9	1
	0-1	2-1	0-0			0-0						2-6		5	1	2	2	4	8						
CLAPTON O				0-0	2-2	4-2								3	1	2	0	6	4	6	2	3	1	8	6
				1-1	0-1	1-0								3	1	1	1	2	2						
COVENTRY				2-1	1-2	5-1								3	2	0	1	8	4	6	2	1	3	9	8
				0-2	1-1	0-1								3	0	1	2	1	4						
CRYSTAL P				2-1	5-1	1-0								3	3	0	0	8	2	6	4	1	1	13	7
				3-2	1-1	1-2								3	1	1	1	5	5						
DERBY	0-2	3-0		0-0	0-0	1-1		2-2	5-0	0-1	3-2	2-1		10	4	4	2	16	9	20	4	9	7	24	3
	1-1	1-1		1-1	0-3	0-1		2-2	0-5	1-6	1-1	1-6		10	0	5	5	8	27						
EVERTON	1-0	3-2	2-1				0-0	2-1	1-0	1-1	3-3			8	4	3	1	11	8	16	6	6	4	20	2
	0-0	0-2	0-5				3-1	0-0	2-5	4-2	0-0			8	2	3	3	9	15						
FULHAM				1-1	0-0	2-0								3	1	2	0	3	1	7	2	3	2	6	6
				0-0	1-3	0-1	2-1							4	1	2	3	3	5						
GRIMSBY											2-5	0-2		2	0	0	2	2	7	5	0	1	4	5	1
											2-2	1-2 / 0-1		3	0	1	2	3	5						
HUDDERSFIELD		2-0	1-1		0-3		1-1	0-0	0-0	1-0	1-0	0-6		9	3	4	2	6	11	17	4	7	6	15	3
		2-5	1-1				0-5	0-0	2-4	2-1	2-2	0-3		8	1	3	4	9	21						
HULL				3-2	1-1	2-0								3	2	1	0	6	3	6	3	2	1	9	6
				3-2	1-1	1-0								3	1	1	1	3	3						
LEEDS				0-0	3-1		2-1	2-2		1-2	3-1	0-0	2-5	8	3	3	2	13	12	16	6	4	6	24	28
				1-0	0-0		0-2	3-2		2-3	1-3	0-5	4-1	8	3	1	4	11	16						
LEICESTER				0-2	3-0	1-0	3-2	1-0	5-2	1-1	2-1	0-0		9	6	2	1	16	8	18	9	3	6	31	2
				1-0	2-2	0-3	3-1	3-2	0-1	1-4	1-4	4-5		9	3	1	5	15	20						

Opponents	1919-20	1920-21	1921-22	1922-23	1923-24	1924-25	1925-26	1926-27	1927-28	1928-29	1929-30	1930-31	1931-32	HOME/AWAY P	W	D	L	F	A	TOTAL P	W	D	L	F	A
Liverpool	0-0	1-1 / 1-2	0-0				3-3	0-1	6-1	2-2	1-2	4-1		10	2	5	3	18	13	20	3	8	9	26	33
	0-0	0-2 / 1-1	1-2				0-5	2-4	0-2	3-2	0-1	1-1		10	1	3	6	8	20						
Man City	1-0	1-1	3-1				1-6			1-2	1-3	1-3		7	2	1	4	9	16	15	3	4	8	18	36
	3-3	0-3	1-4				1-1 / 0-3			2-2	1-0	1-4		8	1	3	4	9	20						
M'brough	1-1	0-1	3-5			2-0			3-0		0-3	4-4		7	2	2	3	13	14	14	5	4	5	25	26
	1-1	4-2	0-2			1-1			2-1		3-2	1-3		7	3	2	2	12	12						
Millwall													2-0	1	1	0	0	2	0	2	1	1	0	3	1
													1-1	1	0	1	0	1	1						
Nelson				0-1										1	0	0	1	0	1	2	1	0	1	2	1
				2-0										1	1	0	0	2	0						
Newcastle	2-1	2-0	0-1				2-1	3-1	1-7	5-0	5-0	4-7		9	6	0	3	24	18	18	6	0	12	36	54
	1-2	3-6	0-3				1-4	2-4	1-4	0-5	1-4	3-4		9	0	0	9	12	36						
Notts Co	0-0			1-1			0-1						3-3	4	0	3	1	4	5	8	4	3	1	17	7
	2-0			6-1			3-0						2-1	4	4	0	0	13	2						
Nottm Forest													3-2	1	1	0	0	2	2	2	1	0	1	4	4
													1-2	1	0	0	1	1	2						
Oldham	1-1	4-1	0-3		2-0	0-1							5-1	6	3	1	2	12	7	12	6	3	3	28	14
	3-0	2-2	1-1		2-3	3-0							5-1	6	3	2	1	16	7						
Plymouth			1-0										2-1	2	2	0	0	3	1	4	2	0	2	5	8
													1-3 / 1-4	2	0	0	2	2	7						
Portsmouth					2-0			2-0	0-0	3-0	0-1			5	3	1	1	7	1	10	3	2	5	9	13
					1-1			0-1	0-3	0-3	1-4			5	0	1	4	2	12						
Port Vale			1-2	5-1	4-0								2-0	4	3	0	1	12	2	11	8	0	3	23	8
	1-0		0-1	1-0	1-2	3-2			3-0				2-1	7	5	0	2	11	6						
Preston	5-1	1-0	1-1										3-2	4	3	1	0	10	4	8	4	3	1	15	9
	3-2	0-0	2-3										0-0	4	1	2	1	5	5						
Reading							2-1							1	0	1	0	2	2	3	0	2	1	4	5
							1-1 / 1-2							2	0	1	1	2	3						
Rotherham				3-0										1	1	0	0	3	0	2	1	1	0	4	1
				1-1										1	0	1	0	1	1						
Sheff United	3-0	2-1	3-2				1-2	5-0	2-3	1-1	1-5	1-2		9	4	1	4	19	16	18	4	4	10	27	39
	2-2	0-0	0-3				0-2	2-2	1-2	1-6	1-3	1-3		9	0	3	6	8	23						
Sheff Weds	0-0			1-0	2-0	2-0			0-0	1-1	2-1	2-2	4-1	9	5	4	0	14	5	19	7	5	7	23	26
	3-1			0-1	0-2	1-1 / 0-2			0-2	2-0	1-2	2-7	0-3	10	2	1	7	9	21						
Southampton				1-2	1-0	1-1							2-3	4	1	1	2	5	6	8	2	4	2	8	7
				0-0	0-0	2-0							1-1	4	1	3	0	3	1						
South Shields				3-0	1-1	1-0								3	2	1	0	5	2	6	4	1	1	10	3
				3-0	0-1	2-1								3	2	0	1	5	2						
Stockport				1-0	3-0	2-0								3	3	0	0	6	0	6	3	0	3	9	6
				0-1	2-3	1-2								3	0	0	3	3	6						
Stoke					2-2	2-0						0-0	1-1	4	1	3	0	5	3	9	2	5	2	12	14
					0-3	0-0						3-3 / 4-2	0-3	5	1	2	2	7	11						
Sunderland	2-0	3-0	3-1				5-1 / 2-1	0-0	2-1	3-0	2-1	1-1		10	8	2	0	23	6	20	11	3	6	39	36
	0-3	3-2	1-2				1-2 / 3-3	0-6	1-4	1-5	4-2	2-1		10	3	1	6	16	30						
Swansea													2-1	1	1	0	0	2	1	2	1	0	1	3	4
													1-3	1	0	0	1	1	3						
Swindon											0-2			1	0	0	1	0	2	1	0	0	1	0	2
														0	0	0	0	0	0						
Tottenham		0-1	2-1				0-0 / 2-0	2-1	3-0				1-1	7	4	2	1	10	4	15	5	5	5	19	25
		1-4	2-2	0-4			1-0 / 2-2	1-1	1-4				1-4	8	1	3	4	9	21						
West Brom	1-2	1-4	2-3				3-2	2-0						5	2	0	3	9	11	10	3	2	5	15	20
	1-2	2-0	0-0				1-5	2-2						5	1	2	2	6	9						
West Ham			1-2				2-1	0-3	1-1	2-3	4-2	1-0		7	3	1	3	11	12	14	5	1	8	18	28
			2-0				0-1	0-4	2-1	1-3	1-2	1-5		7	2	0	5	7	16						
Wolves				1-0		3-0							3-2	3	3	0	0	7	2	6	4	1	1	8	9
				1-0		0-0							0-7	3	1	1	1	1	7						

3. ANALYSIS OF UNITED'S RECORD (CLUB BY CLUB) 1919-1932

*TO MAKE COMPARISONS EASIER, I HAVE AWARDED POINTS FOR WINS AND DRAWS IN THE CUP AS WELL AS IN THE LEAGUE

OPPONENTS	P	W	D	L	F	A	W %	D %	L %	PTS*	AVE PTS
ARSENAL	18	6	2	10	25	29	33	11	56	14	0.78
ASTON VILLA	19	5	3	11	29	41	26	16	58	13	0.68
BARNSLEY	8	3	3	2	8	5	38	38	25	9	1.13
BIRMINGHAM	15	6	6	3	13	11	40	40	20	18	1.2
BLACKBURN	19	4	2	13	17	42	21	11	68	10	0.53
BLACKPOOL	8	1	4	3	4	9	13	50	38	6	0.75
BOLTON	18	3	7	8	22	33	17	39	44	13	0.72
BRADFORD CITY	16	5	8	3	21	14	31	50	19	18	1.13
BRADFORD PA	6	3	0	3	14	10	50	0	50	6	1
BRENTFORD	1	1	0	0	7	1	100	0	0	2	2
BRISTOL CITY	4	2	0	2	5	5	50	0	50	4	1
BURNLEY	18	8	0	10	27	32	44	0	56	16	0.89
BURY	17	5	3	9	19	20	29	18	53	13	0.76
CARDIFF	11	3	5	3	14	16	27	45	27	11	1
CHARLTON	2	0	0	2	0	3	0	0	100	0	0
CHESTERFIELD	2	2	0	0	6	2	100	0	0	4	2
CHELSEA	10	4	3	3	9	11	40	30	30	11	1.1
CLAPTON O	6	2	3	1	8	6	33	50	17	7	1.17
COVENTRY	6	2	1	3	9	8	33	17	50	5	0.83
CRYSTAL PALACE	6	4	1	1	13	7	67	17	17	9	1.5
DERBY	20	4	9	7	24	36	20	45	35	17	0.85
EVERTON	16	6	6	4	20	23	38	38	25	18	1.13
FULHAM	7	2	3	2	6	6	29	43	29	7	1
GRIMSBY	5	0	1	4	5	12	0	20	80	1	0.2
HUDDERSFIELD	17	4	7	6	15	32	24	41	35	15	0.88
HULL	6	3	2	1	9	6	50	33	17	8	1.33
LEEDS	16	6	4	6	24	28	38	25	38	16	1
LEICESTER	18	9	3	6	31	28	50	17	33	21	1.17
LIVERPOOL	20	3	8	9	26	33	15	40	45	14	0.7
MAN CITY	15	3	4	8	18	36	20	27	53	10	0.67
M'BROUGH	14	5	4	5	25	26	36	29	36	14	1
MILLWALL	2	1	1	0	3	1	50	50	0	3	1.5
NELSON	2	1	0	1	2	1	50	0	50	2	1

NEWCASTLE	18	6	0	12	36	54	33	0	67	12	0.67
NOTTS CO	8	4	3	1	17	7	50	37	13	11	1.38
NOTTM FOREST	2	1	0	1	4	4	50	0	50	2	1
OLDHAM	12	6	3	3	28	14	50	25	25	15	1.25
PLYMOUTH	4	2	0	2	5	8	50	0	50	4	1
PORTSMOUTH	10	3	2	5	9	13	30	20	50	8	0.8
PORT VALE	11	8	0	3	23	8	73	0	27	16	1.45
PRESTON	8	4	3	1	15	9	50	37	13	11	1.38
READING	3	0	2	1	4	5	0	67	33	2	0.67
ROTHERHAM	2	1	1	0	4	1	50	50	0	3	1.5
SHEFF UNITED	18	4	4	10	27	39	22	22	56	12	0.67
SHEFF WEDS	19	7	5	7	23	26	37	26	37	19	1
SOUTHAMPTON	8	2	4	2	8	7	25	50	25	8	1
SOUTH SHIELDS	6	4	1	1	10	3	67	17	17	9	1.5
STOCKPORT	6	3	0	3	9	6	50	0	50	6	1
STOKE	9	2	5	2	12	14	22	56	22	9	1
SUNDERLAND	20	11	3	6	39	36	55	15	30	25	1.25
SWANSEA	2	1	0	1	3	4	50	0	50	2	1
SWINDON	1	0	0	1	0	2	0	0	100	0	0
TOTTENHAM	15	5	5	5	19	25	33	33	33	15	1
WEST BROM	10	3	2	5	15	20	30	20	50	8	0.8
WEST HAM	14	5	1	8	18	28	36	7	57	11	0.79
WOLVES	6	4	1	1	8	9	67	17	17	9	1.5

FAVOURITE OPPONENTS (QUAL'N 5+ MEETINGS)
PTS PER GAME

1.5:	CRYSTAL PALACE, SOUTH SHIELDS, WOLVES	1.25:	OLDHAM, SUNDERLAND
1.45:	PORT VALE	1.2:	BIRMINGHAM
1.38:	NOTTS CO, PRESTON	1.17:	CLAPTON ORIENT, LEICESTER
1.33:	HULL	1.13:	BRADFORD CITY, BARNSLEY, EVERTON
		1.1:	CHELSEA

LEAST FAVOURITE OPPONENTS (QUAL'N 5+ MEETINGS)
PTS PER GAME

0.2:	GRIMSBY	0.72:	BOLTON
0.53:	BLACKBURN	0.75:	BLACKPOOL
0.67:	MAN CITY, NEWCASTLE, SHEFFIELD UTD	0.76:	BURY
0.68:	ASTON VILLA	0.78:	ARSENAL
		0.7	LIVERPOOL

FAVOURITE VISITORS (QUAL'N 5+ VISITS)
PTS PER GAME

1.8:	SUNDERLAND*	1.5:	BRADFORD CITY*
1.56:	LEICESTER, SHEFF WEDS*	1.43:	SPURS

4. United Players' Appearances and Goals Season by Season 1919-32

* TOTAL UNITED CAREER RECORDS ARE GIVEN IN BRACKETS

Name	From/To	1919-20	1920-21	1921-22	1922-23	1923-24	1924-25	1925-26	1926-27	1927-28	1928-29	1929-30	1930-31	1931-32	Totals*
Albinson	1919-21		1												1
Astley	1924-28							1	1						2
Bain D.	1922-24				4/1	19/8									23/9
Bain J.	1922-28						1	2		1					4
Ball	1929-30 & 33-34											24/11			24/11 (50/18)
Barber	1922-24				3/1	1/1									4/2
Barlow	1914-22	7	20	3											30
Barson	1922-28				34	19	32	32/2	24/2	11					152/4
Bennion	1921-32			15	14	36	17	7	40/1	41/1	34	28	40/1	29	301/3
Bisset	1919-21	22/6	14/4												42/10
Black	1932-34													3/3	3/3 (8/4)
Boyle	1929-30										1	16/6			17/6
Brett	1921-22			10											10
Broome	1923-24				1										1
Bullock	1930-31												10/3		10/3
Cartman	1922-23				3										3
Chapman	1926-28								17	9					26
Chesters	1929-33											3	4	2	9
Dale	1925-31										19	19	26	4	68
Dean	1931													2	2
Dennis	1923-24					3									3
Ellis	1923-24					11									11
Evans	1923-25					6/2									6/2
Ferguson D.	1927-28									4					4

Player	Years	Per-season figures (apps / goals, earliest → latest)	Total
FERGUSON J.	1931	8/1	8/1
FITTON	1932	8/1	8/1 (12/2)
FORSTER	1916–22	5, 27, 4	36
GALLIMORE	1929–33 & 34	32/6, 25/6	57/12 (76/20)
GIBSON	1921–22	12	12
GOLDTHORPE	1922–25	25/14, 4/1, 1/1	30/16
GOODWIN	1920–22	5/1, 2	7/1
GRIMWOOD	1919–27	24/1, 27/4, 28, 39, 22/2, 40/1, 8, 17	205/8
HALL	1925–27	3	3
HANNAFORD	1925–27	5, 7	12
HANSON	1924–31	3/3, 26/5, 22/5, 35/14, 43/20, 18/5	147/52
HARRIS F.	1920–23	7/1, 28/1, 14	49/2
HARRIS T.	1926–28	4/1	4/1
HARRISON	1920–22	25/3, 21/2	46/5
HASLAM	1921–27	1, 7, 1, 11, 4, 3	27
HAWORTH	1926–27	2	2
HENDERSON	1921–25	10/2, 2/1, 1, 23/14	36/17
HILDITCH	1916–32	34/2, 34/1, 35/1, 43, 31/1, 19, 5, 11/1, 28/1, 29, 18	322/7
HODGE	1910–19	16/2	16/2 (86/2)
HODGES	1919–21	18/4, 2	20/4
HOFTON	1910–13 & 19–22	1	1 (18)
HOPKIN	1919–21	41/5, 33/3	74/8
HOPKINSON	1929–35	19/6, 19/5	38/11 (57/12)
HOWARTH	1921–23	4	4
IDDON	1925–27	1, 1	2
INGLIS	1925–30	7/1, 6, 1	14/1

NAME	FROM/TO	1919-20	1920-21	1921-22	1922-23	1923-24	1924-25	1925-26	1926-27	1927-28	1928-29	1929-30	1930-31	1931-32	TOTALS*
JOHNSTON	1927-29 & 31-32									36/11	12/5			29/11	77/27
JONES	1924-37						16	10	21	38		17	5	12	119 (200)
KENNEDY	1923-25					6/1	12/3								18/4
LEONARD	1920-21		10/5												10/5
LIEVESLEY L.	1932-33													2	2
LIEVESLEY W.	1922-23				3										3
LOCHHEAD	1921-25			32/8	37/13	42/14	37/13	5/2							153/50
LYDON	1928-33												1	2	3
LYNER	1922				3										3
MACDONALD	1923				2/1	7/1									9/2
MANLEY	1930-39													3	3 (195/41)
MANN F.	1923-30				10	27/3	33	41	14	31	27/1	14/1			197/5
MANN H.	1931-33													13/2	13/2
MCBAIN	1921-23			22	21/2										43/2
MCCRAE	1925-26							13							13
MCDONALD	1932-34													2	2 (27/4)
MCLACHLAN	1929-33											24/2	46/2	29	99/4 (116/4)
MCLENAHAN	1927-36									10/1	1	10/6	21/1	12	54/8 (116/12)
MCPHERSON	1922-28					36/2	39/7	36/20	35/16	29/7					175/52
MEEHAN	1917-20	38/2													53/6
MELLOR	1929-37												39	34	73 (122)
MEREDITH	1906-21	21/2	14/1												35/3 (332/35)
MEW	1912-26	44	42	42	44	12		11							195 (199)
MILLER J.	1924					4/1									4/1
MILLER T.	1920-21		27/8												27/8
MONTGOMERY	1915-21	14/1	2												16/1 (27/1)
M...														8	8 (51)

MOORE	1919-21 & 22-31	38	26	12	44	41	40	33	26	39	29				328
MYERSCOUGH	1920-23		13/5	7	14/3										34/8
NICOL	1928-29										5/2	2			7/2
PAGE	1932													9	9 (12)
PAPE	1925					16/5	2								18/5
PARKER	1930-32												8	9	17
PARTRIDGE	1920-29		30/8	38/4	33/1			9	26/5	19	5				160/18
POTTS	1913-20	5													5 (29/5)
PRENTICE	1919-20	1													1
PUGH	1922-23			1	1										2
RADFORD	1920-24		1	27	37/1	31									96/1
RAMSDEN	1927-32									2	5/3	9			16/3
RAWLINGS	1928-29										12/10	20/6	4/3		36/19
REID	1929-33										17/14	13/5	33/20	26/18	89/57 (101/67)
RENNOX	1925-27							4	41/18	23/7					68/25
RICHARDSON	1926-29								36	5	1				42
RIDDING	1931-34													15/3	15/3 (44/14)
ROBINSON J.	1919-22		7/2	12/1											21/3
ROBINSON M.	1931-32													10	10
ROWLEY	1928-31 & 34-37										25/5	41/12	29/7	1	96/24 (180/56)
SAPSFORD	1919-22	2	21/7	30/10											53/17
SARVIS	1922-25				1										1
SCHOFIELD G.	1920-22			1											1
SCHOFIELD P.	1921-22			1											1
SCOTT	1921-22			24											24
SILCOCK	1916-34	41	39/1	36	40	29	40	29	30	29/1	21	25	36		404/2 (449/2)
SMITH A.	1925-27							5/1							5/1
SMITH T.	1924-27						12/4	32/5	35/7	11					90/16
SPENCE	1919-33	33/14	15/7	36/15	37/11	38/10	43/5	46/11	43/19	43/24	38/6	43/12	37/7	38/19	490/160 (510/168)

Name	From/To	1919-20	1920-21	1921-22	1922-23	1923-24	1924-25	1925-26	1926-27	1927-28	1928-29	1929-30	1930-31	1931-32	Totals*
Spencer	1928-30										38	10			48
Spratt	1915-20	1													1 (13)
Steward	1920-32		2	1	1	32	43	37	45	11	39	40	42	33	326
Sweeney	1925-30							3/1	16/4	4/1	8/1	1			32/7
Taylor C.	1924-31						1	6/6		2	4/1	17			30/7
Taylor W.	1921-22			1											1
Thomas	1922-30			3	18	6	3	35/6	16	13/2	20/4	21/1			135/13
Thomson	1928-31										1	1	3/1		5/1
Toms	1919-20	13/4	1												14/4
Tyler	1922-24					1									1
Vincent	1932-35													16	16 (65/1)
Warburton	1929-33											2/1	22/5	7/3	31/9 (39/10)
Whalley	1909-20	25													25 (106/6)
Whittle	1931-32													1	1
Williams F.	1928-31												3		3
Williams H.	1922-23				5/2										5/2
Williams R.	1927-29									16/2	19				35/2
Williamson	1919-21	2													2
Wilson	1926-32								21	38	21/1	29/1	22/1	9	140/3
Wood	1922-23				16/1										16/1
Woodcock	1912-20	30/12													30/12 (61/21)

United's record versus the rest - first three columns indicate United's performance.

Season	Div	Pos	Pts Total	Champions	Relegated Clubs	A	B	Promoted Clubs	Relegated from 2nd Division
1919-20	1	12TH	40	West Brom 60	Notts Co 36, Sheff Weds 23	-20	4	Spurs 70, Huddersfield 64	Lincoln 27, Grimsby 25
1920-21	1	13TH	40	Burnley 59	Derby 26, Bradford PA 24	-19	14	Birmingham 58, Cardiff 58	Coventry 35, Stockport 30
1921-22	1	22ND	28	Liverpool 57	Bradford City 32, UNITED 28	-29	-4	Nottm Forest 56, Stoke 52	Bradford PA 33, Bristol C 33
1922-23	2	4TH	48	Liverpool 60	Stoke 30, Oldham 30	-3	13	Notts Co 53, West Ham 51	Rotherham 35, Wolves 27
1923-24	2	14TH	40	Huddersfield 57	Chelsea 32, Boro 22	-11	7	Leeds 54, Bury 51	Nelson 33, Bristol C 29
1924-25	2	2ND	57	Huddersfield 58	Preston 26, Nottm Forest 24	0	23	Leicester 59, UNITED 57	C.Palace 34, Coventry 31
1925-26	1	9TH	44	Huddersfield 57	Man City 35, Notts Co 33	-13	9	Sheff Weds 60, Derby 57	Stoke 32, Stockport 25
1926-27	1	15TH	40	Newcastle 56	Leeds 30, West Brom 30	-16	10	Boro 62, Portsmouth 54	Darlington 30, Bradford C 23
1927-28	1	18TH	39	Everton 53	Spurs 38, Boro 37	-14	1	Man City 59, Leeds 57	Fulham 33, South Shields 23
1928-29	1	12TH	41	Sheff Weds 52	Bury 31, Cardiff 29	-11	10	Boro 55, Grimsby 53	Port Vale 34, Clapton O 32
1929-30	1	17TH	38	Sheff Weds 60	Burnley 36, Everton 35	-22	2	Blackpool 58, Chelsea 55	Hull 35, Notts Co 33
1930-31	1	22ND	22	Arsenal 66	Leeds 31, UNITED 22	-44	-9	Everton 61, West Brom 55	Reading 30, Cardiff 25
1931-32	2	12TH	42	Everton 56	Grimsby 32, West Ham 31	-12	9	Wolves 56, Leeds 54	Barnsley 33, Bristol C 23

Key - A: number of points away from title/promotion B: number of points away from relegation

Season	Div	Utd In Cup	Lost To	FA Cup Finals	Top Utd Scorer (Lge)	Division 1 Top Scorer	Division 2 Top Scorer
1919-20	1	4	Aston Villa h Div 1	Aston Villa 1-0 Huddersfield	Spence 14	Fred Morris West Brom 37	Sam Taylor Huddersfield 35
1920-21	1	3	Liverpool h Div 1	Spurs 1-0 Wolves	Spence, Miller, Sapsford, Partridge 7	Joe Smith Bolton 38	Syd Puddefoot West Ham 29
1921-22	1	3	Cardiff h Div 1	Huddersfield 1-0 Preston	Spence 15	Andy Wilson Boro 32	Jimmy Broad Stoke 25
1922-23	2	4	Tottenham a Div 1	Bolton 2-0 West Ham	Goldthorpe, Lochhead 13	Charlie Buchan Sunderland 30	Harry Bedford Blackpool 32
1923-24	2	4	Huddersfield h Div 1	Newcastle 2-0 Aston Villa	Lochhead 14	Wilf Chadwick Everton 28	Harry Bedford Blackpool 32
1924-25	2	3	Sheff Weds a Div 2	Sheff Utd 1-0 Cardiff	Henderson 14	Fred Roberts Man City 31	Arthur Chandler Leicester 32
1925-26	1	S/F	Man City n Div 1	Bolton 1-0 Man City	Rennox 17	Ted Harper Blackburn 43	Bob Turnbull Chelsea 29
1926-27	1	3	Reading n Div 2	Cardiff 1-0 Arsenal	Spence 17	Jimmy Trotter Sheff Weds 37	George Camsell Boro 59
1927-28	1	6	Blackburn a Div 1	Blackburn 3-1 Huddersfield	Spence 22	Dixie Dean Everton 60	Jimmy Cookson West Brom 38
1928-29	1	4	Bury h Div 1	Bolton 2-0 Portsmouth	Hanson 19	Dave Halliday Sunderland 43	Jimmy Hampson Blackpool 40
1929-30	1	3	Swindon h Div 3S	Arsenal 2-0 Huddersfield	Rowley, Spence 12	Vic Watson West Ham 42	Jimmy Hampson Blackpool 45
1930-31	1	4	Grimsby a Div 1	West Brom 2-1 Birmingham	Reid 17	Pongo Waring Aston Villa 49	Dixie Dean Everton 39
1931-32	2	3	Plymouth a Div 2	Newcastle 2-1 Arsenal	Spence 19	Dixie Dean Everton 45	Cyril Pearce Swansea 35

Season	Div	Biggest United Win	Biggest United Defeat
1919-20	1	5-1 v Preston (A) 20/9/19	0-5 v Blackburn (A) 24/4/20
1920-21	1	5-1 v Bradford PA (H) 4/12/20	3-6 v Newcastle (A) 1/1/21
1921-22	1	5-1 v Man City (H) 29/12/20 & Sunderland (H) 28/1/22	0-5 v Everton (A) 27/8/21
1922-23	2	6-1 v Notts Co (A) 10/2/23	0-4 v Spurs (A) FA Cup 3/2/23
1923-24	2	5-0 v Port Vale (H) 22/12/23	0-3 v Derby (A) 16/2/24, Stoke (A) 5/4/24 & Huddersfield (H) FA Cup 2/2/24
1924-25	2	5-1 v Coventry (H) 13/9/24	0-3 v Leicester (A) 27/12/24
1925-26	1	6-1 v Burnley (H) 26/9/25	0-7 v Blackburn (A) 10/4/26
1926-27	1	5-0 v Sheff Utd (H) 27/12/26	0-6 v Sunderland (A) 11/12/26
1927-28	1	7-1 v Brentford (H) FA Cup 14/1/28	1-7 v Newcastle (H) 10/9/27
1928-29	1	5-0 v Newcastle (H) 29/9/28	1-6 v Sheff Utd (A) 26/12/28 & Derby (A) 30/3/29
1929-30	1	5-0 v Newcastle (H) 28/12/29	2-7 v Sheffield Weds (A) 16/11/29
1930-31	1	4-1 v Sheff Weds (H) 28/1/31 & Liverpool (H) 6/4/31	0-7 v Aston Villa (A) 27/12/30

6. HIGHS & LOWS - APPEARANCE AND GOALS
(BOTH IN THE DEPRESSION YEARS & IN UNITED HISTORY)

MOST APPEARANCES IN THE DEPRESSION YEARS

PLAYER	CAREER SPAN	LEAGUE	FA CUP	TOTAL
SPENCE	1919-33	453(151)	27(9)	490(160)
SILCOCK	1916-34	380(2)	24	404(2)
MOORE	19-21/22-31	309	19	328
STEWARD	1920-32	309	17	326
HILDITCH	1916-32	301(7)	21	322(7)
BENNION	1921-32	286(2)	15(1)	301(3)
GRIMWOOD	1919-27	196(8)	9	205(8)
MANN F.	1923-30	180(5)	17	197(5)
MEW	1912-26	182	13	195
McPHERSON	1922-28	159(45)	16(7)	175(52)
PARTRIDGE	1920-29	148(16)	12(2)	160
LOCHHEAD	1921-25	147(50)	6	153(50)
BARSON	1922-28	140(4)	12	152(4)

150+ QUALIFICATION, GOAL TALLIES ARE IN BRACKETS

MOST APPEARANCES IN UNITED HISTORY

PLAYER	CAREER SPAN	LEAGUE	FA CUP	LEAGUE CUP	EUROPE	TOTAL
CHARLTON	1956-73	604+2(199)	79(19)	24(7)	45(22)	752+2(247)
FOULKES	1952-70	563+3(7)	61	3	52(2)	679+3(9)
GIGGS	1990-	418+56(94)	47+7(10)	25+5(7)	95+6(23)	585+74(134)
STEPNEY	1966-78	433(2)	44	35	23	535(2)
DUNNE	1960-73	414(2)	54+1	21	40	529+1(2)
IRWIN	1990-02	356+12(22)	42+1(7)	28+3	73+2(4)	499+18(33)
SPENCE	**1919-33**	**481(158)**	**29(10)**			**510(168)**
NEVILLE, G.	1992-	325+15 (5)	38+3 (0)	16+1(0)	94+6 (2)	473+25(7)
ALBISTON	1974-88	364+15(6)	36	38+2(1)	26+1	464+18(7)
SCHOLES	1994-	277+64 (89)	23+9 (12)	12+2 (0)	82+1 (14)	448+21 (49)
KEANE	1993-05	310+16 (33)	44+2(2)	12+2 (0)	82+1 (14)	448+21(49)
McCLAIR	1987-98	296+59(88)	38+7(14)	44+1(19)	17+6(5)	395+73(126)
BEST	1963-74	361(137)	46(21)	25(9)	34(11)	466(178)
HUGHES	83-6/88-95	336+9(120)	45+1(18)	37+1(16)	30+3(9)	448+14(163)
ROBSON	1981-94	326+19(74)	33+2(10)	49+1(5)	26+1(8)	434+23(97)
BUCHAN	1971-83	376(4)	39	30	10	455(4)
SILCOCK	**1917-34**	**423(2)**	**26**			**449(2)**

449+ QUALIFICATION, '+' FIGURES REPRESENT SUBSTITUTE APPEARANCES, GOAL TALLIES ARE IN BRACKETS

Most Goals in the Depression Years

Player	Dates	League	FA Cup	Total	Apps/Gl
SPENCE	1919-33	151 (453)	9 (27)	160 (490)	3.06
REID	1929-33	63 (96)	4 (5)	67 (101)	0.66
HANSON	1924-31	47 (138)	5 (9)	52 (147)	2.83
MCPHERSON	1922-28	45 (159)	7 (16)	52 (175)	3.37
LOCHHEAD	1921-25	50 (147)	0 (6)	50 (153)	3.06
JOHNSTON	27-29/31-32	24 (71)	3 (6)	27 (77)	2.85
RENNOX	1925-27	24 (60)	1 (8)	25 (68)	2.72
H ROWLEY	1928-31	24 (95)	0 (1)	24 (96)	4

20+ QUALIFICATION, APPEARANCE FIGURES ARE IN BRACK

Most Goals in United history

Player	Dates	League	FA Cup	Lge Cup	Europe	Total	Apps/c
CHARLTON	1956-73	199(606)	19(79)	7(24)	22(45)	247(754)	3.05
LAW	1962-73	171(309)	34(46)	3(11)	28(33)	236(399)	1.69
J.ROWLEY	1937-55	182(380)	26(42)			208(422)	2.03
BEST	1963-74	137(361)	21(46)	9(25)	11(34)	178(466)	2.62
VIOLLET	1952-62	159(259)	5(18)	1(2)	13(12)	178(291)	1.63
SPENCE	1919-33	158(481)	10(29)			168(510)	3.04
HUGHES	83-6/88-95	120(345)	18(46)	16(38)	9(33)	163(462)	2.83
VAN NISTELROOY	2001-06	95 (150)	14(14)	2(6)	38(48)	149(218)	1.46
STAN PEARSON	1937-54	128(315)	21(30)			149(345)	2.32
HERD	1961-68	114(202)	15(35)	1(1)	14(25)	144(263)	1.83
GIGGS	1990-	94(474)	10(54)	7(30)	23(101)	134(659)	4.91
SCHOLES	1994-	89(341)	12(32)	8(16)	21(92)	130(481)	3.7
T.TAYLOR	1953-58	112(166)	5(9)		11(14)	128(189)	1.48

128+ QUALIFICATION, APPEARANCE FIGURES IN BRAC

Most League Goals in United history

Player	Dates	Goals	Apps	Apps/Gls
CHARLTON	1956-73	199	606	3.05
J.ROWLEY	1937-55	182	380	2.09
LAW	1962-73	171	309	1.81
VIOLLET	1952-62	159	259	1.63
SPENCE	1919-33	158	481	3.04
BEST	1963-74	137	361	2.64
STAN PEARSON	1937-54	128	315	2.46
HUGHES	83-6/88-95	120	345	2.88
HERD	1961-68	114	202	1.77
T.TAYLOR	1953-58	112	166	1.48
VAN NISTELROOY	2001-06	95	150	1.5
GIGGS	1990-	95	474	4.98
COLE	1995-02	93	195	2.10

93+QUALIFICATION

7. INTERNATIONAL REDS (OFFICIAL INTERNATIONALS ONLY)

PLAYER	COUNTRY	DATES	DEBUT	CAPS AS A RED	GLS AS A RED	TOTAL CAPS	TOTAL GOALS	OVERALL RECORD (FIRST TO LAST CAP)
MEW	ENGLAND	1920	v Ireland Oct 1920	1		1	1	W
SILCOCK	ENGLAND	1921–23	v Wales Mar 1921	3		3		DLW
SPENCE	ENGLAND	1926	v Belgium May 1926	2	1	2	1	WD
MILLER	SCOTLAND	1920–21	v England Apr 1920	2		3	2	LWW
McBAIN	SCOTLAND	1922–24	v England Apr 1922	1		3		WWL
MEREDITH	WALES	1895–1920	v Ireland Mar 1895	26 (3 in Dep Yrs)		48	11	TOO MANY MATCHES TO INCLUDE HERE
R.WILLIAMS	WALES	1921	v Scotland Feb 1921	2		8	2	LDLLDDLL
BENNION	WALES	1925–31	v Scotland Oct 1925	10		10		LLDWWLLDLL
JONES	WALES	1926–30	v N.Ireland Feb 1926	4		4		LDDL
LYNER	N. IRELAND	1919–23	v Scotland Mar 1919	1		6		LDLDLW

DEPRESSION YEARS REDS WHO WON INTERNATIONAL HONOURS WITH OTHER CLUBS

BARSON	ENGLAND	1920	v Wales Mar 1920	0		1		L
RAWLINGS	ENGLAND	1922	v Wales Mar 1922	0		2		WL
SPENCER	ENGLAND	1924–25	v Scotland Apr 1924	0		2		DW
MEEHAN	ENGLAND	1923	v Ireland Oct 1923	0		1		L
PAGE	ENGLAND	1927	v Wales Feb 1927	0		7	1	DWWWWLL

JOE SPENCE WAS THE ONLY UNITED PLAYER TO SCORE AN OFFICIAL INTERNATIONAL GOAL DURING THE DEPRESSION YEARS PERIOD (BILLY MEREDITH DID SCORE IN WALES' 2–0 'VICTORY INTERNATIONAL' WIN AGAINST ENGLAND IN 1919 BUT THE MATCH WAS NOT GIVEN OFFICIAL STATUS).

Below are the league and FA Cup records of the 35 clubs who played First Division football between 1919 & 1932. Final league positions are given on the left, cup records on the right. Entries in italics show how clubs fared in those seasons (if any) they spent outside the First Division and also which division they were in at the time. For example: Birmingham 3/2 means that Birmingham finished 3rd in the Second Division.

Key: W – FA Cup Winners, R/U – runners-up, S/F – losing semi-finalists, 6,5,4,3 – knocked out in 6th round etc., DNE – did not enter, W/D – withdrew: 3S Third Division South, 3N Third Division North, ML – Midland League, SL – Southern League

Opponent	1919/20		1920/21		1921/22		1922/23		1923/24		1924/25		1925/26		1926/27		1927/28		1928/29		1929/30		1930/31		1931/32	
Arsenal	10	4	9	3	17	6	11	3	19	5	20	3	2	6	11	R/U	10	S/F	9	6	14	W	1	4	2	R/U
Aston Villa	9	W	10	6	5	3	6	3	6	R/U	15	5	6	5	10	3	8	5	3	S/F	4	6	2	3	5	4
Birmingham	3/2	5	1/2	3	18	DNE	17	3	14	3	8	5	14	4	17	4	11	5	15	4	11	4	19	R/U	9	4
Blackburn	20	3	11	3	15	5	14	4	8	3	16	S/F	12	4	18	3	12	W	7	6	6	5	10	5	16	4
Blackpool	4/2	4	4/2	4	19/2	3	5/2	3	4/2	3	17/2	6	6/2	3	9/2	3	19/2	3	8/2	3	1/2	4	20	4	20	3
Bolton	6	3	3	3	6	4	13	W	4	5	3	4	8	W	4	5	7	4	14	W	15	3	14	4	17	3
Bradford City	15	6	15	4	21	4	15/2	3	18/2	3	16/2	5	16/2	3	22/2	3	6/3N	2	1/3N	4	18/2	5	10/2	4	7/2	3
Bradford PA	11	6	22	4	21/2	4	2/3N	3	5/3N	3	5/3N	4	2/3N	2	3/3N	1	1/3N	2	3/2	3	4/2	5	6/2	5	6/2	5
Burnley	2	4	1	5	3	3	15	3	17	S/F	19	3	20	3	5	5	19	3	19	4	21	3	8/2	4	19/2	3
Bury	5/2	4	11/2	3	11/2	3	6/2	5	2/2	3	5	3	4	4	19	3	5	4	21	5	5/2	3	13/2	4	5/2	6
Cardiff	4/SL	5	2/2	S/F	4	6	9	3	2	6	11	R/U	16	4	14	W	6	3	22	3	8/2	4	21/2	3	9/3S	3
Chelsea	3	S/F	18	6	9	3	19	4	21	3	5/2	3	3/2	4	4/2	6	3/2	3	9/2	5	2/2	3	12	6	12	S/F
Derby	18	3	21	3	12/2	3	14/2	S/F	3/2	4	3/2	4	2/2	4	12	4	4	5	6	4	2	4	6	3	15	5
Everton	16	3	7	6	20	3	5	3	7	4	17	5	11	3	20	4	1	4	18	3	22	4	1/2	S/F	1	3

Club																										
GRIMSBY	22/2	3	13/3	4	3/3N	3	3N	1	3N	3	3N	1	1/3N	3	17/2	3	11/2	3	2/2	3	18	3	13	5	21	5
HUDDERSFIELD	2/2	R/U	17	5	14	W	3	5	1	3	1	3	1	4	2	3	2	R/U	16	S/F	10	R/U	5	3	4	6
LEEDS	12/ML	DNE	14/2	w/D	8/2	3	7/2	5	18	5	18	5	19	3	21	3	2/2	3	13	4	5	4	21	5	2/2	3
LEICESTER	14/2	5	12/2	9/2	3/2	5	3/2	4	12/2	3	4	6	17	3	7	3	3	5	2	5	8	3	16	3	19	5
LIVERPOOL	4	6	4	4	1	4	1	5	12	6	4	6	7	4	9	5	16	4	5	4	12	3	9	3	10	6
MAN CITY	7	4	2	3	10	5	8	3	11	S/F	10	3	21	4	3/2	3	1/2	5	8	3	3	5	8	3	14	S/F
MAN UTD	12	4	13	3	22	3	4/2	4	14/2	4	2/2	3	9	S/F	15	3	18	6	12	4	17	3	22	4	12/2	3
MIDDLESBRO'	13	4	8	3	18	3	18	3	22	3	13/2	3	10/2	4	1/2	3	22	5	1/2	4	16	5	7	3	18	3
NEWCASTLE	8	4	5	5	7	4	4	3	9	W	6	4	10	5	1	5	9	3	10	3	19	6	17	4	11	W
NOTTM FOREST	18/2	3	18/2	3	1/2	5	20	3	20	4	22	4	17/2	6	5/2	4	10/2	6	11/2	3	10/2	6	17/2	3	11/2	6
NOTTS COUNTY	21	5	6/2	2	13/2	2	1/2	3	10	4	9	5	22	5	16/2	5	15/2	3	5/2	3	22/2	3	1/3S	4	16/2	3
OLDHAM	17	3	19	3	19	4	22	3	7/2	4	18/2	3	7/2	3	10/2	3	7/2	4	18/2	3	3/2	4	12/2	3	18/2	3
OLDHAM																										
PORTSMOUTH	1/SL	1	12/3	3	3/3S	3	7/3S	3	1/3S	3	4/2	4	11/2	3	2/2	4	20	3	20	R/U	13	4	4	5	8	5
PRESTON	19	5	16	R/U	16	3	16	4	18	3	21	4	12/2	3	6/2	3	4/2	3	13/2	3	16/2	3	7/2	3	13/2	5
SHEFF UTD	14	4	20	3	11	3	10	S/F	5	3	14	W	5	4	8	3	13	3	11	3	20	4	15	5	7	4
SHEFF WEDS	22	3	10/2	4	10/2	3	8/2	5	8/2	4	14/2	4	1/2	3	16	4	14	5	1	S/F	1	4	3	4	3	5
STOKE	10/2	3	20/2	3	2/2	3	21	4	6/2	3	20/2	3	21/2	4	1/3N	1	5/2	5	6/2	3	11/2	3	11/2	3	3/2	5
SUNDERLAND	5	5	12	3	12	3	2	4	20/2	3	7	4	3	5	3	3	15	3	4	3	9	3	11	S/F	13	4
TOTTENHAM	1/2	6	6	S/F	2	W	12	6	7	4	12	5	15	4	13	3	21	3	10/2	3	12/2	3	3/2	4	8/2	3
WEST BROM	1	3	14	3	13	5	7	4	2	3	2	6	13	4	22	3	8/2	3	7/2	6	6/2	3	2/2	W	6	3
WEST HAM	7/2	5	5/2	3	4/2	3	2/2	5	13	4	13	5	18	3	6	4	17	4	17	6	7	6	18	3	22	4

9. GIANTS OR DWARFS?

IN ORDER TO GIVE SOME IDEA OF THE PECKING ORDER IN ENGLISH FOOTBALL DURING THE DEPRESSION YEARS, I HAVE DEVISED A ROUGH SYSTEM WHICH HANDS OUT POINTS FOR LEAGUE AND CUP PERFORMANCES IN EACH SEASON.

KEY TO SCORING: 1ST PLACE IN THE FIRST DIVISION EARNS A CLUB 21 POINTS, 2ND PLACE 20, 3RD PLACE 19 ETC. THE FA CUP WINNERS GET 18 POINTS, THE RUNNERS-UP 15, THE SEMI-FINALISTS 12, ROUND 6 LOSERS 9 ETC. NON-DIVISION ONE CLUBS DO NOT EARN ANY POINTS FOR THEIR LEAGUE PERFORMANCES AND NEITHER DOES THE BOTTOM CLUB IN THE TOP FLIGHT. CLUBS WHO WERE KNOCKED OUT OF THE CUP AT THE THIRD ROUND STAGE OR EARLIER DO NOT SCORE ANY POINTS EITHER. ONLY THOSE CLUBS WHO PLAYED FIRST DIVISION FOOTBALL DURING THE DEPRESSION YEARS HAVE BEEN INCLUDED.

	1919-20	1920-21	1921-22	1922-23	1923-24	1924-25	1925-26	1926-27	1927-28	1928-29	1929-30	1930-31	1931-32	Total	Seasons	Titles	Top 3	Bot 6	Rel'd	Cups	R/U	S/F
ARSENAL	15	13	14	11	9	2	29	26	24	22	26	24	35	250	13	1	3	3		1	2	4
ASTON VILLA	31	21	26	16	31	13	22	12	20	31	27	20	20	290	13		2			1	1	3
BIRMINGHAM	6	0	4	5	8	20	11	8	17	10	14	18	16	137	11			4			1	1
BLACKBURN	2	11	13	11	14	18	13	4	28	24	22	18	9	187	13			2	1			2
BLACKPOOL	3	3	0	0	3	9	0	0	0	0	3	5	2	28	2			2				
BOLTON	16	19	19	27	24	22	32	24	18	26	7	11	5	250	13		?	1		3		3
BRADFORD C	16	10	4	0	0	6	0	0	0	3	6	3	0	48	3			1	1			
BRADFORD PA	20	3	3	3	0	6	0	0	0	3	6	6	6	56	2			1	1			
BURNLEY	23	27	19	7	17	3	2	23	3	6	1	3	0	134	11	1		6	1	1		1
BURY	3	0	6	0	0	17	21	3	20	7	0	3	9	89	5			2	1			
CARDIFF	6	12	27	19	29	26	9	26	22	0	3	0	0	179	8		1	1	1	1	1	3
CHELSEA	31	13	13	6	1	0	3	9	0	6	0	19	22	123	7			3	1			2
DERBY	4	4	0	12	3	0	3	13	21	19	23	16	13	131	8		1	2				1
EVERTON	6	24	2	17	18	11	11	5	24	4	3	12	21	158	12	2	2	5	1	1		1
GRIMSBY	0	3	0	0	0	0	0	0	0	0	4	15	7	29	3			2				
HUDDERSFIELD	15	11	26	25	27	21	24	20	35	18	27	17	27	293	12	3	6	1		1	3	5
LEEDS	0	0	0	6	6	4	3	4	0	12	20	7	0	62	6			4	2			

Final Points Table grid (1919–32) — points won against each opponent, with totals in the shaded column:

Team													Total				
LIVERPOOL	27	21	24	27	19	27	18	19	20	10	13	21	255		2	13	3
MAN CITY	18	20	18	14	23	12	16	0	14	25	14	20	200	2	11	4	1
MAN UTD	13	9	0	3	3	0	28	7	13	5	3	0	97		9	2	
MIDDLESBRO'	12	14	14	7	0	0	3	6	6	12	15	4	96		9	4	2
NEWCASTLE	17	23	18	18	31	19	18	27	12	12	8	29	245	1	13	2	2
NOTTM FOREST	0	0	6	2	2	3	9	3	0	9	0	9	52		3	3	
NOTTS COUNTY	7	3	12	0	15	19	6	0	0	0	3	0	65		4	2	1
OLDHAM	5	3	6	0	3	0	0	0	0	3	0	0	23		4	4	
PORTSMOUTH	0	0	0	0	0	3	0	3	17	12	24	20	81		5	2	1
PRESTON	9	18	21	9	4	4	0	3	0	0	0	6	74		6	3	2
SHEFF UTD	11	2	11	24	17	26	20	14	11	5	13	18	193		13	2	3
SHEFF WEDS	0	3	0	6	3	3	0	9	24	33	22	25	142	2	7	1	1
STOKE	0	0	6	4	0	0	3	0	0	0	0	6	28		1	1	
SUNDERLAND	23	10	10	23	19	18	25	19	18	19	23	12	229	4	13	4	1
TOTTENHAM	9	34	32	19	7	16	10	9	0	0	3	0	149	1	8	1	2
WEST BROM	21	8	15	21	15	29	12	0	9	0	18	16	164	2	9	1	1
WEST HAM	6	0	0	6	12	15	4	19	14	24	4	3	124		9	5	1

FINAL POINTS TABLE 1919–32

1	HUDDERSFIELD	293		8	MAN CITY	200
2	ASTON VILLA	290		9	SHEFFIELD UTD	193
3	LIVERPOOL	255		10	BLACKBURN	187
4	BOLTON	250		11	CARDIFF	179
5	ARSENAL	250		12	WEST BROM	164
6	NEWCASTLE	245		13	EVERTON	158
7	SUNDERLAND	229		14	TOTTENHAM	149

15	SHEFFIELD WED	142		22	MAN UTD	97
16	BIRMINGHAM	137		23	MIDDLESBRO'	96
17	BURNLEY	134		24	BURY	89
18	DERBY	131		25	PORTSMOUTH	81
19	WEST HAM	124		26	PRESTON	74
20	CHELSEA	123		27	NOTTS COUNTY	65
21	LEICESTER	121		28	LEEDS	62

29	BRADFORD PA	56
30	NOTTM FOREST	52
31	BRADFORD C	48
32	GRIMSBY	29
33	BLACKPOOL	28
34	STOKE	28
35	OLDHAM	23

10. ATTENDANCES 1919–32

Season	Div	Lge ave	Cup ave	Highest home attendance	Lowest home attendance	Div average*	Utd v. the rest**	Rank***	Best ave att****
1919-20	1	26,540	48,600 (1)	58,661 v Sunderland 14/2/20	13,000 v Sheff Wed 1/9/19	24,016	111%	9th	Chelsea 42,615
1920-21	1	35,525	30,000 (1)	70,504 v Aston Villa 27/12/20	10,000 v Derby 7/5/21	29,252	121%	6th	Newcastle 41,265
1921-22	1	28,510	25,726 (1)	56,000 v Manchester City 29/10/21	9,000 v Bradford C 10/12/21	27,003	106%	9th	Chelsea 37,545
1922-23	2	22,955	27,791 (1)	30,000 v Palace, Soton & Leicester	12,100 v Notts Co 21/2/23	13,474	170%	12th	Liverpool 33,945
1923-24	2	21,125	51,187 (2)	66,673 v Hudd'fl'd (FAC) 2/2/24	7,000 v Coventry 2/1/24	12,682	167%	14th	Chelsea 30,895
1924-25	2	27,995	N/A	59,448 v Derby County 29/11/24	9,500 v Barnsley 8/9/25	14,405	194%	5th	Arsenal 29,485
1925-26	1	27,647	51,831 (2)	58,661 v Sun'land (FAC) 24/2/26	9,116 v Cardiff 28/4/26	22,598	122%	6th	Chelsea 32,355
1926-27	1	26,138	29,122 (1)	50,665 v Spurs 27/12/26	14,709 v Bury 5/3/27	22,881	114%	9th	Newcastle 36,510
1927-28	1	25,555	39,699 (3)	52,568 v Birmingham (FAC)18/2/28	9,545 v Sunderland 25/4/28	22,885	112%	8th	Man City 37,468
1928-29	1	23,659	40,588 (1)	42,555 v Manchester City 5/1/29	12,020 v West Ham 2/2/29	22,712	104%	12th	Man City 31,715
1929-30	1	18,599	33,226 (1)	57,201 v Manchester City 5/10/29	5,656 v Bolton 7/12/29	22,645	82%	19th	Arsenal 35,537
1930-31	1	11,685	22,013 (1)	39,876 v Manchester City 7/2/31	3,969 v Middlesbro' 2/5/31	20,462	57%	33rd	Arsenal 37,106
1931-32	2	13,011	N/A	37,012 v Charlton 25/3/32	3,507 v Soton 2/9/31	12,213	107%	30th	Arsenal 40,547

KEY

NOTES ON CROWDS

WHAT THE FIGURES DO NOT SHOW IS HOW BADLY UNITED'S CROWDS WERE AFFECTED BY 'DEAD' SEASONS. FOR EXAMPLE, IN THE FINAL FOUR HOME GAMES OF THE 25/26 SEASON, UNITED ATTRACTED CROWDS OF 19,606, 10,918, 9,116 AND 9,974. BEFORE THEY LOST THEIR FA CUP SEMI IN LATE MARCH, ONLY TWO OF THEIR HOME MATCHES ALL SEASON HAD BEEN WATCHED BY FEWER THAN 20,000 FANS. IF THE TEAM HAD BEEN EVEN MODERATELY SUCCESSFUL IN THE DEPRESSION YEARS, IT SEEMS FAIR TO CONCLUDE THAT UNITED'S CROWDS WOULD HAVE COMPARED FAVOURABLY WITH THOSE OF ANY OTHER CLUB.

THE ATTENDANCE OF 70,504 FOR THE ASTON VILLA GAME IN DECEMBER 1920 REMAINS THE HIGHEST OLD TRAFFORD ATTENDANCE FOR A UNITED GAME (THOUGH IT WON'T SURVIVE THE NEXT ROUND OF GROUND IMPROVEMENTS).

THE ATTENDANCE OF 66,673 FOR THE HUDDERSFIELD CUP GAME IN FEBRUARY 1924 REMAINED UNITED'S HIGHEST OLD TRAFFORD FA CUP CROWD UNTIL 2001.

THE ATTENDANCE OF 3,507 FOR THE SOUTHAMPTON GAME IN SEPTEMBER 1931 IS THE LOWEST IN UNITED HISTORY.

ACCORDING TO LEGEND, ONLY 13 FANS WATCHED THE OLD TRAFFORD MATCH BETWEEN ALREADY-RELEGATED STOCKPORT COUNTY (WHOSE OWN GROUND HAD BEEN CLOSED AS A RESULT OF CROWD TROUBLE) AND LEICESTER FOSSE ON 7 MAY 1921. IN FACT, THE MATCH FOLLOWED STRAIGHT AFTER UNITED'S FIRST DIVISION GAME AGAINST DERBY AND PERHAPS 2,000 FANS STAYED BEHIND TO WATCH IT FOR FREE. THE CONFUSION WAS CAUSED BY THE FACT THAT ONLY 13 PEOPLE ACTUALLY PAID TO WATCH THE STOCKPORT MATCH. AS THE GATES HAD ALREADY BEEN OPENED TO LET THE UNITED FANS OUT, THOSE THIRTEEN PAYING PUNTERS MUST HAVE EITHER BEEN EXTREMELY HONEST - OR EXTREMELY THICK.

THE INSIDER'S TO MANCHESTER UNITED
Candid player profiles of every post-war United player
by John Doherty
with Ivan Ponting
£20 - 364PP - PAPERBACK

Containing candid assessments on every United player to have appeared in a red shirt since the war, this magnificently illustrated work is penned by one of the few people to have seen nearly every post-war United player in action. Former Busby Babe John Doherty gives his honest opinion of the players he has watched down the years

THE BIRTH OF THE BABES
Manchester United's Youth Policy 1950-57
by Tony Whelan
Landscape A4 Paperback
121pp - includes over 80 photographs

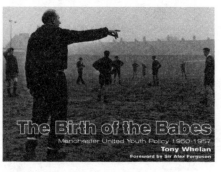

"I did not set out to build a team: the task ahead was much bigger than that. What I really embarked upon was the building of a system which would produce not one team but four or five, each occupying a rung of the ladder, the summit of which was the First XI."

MATT BUSBY

In The Birth of the Babes, current Manchester United Academy coach Tony Whelan examines not only the roots of Matt Busby's socialism, his approach to the care of his players, but illustrates the system of scouts, coaches and trainers that made Manchester United a prototype for the youth systems of today. Beautifully illustrated with photographs and memorabilia culled from the private collections of many of the youth players of the time, The Birth of the Babes is essential reading for anyone interested in the pre-Munich era when United took English football by storm.

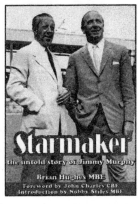

STARMAKER

THE UNTOLD STORY OF JIMMY MURPHY

BY BRIAN HUGHES MBE

£16.95 - 268 PP - HARDBACK

'My first signing and my most important'
SIR MATT BUSBY

The 'greatest coach in the world' trained the likes of George Best, Duncan Edwards, Bobby Charlton and Dennis Viollet and saved the club in the the wake of the Munich air disaster.

THE KING

DENIS LAW, HERO OF THE STRETFORD END

BY BRIAN HUGHES MBE

£18.95 - 403PP - HARDBACK

Denis Law was hero and villain all rolled into one: a player capable of incredible feats of skill and power, all carried off with the knowing smile and villainous touch that put some in mind of a Piccadilly pickpocket. To Mancunians, this son of an Aberdonian trawlerman became part of the fabric of the city; first as a dynamic frontman for the Sky Blues and later as an all-action hero at Matt Busby's United.

VIOLLET
LIFE OF A LEGENDARY GOALSCORER
BY BRIAN HUGHES
£10.95 - 334PP - PAPERBACK

A legendary goalscorer and Busby Babe, Dennis Viollet's career took in tragedy and triumph in equal measure. As a player he thrilled thousands as an outstanding teenage footballer with Manchester United's all-conquering Babes. Later, having survived the Munich air disaster, Viollet broke Manchester United's record for goals in a season - a mark he still holds.

CATCH A FALLING STAR
The Autobiography of Neil Young
£17.95 - Hardback - 224pp

A tall, leggy striker with a venomous left-foot shot, Neil Young scored in every significant game for City in the late 60s. For all the talk in the intervening years of the likes of Summerbee, Bell and Lee, it was the local lad made good who made the greatest impact when it mattered.

In Catch a Falling Star, Neil Young explains what he has been up to in the years since his sizzling shots stung the hands of the country's finest keepers. Here he frankly discusses the problem that faced footballers of the pre-Premiership era:

"When I left Rochdale for the last time one Friday afternoon I had a week's wages... about £60. I drove home and sat in my lounge for two hours, wondering what the hell I was going to do. I had a car on HP, a mortgage, a wife and three children to feed. I was the provider who could no longer provide. I had no savings whatsoever and my wife didn't work. I didn't see it coming. It was a calamity waiting to happen."

COMPLETIST'S DELIGHT
The Full Empire Back List

ISBN	Title	Author	Price
1901746003	SF Barnes: His Life and Times	A Searle	£14.95
1901746011	Chasing Glory	R Grillo	£7.95
190174602X	Three Curries and a Shish Kebab	R Bott	£7.99
1901746038	Seasons to Remember	D Kirkley`	£6.95
1901746046	Cups For Cock-Ups+	A Shaw	£8.99
1901746054	Glory Denied	R Grillo	£8.95
1901746062	Standing the Test of Time	B Alley	£16.95
1901746070	The Encyclopaedia of Scottish Cricket	D Potter	£9.99
1901746089	The Silent Cry	J MacPhee	£7.99
1901746097	The Amazing Sports Quiz Book	F Brockett	£6.99
1901746100	I'm Not God, I'm Just a Referee	R Entwistle	£7.99
1901746119	The League Cricket Annual Review 2000	ed. S. Fish	£6.99
1901746143	Roger Byrne - Captain of the Busby Babes	I McCartney	£16.95
1901746151	The IT Manager's Handbook	D Miller	£24.99
190174616X	Blue Tomorrow	M Meehan	£9.99
1901746178	Atkinson for England	G James	£5.99
1901746186	Think Cricket	C Bazalgette	£6.00
1901746194	The League Cricket Annual Review 2001	ed. S. Fish	£7.99
1901746208	Jock McAvoy - Fighting Legend *	B Hughes	£9.95
1901746216	The Tommy Taylor Story*	B Hughes	£8.99
1901746224	Willie Pep*+	B Hughes	£9.95
1901746232	For King & Country*+	B Hughes	£8.95
1901746240	Three In A Row	P Windridge	£7.99
1901746259	Viollet - Life of a legendary goalscorer+PB	R Cavanagh	£16.95
1901746267	Starmaker	B Hughes	£16.95
1901746283	Morrissey's Manchester	P Gatenby	£5.99
1901746305	The IT Manager's Handbook (e-book)	D Miller	£17.99
1901746313	Sir Alex, United & Me	A Pacino	£8.99
1901746321	Bobby Murdoch, Different Class	D Potter	£10.99
190174633X	Goodison Maestros	D Hayes	£5.99
1901746348	Anfield Maestros	D Hayes	£5.99
1901746364	Out of the Void	B Yates	£9.99
1901746356	The King - Denis Law, hero of the...	B Hughes	£17.95
1901746372	The Two Faces of Lee Harvey Oswald	G B Fleming	£8.99
1901746380	My Blue Heaven	D Friend	£10.99
1901746399	Viollet - life of a legendary goalscorer	B Hughes	£11.99
1901746402	Quiz Setting Made Easy	J Dawson	£7.99
1901746437	Catch a Falling Star	N Young	£17.95
1901746453	Birth of the Babes	T Whelan	£12.95
190174647X	Back from the Brink	J Blundell	£10.95

Originally published by Collyhurst & Moston Lads Club

+ *Out of print*   PB *Superceded by Paperback edition*

To order any of these books email: enquiries@empire-uk.com or call 0161 872 3319.